Cooperating with the Colossus

COOPERATING WITH THE COLOSSUS

A Social and Political History of US Military Bases in World War II Latin America

Rebecca Herman

Oxford University Press is a department of the University of Oxford. It furthers the University's objective of excellence in research, scholarship, and education by publishing worldwide. Oxford is a registered trade mark of Oxford University Press in the UK and certain other countries.

Published in the United States of America by Oxford University Press 198 Madison Avenue, New York, NY 10016, United States of America.

CIP data is on file at the Library of Congress

ISBN 978–0–19–753187–7 (pbk.)
ISBN 978–0–19–753186–0 (hbk.)

DOI: 10.1093/oso/9780197531860.001.0001

9 8 7 6 5 4 3 2 1

Paperback printed by Lakeside Book Company, United States of America
Hardback printed by Bridgeport National Bindery, Inc., United States of America

For my parents

CONTENTS

ACKNOWLEDGMENTS

A few pages of acknowledgments can only begin to register the debts that I've incurred over the ten years that I've been working on this book. In fact, the debts began to accumulate long before that. Jolie Olcott and Grant Farred first drew me toward a career in academia when I was an undergraduate, nearly twenty years ago, with their superb teaching and mentorship. It was also back then that Duke's Center for Latin American and Caribbean Studies funded my first research trip, to Santiago, Chile. I had always loved writing, but the joy of archival work was a revelation, as was the realization that one could, if very lucky, get paid to do both for a living.

Along the circuitous route that I took from college to graduate school, I learned a lot about storytelling and meaning making outside of academia, and I'm grateful to the people who gave me that education and the institutions that supported it. After graduating from college, I moved to Argentina to work with the alliance of human rights organizations, Memoria Abierta. During my time with them, I assisted (in what limited ways my skillset allowed) a remarkable group of activists, archivists, artists, and historians in the creation of a multimedia graphic exhibit that commemorated the thirtieth anniversary of the last coup in Argentina. The architects of that exhibit drove home for me the power of bringing very different kinds of sources together to reconstruct and explain the past in an engaging way. When the exhibit left town to tour the country, I stuck around Buenos Aires for a few more years, punctuated by stints in Bolivia, Brazil, and Boston. The work I did during that period clarified for me that while I was interested in political history, I was best able to make sense of it when it was grounded in the social and cultural lives of "ordinary" people. For their support during those years, I am grateful to the Benenson Award in the Arts, the Lewis Hine Documentary Fellowship, Duke's Center for Documentary Studies, the Jessica Jennifer Cohen Foundation, Roca's

Refugee and Immigrant Initiative, and Catherine Murphy and The Literacy Project.

When I left Boedo for Berkeley, I was fortunate to find a community of smart and supportive peers in graduate school. I'm thankful in particular for Javier Cikota, Bathsheba Demuth, Alberto García Maldonado, Zoe Griffith, Bea Gurwitz, Sarah Hines, Daniel Immerwahr, Samantha Iyer, Erica Lee, James Lin, Pablo Palomino, Tehila Sasson, Sarah Selvidge, Lynsay Skiba, Yana Skorobogatov, and David Tamayo. Mark Healey and Margaret Chowning were exemplary mentors, fostering, with our annual *pan con pavo* festivities, a supportive culture among us Latin Americanists.

Over the many years of research that went into this project, I benefited from the generosity of academics, archivists, and friends encountered across the Americas. In Rio, I am grateful to Martha Abreu, the late Comandante Lucas Antônio Monteiro de Barros Bastos, and the rest of the "Panair family," as well as Major-Brigadeiro Rui Moreira Lima, his son Pedro, and friend Fernando Mauro, for bringing the history of Brazilian aviation to life. Carlo Patti and Alexandre Morelli welcomed me as a Visiting Fellow at the Fundação Getulio Vargas and helped me navigate Brazil's freedom of information request protocol. Larissa Rosa Corrêa and Paulo Fontes not only provided intellectual support, but also a bed to sleep in and the company of sweet Lola. Alexandre Fortes has been an enthusiastic and generous interlocutor over these many years. In Campinas, Fernando Teixeira da Silva shepherded the Brazilian base labor story to publication in Brazil, and he and the other *Trabalho & Labor* volume contributors provided helpful feedback on the work. My research in the Brazilian North and Northeast was enhanced by my conversations with Fred Nicolau, Clyde Smith, and Uilde Monteiro and the company and camaraderie of Courtney Campbell. Guina Alves, Larissa Rosa Corrêa, Cida Carvalhais Cunha, John French, Marcília Gama, Esther Russo Limam, Antonio Montenegro, Gino Negro, and Tom Rogers all gave me helpful advice as I explored Brazilian labor justice records.

In Havana, the Instituto de História (IHC) and the Fundación Antonio Núñez Jiménez sponsored my academic visas over the years. Belkis Quesada embraced me at the IHC and made phone calls on my behalf that opened doors across the country. I will be forever grateful to Ricardo Quiza and Mabel for their advocacy and hospitality. Angelina Rojas went above and beyond in her support for my work, accompanying me to San Antonio de los Baños and facilitating my admission to the Museo when it was otherwise closed. Mercedes García, Servando Valdés, and Marilú Uralde were all generous with their time and advice. Reinaldo Funes kindly helped facilitate my visa ahead of travel. Eduardo Valido and Damila Hechavarría

Argudin enabled my access to the Cuban Foreign Ministry records. Tony and Marina gave me a home in Vedado and received me like family each time I returned. In Camagüey, Elda Cento oriented me to the city and its archives. The librarians at the Biblioteca Provincial Ramón González Coro in Pinar del Rio, who helped me and other patrons on the sidewalk when the electricity was out for prolonged periods of time, have my greatest admiration. In Panama City, where my research was remarkably streamlined by comparison, I am grateful to the staff and archivists at the National Archive, the National Library, and the Panamanian Foreign Ministry Archive, especially Mireya Jaramillo and Ana Belkis Castro. In College Park, David Langbart at the US National Archives taught me the fourth language required for research on this project: the language of the State Department's Central Decimal Files.

The success of many of these research trips also relied on practical advice from scholars who had been there before. That sort of assistance is invaluable, and I've endeavored to pay it forward. Courtney Campbell, Frank Guridy, Gillian McGillivray, Aaron Coy Moulton, Alejandro de la Fuente, Lou Pérez, Jenny Lambe, Raúl Fernandez, Anita Casavantes Bradford, Jana Lipman, Renata Keller, Matthew Scalena, Blake Scott, Heather Roller, Frank McCann, and Jen Van Vleck all took the time to give me logistical advice ahead of various trips. Courtney, Paul Clemans, Felipe Cruz, Alexandre Fortes, Frank McCann, and Kara Vuic generously shared sources with me. Joshua Michelangelo Stein helped me track down court records and patiently talked me through a number of legal questions.

Multi-sited research doesn't only take a lot of help, it takes a lot money, and I am thankful to the many institutions that provided research funding: the Social Science Research Council, the Council on Library and Information Resources, the Smithsonian National Air and Space Museum, the Society for Historians of America Foreign Relations, the George C. Marshall Foundation, the Rockefeller Archive Center, the FDR Presidential Library, UC Berkeley's Institute for International Studies, UC Berkeley's Center for Latin American Studies, UC Berkeley's Graduate Division, the UC-Cuba Educational Initiative, and the University of Washington's Jackson School of International Studies.

The very long list of scholars who provided feedback on the substance of this project over the years, from grad school papers to manuscript chapters, gives lie to the notion that writing a book is a solitary undertaking. Brooke Blower, Mark Brilliant, Ben Coates, John Connelly, Evan Fernandez, Ada Ferrer, Brodie Fischer, Alexandre Fortes, Victoria Frede, Sarah Gold McBride, David Henkin, Daniel Immerwahr, Kyle Jackson, Craig Johnson, Patrick William Kelly, Paul Kramer, Fred Logevall, Erez Manela,

Dan Margolies, Katherine Marino, Gillian McGillivray, Alan McPherson, Harvey Neptune, Aaron O'Connell, Vanessa Ogle, Christine Philliou, Maria Reis, Tom Rogers, Elizabeth Schwall, Diana Schwartz Francisco, Elena Schneider, Jonathan Sheehan, Fernando Teixeira da Silva, Brad Simpson, Ronit Stahl, Christy Thornton, James Vernon, and the participants of Harvard's International and Global History seminar and the Social Landscapes of Military Bases workshops all enriched this book with their comments, as did conversations about the project with Shanon Fitzpatrick, Kate Marshall, Amy Offner, and Stuart Schrader. Richard Candida Smith, Margaret Chowning, Brian DeLay, Mary Dudziak, Laura Enriquez, Susan Ferber, Mark Healey, Emily Rosenberg, Daniel Sargent, Barbara Weinstein, and a helpful slate of anonymous reviewers generously provided comments on full drafts of the manuscript at different stages. Special thanks to Margaret, who read many drafts and has been a sounding board from start to finish, and to Diana Schwartz Francisco, who has been a constant companion and accountability partner throughout these last few years.

My editor, Susan Ferber, provided expert guidance throughout the peer review and publication process, and I'm also grateful to the OUP faculty delegates who went above and beyond in offering additional thoughts on the manuscript. Parts of Chapter 4 of this book appeared in an article I that published in the *American Historical Review* and a Portuguese translation of parts of Chapter 3 appeared in *Trabalho & Labor: Historias compartilhadas Brasil–Estados Unidos*, published in Brazil by Editora Sagga and coedited by Fernando Teixeira da Silva and Alexandre Fortes. This book benefited from the editorial processes behind the publication of both shorter pieces.

Over the years that I spent working on this project, I moved from San Francisco to Seattle and back again. The University of Washington's Jackson School of International Studies was an outstanding place to be. I'm particularly grateful for the friendships of Danny Bessner, Vanessa Freije, Tony Lucero, and Adam Warren. Returning to UC Berkeley's History Department as a faculty member, I had the good fortune to become friends with colleagues I had previously only known through occasional hallway sightings and to continue to work with terrific people I had known for years. Berkeley's Humanities Research Fellowship, the UC Regents' Junior Faculty Fellowship, and a Manuscript Conference grant from the Institute for International Studies supported the book's completion. I'm grateful to Clare Ibarra for providing research assistance in the homestretch, to Miriam Pensack for helping me to confirm image permissions in Panama on the eve of publication, and to Kyle Jackson for creating my index. As both a graduate student and a faculty member, I benefited from the wisdom and patience of our department's incredible staff, especially

Marianne Bartholomew-Couts, Kim Bissell, Erin Leigh Inama, Mabel Lee, Janet Flores, and Jan Haase.

Another form of institutional support that was critical to this project was parental leave. When I first heard of the "motherhood penalty" in academia as a graduate student, I did the math and recognized that, if one day I had both job security and children, I was not likely to come by them in that order. UC Berkeley's parental leave policies are among the most supportive of any I've seen in the United States and made me think it was possible to have children on the tenure track. I don't take it for granted. The six months of paternity leave that my husband's employers provided—some of it spent hanging around outside of archives, soothing our infants—was also indispensable and still, in this country, an enormous privilege.

Finally, as we all know, sustaining a project for ten years requires more than intellectual and financial support. Besides giving my life meaning, the friends and family who have surrounded me over these years, most of whom will never read this book, are most responsible for its completion. My friends, especially Erica Mutchler, Macy Parker, Danny Kedem, and Alaine Newland, and my neighbors and community in the Outer Sunset, kept me sane while I nudged my book forward against the headwinds of early parenthood and the pandemic. Jane and Chuck Weber enriched my research visits to DC with their company and a home in Alexandria, and have rooted for me at every turn. My parents, Gary Herman and Sandra Viar Herman, their partners Gail Graham and Rob Cunningham, my sister Stephanie Plaisier, niece Avery Plaisier, and aunt Emily Viar often came to the rescue with child care, cooked meals, comic relief, and company on long walks. My husband, Chris Weber, was sitting beside me on the couch when I first stumbled onto this story in an old Life magazine, and has been an unwavering companion on the long journey since. Jack and Zoe, little agents of chaos, counterintuitively force balance on our lives.

As I type these last words before sending the book to production, we are in the throes of a fourth surge in coronavirus cases and entering the third year of the pandemic. It has been relentless and we are tired. I take inspiration from the people I see muddling through, a day at a time, with kindness and grace for themselves and others—among them, my parents. I dedicate this book to them, grateful for every day that we have.

Cooperating with the Colossus

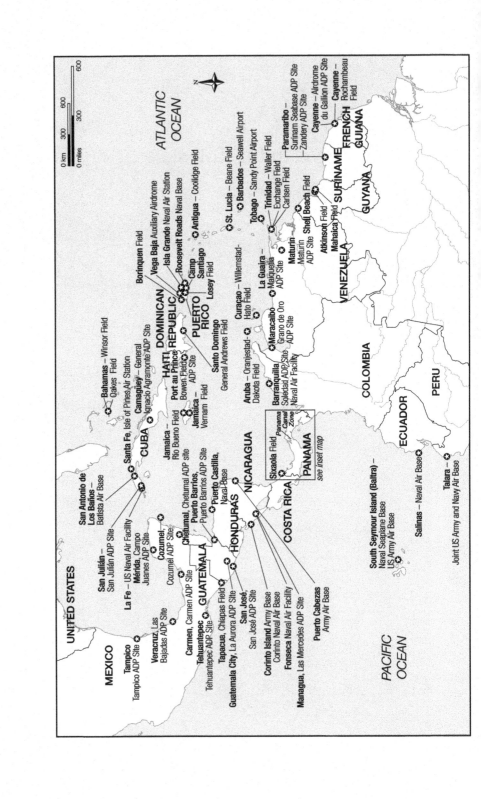

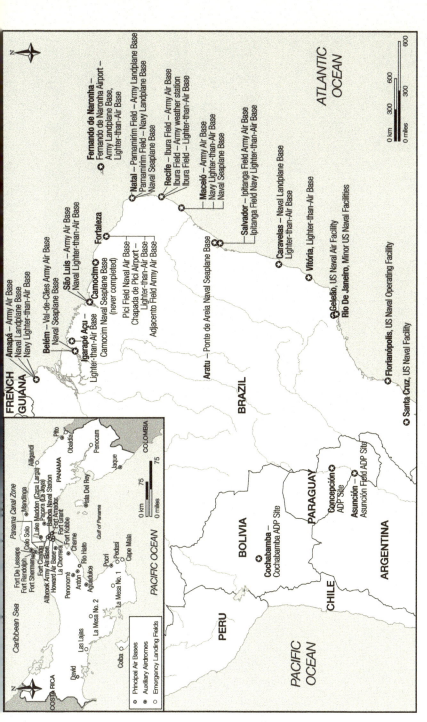

Maps of US defense sites in Latin America and the Caribbean during World War II. I compiled the list of sites included here from various sources over the years, and the list may still be incomplete. The inset map of Panama shows only air defense sites and does not include all of the 134 sites that the US government leased in the Republic of Panama outside of the Canal Zone during World War II.

Key sources: War Department Army Service Forces, Office of the Chief of Engineers, Secret Synopsis of Airport Development Program, November 1, 1945, Box 2009, Entry 433: Correspondence and Reports Relating to the Central and South American Airport Development Program, Record Group 165: Records of the War Department General and Special Staffs, NARA; Captain Bynum E. Weathers, Jr. "US Air Force Historical Study Nr 63: Acquisition of Air Bases in Latin America June 1939–June 1943," USAF Historical Division, Research Studies Institute, Maxwell Air Force Base, Alabama; Paolo Enrico Coletta and K. Jack Bauer, eds, *United States Navy and Marine Corps Bases, Overseas* (Westport, CT: Greenwood Press, 1985).

Introduction

During World War II, the United States established over 200 defense installations on sovereign soil in Latin America. Predictably, it proved to be a fraught affair. When US military planners first called for the acquisition of airbases across the region in the late 1930s, their counterparts in the State Department recognized the truly poor timing of it all. Just a few years earlier, in a bid to improve relations in the Western Hemisphere, the US government had agreed to end three decades of military incursions in Latin America. Under the banner of a new "Good Neighbor" policy, the United States had pulled troops from occupations in Haiti and Nicaragua, renounced the right to meddle in Cuban politics, and renegotiated the terms of governance over the Panama Canal. State Department officials worried that if the United States attempted on the eve of war to extend its military footprint deeper into Latin America than ever before, Washington would burn through the goodwill it had just recently earned, at the precise moment when goodwill in the Americas, thought to be a safeguard against Nazi inroads, had become a national security imperative.

Latin American leaders, for their part, were poorly positioned to greet US appeals for bases favorably. A wave of revolutionary nationalism that began to sweep the region with the Mexican Revolution in 1910 had gained momentum over the succeeding decades. Across the diverse political projects that competed with one another for legitimacy during these revolutionary years, one general point of consensus prevailed that would bear on the wartime story: national sovereignty was the order of the day.[1] The 1933 commitment to non-intervention that Latin American jurists, diplomats, and activists had finally elicited from the United States after

Cooperating with the Colossus. Rebecca Herman, Oxford University Press. © Oxford University Press 2022.
DOI: 10.1093/oso/9780197531860.003.0001

decades of lobbying was widely celebrated. Even as popular support for the Allied cause grew, leaders in Latin America would need to find ways to cooperate in the defense effort without diminishing their nationalist credentials and ensure that a wartime alliance did not merely turn their nations into staging grounds for the US military.

In this context, politicians and diplomats in the Americas, North and South, framed the wartime partnership in novel terms: as an alliance between sovereign peers in a shared project of hemisphere defense. This framing suited the political constraints of the moment well. The project of collective security hung nicely on the multilateral scaffolding built at Pan-American Conferences over the preceding decades, fortified by US affirmations of the sovereign equality of all American Republics. Pan-American unity with the Allied cause acquired an almost mythical quality: the natural fate of New World republics forged in the fight against tyranny. It was not all ideological; the alliance also proved lucrative, as unprecedented sums of US military aid and development assistance greased the wheels of hemispheric cooperation. Investments in roads, railways, airfields, public health infrastructure, military modernization, resource extraction, and cultural and educational exchanges all addressed a mix of US defense interests and Latin American development goals. The general spirit surrounding wartime cooperation when the war drew to a close was one of celebration, and the war period is still regarded as perhaps the brightest point in the otherwise dark history of twentieth-century US–Latin American affairs.

But the matter of basing was contentious. As they negotiated the terms of defense construction and the US military presence, Latin American leaders guarded against any stipulations that might openly diminish their nations' integrity. Questions of legal jurisdiction and governance surrounding the new defense sites were especially problematic, as they transparently threatened that most sacred principle of territorial sovereignty. Diplomats often sidestepped such questions entirely in formal agreements for the sake of expediency and political concord. But on the ground near the bases, the practical details of governance could not be politely ignored. Larger bases were plagued from the beginning by struggles over legal and cultural authority that drew local residents' attention to the very questions of sovereignty that US and Latin American leaders alike had hoped to avoid. Workers demanded that US defense contractors observe local labor laws, police scrambled for the power to patrol the behavior of US personnel, and courts vied for jurisdiction over US troops. The attitudes of racial and cultural superiority that had informed generations of US policy in Latin America, from which Good Neighbor Washington sought to distance itself, were evident in the behavior of US personnel who traveled south for the war effort. On and around the bases, inter-American politics became inter-personal, and these encounters with US power frequently belied the war-time rhetoric of Pan-American fraternity and equality.

This book reconstructs the history of US basing in World War II Latin America, from the elegant chambers of the American foreign ministries to the cantinas, courtrooms, plazas, and brothels surrounding US defense sites. Steeped in conflict, the story of wartime basing certainly departs from the celebratory triumphalism commonly associated with this period in US–Latin American relations, but this book does not wholly upend the conventional account of wartime cooperation. Rather, the history of basing distills, cleanly and dramatically, a central tension that has infused regional affairs since a wave of independence movements first transformed the Americas into a so-ciety of nations: though national sovereignty and international cooperation are compatible concepts in principle, they are difficult to reconcile in practice.

Over the pages that follow and the thousands of miles they traverse, this book considers how a diverse cast of characters sought to reconcile cooperation and sovereignty in the manner that best suited their interests. The US government improvised creative new ways to achieve controversial basing objectives in the region while proclaiming itself within the bounds of the Good Neighbor policy. Latin American heads of state and their for-eign ministers used basing rights as bargaining chips to advance their nation-building agendas with US resources, while limiting overreach by the "Colossus of the North" as best they could. While US and Latin American leaders managed to strike mutually beneficial agreements regarding basing in the realm of high politics, noise from below routinely threatened the peace. Residents of the cities, towns, and villages that came to host US de-fense sites often welcomed the employment and commercial opportunities that US basing projects presented, but the economic benefits of cooperation were overshadowed by social and political turmoil. As the basing project stumbled forward, it ensnared matters of increasing importance in Latin American political contests in the 1930s and 1940s: the consecration of so-cial rights, the role of the state in ensuring social welfare, the relationship between race and citizenship, the propriety of the "modern woman," and the fate of conservative visions of patriarchal honor. Reopening debates in the diplomatic realm that had previously been left unresolved, these conflicts on the ground forced a reckoning. Moving between the local, national, and international spheres in which the wartime basing project unfolded, this book examines the intertwined hierarchies that shaped do-mestic and international politics in the Americas at mid-century.

Historians have not attributed much importance to World War II in the broader trajectory of twentieth-century US–Latin American relations. In overviews of the region's past, the war period is usually portrayed as an atypical moment of harmony that was cut short, and rendered inconsequential, when Cold War security concerns drove US officials to abandon Good Neighbor cooperation and "return" to the interventionism of the past.[2] But that account errs both in taking wartime cooperation at face value, and dismissing postwar cooperation as a charade. This book instead views cooperation critically as an under-scrutinized through-line in the region's past in which the war period was pivotal.

The fact that cooperation has not been a prominent theme in the scholarship on US–Latin American relations may have to do with the political perils of taking it seriously. Cooperation with the United States can appear at first glance as something that forever thwarted democracy and social justice in the region, whether at the hands of *vende-patria* liberal elites in the nineteenth century or *entreguista* dictators in the twentieth. The violence that right-wing military regimes committed in Cold War collaboration with the United States, resulting in the murder, disappearance, and displacement of hundreds of thousands of civilians in the Americas, only made the notion that the word "cooperation" could be used in accounts of US–Latin American relations without placing it between scare quotes all the more dubious. The disinclination to do so lingers in contemporary politics. When, in 2014, Ecuadorian president Rafael Correa expelled fifty US military attachés who had been in Ecuador in the name of inter-American military cooperation, he astutely remarked, "We must be careful when speaking of cooperation. All manner of sins have been committed in the name of cooperation in Latin America."[3]

But the quest for beneficial engagement with the United States has never been the sole purview of oligarchs and anti-communists. Rather, people across the ideological spectrum, inside and outside of the state, have entertained the idea that, with the proper guardrails in place, perhaps something good could come of cooperation with the Colossus of the North. At the center of this study is an understanding that nation building is an inherently international undertaking. This is true for more powerful nations like the United States, whose wealth and international influence feed one another, as well as for less powerful countries. National sovereignty, in the absence of preponderant military power, requires international recognition. Economic development, in the absence of substantial national wealth, requires foreign capital. From the age of independence, Latin American leaders, liberal and conservative alike, endeavored to put the resources of foreign interests in the service of their own agendas, while promoting international norms and institutions that would protect their integrity. Along the way, a curious political ecosystem emerged in which US and European imperialism in the region in the modern era were often built on the back of Latin American nation building, and vice versa. That the material business of nation building has frequently aligned with foreign interests, while the more intangible project of constructing egalitarian democratic societies has not, is the great tragedy at the heart of this configuration, and all the more reason to analyze cooperation as a vital field of contest.

Recently, scholars have begun to do just that, if not entirely self-consciously. The broad intellectual project underway over the last couple of decades to restore Latin American agency to histories of US–Latin American relations has developed in a number of ways that lend themselves to a more nuanced consideration of cooperation. One trend has been to recognize Latin American dictators and other powerful elites as complex historical figures, rather than US lackeys, with their own motivations for enlisting US power.[4] Another has been to examine the work of Latin American diplomats, jurists, and intellectuals as architects of multilateral institutions and international laws that could safeguard the well-being of less powerful nations, while still others have brought renewed attention to collaboration and exchange in economic development and thought.[5]

Other scholarship, concerned more with social and cultural histories than high politics and diplomacy, has found an examination of "close encounters" with US power on the ground in Latin America to be an effective means of understanding the agency of less powerful figures such as peasants, miners, and plantation workers. While resistance remains a popular analytic theme of these ground-level accounts, that portrait of resistance often includes the ingenuity of ordinary people channeling foreign resources toward their own ends, just as the elites of the high political realm did on the international stage.[6] Still further scholarship contemplates transnational solidarity in the Americas outside of the realm of the state by women, workers, and Afro-descended people mobilizing across national lines to contend with the transnational forces of patriarchy, capitalism, and white supremacy.[7] In all of these distinct narratives, there is a common pattern: Latin American actors trying to make the most of partnerships with powerful and well-resourced counterparts from the United States and elsewhere, while also confronting and trying to mitigate the inequality that structures their relationships.

In this book, understanding the tensions between cooperation and sovereignty requires some reconciliation between the top-down and bottom-up frameworks that tend to divide the historical literature. To tell the history of US basing in Latin America from only the perspective of high politics would give a deceptively benign picture of wartime cooperation, blind to the social, cultural, and legal terrain on which struggles over sovereignty played out on the ground, and to the misalignment between principle and practice. At the same time, a single, ground-level account told in isolation would miss the complicated balancing act that leaders engaged in as they navigated the competing demands of nationalism and US partnership, the significant innovation of local adaptations of the regional agenda, and the ways that local conflict shaped US strategy. As scholar Fernando Coronil cautioned, "lest we miss the forest for the trees, the task remains to understand the complex architecture of parts and whole."[8]

To that end, this book brings the diplomatic and social histories of basing together. And, to move nimbly between the local, national, and international spheres, it centers three countries deemed especially vital to US defense planning on the eve of Pearl Harbor: Panama, Brazil, and Cuba. Panama's importance to US defense planning was perhaps the most obvious, as the country was the site of the United States' greatest strategic asset: the Panama Canal. Brazil, a nation previously peripheral to US conceptions of national security, became the second greatest source of strategists' anxiety at this juncture in the aerial age. Military planners deemed the northeastern Brazilian coastline, which extended 1,600 miles across the Atlantic from West Africa, the most likely point of entry for a trans-Atlantic invasion of the Americas. Cuba, long a vital node in the US strategic imaginary, remained an important gateway to the Caribbean and a crucial stepping stone between the continental United States and new fortifications under development in Puerto Rico.

Centering three countries, the book does not give comprehensive coverage to the particular experiences of all sixteen republics that hosted US defense sites or the myriad locations at which they were built. Inter-American security cooperation has, since its inception, impacted different countries in disproportionate ways. During the war, US security interests in Panama were far greater than they were in Paraguay. A country like Brazil enjoyed greater flexibility in responding to US appeals for cooperation than did the Dominican Republic. Mexico, with its long contiguous border abutting the United States, presented US officials with a number of urgent strategic concerns that did not apply to any other nation in the region. And Argentina and Chile, which did not sever ties with the Axis powers until years after their neighbors did, participated only minimally in the wartime arrangement at all. Moreover, struggles over labor rights, women's rights, national belonging and social norms obviously diverged considerably, not only between the nations of Latin America, but also between communities and regions within them. But if Brazil, Cuba, and Panama do not stand in wholesale for their neighbors, this is still a book about a region—the relationship between its parts and the whole. By surveying the common conflicts that arose across these very distinct settings and the locally specific solutions improvised to settle them in each place, the book illustrates the brilliant flexibility and adaptability of this nascent practice of security cooperation as an instrument of US power, a resource of Latin American political and military elites, and an interloper in local social and political conflicts.

The chapters of the book take an hourglass shape as they move between scales, beginning at the regional level, shifting into the bilateral realm, then down to the ground of the bases themselves, and back again. Chapter 1 begins by surveying the problem of basing in the Western Hemisphere from the perspectives of its various constituents. The United States' existing military footprint on sovereign soil in Latin America when the war began consisted of the Guantanamo Naval Base and various installations inside the Panama Canal Zone. Holdovers from the heyday of early twentieth-century US interventionism and lightning rods for anti-US sentiment, these spaces haunted wartime efforts to acquire defense installations in a purportedly new era in inter-American affairs. While the American Republics made strides in advancing multilateral commitments to neutrality and mutual security at Pan-American Conferences, basing as a feature of hemisphere defense remained a delicate topic relegated to the back rooms.

And yet US defense sites soon appeared across the region. Through a number of different programs, most prominently a covert defense construction program carried out by the commercial airline Pan American Airways, the United States ultimately established two chains of airbases that encircled a substantial portion of the Americas. One ran through the Caribbean, along the northern coast of South America and around the "Brazilian bulge," and the other through Mexico and Central America, joining the first chain along the northern coast of South America. After the attack on Pearl Harbor, further bases were established on the Pacific, in Peru, mainland Ecuador, and in Ecuador's Galápagos Islands; additional airfields were built in Bolivia and Paraguay; and a new state-of-the-art airbase was constructed in the Cuban town of San Antonio de los Baños. Panama alone hosted a total of 134 US defense sites on land located outside of the Canal Zone, in addition to the defense installations that dotted the landscape within the Zone. The bases ranged in size and scope from freshly paved runways guarded by plainclothes technicians in Mexico to the largest

US airbase outside of US continental borders in the Brazilian Northeast, teeming with men in uniform.

Chapter 2 explores how Latin American leaders deftly engaged US appeals for basing rights. While the multilateral arena set the tone for Pan-American solidarity, the nuts and bolts of wartime defense cooperation were worked out bilaterally between the United States and each American Republic. Accordingly, this chapter departs the multilateral realm to focus on the particular experiences of the three countries at the heart of this study. Arnulfo Arias and Ricardo de la Guardia in Panama, Getúlio Vargas in Brazil, and Fulgencio Batista in Cuba each navigated the prospect of a wartime alliance with the United States mindful of the constraints posed by the particular political contests ongoing around them, and careful to calculate what forms of cooperation with the United States might bolster their power and what forms might diminish it.

The attack on Pearl Harbor and relentless German submarine warfare in the Caribbean and South Atlantic rallied greater popular support for the Allied cause across the Americas, making US bases and the soldiers that would staff them less politically risky for Latin American leaders to permit after December 1941. The end of the Nazi-Soviet pact earlier that year and the subsequent alliance between the United States and the USSR helped to bring communists and other popular front affiliates in Latin America on board with inter-American designs for hemisphere defense, and quieted the anti-imperialist critiques of US power in Latin America that would otherwise have found productive propaganda in the opening of US bases. Nonetheless, leaders of all three countries sought to place firm constraints on the US military presence while soliciting quid pro quo military and development aid in return for the bases, with varying degrees of success.

Even as security cooperation moved forward at a high political level, local conflicts began to arise as ground broke on new defense sites. Chapters 3 through 6 zero in on particular bases in Cuba, Panama, and Brazil and the communities in which they were built. Each of these chapters focuses on a specific governance issue that arose at defense sites over the course of the war. Chapter 3 examines struggles over labor rights that erupted at defense sites in Cuba and Brazil when workers denounced the United States' violation of certain provisions of labor law recently instituted in each country. Chapter 4 explores the threat that race- and nation-based discrimination against workers from across the circum-Caribbean who were recruited for defense construction in Panama posed to the project of Pan-American unity. Chapter 5 considers how the arrival of US soldiers at bases in all three countries upset local social practices and fueled the growth of sex industries, leading community members to lament the degrading moral influence of the US presence. US officials' efforts to mitigate the ill will that the soldiers' presence inspired in this arena, from the provision of "healthy" recreation options to the improvisation of new systems for regulating red light districts, often simply caused greater offense. Chapter 6 considers the enduring struggles surrounding questions of criminal jurisdiction over US soldiers in Latin America as US authorities asserted extraterritorial authority over US personnel, while an array of residents, police officers, judges, and foreign ministers insisted that the right to enforce national laws within national borders was an essential feature of national sovereignty.

In the absence of formal agreements regarding governance, local battles over law, rights, culture, and authority pulled at the seams of diplomatic cooperation. Something more was at stake than the narrow technical questions of legal authority around which they pivoted. When US firms denied workers' rights or US soldiers failed to appear in court, when US military authorities took it upon themselves to monitor local sex industries or to segregate their workforce, US power was brought to bear on charged matters of state formation. Sometimes conflicts were resolved locally, but often, residents near base sites appealed to their national leaders, or sometimes directly to Washington, in protest. On those occasions, Latin American authorities found themselves pegged between conflicting domestic and international political prerogatives. Leaders in Cuba, Brazil, and Panama responded in a number of ways: informally stripping local authorities of their power, leaning on courts, suspending social laws, or simply looking the other way as US personnel improvised extraterritorial rule on the fly. The particular resolutions to conflicts were as varied as the settings in which they played out, but across them, a trend is evident: careful to preserve national sovereignty in principle and proclaim it in rhetoric, leaders of these countries quietly and selectively diminished sovereignty in practice.

Chapter 7 examines the postwar fate of wartime bases and the broader legacy of World War II security cooperation in the region. When the war concluded, actors of all stripes attempted to shape what might remain of the wartime experiments. If Chapters 3 through 6 largely demonstrate the ability of international relations to constrain domestic politics, the postwar history of basing protests in Chapter 7 more clearly shows that the opposite was also sometimes true. That prewar rise of mass politics in the region crested in a democratic spring in Latin America as the war drew to a close; across the region, dictators fell and an ideologically diverse political left flourished. Even where Latin American leaders were willing to use extended basing rights as a new bargaining chip in the postwar era, as in Brazil and Panama, popular protests successfully thwarted those endeavors.

In the international arena, meanwhile, Latin American jurists and diplomats sought to lock in the synergy between US foreign policy practices and Latin American development goals, foregrounding social and economic challenges as central tasks that the nations of the Americas, and the world, should collectively tackle through the new Organization of American States, the new economic order conceived at Bretton Woods, and the new United Nations. The failure of a "Marshall Plan for Latin America" to materialize, however, imbued the postwar years in inter-American affairs with a deep sense of disillusionment from which inter-American multilateralism never recovered. The CIA-orchestrated coup against democratically elected President Jacobo Árbenz of Guatemala, the last survivor of the democratic spring, signaled to many the final nail in the Good Neighbor's coffin.

Rather than mark the end of a brief era bookended by interventionism, however, World War II is better understood as a profoundly important pivot point. The political economy of security cooperation forged in World War II lived on as the war's greatest legacy, deeply consequential in the Cold War years. If US imperialism and Latin American politics had long been intertwined, World War II put security more squarely at the center of that relationship. From anti-communist authoritarians to leftist and centrist democrats, Latin Americans in or seeking power became proficient in the language of US security interests and skilled at translating their nations' needs into the dialect. For US officials, security cooperation remained a more discreet mode of intervention, born of a period conventionally hailed for its non-interventionism. When the perceived threat to hemispheric security changed during the Cold War from "external assailant" to "domestic insurgent," the toolkit devised through wartime horse-trading—military and police training, weapons transfers, development aid, and a multilateral rhetoric of unity undergirded by bilateral quid pro quo—was repurposed, to devastating effect.

But this history is not a mere prelude to the Cold War. In some sense, the domestic and international stories woven together in this book chart the long-term struggles of people in the Americas trying to make good on two abstract political concepts that existed in principle in the Americas since the region became populated by independent republics: equal political citizenship in the domestic sphere, and sovereign equality in the international sphere. By the late 1930s, important strides had been made in the quest for a more dignified politics at home and on the global stage. But these gains were tenuously held on the eve of World War II. It was one thing to draft a new constitution full of progressive social rights, as many countries in the region did during this period, but another to enjoy them. And it was one thing to declare Latin American nations equal peer republics of the United States, but another to see them treated as such in the execution of international affairs. The precariousness with which the gains of mass politics and the Good Neighbor policy were held at this moment made the stakes all the greater. The dust had not yet settled on revolutions in domestic politics and US–Latin American relations when the logistical demands of global war were brought to bear on both.

CHAPTER 1

The Specter of Guantanamo

Despite the US government's general success in obtaining most of the defense sites that US officials sought in Latin America during World War II, there was one particularly instructive failure. In 1940, the United States tried to enlarge the Navy's existing base in Guantánamo Bay but after two years of frustrated negotiations with the Cuban government, the project fell apart. The weight of history in Guantánamo proved too heavy a load for Pan-American unity to bear.

The base had been a prize of US intervention in Cuba's War of Independence from Spain. After intervening in the war in 1898, the US government imposed four years of military occupation on Cuba, which US officials framed, condescendingly, as a gift of tutelage for a people not yet fit for self-government.[1] Washington made the end of the occupation contingent upon Cubans' agreement to add to their new constitution a number of stipulations that ran contrary to the principle of national sovereignty. Through what came to be known as the Platt Amendment, the United States formally reserved the right to intervene in Cuba's domestic affairs, to oversee Cuba's foreign relations, and to establish naval stations on the island, with the site in Guantánamo Bay already chosen for its advantageous position in the Windward Passage.[2]

The text of the 1903 lease of the Guantanamo base, which declared Cuba's "ultimate sovereignty" over the leased lands and waters, but granted the United States "complete jurisdiction and control" therein, seemed to capture in distilled form Cuba's broader predicament as a new nation whose independence was riddled with caveats: sovereignty without jurisdiction was farcical.[3] The Platt Amendment justified a number of further

Cooperating with the Colossus. Rebecca Herman, Oxford University Press. © Oxford University Press 2022.
DOI: 10.1093/oso/9780197531860.003.0002

US interventions in Cuban affairs over the following decades, including two subsequent military occupations, and US economic and military power became integrated features of the domestic political landscape.

The effort to expand the base in Guantánamo Bay in 1940 ran headlong into new constraints on US power—within Cuba and in Latin America more broadly—that were quite different from what they had been at the turn of the century. In Cuba, thirty years of frustration with the unfulfilled promises of the wars for independence precipitated a revolution in 1933. In the wake of the revolution, the Cuban government abrogated the Platt Amendment and denounced the US base in Guantánamo Bay in the name of national sovereignty. In 1940, Cubans authored a new constitution to replace the one written under US occupation, and while Cuba's first constitution had facilitated the base in Guantánamo Bay, its second expressly prohibited foreign powers from leasing any further territory.[4] A treaty to enlarge the base during World War II would have to clear the Cuban Senate and might require an amendment to the months-old constitution, ensuring ample public debate. A larger US base in Guantánamo Bay was not a hill than any Cuban politician was eager to die on.

The international climate had also changed in ways that further constrained US designs for Guantanamo by 1940. The relentless efforts of Latin American jurists, diplomats, and activists to curb US and European meddling in the region, as well as the shifting priorities of the US government, led Washington to reposition itself as a "Good Neighbor" in Latin America. At an Inter-American Conference in Montevideo in 1933, the US government formally conceded to a principle of inter-American relations that US administrations had refused to endorse at nearly every previous conference: "No state has the right to intervene in the internal or external affairs of another."[5] In the spirit of the Good Neighbor policy, the United States yielded to Cuba's abrogation of the Platt Amendment, but Washington rebuffed Cuban calls to close the base in Guantánamo Bay. So the US Navy lingered, as did ample skepticism about whether the United States would honor its new commitments.

Both the Good Neighbor policy (as a source of goodwill) and the Guantanamo Naval Base (a persisting source of ill will) became all the more important to US interests over the course of the decade, as a second global war appeared increasingly likely. When Washington called on all American Republics to unite and cooperate in the defense of the hemisphere, the task of squaring the United States' multilateral vision for hemispheric unity with its unilateral basing agenda was complicated. Guantanamo represented a politics from which US diplomats and Latin American leaders alike were eager to distance themselves. And yet, US defense strategy at the end of the 1930s called for more defense infrastructure in Latin America, not less. The specter of Guantanamo and all it signified would haunt that enterprise in Cuba and beyond. No matter the strides made in reframing the nature of US intentions in the region in terms that celebrated equal partnership, the practical matter of bases perpetually dredged up the past.

BASING, SOVEREIGNTY, AND ANTI-IMPERIALISM IN THE AMERICAS

As the US and Cuban governments considered various ways to meet the desires of the US Navy in Guantánamo Bay, Laurence Duggan, chief of the Division of the American Republics in the US State Department, opined that even if their Cuban counterparts could "wangle some legal technicality" that would allow the United States to enlarge the Guantanamo base without the approval of the Cuban Senate, he thought it inadvisable. He argued that whatever strategic gains that might come from a larger Guantanamo would not likely outweigh the political costs, and advocated instead "some cooperative arrangement." It was one thing, Duggan reasoned, to secure exclusive bases on British territory in the Caribbean, but another entirely to do so in the independent American Republics.[6]

Duggan's understanding of the distinct possibilities for US basing in the British territories of the Caribbean compared to the Spanish American Republics located beside them captured a basic reality of overseas basing in the 1930s. It was what made them so objectionable from the perspective of Latin American nations guarding their sovereignty: bases were a distinctly colonial institution. The United States' existing military footprint on the eve of World War II bore this out. Though the nation today maintains some 800 defense sites in sovereign countries around the globe, on the eve of World War II, US bases outside of US continental borders numbered only fourteen and mapped, almost exclusively, onto the United States' colonial possessions: Hawaii, Puerto Rico, Alaska, the Midway Islands, Johnston Atoll, American Samoa, the US Virgin Islands, Wake Island, the Philippines, and Guam.[7] Others were located at ports in Asia among populations that the United States and Western European powers did not recognize as entitled to the full privileges of Westphalian sovereignty.

Officials like Duggan recognized what a tall order US basing on Latin American soil would be at a time when territorial sovereignty was sacrosanct. The integrity of national sovereignty had been a central concern of Latin American nations since the time of their founding. It was a concern of US officials as well. In 1823, US president James Monroe famously pronounced the Western Hemisphere off limits to further European colonization. The Monroe Doctrine, through various reinventions, would remain a central pillar of US policy in the Americas, and would become a persisting source of tension in inter-American relations. No Latin American republic disagreed with the Monroe Doctrine's rebuke of European colonialism, but neither did Latin Americans want the cost of freedom from European colonization to be US imperialism.

Washington gave those wary of US power in the Americas cause for concern. The United States' mid-nineteenth-century war against Mexico, through which Mexico lost half of its national territory, rendered the idea of the US as a guardian of Latin American freedom laughable. So too did recurring US filibuster expeditions to conquer Latin American territories in the Caribbean and Central America in the nineteenth century. The United States was not the only interventionist power to assume control of independent territory in the Americas at this time—most notably, France occupied Mexico and Spain annexed the Dominican Republic in the 1860s. Inter-American border wars continuously reshaped the contours of Latin American Republics, further reifying anxieties around territorial integrity. But by the early twentieth century, the danger of European recolonization had largely dissipated, borders were somewhat less embattled, and the United States emerged as the greatest perceived threat to sovereignty in much of Latin America.

The only defense sites that the United States occupied on purportedly sovereign land in Latin America on the eve of World War II—in Guantánamo Bay and the Panama Canal Zone—were both conquests of the early twentieth century, a period noteworthy for the overt and unapologetic nature of US interference in the governance of Spanish American Republics in and around the Caribbean basin. The same year that the United States signed the lease for the base in Guantánamo Bay, it also sent warships to the isthmus of Panama to back a cohort of Panamanian elites who declared their independence from Colombia. In return for US support, Panamanians granted Washington rights to build a trans-isthmian canal on terms that the Colombian legislature had just recently rejected on the grounds that they were too offensive to Colombian sovereignty.

The Hay–Bunau-Varilla Treaty, signed between the United States and Panama in the days following Panamanian independence, permitted the United States to build a canal and to control a ten-mile strip of land running along the waterway, cutting the new nation in two. The resultant Canal Zone was a 553-square mile territory, a space strikingly similar to Guantanamo insofar as governance was concerned. While the treaty recognized that the sovereignty of the Canal Zone territory was "actually vested" in Panama, it gave the United States "all the rights, power and authorities within the zone . . . which the United States would possess and exercise if it were the sovereign."[8] That condition of sovereignty without jurisdiction within the Canal Zone, as in Guantánamo Bay, appeared a poetic commentary on the nature of Panama's relationship to the United States, as the treaty also granted the United States a broad mandate to intervene in Panama's domestic affairs as well as a number of responsibilities in Panamanian governance ordinarily possessed by the national government of a sovereign state.

Comparing British imperial expansion to that of the United States, Theodore Roosevelt laid bare the colonial logic that underlay his government's actions in the Caribbean: racialized skepticism regarding Latin Americans' capacity for self-government. Writing to Cecil Spring Rice in the British Foreign Office, Roosevelt explained, "It was a good thing for Egypt and the Sudan, and for the world, when England took Egypt and the Sudan. It is a good thing for India that England should control it. And so it is a good thing, a very good thing, for Cuba and for Panama and for the world that the United States has acted as it has actually done during the last six years. . . . The politicians and revolutionaries at Bogotá are entitled to precisely the amount of sympathy we extend to other inefficient bandits."[9]

The concurrent timing of the United States' acquisition of the Guantanamo Naval Base and the Panama Canal Zone was not coincidental. In the 1890s, naval strategist Alfred Thayer Mahan had famously advocated the importance of a canal and two-ocean navy to the growth of US commercial and military power.[10] The base in Guantánamo would enable the aspiring global power to stand guard in the Caribbean and control the essential Windward Passage through which ships traveled between the site of the future canal and the eastern seaboard of the United States. Together, they formed part of a broader geography of US power projection cobbled together during this period. Through the War of 1898, in addition to the Guantanamo base, the United States acquired rights to build a second base in Bahía Honda, Cuba, as well as formal colonies in Puerto Rico, Guam, and the Philippines.[11] Washington annexed the Hawaiian Islands the same year and Samoa two years later. The completion of the Panama Canal in 1914 and the acquisition of the US Virgin Islands in 1917 rounded out a map of US power projection within the Caribbean and toward the Pacific.

Disregard for the sovereignty of Latin American Republics in and around the Caribbean became a persistent source of resentment in Latin America. While the Guantanamo base and the Panama Canal Zone were unique in many ways, the farce of sovereignty-without-jurisdiction resonated, to varying degrees, with the experiences of American Republics across the

Caribbean basin in the first decades of the twentieth century whose autonomy was circumscribed by US meddling. In 1904, Theodore Roosevelt pledged that the United States would act as the hemisphere's "international police power," inserting itself into the domestic affairs of Latin American Republics if and when they "require[d] intervention by some civilized nation."[12] What came to be known as the Roosevelt Corollary to the Monroe Doctrine justified US intervention on the grounds that in order to keep Europe out, the United States would have to intercede in any political or economic instability that might otherwise give European powers cause to intervene. The pledge justified over thirty US military interventions in as many years—in Mexico, Honduras, Guatemala, Nicaragua, Haiti, the Dominican Republic, Costa Rica, and Panama—and made clear to the American Republics of the Caribbean basin that, though they were not colonies of the United States, neither did the US government consider them equal peers.[13]

The South American Republics fit within the imaginary of the United States' sphere of influence and were included, rhetorically, in declarations such as the Monroe Doctrine, but the hierarchy in early twentieth-century inter-American relations had multiple tiers, and US diplomats tended to perceive the larger republics as a class apart from the smaller nations whose "chronic wrongdoing" seemed to demand such extensive US tutelage.[14] The countries of South America were more closely tied to Europe, both culturally and economically, than they were to the United States at that point. And geographically, they were simply too far away from US borders in the naval age to possess the same immediate strategic importance in the minds of US officials that the countries in and bordering the Caribbean did.

However, though US interventions were concentrated in one region within the Americas, the anti-imperialism that those interventions incited was not. Campaigns against US intervention spanned from Mexico to Argentina. In fact, the threat of intervention, not just from the United States but also from Europe, had been a unifying anxiety through which anti-imperialists in the Americas had first forged "Latin America" as a regional identity in the 1860s.[15] During the same period, Argentine jurist Carlos Calvo, recognizing international law as a promising tool that could safeguard the sovereignty of the Latin American Republics despite the asymmetries of economic and military power that disadvantaged them on the international stage, championed a legal doctrine that would proscribe the use of military or diplomatic intervention to collect on debts.[16] The broader ideological work of building a distinctly Latin American anti-imperialism extended far south as well; literary denunciations of the United

States were not just the purview of Cuban José Martí or Nicaraguan Rubén Dário, but also Uruguayan José Enrique Rodó.

Pressure from Latin America to halt US intervention only grew during the twenty-four years between the presidencies of the two Roosevelts, augmented by the rise of revolutionary nationalisms across the region. Though the quest for national sovereignty was an international project in many respects, it was also a matter of domestic concern. Nationalists understood the deep socioeconomic stratification within Latin American societies and Latin American nations' international subordination to Europe and, increasingly, the United States, to be mutually reinforcing. That entanglement of domestic and international power imbued twentieth-century revolutionary political agendas in Latin America with inexorable international dimensions, even when focused primarily on achieving domestic political change. Beginning with the Mexican Revolution in 1910, mass political movements arose across the region that endeavored to create more inclusive political and economic systems and condemned the complicity of foreign interests in the anti-democratic nature of early twentieth-century governance. The Great Depression only exacerbated the crisis of the old liberal order. Both fascism and popular front anti-fascism blossomed during this period, and the adherents of these opposing perspectives shared at least one tenet in common: an abiding commitment to anti-imperialism.

At the same time that popular nationalism gained strength across the region, the project to advance international norms that would protect the sovereignty of Latin American Republics proceeded at Inter-American Conferences. US secretary of state James G. Blaine had convened the first of these meetings in 1889 with the objective of advancing US economic interests in the region. While few would dispute that these conferences largely worked as intended in that regard, Latin Americans also sought to use them as a venue for pushing back against US overreach.[17] The goal of halting US military intervention became a particular fixation at these conferences from the time of Theodore Roosevelt's presidency onward. At every principal conference held from 1906 to 1933, representatives of different countries—Argentina, Uruguay, Costa Rica, and Mexico—introduced resolutions that insisted, in one way or another, on the two basic principles that they hoped to make the keystones of an emerging inter-American system: the juridical equality of all American nations and the principle of non-intervention.

During these decades, meanwhile, thinking around US policy in Latin America was shifting within the White House and the State Department. Though Franklin Roosevelt is most commonly associated with the policy of non-intervention in Latin America, the preceding administrations of Calvin Coolidge and Herbert Hoover had also both recognized that occupations and interventions in the Caribbean basin seemed to create more problems than they solved. The Great Depression only reified that conclusion, as the US government sought to redirect scarce resources away from costly occupations overseas to attend to more pressing matters at home. After signing on to the principle of non-intervention in Montevideo in 1933, Roosevelt's administration moved to end the most flagrant persisting violations of that principle by removing US marines from Haiti and revising the treaties with Cuba and Panama that sanctioned US interference in those countries' domestic affairs.

The Guantanamo Naval Base and the Panama Canal Zone both survived the Good Neighbor reorientation in US policy towards Latin America, but they did so awkwardly. Cuban and Panamanian leaders at the helm of negotiations with US officials as they hashed out new treaties had to navigate the surge of anti-imperialist nationalism that had transformed their countries in recent years, while grappling with the continued preponderance of US power. Good Neighbor diplomats eager to distance themselves from the old paternalist approach professed that going forward, the United States would engage Cuba and Panama and the other Republics as juridically equal sovereign peers, but what that might mean in practice remained to be seen.

US DEFENSE AS A HEMISPHERIC UNDERTAKING

The imperialist connotations of overseas basing, at a time when the United States sought to assuage concerns of US imperialism in Latin America, became only more problematic when US defense planners reimagined national security as a hemispheric undertaking that extended beyond the traditional focus on the Caribbean. Advances in aviation and weapons technology over the 1920s and 1930s, particularly the development of the naval aircraft carrier and long-range bomber, dramatically changed the way that defense strategists and leaders in Washington understood US vulnerability. This shift became evident as tensions mounted in Europe. By the fall of 1938, Roosevelt was convinced that the United States would only be safe as long as no hostile power gained a foothold anywhere in the Americas.[18] As he explained at a press conference, "as a result of scientific advancement in waging war, the whole orientation of this country in relation to the continent on which we live—in other words, from Canada to Tierra del Fuego . . . has had to be changed."[19]

In November 1938, a Joint Planning Committee of officers from the War Plans divisions of the Army and Navy sketched out the infrastructure required for the United States to unilaterally defend the Americas from Axis aggression. The final report, concluded in April of the following year, and the series of War Plans that the services developed once that report was approved, became the basis on which US officials from the State, War, and Navy departments would strategize the growth of the US military footprint in Latin America.[20]

The most pressing site of concern was the Panama Canal, which permitted the US military crucial mobility between the Atlantic and Pacific oceans. Existing US military infrastructure in the Canal Zone was originally designed with naval defense of the canal in mind, but aerial defense of the canal would require defense infrastructure beyond the limits of the zone, including radar installations and a network of outlying bases in Panama and neighboring countries. The Brazilian northeast, which extended a mere 1,600 miles across the South Atlantic from French West Africa, was the other major focal point of US defense anxiety at this time. Were France to fall, the thinking went, it would not be difficult for German forces to make their way across the ocean, but it would be nearly impossible to dislodge them once they arrived. From the Brazilian northeast, German troops might move north across the Caribbean to invade the United States or attack the Canal.

Recognizing the challenges inherent to basing on sovereign soil in Latin America, US officials looked to their own colonies as well as those of Great Britain to meet as much of the infrastructural need in the Western Hemisphere as possible. Washington poured money and men into Puerto Rico, endeavoring to turn the island into the "Gibraltar of the Caribbean." The commanding general of the Panama Canal Department advocated the formal acquisition of new island territories that would enhance the defense of western approaches to the canal— Ecuador's Galápagos Islands and Costa Rica's Cocos Island—but the recognition that territorial expansion in the Americas would surely invite the ire of Latin American anti-imperialists led the War Department to ultimately desist.[21] Finally, in the famed "Bases for Destroyers" deal struck with Great Britain in September 1940, the United States gave Britain fifty US Navy destroyers in return for ninety-nine-year leases on land in British colonial territories, where the United States could establish air and naval bases. In fact, it was only once the US military base in Jamaica was nearly completed that the US government finally abandoned its frustrated efforts to expand the size of the base in Guantánamo Bay.[22]

But bases in colonized territories alone were inadequate to meet the demands of US defense planners at this early moment in the aerial age. If advances in aviation technology meant that the United States would now need airfields in the Western Hemisphere, the persisting limitations of that technology meant that the United States would need a lot of airfields. Planes could fly farther without refueling, but their range was still limited. Even transit between the continental United States and a major base in Puerto Rico could require the use of intermittent airfields in Cuba or Haiti. In August 1939, Roosevelt approved plans for the "aeronautical development of Latin America," which called for primary facilities at 400 mile intervals and smaller, intermediate facilities at 130 mile intervals.[23] In addition to adequate runways for the movement of different types of military aircraft, the Army called for the development of appropriate meteorological equipment, refueling and servicing facilities, radio aids, and housing for personnel.[24]

Further complicating matters, the invasion scenarios that drove US defense planning typically included some element of Latin American complicity in Axis designs, which underscored the importance of securing not just the borders of the American Republics but also the loyalty of their citizens and governments. Though historians now agree that the Axis threat to Latin America was largely overblown, rumors abounded of a fifth column of Nazi sympathizers who could help to facilitate a German invasion. US officials eyed the 1.5 million German nationals who lived in various pockets across the region, as well as the large Japanese communities in Peru and Brazil, with suspicion. Rumors touted Germany's involvement in fomenting revolutions in Brazil, Uruguay, and Argentina, and still others described Japanese efforts to acquire islands off the Pacific coast of South America and engage in reconnaissance missions under the guise of commercial fishing operations.[25]

Beyond these more outlandish fears of Axis domination, US officials also worried about the more realistic possibility of Axis sympathies or agnosticism in the Americas. It was not unfathomable that Latin American leaders might look at the global contest and view the prospect of taking sides as detrimental to their economic fortunes.[26] Some, like Argentina, might even conclude that their interests were best aligned with the other side. During the 1930s, Germany had made significant economic inroads in Latin America, advancing preferential trade deals that expanded Germany's share of trade. In the 1930s, many Latin American leaders, from Mexico to Brazil, favored corporatist political structures not unlike those of fascist Europe, and it was no secret that some military leaders in the region admired the German military machine or that many had received training from German military advisers. Fascist organizations like the Brazilian Integralistas grew in number during these years, and Francisco Franco's victory in Spain thrilled Falangists in the region who touted Hispanicism as an alternative to Pan-Americanism.

The fact that long-standing anti-US sentiment so rampant in the region could prove a powerful asset for Axis propagandists made the Good Neighbor policy and the goodwill that it generated more important to US interests than ever before. The challenge that officials concerned with US defense faced by the end of the decade was that the principal objectives of defensive planning in Latin America in the late 1930s—basing and goodwill—seemed to run at cross purposes. The State Department formally opposed new defense construction on sovereign Latin American soil by any official US government agency, contending that the backlash against base-building could offset the gains achieved by the Good Neighbor Policy, imperiling one security objective in pursuit of another.[27]

Important

THE MULTILATERAL MONROE DOCTRINE

The United States' vision for hemisphere defense in World War II was, in many respects, yet another iteration of the Monroe Doctrine. Whatever else had changed in US policy in Latin America in recent years, that 100-year-old project of "keeping Europe out" continued. Franklin Roosevelt attempted to reinvent the Monroe Doctrine in terms that denounced the bullish unilateralism of the (Theodore) Roosevelt Corollary. He championed a "continental solidarity in which we are *one* of the republics" and insisted that hemisphere defense would be a collective endeavor.[28] At Inter-American Conferences from 1936 onward, Roosevelt's administration pitched a multilateral framework for hemisphere defense that enlisted the other American Republics as partners in maintaining neutrality in the region and, later, in joining the Allied cause.

Historians typically point to a series of consultations and key resolutions passed at inter-American Conferences over the late 1930s and early 1940s as evidence of the Good Neighbor policy's success in achieving unity in the face of war. The American Republics took initial steps toward creating a system of mutual security at the Conference for the Maintenance, Preservation and Reestablishment of Peace in Buenos Aires in 1936, where representatives agreed to consult and cooperate with one another when peace in the Americas was threatened. At a subsequent conference in Lima in 1938, the American Republics created a formal protocol for consultation through emergency meetings of the American foreign ministers on an as-needed basis. The first such meeting convened in Panama the following year, after France and Great Britain declared war on Germany. There, the foreign ministers affirmed their commitment to continental solidarity and neutrality and established a neutrality zone around the Americas from which belligerent ships would be excluded.[29]

At a Second Meeting of the American Foreign Ministers that was convened after the fall of France in 1940, diplomats agreed to an essential principle of hemispheric solidarity: an attack on any one American Republic would be treated as an attack on all.[30] By the time that the foreign ministers met a third time, a few weeks after the attack on Pearl Harbor, twelve of the twenty Latin American Republics had already broken diplomatic relations with Axis powers and nine of them had also declared war. The meeting concluded with a recommendation that all American Republics sever ties with the Axis powers, which all but two, Chile and Argentina, proceeded to do. Eventually, though quite a bit later, even the holdouts relented and declared war as well—Chile in 1943 and Argentina in 1945—creating unanimous American support for the Allies by the war's conclusion.

The success of the multilateral pitch for hemisphere defense is not surprising considering the long-held desires within Latin America for a more collaborative inter-American system that could deliver real benefits to its constituent members. Early twentieth-century architects of American international law—prominent lawyers like Argentine Luis María Drago, Chilean Alejandro Álvarez, and Uruguayan Baltasar Brum—had explicitly advocated a multilateral Monroe Doctrine through which the nations of the Americas would work together to prevent European intervention, but they were rebuffed by the unilateral impulses of US policymakers.[31]

Wartime cooperation was also attractive for the extent to which it extended beyond military matters to include various forms of economic cooperation and technical assistance. The most devout proponents of the goodwill security imperative in Roosevelt's administration argued that improving social welfare in Latin America was a matter of US security, worthy of US support and investment. "Nazism has offered a 'better' political and economic way of life, a positive program of action, an incentive and a goal, in short—a hope," wrote Vincenzo Petrullo of the Office of Strategic Services in a memo to the State Department. To the contrary, "the Democracies have been depending on diplomatic accords, polite expressions of faith, and the hit or miss goodwill of commercial entrepreneurs. . . .Very little has been tried in fields which affect the daily life of the ordinary citizen and no direct action has been taken to sell the democratic way of life to the people at large."[32] US aid for Latin American development could hold off Axis inroads, officials like Petrullo thought, by promoting feelings of goodwill toward the United States and making fascism less appealing as a political and economic project. The economic disruption in Latin America caused by European conflict had only made the matter more urgent.

Convinced of the economic and cultural dimensions of hemispheric security, Franklin Roosevelt established a new wartime agency called the Office of Coordination of Commercial and Cultural Relations between the American Republics in 1940, under the leadership of Nelson Rockefeller. Later renamed the Office of the Coordinator of Inter-American Affairs (OIAA), the agency's mission was "to provide for the development of commercial and cultural relations between the American Republics thereby increasing the solidarity of this hemisphere and furthering the spirit of cooperation between the Americas in the interest of hemisphere defense."[33] The OIAA's best-known work was in the field of cultural diplomacy and propaganda. The agency flooded the region with Pan-American and pro-Ally messaging by sponsoring radio programming and distributing news features, photographs, and pamphlets that painted the United States as a good neighbor. Enlisting high-profile artists like Walt Disney, the Motion Picture Division produced and distributed both feature films and educational materials, in addition to the physical equipment required to screen them.[34]

But the Coordinator's Office also undertook development programs involving public health, railroad and road building, and food supply throughout the region. The perceived value of each initiative to hemisphere security was multilayered and demonstrated the ways that US security interests could overlap with Latin American nation-building concerns. For instance, the stated objectives of public health programing included protecting the health of the US armed forces stationed in the region, increasing the productivity of workers involved in the extraction of important raw materials, and achieving a broader goodwill security objective, "to demonstrate by deeds as well as words the tangible benefits of democracy in action and to win active support of the civilian population."[35] Road-building projects and food supply programs could similarly meet concrete strategic objectives related to the defense effort in addition to inviting broader goodwill by providing states with needed infrastructure.

The wide-ranging agenda for hemisphere defense reached its most capacious framing at the Third Foreign Ministers meeting held in Rio in January 1942, when representatives from foreign ministries across the Americas described their work as a matter of "joint cooperation in the solution of the outstanding problems of the continent."[36] The Final Act called for collaboration in endeavors of obvious military value, such as the production of strategic materials; the improvement and accessibility of air, rail, road, and maritime transportation and communication infrastructure; and the fight against subversive activities. But it also called for cooperation in matters whose connection to hemisphere defense was a bit more removed, such as the improvement of health and sanitation, the maintenance of internal economic stability, national development, and the development of "civilization and culture."[37]

An expansive understanding of mutual security that included economic and social issues aligned with long-standing visions for the inter-American system coming from Latin America, where activists, labor leaders, scientists, intellectuals, and others bought into the promise of inter-American exchange and Pan-American cooperation. In addition to the principal Inter-American Conferences attended by diplomats from across the Americas, the emerging inter-American system also grew from more specialized meetings convened by actors and activists committed to developing international solutions to wide-ranging shared dilemmas. By one count, between 1889 and 1940, at least 159 specialized inter-American meetings took place.[38]

Even as nationalism surged in the 1930s, the period was also a dynamic one for Pan-American projects, invigorated by the opening that the Great Depression provided for imaginative ways of rethinking social, economic, and political life. Feminists met at Pan-American conferences where they advocated an international agenda for women's rights.[39] International labor organizers complemented their active participation in the International Labor Organization (ILO) with a regional counterpart, the Latin American Labor Confederation (Confederación de Trabajadores de América Latina, or CTAL). Latin American economists, meanwhile, pushed to create an Inter-American Development Bank that could change the nature of international economic governance in the Americas in ways that better suited the interests of debtor nations.[40] Each of these endeavors was shot through with the inevitable tensions resulting from regional power asymmetries, but common to them all was belief in a certain promise of engaging in inter-American cooperation despite its pitfalls: if the domestic and international hierarchies of the old liberal order were mutually reinforcing and under assault, perhaps a more dignified international order could support a more dignified domestic politics. More than perhaps any time before or since, the old promise of Pan-Americanism was manifest. The typically divergent US and Latin American visions for inter-American cooperation finally seemed to align.

A project of continental solidarity in addressing the hemisphere's social and economic problems mapped well onto the recent turn in US–Latin American affairs, but the fact remained that a large-scale US overseas basing agenda did not. At the same time that the Roosevelt administration built up the multilateral vision of hemisphere defense at inter-American meetings, it pursued basing objectives through less public channels.

After Roosevelt first approved of the general plan to build strategic airfields across Latin America in the fall of 1939, the sense of urgency around the project briefly subsided and US defense planning went into a lull over the winter. But when Germany invaded the Low Countries and France in May 1940, efforts to obtain the desired base sites in Latin America became an urgent priority once more and planning resumed at a faster clip. The US government dealt with Cuba and Panama directly in their efforts to expand the Guantanamo base and Canal Zone defense infrastructure, but authorities were uncertain about how to obtain defense sites in new locations. The problem was two-pronged: figuring out how to build the airfields and infrastructure across Latin America that defense planners desired, and obtaining permission from Latin American governments to use them once built.

An interdepartmental committee of the War Department, Civil Aeronautics Authority, and the State Department convened to consider a plan for defense construction. In considering various solutions to the problem the committee emphasized three interconnected priorities: speed, the ability to avoid "enabling legislation," and "the maintenance of friendly relationships with the other sovereign states in the Western Hemisphere."[41] Though it was the War Department representative's preference to formally lease desired sites along the lines of the existing Guantanamo lease, State Department officials noted that a number of Latin American constitutions prohibited leasing land to foreign countries, and, where legally possible, doing so would still be politically objectionable.[42] US Under Secretary of State Sumner Welles insisted that if the State Department were to undertake negotiations with the various Latin American countries involved in order to obtain formal rights to build the desired defense sites, the delays incurred in the process could threaten the entire enterprise, and in some instances, final agreement on the matter would prove impossible to reach.[43]

The committee ultimately determined that the most expeditious path forward was to enlist the commercial airline Pan American Airways to establish and maintain the desired airfields under the guise of commercial expansion. Pan American Airways was an obvious candidate for the work.

The airline had gotten its start with a US government contract to carry airmail between Key West and Havana in 1927, and Pan Am soon expanded to other destinations throughout Latin America, often with diplomatic assistance from the State Department. There was an ideal in play that business was simply more nimble than government. And indeed, *Time* magazine would remark of Pan Am's defense contributions in 1941 that the airline worked "so effectively that it has sometimes seemed that the rest of the defense effort, still largely composed of creaks and groans in Washington, should become an arm of Pan American."[44]

Figure 1.1 A wartime advertisement touts Pan American Airways as a goodwill ambassador in Latin America. Courtesy of the John W. Hartman Center for Sales, Advertising & Marketing History, Rubenstein Library, Duke University.

Through what came to be known as the Airport Development Program (ADP), the War Department contracted a newly created Pan American Airways subsidiary called the Pan American Airports Corporation to build airfields across the Americas according to the specifications indicated by the Joint Planning Committee, with money from the President's Emergency War Fund.[45] Pan Am would negotiate any necessary permits for airfield construction and improvement directly with Latin American governments, and often executed the work through local subsidiaries. The airline's ongoing transition from seaplanes to landplanes lent an easy rationale for the construction of expanded facilities and improved runways. By the end of the war, Pan Am's Airport Development Program had built or improved airfields and attendant facilities at fifty-five locations in twelve Latin American countries.[46]

In the near term, the Pan Am contract seemed to solve the problem of infrastructure for US defense planners, but there remained the problem of access. To this end, at the same time that the War Department began negotiating a contract with Pan Am, the State Department arranged for representatives of the US armed forces to meet with their counterparts in each Latin American country to undertake bilateral conversations about security matters. These Staff Conversations were designed as an opportunity to discuss what each Republic might offer the project of security cooperation in the event of extra-hemispheric aggression, but a central objective, as far as the US government was concerned, was to obtain a commitment from each country that the United States would be permitted to use its nation's airfields in the event that it became necessary.[47]

The Staff Conversations were meant to remain secret, to prevent domestic dissenters or Axis propagandists from exploiting sensitive discussions.[48] A scandal in Uruguay validated the inclination toward secrecy, when news reports that the Uruguayan government had secretly agreed to make military bases available to the United States set off a political firestorm. Uruguayan president Alfredo Baldomir Ferrari, elected in 1938, had emerged a prominent ally in the Pan-American defense effort, reassured by Roosevelt's Good Neighbor posturing in the region and the multilateral framing of hemisphere defense efforts. In December 1939, in violation of the inter-American neutrality zone, German and British naval cruisers clashed off the Uruguayan coast in the Battle of the River Plate, bringing the shadow of war to the Southern Cone at the same time that rumors of German plans to colonize Uruguay were circulating.[49] The Uruguayan public generally held both Baldomir and Roosevelt in high regard, and the perception that the two nations must cooperate in hemisphere defense enjoyed widespread support. But when news broke of an alleged secret basing agreement between Uruguay and the United States, the rumors provoked outcry from all political corners.

In public debate over the affair, even those sympathetic to the vision for cooperation in hemisphere defense insisted that while Uruguay must actively and eagerly participate in the defense effort by building up military capacity and mobilizing raw materials, permitting US basing on Uruguayan soil was an entirely different proposition because of the threat that it posed to Uruguayan sovereignty. A prominent senator publicly declared that a US base would be a "double-edged sword" because even if it proved effective for hemisphere defense during the war, it could one day be used against Uruguayans or their neighbors.[50] A news article cautioned that leasing any Uruguayan territory to a foreign power under the pretext of collective defense would render the nation a "de facto protectorate."[51] The specter of Guantanamo hovered closely, as the article listed the "living examples" that Uruguayans should look to as cautionary tales: "Santo Domingo, Nicaragua, Panama, Puerto Rico, and the Philippines, not to mention Cuba which, despite having broken free from the chains of the famous Platt Amendment . . . has not been able to eliminate the United States' de facto occupation of the naval station in Guantanamo."[52]

The scandal made clear that, if US basing in Latin America was an international political problem for US foreign policymakers, it was also a domestic political problem for those Latin America leaders to whom US officials appealed for basing rights. Baldomir's conservative political opposition, led by Senator Luis Alberto de Herrera, seized the issue as a rallying cry. Herrera's newspaper, El Debate, demanded in article after article that Uruguayans "loudly denounce the damage that such agreements would do to national sovereignty."[53] Herrera and his colleagues brought the debate to the Senate floor, where Herrera argued that the basing negotiations made clear that the United States was taking advantage of the international emergency as an opportunity to advance its long-standing project of imperialist expansion in the Americas. In his highly publicized speech, Herrera offered a rapid-fire history lesson on "imperialismo yanqui," ticking off the offenses one by one, much as the press had done, citing "the annexation of Texas and California, that whole Cuba matter, Panama, the Hawaiian islands, Nicaragua, etc."[54]

Uruguayan Foreign Minister Alberto Guani, called to testify before the Senate, attempted to convey the nuance of the discussions that had taken place between the US and Uruguay. Any base under consideration would be Uruguayan, he explained, built and run by Uruguayans, and made available to *all* the American Republics if and when circumstances required. Such a plan, he insisted, aligned perfectly with the multilateral inter-American defense project that enjoyed such widespread support among Uruguayans. He accused conservatives of distorting the issue for political gain. But despite his efforts, at the conclusion of an extraordinary eight-hour session, just after 2 o'clock in the morning, the Senate passed two resolutions. The first declared that the Uruguayan Senate would not, under any circumstances, approve "treaties or conventions which authorize the creation in our territory of air or naval bases which imply a servitude of any kind or diminution of national sovereignty."[55] Though Herrera's party controlled only half the Senate, the vote in support of this resolution was a resounding 25 to 1. In a second, unexpected vote, the Senate also censured Guani.[56]

Nationalists throughout the Americas closely observed the events in Uruguay. One Colombian newspaper declared, "Yesterday, the Uruguayan Senate offered a lesson for Colombians and for all Spanish American countries, when it rejected, by an overwhelming majority of 25 to 1, the authorization to establish air and naval bases in its territory." Bringing the battle to bear on the Colombian domestic political tensions surrounding US-Colombian relations and the prospect of wartime cooperation, the article sniped, "the transcript of this dramatic session of Congress should be read and memorized by the "*jefes* of Colombian *entreguismo* (traitors/sellouts)."[57] Echoing the position held by many in Uruguay, that the boundaries of acceptable forms of cooperation with the Colossus of the North must be carefully policed, the article insisted, "We have said and repeated thousands of times that we are not enemies of the United States, and that . . . we should maintain with that powerful country a politics of friendship and cooperation, founded in equality and mutual respect." But wartime cooperation must not simply lead to further economic and political subordination to the United States, and Colombians must not allow any wartime arrangements to "endanger" their sovereignty.[58]

The episode in Uruguay and its reverberations throughout the Americas underscored the extent to which US and Latin American leaders alike were constrained by popular perceptions and the weight of the past. The international politics of building US bases, and the domestic politics of permitting US bases to be built, seemed to doom the project from the beginning. And yet, the United States would enjoy great success in advancing the infrastructural designs laid out in 1939. Though it struck out in expanding the territorial limits of Guantanamo, Washington successfully obtained installations in sovereign territory spanning the region. How did they manage it? The multilateral program for hemisphere defense set forth at the inter-American conferences was, as one historian put it, "more a spiritual than a tangible military foundation."[59] The details of security cooperation were worked out bilaterally between US officials and their counterparts in each Latin American country, shaped by the divergent circumstances of each prospective partner in defense.

Concerned about growing security (hemispheric) concerns. The US had to adopt a multilateral approach to installations to both forward the Good neighbor policy and balance the political climate in each Latin American country

CHAPTER 2

High Politics and Horse-Trading

"When they write the history of negotiations between the US and Panama, across distinct periods and issues, the story of Panama's cooperation in hemisphere defense and Canal security will stand out," an editorial in Panama's *Acción Comunal* newspaper declared in June 1941. "For the first time, negotiations with our powerful neighbor to the North have been carried out at a roundtable in a plane of perfect equality. Economic and military power have not forced the scales to tilt in a particular direction. We are negotiating equal to equal, as good neighbors." The article credited this unprecedented situation to the man at the helm of Panamanian politics at the time, staunch nationalist (and Acción Comunal leader) Arnulfo Arias, who, the piece contended, refused to consider any proviso of hemisphere defense that "cast even the slightest shadow over our nation's freedom and sovereignty." "For every concession we make, we demand one in return," the editorial affirmed, "and those fateful times when one often heard the refrains 'PANAMA CEDES,' 'PANAMA SURRENDERS,' 'PANAMA RELINQUISHES' seem so distant to us now."[1]

This was not a particularly accurate picture of the status of the basing negotiations between the United States and Panama as they stood in June 1941. The US government was, at the time, well on its way toward occupying 134 defense sites in the Republic of Panama, a nation smaller than the state of Maine. Those 134 sites did not include the additional bases located within the 553 square mile Canal Zone that the United States military already occupied in Panama, which swelled with ever-larger numbers of US military personnel. Arias had indeed pushed back against the more onerous terms that the United States proposed for the new defense sites,

Cooperating with the Colossus. Rebecca Herman, Oxford University Press. © Oxford University Press 2022. DOI: 10.1093/oso/9780197531860.003.0003

such as 999-year lease terms. And he had issued a number of bold requests for compensation for the sites, not only in the form of rental payments for the sites themselves but also indirect compensation in the form of US assistance in advancing a number of infrastructural projects in Panama. But in June 1941, progress on Arias's efforts to obtain quid pro quo benefits had momentarily stalled, and though the two nations were still nearly a year away from reaching an agreement, US troops had already begun to occupy the tracts that the US military most urgently desired. Officials in the US War and State Departments regarded Arias as neither a good neighbor nor an equal, but as a temperamental, fascist-leaning threat to canal security whose removal from office by coup they would warmly welcome just four months later.

However inaccurate its depiction of the status of negotiations, the *Acción Comunal* editorial reflects something else quite accurately: Roosevelt and his State Department were not the only authorities with a vested interest in selling the Good Neighborliness of wartime cooperation to Latin Americans at large in the early 1940s. Those leaders tasked with navigating US wartime security requests against a backdrop of revolutionary nationalism were also invested in the myth of equal partnership in hemisphere defense and dedicated themselves throughout the war years to two general objectives as they navigated the competing impulses of international cooperation and national sovereignty: they sought to make good on the promises of the Good Neighbor creed where they could, and they worked to control the optics where they could not.

PANAMA

Panama was unique among the American Republics not only because it hosted the canal, but also because the treaties governing the canal created a basis for security cooperation that officials could use as a departure point when seeking to expand US defense infrastructure in the Americas on the eve of World War II. While US authorities pursued new defense construction quietly through Pan Am's Airport Development Program (ADP) elsewhere in the region in 1940, Washington approached the Panamanian government directly. Still, when US officials expressed their desire to obtain numerous tracts outside of the Canal Zone for aerial defense of the canal, both governments were cautious not to incite the anti-US sentiment that had become so powerful in recent years and had helped to bring about a sea change in Panamanian politics.

During the first three decades following Panama's 1903 secession from Colombia, an elite cohort consisting mainly of wealthy merchants and urban landlords held political power, often with the assistance of the US marines. Disillusionment with the nature of Panamanian political and economic governance became increasingly acute as a number of crises triggered popular mobilization. In the 1920s, flailing sugar, banana, and coconut markets drove a severe decline in the nation's agricultural sectors and rural residents migrated to urban areas, overwhelming already taxed infrastructure. The Great Depression only made things worse. A decrease in canal traffic caused further economic misery and contributed to rising unemployment. The crisis invigorated a number of sources of political agitation as labor organizing, student mobilization, renters' strikes, and an increasingly vocal sector of the disgruntled middle class began to make new demands on the state. The latter formed the nationalist civic association called the Acción Comunal that condemned ruling elites as antidemocratic authoritarians who prioritized their own economic wealth over the well-being of Panama's people and relied on the complicity of the equally self-interested US government to do so.

In January 1931, prominent figures in the Acción Comunal took power in a coup, ending nearly thirty years of elite rule on the isthmus. The Hoover administration, disinterested in continuing the United States' interventionist policies in Latin America, opted not to intervene on behalf of the overthrown administration, and a new class of nationalist politicians went on to hold power for the better part of the decade that followed. Though the coalition that supported the coup fractured in subsequent years, the nationalism of the group indelibly shaped the period.[2] The successive governments led by Acción Comunal leaders advocated for the kinds of social welfare policies that gained greater popularity elsewhere in the wake of the Depression. US imperialism proved a worthy culprit for Panama's social and economic ills and gave politicians a rallying cry that transcended class concerns. Harmodio Arias, president of Panama from 1932 to 1936, traveled to the White House in 1933, where he demanded a new deal for Panama, and Franklin Roosevelt, who had just recently entered office with a promise to make the United States a good neighbor, agreed to explore one.

It took 110 meetings over three years for US and Panamanian officials to bring the much-reviled Hay-Bunau-Varilla Treaty into line with the spirit of the Good Neighbor era. Article by article, at conference after conference, US Under Secretary of State Sumner Welles and Panamanian statesman Ricardo Alfaro debated the merits and sins of the treaty that had given the US rights to build the Panama Canal in 1903 and had since become the bedrock of anti-US sentiment on the isthmus.

The Hull-Alfaro Treaty (formally called the General Treaty of Friendship and Cooperation), signed in March 1936, was a first attempt at reconciling national sovereignty and international cooperation in US-Panamanian relations once the United States had professed, as a matter of principle, to take Panamanian sovereignty seriously. Tense treaty negotiations between Alfaro and Welles illustrated the lopsided stakes of cooperation between unequal partners and previewed the tensions to come in international negotiations over wartime bases in the Americas more broadly. When Alfaro refused to concede to a particular US request to supervise Panamanian radio communications, Welles said to him, "We are asking for cooperation for our common interests, the same as you have asked from us and we have been very glad to offer throughout these negotiations," to which Alfaro replied, "Your cooperation is not at the expense of your sovereignty and ours is."[3]

US defense planners concerned with canal security opposed the Hull-Alfaro Treaty's concessions to Panamanian sovereignty that seemed to impede the United States' ability to take quick and unfettered action to defend the canal. In the original 1903 treaty, the United States had obtained the right to "use, occupy and control" any Panamanian land or water outside of the Canal Zone that it deemed necessary for canal defense, and the United States could occupy those sites in perpetuity. US and Panamanian diplomats endeavored to update this provision in a manner more respectful of Panamanian sovereignty, but US officials were unwilling to renounce the right to act unilaterally. The two nations ultimately settled on a vague agreement that, in the event of an international conflagration, any actions taken to defend the canal that would affect Panamanian territory would be "the subject of consultation between the two Governments."[4] The US Army thought that even this provision surrendered too much and opposed the Treaty even after the diplomats had signed it. The US Senate dragged its feet on ratification, in part due to the Army's opposition, and only agreed to approve it in August 1939, when, in light of events in Europe, the US government could afford neither the inconclusiveness of a signed but not yet ratified treaty, nor the popular resentment that the delayed ratification had caused in Panama.

As hostilities mounted in Europe, the United States moved to shore up canal defenses by sending reinforcements to the Canal Zone, installing equipment in the lock chambers that could detect underwater mines and bombs, and implementing new inspection policies for ships passing through. In Washington, Congress approved funds to build a third set of canal locks that could accommodate larger war ships. The US War Department had relatively free rein to do what it could to enhance canal security within the borders of the Canal Zone, but anything beyond those borders required consultation with the Panamanian government. While the Zone itself had been sufficient space for ensuring canal defense in the naval age, aerial defense called for a wider berth.

For a few years, the US Army had been leasing an airfield in Rio Hato from a private owner, but it was not enough—the Army wanted further tracts for emergency and auxiliary landing fields, mechanical aircraft warning stations, and the operation of searchlights. In 1939, the commanding general of the Zone appealed to the Panamanian government for leases on around a dozen defense sites in the Republic, but little came of the effort. By the time that negotiations began in earnest in the fall of 1940, the number of desired sites had increased to over seventy and the list would continue to grow.[5]

Arnulfo Arias assumed the presidency in October 1940, just as the frenzy around airfield acquisition efforts was getting fully underway. Arias was far more critical of US power on the isthmus than his predecessor, Augusto Boyd, had been. Younger brother of former president Harmodio Arias, Arnulfo was a Harvard-trained physician who had been a leading figure in the 1931 coup.[6] He had since spearheaded a movement called *panameñismo* that trumpeted the slogan "Panama for Panamanians" and rejected all non-Hispanic influence in Panamanian society and politics. His political and economic agenda for Panama during his first brief tenure as president was in many ways characteristic of this moment of rising mass politics in Latin America. Seeking to expand the size and role of the national government in social and economic life, he created the nation's social security system, embarked on experiments in Import Substitution Industrialization, and created state banks intended to foment agricultural and urban development. In January 1941, the Panamanian National Assembly ratified a new constitution embracing this new social and economic program. Though Arias was resolutely nationalist above all else, he had previously served as ambassador to Italy, and US officials suspected him and several of his cabinet members of sympathizing with Axis powers.

When US ambassador William Dawson approached Arias seeking 999-year leases on more than seventy defense sites in Panama, his reluctance to quickly accede was not surprising. Responding to Dawson's requests, Arias and his foreign minister, Raúl de Roux, used the language of the Good Neighbor and the multilateral vision of hemisphere defense to frame both their willingness to cooperate and their reluctance to accept the terms that the US proposed. The administration insisted on its "very heartfelt desire to make a reality the politics of the Good Neighbor that his excellency President Franklin D. Roosevelt acclaims," but insisted that such cooperation "cannot include an obligation that violates the sovereignty or independence of an American nation," and noted, "no Latin American nation, if they were consulted, would ask of Panama such a sacrifice."[7] To permit the US armed forces to occupy defense sites throughout the Republic for centuries to come would signal significant backsliding in US-Panamanian relations and would be detrimental to the collective project of hemispheric unity in the Americas.[8] Calling Washington's bluff Arias asserted, "the military authorities of the Canal Zone can, if they believe it convenient and would like to break with inter-American solidarity, violate Panama's rights as a free and independent republic: enact the desired occupation by force."[9]

Whether he knew it or not, Arias was in fact stressing the fault lines between the State Department and the War and Navy departments, which tended to be less invested in Good Neighbor appearances and more concerned with immediate strategic demands. General Daniel Van Voorhis, commander of the Canal Zone forces, devised plans for the emergency occupation of the Panamanian Republic with or without the government's consent. A study of Panama produced by the Military Intelligence Division in 1940 betrayed the extent to which the racialized condescension that had informed US policy toward the Caribbean basin for decades still lingered when it noted "a small country with the temperamental instability characteristic of mixed races is not too dependable" and insisted that US planning must, therefore, be "based on hard practical facts, rather than any fatuous illusions of fraternalism."[10] While Arias walked the line between popular nationalism and US partnership, Dawson, Welles, and others attempted to mediate the tensions between Arias's stance and the War Department's requirements.

Throughout the negotiations, the Arias administration pursued two principal goals: to limit the extent to which the new basing agenda would facilitate a greater US encroachment in Panamanian affairs, and to obtain as much benefit for Panama as possible in return for the coveted defense sites. On the matter of limiting US overreach, Arias countered the 999-year lease term proposal with which US officials opened discussions with a counter-proposal of only four to seven years.[11] He insisted that Panama retain full jurisdiction over the territories in question, in contrast to the Canal Zone, where the US exercised complete jurisdiction.[12] And he proposed the creation of a joint US-Panamanian commission for the study of the suggested tracts, to make the endeavor less unilateral in nature.[13] In descriptions of the proposed sites, where the size of the suggested tracts were indicated, Foreign Minister Octavio Fábrega (de Roux's successor) substituted the word "approximately" with the word "maximum."[14]

As for compensation for the leased defense sites, Arias pursued quid pro quo remunerations in a number of ways. Most directly, he requested that the United States pay rent for the defense sites at a price commensurate with "the burdens, dangers and moral sacrifices that such concessions impose on the country."[15] Alternatively, his administration floated the idea that Panama's debt be forgiven in return for the leases, or that fifty years of canal annuities be paid in advance so that Panama might use that money to pay off US bondholders.[16]

When the State Department proved disinclined to compensate Panama directly for the defense sites, Arias's administration insisted that they do so "indirectly" instead and listed a number of "pending matters" that had long been on the nationalists' wish list that might be resolved in exchange for basing rights, such as the transfer of control of an aqueduct and waterworks to Panama, redress for Panamanians' continuing frustration with Canal Zone commissaries, the reassertion of Panamanian jurisdiction over land under the control of the Panama Railroad Company, the construction of a tunnel below the canal to alleviate traffic, the relocation of the railroad station in Panama City to another site, and other matters that the Panamanian government considered to be "of prime importance to the economic, industrial, and political development of the country."[17]

Arias ultimately assembled his various requests into a list that came to be known as the Twelve Points.[18] US officials responded officially that the government would not compensate Panama for merely upholding her duty, but behind closed doors, they began to consider which ones they might be willing to grant, "in lieu of other compensation for the defense sites."[19] As they considered the matters at hand, State Department officials were most disposed to acquiesce on requests that advanced US interests as well. As Sumner Welles put it, "I think it is worth a few millions of dollars to us to prevent trouble with the Panamanian Government at this time provided the money we make available to them is for projects which are really in our own defense interest."[20] In a sense, they all were, as Ambassador Dawson calculated that the extent to which the United States was willing and able to meet Arias's requests would "prove an important and probably controlling factor in determining how rapidly, smoothly, and satisfactorily we attain our own objectives."[21]

As negotiations moved forward, Arias tried to stay ahead of the backlash that he was likely to face as a result of his cooperation with the United States by controlling the narrative of US-Panamanian cooperation domestically. As in most countries in Latin America, the actual work of US basing got going well before military agreements were completed or signed. US soldiers began to occupy new Panamanian defense sites in March 1941 even though the two governments would not conclude a lease agreement until May 1942. In March, Arias issued a press release that addressed the Panamanian public, letting them know that US soldiers were permitted to begin occupying more urgently needed defense tracts but emphasizing that the Panamanian government, in defense of "the legitimate rights of Panama with respect to its territorial integrity and its political independence," had demanded and received concessions in regard to compensation, lease duration, and jurisdiction.[22] He announced that the sites would only be used for the duration of the war and would be evacuated promptly thereafter. This was news to US officials, who had not yet agreed to those terms. The *Acción Comunal* newspaper ran stories celebrating Arias's negotiating prowess, and the equality of the US-Panamanian relationship, to differentiate Arias's position from those of his predecessors whom he had denounced as traitors.

Throughout, Arias used his concern about popular backlash as a negotiating tactic, insisting in conversations with the US ambassador that they must take into account "public opinion" as they settled the terms of their cooperation.[23] When scheduled to give public addresses, he pressured US authorities for concessions that he might publicize to the Panamanian people as evidence of fair treatment.[24] Dawson was sensitive to his plight, noting that allowing Arias such opportunities would be beneficial to both countries. "I believe that President Arias himself would be glad to negotiate leases as rapidly as possible," Dawson insisted, but "he desires also to be in a position to tell his people that he has obtained something substantial in return."[25] Perhaps ironically, Arias's own political predicament made him invested in keeping the myth that the United States itself was peddling alive. For Arias to be a different kind of leader, he needed to be partnering with a different kind of United States, so when an *Acción Comunal* editorial lauded Franklin Roosevelt as an "apostle of democracy and of the right of weak nations," it was not necessarily due to an about-face in feeling toward US power but instead the extent to which their fates were now intertwined.[26]

Or so it seemed. Before he was able to reach a final lease agreement on the defense sites, Arias was deposed in a coup. He had won the presidency through an election that his opponent's supporters boycotted, and his legitimacy had long been called into question. Through a series of policy and personnel decisions after his election, he lost the crucial support of the National Police. Those officials in the US government who saw Arias himself as a potential threat to canal security would not be sorry to see him go.[27] The National Police appointed Minister of Government and Justice

Ricardo de la Guardia as Arias's replacement in October 1941, and he received a warm welcome from Washington.

Ricardo de la Guardia was far more US-friendly in his politics and rhetoric, but his appointment did not significantly change the course of basing negotiations; in fact, with questionable nationalist credentials and no electoral legitimacy, de la Guardia had even more to prove to the Panamanian public than Arias did in ensuring that Panama did not accept a rotten deal.[28] The US ambassador was aware of this predicament and urged the US government to meet Arias's demands in order to protect de la Guardia from the liabilities of his US-friendly disposition.

The presence of US soldiers in the Republic only made the need to publicize the positive gains for Panama all the more urgent. US military personnel were already proving to be "constant sources of irritation." The ambassador reported, "the public in general (and in particular the political opposition including supporters of the previous administration who are becoming much more active of late because of this situation) are demanding [to know] what the Government is doing to protect Panamanian interests." Failing to meet Panamanian demands could soon create hazards for US security, he contended. "Unless we can soon place the Panamanian Government in a position to announce a satisfactory conclusion of the negotiations with the benefits accruing to Panama we shall run the risk of drifting into a situation in which incalculable damage may be done to the friendly and cooperative atmosphere which has been built up here."[29]

The attack on Pearl Harbor in December 1941, six months before the lease agreement would be finalized, accelerated the deployment of the US Army across the country. The lack of formal agreement made the process by which new sites were occupied all the more sloppy and problematic. US troops and construction crews often appeared before an accurate survey of a given tract had been conducted or the owners of that land identified and contacted. Surveys were required in order to establish the proper rent of the land to be offered as compensation, so financial remuneration lagged well behind occupation.

Bewildered Panamanians suddenly and unceremoniously removed from their land, their crops left to wither in the fields and livestock without pasture, looked to their president for some explanation. "We are prepared to make sacrifices to defend the nation's threatened independence," one landowner wrote, "but not to be subject to violent eviction."[30] Landless peasants fared worse, as they were not entitled to rent from the US government and they lost not only their homes and employment but also access to the subsistence plots that they farmed for their family's own consumption.[31] De le Guardia's government assembled a claims commission to handle such disputes and in some instances, the Panamanian treasury fronted the cash to displaced citizens that it hoped the US government would someday provide, but the process of eviction and occupation held echoes of the traumatic depopulation of tens of thousands of Panamanians from the territory that had become the Canal Zone not thirty years earlier.[32] The effort to distinguish the World War II alliance from prior US policies on the isthmus was not going particularly well.

The United States and Panama finally concluded the lease agreement in May 1942, and Arias and de la Guardia's efforts to use the goodwill security imperative to force the United States to accept some clear limits on its power and to secure material benefits for Panama were successful in some significant ways. Negotiations over Arias's Twelve Points produced concrete results and when the agreement was published in Panamanian newspapers, it appeared alongside the Twelve Points. The Lease Agreement itself reflected further successes. The term limits for the leased sites came down from the initially proposed 999-year term to the duration of the war plus one year. The United States would pay $50 per hectare per year for most of the defense sites and $10,000 annually for the prized site at Rio Hato. The United States committed to returning various tracts of land and infrastructure to Panamanian jurisdiction, further expanding Panama's highway infrastructure, building a bridge across the canal, and compensating Panama for wear and tear on roads used by the US military. Though Panama did not receive military aid through Lend Lease as most other Latin American countries did, the Panamanian government was provided with war materiel outside of the bounds of that program and a permanent military mission that trained the increasingly militarized Panamanian National Police.[33]

Beyond the explicit terms of the deal, Panama benefited from wartime cooperation in other ways. Between defense construction and road-building, Panamanian unemployment rates bottomed out. With so many mouths to feed, the US government purchased vast quantities of food from local producers, revitalizing the agricultural sector. But the trade-offs were substantial, and the goodwill security imperative would prove harder to advance in the field than it was in the foreign ministry.

CUBA

Parallel projects underway in Cuba pursued different, inventive tracks. The US Navy and War departments both sought new defense infrastructure on the island in 1940—the Navy attempted to expand the territorial limits of Guantanamo, while the War Department wanted to build up an airfield in Camagüey. The Navy Department worked through official channels, while the War Department's construction advanced quietly through Pan Am's Airport Development Program. Though both endeavors were initiated the same month, by the time that the Navy Department abandoned the Guantanamo project two years later, the first ADP airfield was long since completed and a second ADP project was underway in the western region of the island. The comparative success and failure of each of these initiatives illustrates the constraints under which US and Latin American officials operated at the time, and the extent to which the Good Neighbor policy and the climate of popular nationalism, rather than simply protect territorial sovereignty, inadvertently incentivized clandestine infringements on sovereignty instead.

For most of World War II, from 1940 to 1944, Fulgencio Batista occupied the Cuban presidency. Though Batista was later best remembered as the US-friendly dictator that Fidel Castro battled in the 1950s, in the early 1940s he served a term as a democratically elected populist president. Sitting down with US officials shortly after his election to consider their requests for wartime collaboration, Batista found himself in a delicate position. As in Panama, US appeals for Cuban cooperation in the war advanced under the shadow of long-standing popular frustrations with US power in the country that had boiled over in recent years.

Batista himself had risen to power through the Revolution in 1933 whose legacy remained contested. The first three decades of Cuban independence, compromised by the terms of the Platt Amendment, had been rife with US intervention and electoral illegitimacy. In the 1920s, as plunging global sugar prices devastated the Cuban economy, workers, students, and intellectuals mobilized against Cuban president Gerardo Machado, who relied on ever-greater repression to maintain order. Efforts by US officials to mediate a resolution that would halt the rising tide of popular discontent failed, and riots continued even after Machado was removed from office. Batista, then a thirty-one-year-old sergeant in the Cuban Army, joined a group of fellow sergeants, corporals, and enlisted men in a rebellion that quickly gained the support of the student organizations that had been clamoring for change. After the revolt, university professor Ramón Grau San Martín assumed the presidency and oversaw the most progressive phase of the revolution, promulgating a number of social welfare policies in quick succession.

As far as US power on the island was concerned, Grau abrogated the Cuban Constitution of 1901, and the Platt Amendment along with it, and called for the shuttering of the Guantanamo Naval Base. The United States refused to recognize Grau's government, emboldening opposition groups in Cuba to continue their resistance. Sumner Welles, US ambassador to Cuba during this period, advocated US military intervention to arrest Batista and remove Grau from office, but Roosevelt and Secretary of State Cordell Hull declined, unwilling to delegitimize the Good Neighbor policy just months after pronouncing it. Welles continued to plot with Grau's opponents behind the scenes, and though he departed from his post in Havana in December of that year with Grau still in office, the months of non-recognition effectively alienated Grau's administration.

Batista's relationship to the revolution in the months and years that followed was complicated and circuitous. As the chief of the armed forces, Batista replaced the beleaguered Grau after just four months in office with a more moderate figurehead who was more acceptable to the US government, earning him favor with Washington. Over the following years, Batista continued to repress the more progressive impulses of the revolutionary movement in the name of order and economic stability, while managing politics from behind the scenes. Grau organized his supporters into a new political party, the Partido Revolucionario Cubano Auténtico (the Authentic Cuban Revolutionary Party or, simply, the Auténticos). In the late 1930s, Batista shifted left and made common cause with Cuban Communists, who offered him political support in return for the legalization of communism and a privileged relationship with the Cuban Ministry of Labor. Batista had ushered seven men in and out of the Cuban presidency over the 1930s, but in 1940, he removed his uniform and, after campaigning on a nationalist platform characteristic of the period, he assumed the presidency himself.[34]

During this stint in office from 1940 to 1944, Batista enjoyed electoral legitimacy for the only time in his long and influential career in Cuban politics, but his political opposition had also fared well electorally and so his grasp on political power as a civilian was precarious. In the November 1939 elections for the Constituent Assembly that would craft a new constitution, supporters of the Auténticos had secured 41 of the 76 seats. In the 1940 elections that brought Batista to the presidency, his opponents secured a majority in Congress. This robust political opposition painted Batista as the conservative darling of the United States. In an era in which being seen as an accomplice to US power was a political liability, Batista trod carefully. As an adviser to the US embassy explained just months into Batista's presidency, "He has been at the crossroads of the all-important decision as to whether his Administration would follow a policy of cooperation with, or antagonism toward Washington."[35] On the one hand, Batista was eager to assert his independence to maintain his populist credentials. On the other hand, if properly managed, he knew from experience that US support was a significant asset. As he asserted civil authority, Batista faced opposition from within the Cuban armed forces, and US support was a powerful safeguard against insurgents within the ranks of Army leadership.[36] And, in the spirit of Good Neighbor cooperation, Batista had appealed to Washington for a $50 million loan that would allow him to advance a number of nation-building projects.[37]

These were the circumstances under which Batista calculated his response when the embassy approached his foreign minister, José Manuel Cortina, in November 1940, just one month into his presidency, about the prospect of expanding the Guantanamo Naval Base. The new Cuban Constitution of 1940, which took effect the previous month, expressly prohibited "agreements or treaties which in any manner limit or diminish the national sovereignty or the integrity of the territory."[38] A new treaty with the United States that expanded the limits of the Guantanamo base would have to be approved by the Cuban Senate, where his political opposition held the upper hand, and might require a constitutional amendment. The negotiations over the Guantanamo expansion revealed the challenges of turning the multilateral talk of partnership in hemisphere defense into practice.

The Navy Department's initial concerns about the territorial boundaries of the base had to do with the fact that the base's water supply was located outside of its borders, leaving the base vulnerable to sabotage.[39] Cuban soldiers were stationed to keep guard over the intake and fresh water pumping plant that supplied the base, but the Navy wanted to station US marines there instead. As Captain George Weyler, commanding officer at the Guantanamo base, dismissively explained of the Cuban guards, "naturally we do not put much faith in such protection and would rather they were not there."[40] The US embassy objected to the Navy's desire to send US marines to do a job that could be reasonably done by Cuban forces; as concrete evidence of inter-American cooperation went, this seemed to the State Department like low-hanging fruit.[41] Besides, US Ambassador George Messersmith contended, US marines stationed on formal duty on Cuban soil beyond the base's borders would only "provide more fuel for the demagogues and their allegations respecting derogation of Cuban sovereignty."[42]

The Navy's concern about the vulnerability of the base's water supply reinvigorated an earlier held desire for a larger base that incorporated the water supply into the base's borders. A larger footprint in Guantánamo Bay was even more strategically appealing in 1940, when the Navy sought to turn it into a viable primary base for the Atlantic Fleet. To this end, the Navy also sought additional territory for the operation of fleet patrol planes and to install anti-aircraft defenses. Navy officials appealed to the

State Department to approach the Cuban government about a fifty-year lease on additional territory for these purposes.[43]

José Cortina, Cuban minister of foreign relations; Domingo Ramos, Cuban minister of defense; and US Ambassador George Messersmith all concurred that a unilateral extension of the Guantanamo base was "out of the question."[44] Attempting to align the Navy's desire for base expansion with the Cuban constitutional prohibition and the Good Neighbor project of wartime cooperation, the State Department proposed an alternative idea: perhaps Batista could create a Cuban Naval Reserve in the area surrounding the US base that US forces would be permitted to use for cooperation in defense.[45] So began two years of negotiations between State, Navy, and Havana that, in the end, bore no fruit. Navy officials resisted true cooperation and sought to use the premise of a Cuban base as a mere façade (proposing, for instance, that the Navy enjoy "exclusive access" to areas within the Cuban Zone), while Cuban officials attempted to make of the proposal something less cynical—a Joint Military Zone where a Joint US-Cuban Commission would reign and the armed forces of the two nations would operate in partnership.[46]

Discerning the motivations behind the various diplomatic appeals made by Ramos, Cortina, and Batista over the years that followed requires some speculation. In contrast to the Foreign Ministry Archives of Brazil and Panama, very little documentation is available for consultation at the Cuban Foreign Ministry Archive in terms of internal communications between Batista and his cabinet members. Instead, State Department records must be read critically against what is known about the men and the broader political context that they navigated.

Foreign Minister Cortina was a distinguished Cuban statesman who began his career in public office in Cuba in 1908 as a member of the House of Representatives and went on to serve in the Senate. As president of the Committee on Foreign Relations in the Cuban Senate and Cuban delegate to the League of Nations, Cortina developed his own ideas about the promises of internationalism in safeguarding the sovereignty of less powerful nations like Cuba, which he laid out in a publication called *Cuba's International Ideals*.[47] In that publication, after touting Cuba's natural inclination toward internationalism as a strategically located island nation born of a century-long struggle for independence, he celebrated the promise of Pan-Americanism and international law if properly executed and upheld. "Harmonizing the interests of a nation of such extraordinary power as the United States with the independence of a small country has been the arduous task that has tested the vitality of the Cuban people and the wisdom of Cuban statesmen," Cortina wrote in 1926.[48] Harmonizing those interests was precisely his plight in 1940.

Throughout the Guantanamo negotiations, Cortina declared complete dedication to the principles of inter-American cooperation and even at times professed complicity in helping to facilitate what would, in effect, be an expanded US base "dressed up in better form."[49] But as he did so, he retained the confidence of the US embassy while quietly nudging the terms of Cuba's partnership further in the direction of equality. From early on, Messersmith was of the mind that the new military zone should be created through an exchange of notes between the two governments, rather than a formal treaty that would require Congressional approval.[50] But Cortina pushed back against the suggestion, asserting that a treaty approved by the Cuban Senate would ensure greater buy-in from the Cuban people. This approach also meant that the substance of the agreement between the United States and Cuba would be made public, which enabled Cortina to point to Cubans' concerns about national sovereignty as a rationale for requesting that Washington make further concessions to Cuban interests.[51] US Secretary of Navy Frank Knox was perhaps more attuned to Cortina's strategy than Messersmith, as he remarked, "although the Cuban Foreign Minister has from time to time given verbal assurances that the Cuban Government proposes to take a very liberal position . . . it is noted that changes he has made in [treaty] drafts from A to I have made further restrictions on the authority he proposes to grant the United States."[52] Cortina rejected Washington's proposed terms regarding US jurisdiction in the Zone, and the State Department eventually dropped all mention of jurisdiction from the agreement entirely.[53] And like Arias, Batista's administration managed to leverage basing needs into indirect benefit for Cuba in other areas of the economy as well. When US-Cuban negotiations over a sugar purchasing deal encountered trouble, Cortina stalled on Guantanamo negotiations until progress was made on sugar.[54]

Of course, Cortina and Batista, like Fábrega and Arias in Panama, were also concerned about the optics of any public agreement and so, even as some changes Cortina suggested reflected real concessions for Cuba, others appeared more concerned, as Messersmith described it, with "saving the face of the Cuban government and the Cuban Army and Navy."[55] While the United States suggested that the base extension be called a "Joint Defense Zone," Batista and Cortina insisted that the terminology employed instead be "Cuban Military Zone" in order to prevent any impression that the agreement violated the Constitution.[56] Though the United States intended to compensate Cuba for use of the military zone or for lands expropriated, Cortina requested that no mention of money be included in the formal agreement, as the exchange of funds would make it appear that further territory was being rented, in violation of the Constitution.[57]

Messersmith himself reported that the domestic politics of US basing in Cuba definitely shaped the proposal as it approached its final form in late 1941. "The opposition parties in Cuba, while professing full cooperation with us and while, I believe, on the whole friendly to us, do not miss any opportunity to make difficulties for the President and they will attack any agreement which in any way gives any grounds, even most indirectly, for saying that the sovereignty of Cuba has been violated," Messersmith explained to the State Department official charged with persuading the Navy to accept the terms of the agreement. "The whole agreement has been drawn up with the thought in mind . . . that there is nothing in it which the opposition parties can attack."[58]

In April 1942, the Navy Department abandoned the project of extending its access to the land around the Guantanamo base. Circumstances by then had changed. The strategic importance of the Guantanamo expansion diminished with the construction of new base facilities in the British Caribbean and Puerto Rico, where the political calculations surrounding sovereignty and jurisdiction were different. In Cuba, the Navy maintained its reservations around the cooperative nature of the proposed Cuban military zone, and both Navy and State were concerned that any agreement they reached with Cuba could be used as a model in similar negotiations with other Latin American countries and they did not want to set such a limiting precedent.[59] This is not to say that Guantanamo remained unchanged through the war. To the contrary, the Navy invested heavily inside the existing borders of the base. All in all, they spent around $34 million on improvements to the base to fortify it against sabotage and better service the Atlantic fleet, including work on water treatment and storage plants, an anti-aircraft training center, piers, and railroads.[60]

The ADP was a very different undertaking. In November 1940, the same month that Ambassador Messersmith approached the Cuban government about the prospect of Guantanamo expansion, the US War Department concluded its secret contract with Pan American Airways to build and expand airfields in strategic sites across Latin America under the guise of commercial expansion. An airfield in Camagüey, Cuba was number one on the War Department's ADP priority list. There, the War Department sought to build two new runways, a connecting taxiway, augmented fueling, radio and electric facilities, and improved service buildings, all of which would greatly facilitate transit between the continental United States and new major installations under development in Puerto Rico. As Messersmith haltingly advanced his conversations with Cortina and Batista about Guantanamo, Pan Am's own negotiations with the Cuban government began.

The airline had a robust foundation to build on. It had been operating in Camagüey since 1928. To begin the process of seeking any necessary approvals for the Camagüey work, the company's lawyer in Cuba, Mario Lazo, appealed to Minister of Defense Domingo Ramos, who had in the past helped Pan Am to secure a gasoline tax exemption. Lazo described Ramos as one of his "closest and oldest friends."[61]

Though the program was designed to be covert, Batista, Ramos, and Cortina knew who was behind it. Lazo presented the project to Ramos as one of commercial expansion, but the strategic utility of the airfield was immediately apparent to the "astute" defense minister.[62] After all, just a few months earlier, the United States and Cuba had engaged in Staff Conversations in which confirming Cuba's willingness to permit the United States to use Cuban airfields in the event of an emergency had been a top priority for the US representatives. When Ramos commented right away on the military significance, Lazo proclaimed himself uninformed of any defense purposes and played up the commercial value of the airports as Pan Am transitioned to landplanes, but he also noted in his reports to Pan Am executives that "it would have been futile to deny that this angle of the matter played any part in the program."[63] When Batista became involved in the process and was contemplating a supportive decree that Pan Am sought, he demanded to know where else the ADP was building in Latin America. With the State Department's blessing, Pan Am told him, though they asked that he keep it to himself.[64]

Knowledge of the program's true "sponsor" did not dissuade Batista's administration from permitting Pan Am to proceed. US involvement remained a secret to the Cuban public and to Batista's political opponents. If anything, the secrecy surrounding the ADP gave Batista room to maneuver, freeing his administration from many of the constraints that prevented progress on the Guantanamo negotiations. The ADP required no bilateral treaty and no vote in Congress. And Batista's assent to ADP work did not tether him to US defense strategy; his agreement was only for construction of the airfield and attendant facilities. It did not permit US military aircraft to use the airfield, nor did it allow for US military personnel to be stationed there. These decisions would presumably have to be decided separately and through formal channels.

Besides the diminished political costs of permitting covert defense construction to proceed, there were ample reasons to support ADP development. Beyond recognizing the military value of the airfields, Ramos also recognized the "tourist and commercial advantage to Cuba."[65] In effect, the

ADP expanded civil aviation infrastructure on Washington's dime at a time when such infrastructure was becoming increasingly vital to any nation's commercial and strategic well-being. In fact, Batista would later request that the United States undertake further airfield construction in other regions of Cuba, appealing to US security concerns by noting that this would "increase the power of Cuba to cooperate in a military and naval way."[66] Though the ADP did not allow Batista the same opportunities to negotiate quid pro quo compensation in the way that the Panamanian presidents' direct negotiations did, Batista turned the ADP itself into a form of aid, insisting that the facilities built by Pan Am with US funds become, at the end of the war, the property of the Cuban government.[67]

Despite the commercial façade of the ADP, all interested parties largely treated it as one more element in US-Cuban wartime negotiations. The embassy urged Pan Am to hold off on reaching out to Batista regarding ADP requests as long as the two nations were stalled on both Guantanamo and the proposed $50 million loan, concerned that the ADP would introduce a new bargaining chip for Batista to use in order to make progress on those other, formal discussions.[68]

While treaty negotiations over Guantanamo dragged on for nearly two years, construction to develop the Camagüey airfield began within months of the topic first being broached. When Japan attacked Pearl Harbor in December 1941, the project in Camagüey was nearly complete, and the first contingent of US military personnel arrived at the site shortly thereafter. They set up a tent to operate as a temporary headquarters and lived in a rented house near the field, but the most important strategic work that would facilitate the movement of aircraft was done.[69] By the time the Guantanamo negotiations completely unraveled, a second ADP site was under construction in western Cuba at a previously undeveloped site in Pinar del Rio, and a new round of ADP construction to build army barracks, mess halls, a hospital, a recreation hall, and other facilities in Camagüey began later that year.

The ADP was not a perfect instrument. Mario Lazo, often acting in a dual capacity as adviser to the US embassy, informed George Messersmith of the ADP's proposed course of action as a matter of courtesy, but Messersmith inserted himself and the State Department into the process in ways that were cumbersome and unwelcome. In effect, the State Department was drawn into the matter in a way that caused precisely the sorts of delays that the ADP was intended to circumvent.[70] There were also tensions between the State Department and Pan Am insofar as the ADP introduced a private commercial enterprise's interests into calculations around airfield construction. Messersmith and others in the State Department were loath to see the defense program perverted or delayed by Pan Am's long-term commercial strategy. Finally, pretending that the project had nothing to do with defense and was not an official US government program made it more difficult to obtain exemptions from costly labor laws or duty exemptions on construction equipment on grounds that this was a project for mutual defense. Yet, despite its shortcomings, the ADP proved an effective tool in the early days of the defense effort.

Between the initiation of Guantanamo and ADP negotiations and the attack on Pearl Harbor, a number of changes created a climate more propitious for the arrival of US servicemen. When the Soviet Union joined the Allies in June 1941, the Communist Party in Cuba, upon whose support Batista heavily relied, became unlikely advocates of collaboration with the United States and remained throughout some of Cuba's most ardent supporters of the war effort. Everywhere in the Americas, the attack on Pearl Harbor triggered the contingency upon which so many conversations about defense collaboration had hinged, freeing governments to offer the support discussed in hypothetical terms in Staff Conversations a year and a half prior. After the attack, Cuba swiftly declared war on Japan and a few days later declared war on Germany and Italy as well. US soldiers arrived at Cuban airfields, with their entrance authorized by an exchange of notes (which, not being a formal treaty, required no Senate approval). The escalation of German submarine warfare in the Caribbean in 1942 further cemented Cubans' commitment to the Allies. In May 1942, Batista and his foreign minister approached the US embassy about establishing a formal military alliance, which they signed that September. In this distinct climate, the United States and Cuba agreed to the construction of a new military base in Cuba that would be called (for a short time) the Batista Airbase, the largest of any constructed in Cuba during the war. This one was negotiated in an aboveboard manner and was not built covertly.

Though Messersmith's successor in the embassy, Spruille Braden, would often lament what he perceived as Cubans' apathy toward the war and complain about Batista, Cuba's record on cooperation was strong and so too were the benefits that Cuba extracted in return for its partnership. Expressing a desire to better serve as a partner in defense, Batista sought Lend Lease aid to build additional barracks and buy rifles for training new recruits and ultimately received $7.2 million worth of war materiel. Upon his request, US military training missions were established in Cuba and US officials oversaw the expansion of Cuban intelligence infrastructure. They also created more extensive opportunities for members of the Cuban armed forces to train in the United States.[71] Meanwhile, the US need for nickel prompted investment in Cuba's mining industry, helping to advance a long-held Cuban desire to diversify the Cuban economy.

Cuba also benefited from the more expansive view of security cooperation that encompassed economic and social welfare. The $50 million loan that Cuba sought from the United States in 1940 for work like highway construction, development of the mining industry, and agricultural development, including rice growing, reforestation, irrigation, and the funding of public works and sanitation systems, stalled out as US officials balked at the amount that the Cuban government requested. Over time, however, as Cuban economic stability and the prestige of Batista's administration became increasingly important assets to US national security, the calculation changed. Appealing to the State Department on Cuba's behalf, the US ambassador to Cuba argued, "probably no other American republic has taken so completely cooperative an attitude as Cuba in matters of defense." To Cuba's credit, "so far this cooperation has not been a matter of *quid pro quo*," but, he went on to note, "there appears to be, therefore, on the whole a fair balance on the side of Cuba and if we wish to maintain the very considerable market we have for American goods, to maintain economic, social and political stability and to keep the way open for the most complete cooperation in defense, there are certain measures which we shall in all prudence have to take." He recommended that the State Department take action on a number of broad measures including financing sugar production and other agricultural products as well as public works projects, and immediate consideration of Cuba's request for technical assistance in the establishment of a central bank.[72] In other words, once cooperation was cemented as the means of protecting US interests in the region, US assistance of all sorts need not be negotiated as direct compensation for basing rights. Rather, a friendly government's very economic and political viability was itself a US security concern.

BRAZIL

Brazil occupied a very different position in relation to the United States than did Cuba or Panama. Brazil's size, economy, and geopolitical positioning were obviously distinctive. Brazil's historical relationship with the United States was also markedly different, largely free of the specific burdens that weighed on Panamanian and Cuban efforts to chart a new path in the Good Neighbor era. Like the other large countries in South America, Brazil was economically tied more closely to Great Britain and worried little about the prospect of direct US intervention in its own affairs. Indeed Brazil's greatest territorial threats came from border disputes with its Spanish-speaking neighbors. The Brazilian Foreign Ministry, under the leadership of the Baron de Rio Branco between 1902 and 1912, had pursued a calculated policy of cultivating a "special relationship" with the United States, hoping that cooperation with the United States might help to balance the pressures Brazil faced from Europe and Argentina.[73]

Despite these fundamental differences, many of the same constraints would hinder US efforts to advance defense plans in the Brazilian Northeast. Though Brazilian policymakers historically embraced the potential of allying with the United States, Brazilian intellectuals had joined the chorus of critics of US hegemony in the region.[74] And, as elsewhere in the region, Brazilian domestic politics underwent a dramatic sea change in the 1930s that upended the earlier status quo and brought to power the man who occupied the presidency during World War II, Getúlio Vargas.

The Brazilian Revolution of 1930 ended a period known as the First Republic (1889–1930). During this era, Brazil had been a large federation of vastly unequal states that exercised autonomy so great that they could negotiate with foreign governments, and some maintained police forces more powerful than the nation's military. Presidential power rotated back and forth between the oligarchies of Brazil's two wealthiest and most powerful states, and politics were the purview of a narrow elite. Literacy requirements for suffrage disenfranchised the vast majority of the Brazilian population and those who did participate in the electoral system often exchanged their votes for resources in a deeply entrenched system of patronage.

Vargas, a relative political outsider by the norms of the day, rose to power through a military coup when he and his supporters denounced the results of a fraudulent presidential election in which he was a candidate. Though the Revolution of 1930 was not an especially "bottom-up" affair, it dramatically upended the nature of Brazilian politics. Vargas's supporters represented a broad ideological cross section of society and Vargas was himself a notorious shape-shifter who moved among his diverse poles of support skillfully as circumstances required. Despite the challenges of pinning down his ideology, some central tenets of Vargas's agenda remained fairly consistent throughout his time in power, including centralization of power in the national government, economic development and diversification, a more robust social safety net, and a commitment to Brazilian nationalism.

For US defense planners, the Brazilian Northeast was an area of concern in hemisphere defense planning second only to the Panama Canal. The United States sought more bases in Brazil than in any other Latin American country besides Panama—initially, to deflect an attack from across the South Atlantic, though the bases ultimately proved most useful for combating submarine warfare in the South Atlantic and for ferrying supplies and people across the ocean. The so-called Brazilian bulge—the northern and northeastern coastline of the country—was largely undefended in the late 1930s. Most of the Brazilian military's 60,000 men were stationed in the south of the country, reflecting the fact that Brazil's defense planning was more oriented toward threats from Argentina than any that might loom in Europe or Africa.[75] Limited transportation infrastructure in Brazil would make the mobilization of Brazilian troops to the North and Northeast problematically slow, even if US military planners were inclined to trust their competence in deflecting a foreign attack.[76]

US concerns about the vulnerable Northeast were exacerbated by other concerns about Axis influence in Brazil. US officials prone to such worries saw evidence in a number of places. The country was home to sizable German, Italian, and Japanese populations. A fascist political party called the Ação Integralista Brasileira was prominent in Brazilian public life in the 1930s and, though devoutly nationalist in orientation and staunchly opposed to all foreign influence in Brazil, the group resembled European fascist parties and was popular among enlisted men and noncommissioned officers in the Brazilian military. Vargas's foreign minister, Oswaldo Aranha, was distinctly pro-US, but US officials worried about other leading figures in Vargas's inner circle. Most notably, throughout the war, they worried that the Brazilian Army Chief of Staff Pedro Aurélio de Góes Monteiro and Brazilian Minister of War Eurico Dutra harbored Axis sympathies. Vargas's own preference for corporatist political structure also concerned US officials. In 1937, he declared a self-coup and launched a period of dictatorship called the "Estado Novo"—a titled shared with the authoritarian regime in Portugal, which did not go unnoticed in Washington.

Economically, Brazil and Germany had become closer in recent years. In the 1930s, as part of a concerted German effort to expand its presence in Latin America, trade between Brazil and Germany doubled.[77] In 1938, Vargas concluded negotiations for a large order of weapons and artillery from Germany, to be delivered over the course of five years. Despite all the anxiety that these various factors caused US observers at the time, the archival evidence suggests that Brazil was always inclined to see the United States as the logical partner in the event of global war.[78] That the United States feared otherwise, however, surely played to Brazil's advantage when Vargas's administration sought to extract as much material benefit as possible from its wartime partnership.

Negotiations between the United States and Brazil over the terms of their alliance began in earnest in 1939, when US Army chief of staff George

Marshall visited Brazil, and his Brazilian counterpart, Góes Monteiro, in turn, visited Washington. Góes Monteiro recognized immediately the opportunities presented by Brazil's position in relation to US defense concerns. He wrote to Vargas from Washington, "With respect to the possibility of increasing our military power . . . I am certain that we will never have another opportunity like this one—to lose it would be absolutely ridiculous and unpatriotic."[79] In his meetings with Marshall, Góes Monteiro agreed to make bases available to US air and naval troops in the event of an aggression, but he requested technical assistance in developing them. And he insisted that, if Brazilians were truly being called on to share the burden of hemisphere defense, as US officials claimed, then they would require modern weapons.[80] Though Góes Monteiro and his counterparts in Washington were in general accord in 1939, it would be another three years before they signed a comprehensive agreement.

This quid pro quo—weapons for bases—remained the central dynamic in the United States' quest to obtain defense sites in Brazil. The delays in acquiring bases were largely due to the United States' inability to deliver on its commitments to supply Brazil with weapons. That Vargas had just recently ordered weapons from Germany was troubling to US officials not only because Germany appeared a more trustworthy purveyor of weapons than the United States, but also because they recognized that weapons provisions could provide the seed for a much more robust, long-term relationship. German military advisers would likely follow the weapons, for training purposes, and future purchases of replacement parts and ammunitions would necessarily be made from German manufacturers as well.

In consenting to collaborate with the United States, Brazilian officials had their own strategic concerns in mind, both domestic and international. In terms of national security, Brazil's greatest concern was Argentina. Defensive support from the United States in the North and Northeast would allow Vargas to maintain the majority of Brazilian troops in the South while building up the size of the military. A massive influx of weapons stood to shift the balance of military power in the region away from Argentine predominance. The prospect of obtaining modern weapons by collaborating with the United States also suited Vargas's domestic political concerns. His rise to power in 1930 and his permanence in office fundamentally relied on the support of the military, which was inspired to support him due to his proclaimed commitment to bolster the prestige and strength of the institution. Thus Vargas needed to make good on that promise to ensure his own survival. Since leaders in the armed forces were among those who were most resistant to an alliance with the United States in World War II, positioning them as the greatest beneficiaries of that alliance helped to clear a path.

Stymied by the impasse that the difficulties in delivering weapons to Brazil created, US officials tried to find surreptitious ways of getting US military personnel to the region. For instance, when a Brazilian general proposed establishing a US training center near Natal or Recife to instruct Brazilian servicemen in the use of modern coastal defense weaponry, US strategists seized the proposal as a way of getting US troops to the vulnerable Brazilian bulge without it looking like an occupation. However, when the Army came back with a plan that entailed sending 1,400 US troops to Brazil as part of the "training center" and the United States continued to fail to supply the promised weapons, the general refused to sell the plan to Vargas.[81] In 1941, another plan to get US troops into Brazil without formally stationing them there—by having them participate in Brazilian Army maneuvers—also fell through when Brazilian authorities recognized the effort as "a wolf in sheep's clothing."[82]

Such efforts, which Vargas, Dutra, and Góes Monteiro recognized as a ruse, only inflamed further resentment and distrust among Brazilian authorities and contradicted the broader rhetoric of collaborative defense. Dutra, writing to Vargas in June 1941, lamented that Brazil was willing and able to cooperate in the defense of the Northeast, if only they had the weaponry with which to do so. "Rather than our cooperation, as armed and competent forces, they only want the possession of bases, to come and defend our land as foreigners," Dutra wrote. "They want dominance under the guise of alliance. We ask for arms for our troops, they offer their own armed troops instead." Sounding the protest heard elsewhere, and striking at the very core of the colonial connotation of basing, Dutra further lamented that arrangements such as those that the US military seemed to be pursuing were "more appropriate for the African colonies or Asian possessions, intolerable for relations between free countries in a common struggle."[83] Vargas, in conversation with Góes Monteiro, maintained, "We need the Americans to deliver the promised materiel so that we can defend ourselves, we won't agree to foreign occupation."[84]

Meanwhile, Pan Am's Airport Development Program provided an ideal vehicle for airfield construction and enhancement from both the US and Brazilian perspectives. In Brazil, the ADP would go on to build or enhance twenty-nine bases, a mix of land, sea, and lighter-than-air bases operated by the Army and Navy. This was by far the largest number of ADP sites in any single country. But the ADP did not exactly constitute a program of covert intervention in Brazil. Rather, like in Cuba, the Brazilian government was unofficially consulted on the matter. Pan Am determined that for appearance's sake, the ADP work in Brazil would be carried out by Pan Am's Brazilian subsidiary airline, Panair do Brasil, and the head of Panair, Cauby Araújo, was tapped to meet with Vargas and acquire the necessary permissions. From their very first meeting in January 1941, Araújo was transparent with Vargas about the US role in sponsoring the program.[85] Vargas gave his informal consent for Panair to begin construction but requested that Araújo submit a formal application that Vargas would approve by decree.

For Vargas, like Batista, airfield construction with foreign funding and technical expertise was welcome, even if the US sought the airfields for reasons unrelated to Brazil's own development goals. Given Vargas's centralizing objectives, the growth of aviation infrastructure, in a region of the country that faced large barriers to transportation and communication, was a huge asset.[86] His government allowed construction to begin in January 1941, and in July of that year, a few days after the first shipment of US weapons arrived, Vargas issued a decree formally granting Panair do Brasil permission to build airfields in eight locations in the North and Northeast.[87] Like Cuban Minister of Defense Domingo Ramos, Brazil's foreign minister recognized the long-term value that this construction offered, remarking that the benefits of this construction to the North and Northeast would be "incalculable in peacetime" and they would play a "decisive role in the future of Brazil."[88] Military officials largely concurred, with a Brazilian naval commander in the Northeast remarking that the US airfields would represent "a significant inheritance to be left to our fatherland when our American friends leave."[89] In the decree, Vargas stipulated that Panair must submit the plans for each site to the Brazilian government for approval, and that all the new airfields and installations would become Brazilian government property once constructed. When additional facilities, ranging from hospitals to barracks to munitions depots, were added to the ADP agenda later on, Vargas's administration continued to insist that all such facilities be turned over to the Brazilian government at the war's conclusion.[90]

Brazil's declared neutrality before the war made the ADP's commercial façade important to Vargas. Despite some frustrations and delays similar to those encountered in Cuba, the ADP made quicker progress than official US military construction would have. But successful progress on airfield construction presented US authorities with a new problem: the airfields existed, but they were unstaffed. If anything, the new airfields simply paved a pathway for German penetration of the Americas. Eager to put personnel on the ground to defend the airfields, US officials redoubled their pleas to Brazil to permit the United States to send troops to the Northeast, but Brazilian authorities responded by building up Brazilian garrisons in the Northeast instead and maintained their position that, if the United States made good on its commitments to send the promised war materiel, then the coast would be secure.[91]

The attack on Pearl Harbor changed this calculation, just as it did elsewhere. Prior to the attack, Brazilian officials commonly believed that the war was not really Brazil's concern, but Pearl Harbor and the subsequent escalation of submarine warfare in the South Atlantic changed that perception. In the days following the attack, Brazil agreed to allow the United States to send three fifty-men Marine companies, and the two nations formed a Joint Board for the Defense of the Northeast.[92] By this time, the Lend Lease Act had created the legal means for the United States to supply weapons to Brazil, but results were still slow-going; by December 1941, only a small shipment of light tanks, automotive equipment, and a few searchlights had been delivered. Other weapons offered were obsolete, adding insult to injury. Brazilian military leaders encouraged Vargas and Aranha to delay any diplomatic break with Germany until after the country was properly armed, but at the meeting of the American Foreign Ministers held in Rio in January 1942, Brazil broke ties with Germany, gambling on the United States.

Still, further concessions to the United States would come at further price. When the US Army requested to send hundreds more personnel to the Brazilian bulge, Brazil sat on the request until a new Lend Lease agreement provided for twice as much war materiel as the original agreement signed the year before. Just six days after signing that agreement, Vargas approved 800 additional US servicemen in the Northeast, new defense construction, and unrestricted Army aircraft flight privileges. Two days after that, Welles and Aranha agreed to a draft of a far-reaching bilateral defense agreement.[93]

Throughout, Vargas's authoritarian rule permitted his administration agility in controlling the optics of Brazil's wartime alliance with the United States. Brazil's Department of Information and Propaganda (DIP) censored news coverage of the US bases in Brazil.[94] Recognizing Vargas's public relations concern, the chief of the US Military Mission, Lehman Miller, encouraged his administration to begin to "psychologically prepare" Brazilians for the presence of US military personnel.[95] When Vargas agreed in the wake of the attack on Pearl Harbor to permit US personnel to arrive, he initially insisted that they arrive in plain clothes and be unarmed. Ultimately they were allowed to arrive in uniform but kept their weapons crated.

As time went on, the US-Brazilian alliance grew steadily stronger. When a German submarine campaign sank five Brazilian ships in a three-day period in August 1942, Brazil declared war on Germany and Italy. Once Brazil had joined the war, what news coverage of the US defense sites did go to press touted the partnership of the US and Brazilian forces working "shoulder to shoulder" at the northern and northeastern defense sites, and ensured the public that the new installations would become Brazilian at the war's conclusion.[96] The US armed forces established regional headquarters for the South Atlantic in Recife and Natal. And Brazil ultimately became one of two Latin American countries (along with Mexico) to send combat troops, when the Força Expedicionária Brasileira (FEB) departed for Italy in 1944, where it served under US command.[97] By the end of the war, over half of the funding spent on the ADP was spent on defense sites in Brazil, and the two countries agreed to additional air and naval facilities built outside of the ADP's scope. The number of US servicemen stationed in Brazil grew to 16,000, not accounting for the number of military personnel that passed through the nation's northern and northeastern cities every day in transit. Natal, where the United States operated its largest airbase on foreign soil, has come to be known proudly in Brazil as the "springboard to victory."

The quid pro quo of bases for weapons occupied the vital center of a broader framework of security cooperation between the United States and Brazil that grew to encompass all manner of technical, material, and development assistance. As in Cuba, US officials recognized the stability and well-being of their ally as a national security imperative and, as one historian put it, the United States "committed itself to underwriting the Vargas government militarily and economically for the duration of the war."[98] By the end of the war, Brazil had received two-thirds of all Lend Lease aid that went to Latin America.[99] With this massive influx of war materiel, Brazil surpassed Argentina as the leading military power in South America. The United States established training missions within Brazil, collaborated in the development of Brazilian counterespionage, and accepted vastly increased numbers of Brazilian servicemen into US military academies. The 25,000 Brazilian troops sent to participate in the Allied invasion of Italy were equipped by the US government and served under US commanders. Franklin Roosevelt visited the airbase in Natal in 1943, seeming to cement the international prestige that Brazil hoped its wartime partnership would reap.

Vargas advanced a number of other key agenda items through his wartime cooperation. The United States committed to purchasing a number of raw materials from Brazil, including rubber, iron ore, crystal quartz, and

Figure 2.1 Franklin Roosevelt and Getúlio Vargas visit defense installations in Natal, Brazil, January 28, 1943. United States Library of Congress.

other minerals, which helped to counteract the disruption of trans-Atlantic trade in wartime.[100] The US also helped to finance the erection of a massive steel mill in Volta Redonda, which advanced Brazilian goals of industrialization and became a major symbol of Brazilian economic nationalism. In 1942, a US technical mission traveled to Brazil with the objective of working with Brazilian economists and technicians on ways to "soften the impact" of the loss of imports in wartime, including by fostering local production of previously imported goods.[101] The Coordinator's Office of Inter-American Affairs advanced some of Vargas's developmental goals for the North and Northeast by working with Brazilian officials and practitioners to launch health and sanitation projects, nutrition and food supply programs, and training programs in related fields such as farming, nursing, and midwifery. The public health service initiated through the Coordinator's Office would ultimately become an integral part of the nation's Ministry of Health.[102] In the context of all of this close cooperation, trade between the two countries grew ever greater. By the end of the war, the United States purchased 50 percent of Brazilian exports, and about the same ratio of Brazil's imports came from the United States.[103]

The experiments in hemisphere defense undertaken during the war congealed by the war's end into a comprehensive and wide-ranging program of security cooperation. The countries perceived to be most valuable to US defense plans fared best in terms of reaping material reward for their collaboration, while Chile and Argentina, which failed to join the Allied cause until nearer the war's conclusion, largely missed out. But security cooperation left no nation in the Americas untouched. During the war, US military aid and training became region-wide initiatives. In 1938, there were only two US military missions present in Latin America—a four-person naval mission in Brazil and a single man in Guatemala—and the United States had only six military attachés stationed in the region.[104] By the end of 1941, US military advisers were at work in every Latin American republic.[105] Establishing military training missions in countries across the region, the US armed forces displaced European training missions as the primary source for guidance for Latin American security forces.

Many Latin American countries also requested and received FBI assistance for developing their own intelligence agencies and counterespionage practices.[106] Such programs often helped to centralize power over police with national governments, a boon to the power of executive leaders. Fifteen Latin American countries cooperated with the United States in a deportation program, often under immense pressure, through which they sent German, Italian, and Japanese residents to US internment camps. Some Latin American leaders turned this program to their advantage by using it to expel political opponents or to seize property.[107] All these programs drew US officials into relationships with Latin American police forces to an extent never before seen outside of the context of US occupations.[108] And security assistance was not just of an advisory nature—the United States ultimately granted Lend Lease aid to all Latin American countries over the course of the war, with the exceptions of Panama (which had no military but did receive police aid) and Argentina.

Of course, collaboration with security forces was only a part of it. The Office of the Coordinator of Inter-American Affairs undertook programs in every country in the region, including public health work, railroad and road building, and food supply programs. Further buttressing the wartime alliance was the most concerted government-run effort to date to foster mutual understanding among the people of the Americas.[109] The Coordinator's Office circulated pro-Ally propaganda throughout the region, collaborating with local media outfits in Latin America to sponsor radio programming, and distributing news features, pamphlets, magazines and photographs. The Motion Picture Division produced and distributed new blockbuster films. In the United States, the Office worked to eliminate denigrating portrayals of Latin American characters while boosting the careers of "new faces" from Latin America like Carmen Miranda.[110] Finally, the US government fostered awareness and education about Latin America within the United States—investing funds in Spanish language education, translations of Latin American literature, and "Pan America Day" celebrations across the country—prefiguring the "area studies" boom of the Cold War.

The US government, for its part, did well by its investment. Besides garnering unity in the Americas, it developed over 200 defense sites across the region by the war's end. Though fears of a German invasion dissipated with Allied victories in Africa, the base network proved immensely valuable for ferrying supplies to the Allies across the South Atlantic. The region also provided the United States with access to vital strategic raw materials like rubber in Brazil, nickel in Cuba, and oil in Venezuela.

The growing reach of various US agencies into Latin America also allowed for the creation of the most widespread US counterintelligence infrastructure in the region to date. The Office of Naval Intelligence (ONI), Military Intelligence Division (MID), and the FBI's Special Intelligence Service (SIS), created in 1940, all undertook intelligence-gathering activities in Latin America during the war, and were able to do so inconspicuously by burying such activities beneath the state-sanctioned ones that justified their presence. Most often, SIS agents operated without the knowledge of their host governments as undercover agents posing as employees of US corporations like Firestone, General Motors, or Pan American Airways, or they were posted at US embassies as "legal attachés" or stationed with US servicemen.[111] The Office of Strategic Services (OSS), the predecessor to the CIA, was created in 1942 and became active in Latin America during this period as well, engaging not only in intelligence gathering but also in covert anti-Axis activities in the region.

Finally, to the extent that the United States had in the 1930s viewed growing German economic influence in Latin America as a challenge to US economic interests, the policies pursued in the name of security also helped to diminish that threat. The disruption to trans-Atlantic trade caused by World War II carved out a greater share of Latin American markets for US products and more tightly wove the American Republics together economically. A US-led coordinated assault on German businesses and properties in Latin America was a boon to US private interests as US companies largely stepped in to fill the void created by the elimination of Axis-dominated aviation, mining, and industrial enterprises.

When US diplomats and representatives from the armed forces fanned out across Latin America, country by country, appealing to their counterparts for assistance in hemisphere defense, a period of ad hoc negotiations and patchwork commitments ensued that would ultimately produce not just a practical framework for hemisphere defense, but a broader political economy of security cooperation. The war presented an opportunity for Latin Americans of various political persuasions to try to realize a vision long held of the Americas as a society of nations that could work together toward mutual interests. As negotiations wore on, "security" became an increasingly capacious category that expanded from the basic ability to defend the coast or excavate strategic raw materials to include diverse programs ranging from mosquito abatement to cultural exchange.

US basing was such a delicate proposition that it served as a valuable bargaining chip in these broader negotiations. Trading unpopular US basing rights for military aid and development assistance, many leaders in the Americas found ways to dovetail US security objectives with their own nation-building agendas. At the same time, they worked to delimit the reach of US power in concrete terms and prevent the proliferation of little Canal Zones across the region. By doing so, nationalist nation-builders hoped that their collaboration with the United States might strengthen their prestige and power in this era of mass politics, rather than diminish their chances of political survival.

Motivating these actions in the high political realm, of course, was a concern about ordinary people. Popular perceptions of inter-American interactions mattered in an age of nationalism and mass politics. Basing, in particular, was a facet of hemisphere defense that manifested concretely in the lives of Latin American civilians who lived near the defense sites. While leaders batted back and forth the terms of basing and compensation in the high political realm, the political economy of security cooperation was not suspended there. Against a backdrop of grand proclamations about the sovereign integrity of Latin American countries and the inherent equality of American people, Latin Americans encountered US defense contractors, military personnel, and technical advisers in their cinemas, laundromats, restaurants, and living rooms, where the power asymmetries of inter-American relations were made manifest in everyday life. As the following chapters will demonstrate, the complicated relationship between sovereignty and cooperation looked different from the ground up.

CHAPTER 3
Base Labor

Early one November morning in 1944, Vicente Baños Rodriguez traveled to his job at the US military base in San Antonio de los Baños, Cuba. He got off a public bus across from the main gate as usual, but as he crossed the street, he was hit by a car. First responders rushed Baños to the base hospital for emergency treatment and he was later transferred to Havana for further care. All told, he was hospitalized for three months at a total cost of US $310, which he declined to pay. While US workers' compensation law only covered injuries sustained on duty, the Cuban equivalent, the *Ley de Accidentes*, was more expansive and covered workers while in transit to and from their workplace.[1] Cuban law held the US government liable for the medical expenses, while US law left the bill with Baños. The question of who should bear the cost of Vicente Baños's medical treatment was laden with political import. For years, the Cuban government had struggled to manage conflicting pressures coming from the US officials who wanted to avoid the costs and red tape of Cuba's new, progressive labor laws and those coming from the Cuban workers, like Baños, who sought to prevent them from doing so.

On the ground at bases and in the areas surrounding them, further contours of a political economy of security cooperation took shape in daily life. In some ways, the prospect of base construction appeared to offer untold material benefits, and many living near the new defense sites welcomed their arrival. This was true in San Antonio de los Baños, a small town of around 13,000 residents in the province of Havana, just over twenty miles from the nation's capital.[2] Members of the local chamber of commerce wrote of the "flood of gold" that would accompany the construction of an airbase

Cooperating with the Colossus. Rebecca Herman, Oxford University Press. © Oxford University Press 2022.
DOI: 10.1093/oso/9780197531860.003.0004

there and provide relief from ongoing economic crisis and unemployment.[3] Purveyors of construction materials, landowners with desirable tracts, and owners of heavy machinery all stood to benefit from the demands of construction. The influx of US troops would prompt the creation of new businesses and restaurants. And the presence of the base would imbue the town with enhanced importance on the national stage, permitting local officials to insist on long-desired facilities and improvements to the town with greater authority. Indeed, over the years, local leaders upheld the importance of the base in making the case for a new bank headquarters, a new hospital, paved roads, new schools, and the promulgation of new sanitary codes.[4]

But the optimism with which some residents viewed base construction existed alongside the dismay of others. San Antonio de los Baños came to resemble a boomtown, for better and for worse. The influx of migrants who sought employment on the base and the subsequent arrival of US troops did bring clientele for new businesses, but they also brought a housing crisis when landlords evicted their existing tenants to charge higher rates from the newcomers. Shantytowns cropped up on the outskirts of the base and local papers lamented in xenophobic tones the sudden ubiquity of vagrants. Community leaders worried about the impact of the US presence on local culture and customs, particularly among the town's women and youth as dance halls and bars created new spaces of socialization that ran counter to the small town's prewar norms. Locals deplored the contractor's practice of hiring laborers in the capital instead of prioritizing the town's residents. And those who did get jobs denounced the company's violation of Cuban labor laws. Where there was meant to be abundance, there was instead a sense of loss, with one editorial declaring of San Antonio de los Baños, *"este pueblo se aquila"*—this town is for rent.[5]

Over the war years, all sorts of people living near US defense sites in Latin America sought to do on the ground what heads of state and their foreign ministers were themselves attempting in the high political realm: to engage US power and resources productively and make the most of wartime cooperation, while contending with the vast asymmetries of power that structured the whole affair.

Often, efforts to constrain US overreach on the ground pivoted around conflicts over governance. The integrity of national labor legislation proved an early and enduring arena of struggle. New provisions of labor law that were formulated with the rise of social welfare and the expansion of mass politics in many parts of Latin America in the first decades of the twentieth century obstructed US goals of rapid and economical defense construction. This was especially the case in Cuba and Brazil, which emerged from the

1930s with particularly progressive social legislation.[6] But in both countries, whether and how these new social rights would be upheld and enforced remained to be seen. As the US government cut corners to decrease costs and speed up construction, ongoing domestic political contests surrounding labor and "the social question" intersected unexpectedly with the demands of international politics. A simple question like "who should pay Vicente Baños's medical bills?" forced Cuban and Brazilian leaders to navigate the competing demands of domestic and international political agendas.

THE LABOR POLITICS OF BASE-BUILDING IN CUBA

US officials initiated base construction in Cuba during a pivotal moment for Cuban labor. The Constitution of 1940, the belated product of the 1933 Cuban Revolution, was considered by many to be the most progressive constitution in the hemisphere at the time. It enshrined a number of labor rights that were first advanced in the months following the revolution but had been suppressed during the counterrevolutionary period spearheaded by Batista in the mid-1930s. These were later resuscitated during the so-called Pax Batistiana at the end of the decade, which resulted from a strategic alliance that Batista struck with the Communist Party, through which the Communists offered Batista political support and, in return, Batista legalized the party and permitted the organization of a Communist-led labor confederation, the Confederación de Trabajadores Cubanos (CTC). Labor activists actively lobbied the Assembly that convened to draft the new Constitution through letter-writing campaigns and public demonstrations, and ultimately, the Constitution consecrated the eight-hour workday, forty-eight hours of pay for a forty-four-hour workweek, paid maternity leave, and one month of rest for every eleven worked. It was a victory to see these provisions laid out in the Constitution, but several of them would require the drafting of new, complementary legislation to become enforceable, and only time would tell whether Congress would follow through.

The first US defense construction project to move forward in Cuba was Pan Am's Airport Development Program (ADP) project in Camagüey. It was the top ADP priority when the War Department concluded its contract with Pan Am in late 1940. Defense construction and the US military presence in Camagüey were less conspicuous and impactful than base construction in San Antonio proved to be. It was one of the oldest and largest cities in Cuba, the capital of a province of the same name. What's more, the scope of construction and the size of the military presence were smaller in Camagüey, and less conspicuous. Rather than build an entirely new airbase from scratch, as the US government would go on to do in Pinar del Rio and in San Antonio de los Baños, the War Department planned to turn an airfield that Pan Am had owned and operated in Camagüey since 1928 into a strategic airbase by adding two new runways, augmented radio, electrical and fueling facilitates, and new service buildings. A second phase of the project in 1943 added army barracks and attendant facilities to the field to house the soldiers who, until then, rented lodgings in town.[7]

From the outset of the project, Pan Am's attorney, Mario Lazo, recognized that employment practices on the construction site would be the primary space in which Pan Am would interface with local residents, and he wanted the company to make a good impression. He advised Pan Am to hire as many Cuban workers as possible, particularly for lower-level positions. Labor nationalism had been a prominent theme in the Cuban labor movement over the preceding decade, in part in reaction to preferential treatment given to Spaniards in employment opportunities on the island and also as nativist backlash to the large numbers of Haitian and Jamaican workers who migrated to Cuba to work in the sugar industry after World War I. Though the racial politics of labor nationalism had changed over time, a Nationalization of Labor law remained on the books that privileged Cuban citizens in hiring, and it remained in the company's interest to rely on a Cuban workforce to the greatest extent possible. Lazo was able to secure permission from the Cuban government for US citizens to travel to Camagüey for roles of a more technical nature, but he urged the company nonetheless to hire a Cuban engineer from Camagüey, if only for "cultivating good-will."[8]

Though Pan Am largely followed Lazo's advice to hire Cuban workers in Camagüey, the company proved less inclined to observe other important Cuban labor provisions in their management of Cuban workers. The labor rights that US defense contractors working in Cuba throughout the war were most likely to violate were those that made construction or production slower and more costly: laws that limited the workweek, regulated overtime pay, required the payment of four additional hours per week, and dictated vacation allowances.[9] In 1941, workers hired on the Camagüey project began filing complaints about payroll violations with the Camagüey Labor Office, and an inspector from that office, after visiting the worksite, found ample support for the complaints. The inspector determined that the ADP regularly worked employees on the site ninety hours per week and failed to provide the additional four-hour payments and vacation allowances. According to Cuban law, the penalty for such violations included fines in the order of $1,000 or imprisonment up to sixty days, and if each worker whose rights were violated counted as one violation, the penalty would be cumulative.[10]

ADP officials were not interested in paying the fines, nor were they interested in observing the forty-four-hour workweek. And even as Lazo sounded the alarm about the labor investigations at the ADP site, the pending court hearing, and the potential penalties involved, he commented that though the Constitution technically permitted no exceptions to the eight-hour workday, in practice, the Ministry of Labor recognized that the limitation was often "impracticable" and that both the Labor Ministry and the Courts were "inclined to be lenient" on the matter.[11] Lazo thought such leniency might be particularly easy to come by if the urgent, strategic nature of the work was impressed upon those officials.

As they strategized how to obtain exemption from these requirements, an irony of the ADP's structure emerged. When Pan Am began the work, the clandestine nature of the defense construction had the desired effect of accelerating progress. The company took advantage of existing relationships with Cuban government officials to obtain the required permits for construction and insisted on the private, commercial nature of their endeavors to avoid the political burden of open US government involvement. But, when it came to labor policy, the company confronted the fact that the clandestine nature of the ADP created new obstacles at the same time that it eliminated others. That is, Pan Am could not easily appeal to the Cuban government to declare the company relieved of the obligations of Cuban labor law in the name of cooperation in defense, having so carefully built a commercial façade.

Pan Am officials pursued informal exemptions from labor legislation provisions on their own by appealing to those individuals who could decide whether or not to enforce them.[12] Pan Am's legal counsel met with the judge who would hear the case in Camagüey and with officials from the Camagüey Labor Office. After denying the defensive nature of the project in order to get it started, in these meetings, Pan Am privately emphasized the defensive value of the project in order to keep it going. Lazo also appealed to his old friend, Cuban Minister of Defense Domingo Ramos, to support their case by affirming the strategic importance of the Camagüey airfield. As a result of these conferences, labor officials agreed to cooperate in "discouraging further claims against ADP," and the Camagüey Correctional Court judge seemed similarly amenable to assisting Pan Am.[13]

The conflict remained tied up in court until January 1942, by which time circumstances had changed. With the United States and Cuba having declared war on the Axis powers and become formal allies, the fictional premise of the ADP was no longer essential to defense construction in Cuba. The Camagüey Correctional Court dismissed the complaints regarding the limited workweek at the Camagüey ADP site.[14]

Moving forward, the Cuban government was instrumental in shielding US contractors from the obligations of Cuban social legislation. In June 1942, the United States and Cuba signed a military agreement that permitted the construction of the Batista Airbase in San Antonio de los Baños. The Cayuga Construction Corporation, a New York–based company with no experience in overseas construction, won the contract. Far more expansive than the ADP project in Camagüey, particularly in relation to the town in which it was undertaken, the project would become the major source of employment during the war. At its peak, Cayuga employed 11,000 Cuban workers in a town that had been home to only 13,000 residents at the war's outset.[15]

When work began on the new site, the question of whether Cuban labor legislation should apply arose again. In contrast to the ADP site in Camagüey, in San Antonio de los Baños the construction underway was openly associated with hemisphere defense. The official stance of the US embassy was that US contractors should respect all local labor law, but the State Department was open to circumventing provisions of Cuban law if it could be done in a way that was politically sanctioned by Cuban authorities and justified in the name of the Allied war effort.[16] To this end, US officials lobbied the Cuban Ministry of Labor, formally pursuing the same sorts of labor exemptions that Pan Am had sought informally in Camagüey.

Cuban workers' responses to US efforts to suspend certain provisions at the Batista Airbase were constrained by a cross section of alliances. Not only was the CTC enmeshed in a strategic alliance with Batista, they were also by this time vocal supporters of the war. The CTC had originally advocated isolation, but when Stalin endorsed the Allies in 1941, Cuban Communists became among the biggest champions of the Allied cause in Cuba. In mid-1942, just as the construction of the Batista Airbase was getting underway, the CTC publicly proclaimed that it would avoid strikes that "in these decisive hours, could cause setbacks in the war effort and debilitate the unity that is indispensable to the achievement of victory."[17]

It seemed as though US power, the wartime alliance, and the CTC's alliance with Batista would all close off options available to Cuban workers in asserting their rights on US bases. Nonetheless, at the Batista Air Base, workers and local residents fought to compel the Cayuga Construction Corporation to uphold the newly accorded rights. In early July 1942, a commission claiming to represent some 4,000 workers seeking employment with Cayuga reported to the offices of the leftist newspaper *Hoy* and published a request that the Cuban government compel Cayuga to comply with Cuban social legislation.[18] Workers employed by Cayuga subsequently formed the "Pro-Workers of the San Antonio Airbase Committee" led by Eduardo Torriente under the General Syndicate of Workers in the Building Trades. The committee devised a list of demands and versions of the list were presented to Cayuga management, published in *Hoy*, and circulated on printed handbills around the base.[19] The list included demands that the company recognize the union, that the workday be set at eight hours in accordance with the Constitution, and that the company agree to a minimum salary, hygienic working conditions, the construction of housing, and the provision of transportation for workers employed on the base.[20]

In a context in which dissenting labor risked appearing disloyal to the war effort, Torriente and his peers carefully underscored workers' commitment to cooperation with the US government and to Allied victory. They portrayed Cayuga as the real threat to the Allied cause, a self-interested corporation capitalizing on war. One article in *Hoy* declared, "What we won't accept under any condition is that Cayuga is taking advantage of the circumstances and of our selfless cooperation for its own benefit."[21] Workers alleged that Cayuga officials were selling jobs for 10 pesos each and pocketing the cash. Others asserted that the maltreatment of Cuban workers by US personnel was tantamount to fifth columnist sabotage, a subtle effort to slow down the progress of base construction.[22]

Seeking common cause with the US government, the Pro-Workers Committee circulated a handbill with a printed quote from US ambassador Spruille Braden in which he declared, "Integral collaboration and united action are imperative and those are the terms on which the Cuban government and I work with one another. It's a pleasure to work under these conditions, especially when it is so evident that the authorities reflect in these matters the profound desires of the Cuban people." Below Braden's quote, the handbill stated, "We, the Pro-Workers of San Antonio Airbase Committee agree with the Ambassador; but not with the Cayuga Construction Corporation, which is employing totalitarian methods." The handbill then listed a series of demands, first among them: "The Company must comply with Social Legislation!"[23]

The argument that Cayuga and the US government were two actors with conflicting values was not entirely wrong. Though the embassy advocated on behalf of the company, embassy officials were frustrated with Cayuga from the beginning of the project. Cayuga sought greater exemptions from Cuban law than the embassy was willing to request.[24] There was also the matter of corruption; State Department investigations legitimated Cuban workers' allegations of job-selling. The embassy also frequently expressed frustration at Cayuga's excessive employment of US civilian personnel. They had urged the company to keep the number of US employees to a minimum and insisted that no US citizens should be employed for so-called unskilled or semi-skilled work that could easily be done by Cuban workers.[25] Employment seemed one of the clearest ways that defense construction could benefit local residents, and to hire US citizens for jobs that Cubans could do just as well threatened to convey the sort of US chauvinism and superiority that endangered Pan-Americanism.

All these factors led several embassy officials to lament that Cayuga, as a US contractor, had been a "most unfortunate choice" and when seeking bids from contractors for future construction projects, they strategically avoided entertaining bids from Cayuga.[26] Braden himself made the connection between Cayuga and the legacy of early twentieth-century US imperialism, when he noted, "the Cayuga Construction Corporation has left a very unsavory reputation in Cuba; in fact it has left a taste in the mouth not unlike the Magoon administration," referencing the US official who served as the governor of Cuba during the 1906–1909 US occupation of the island, and governor of the Panama Canal Zone before that.[27]

Nonetheless, State Department efforts to advocate on behalf of Cayuga culminated in a series of resolutions passed by the Ministry of Defense and the Ministry of Labor that effectively created a special set of labor regulations that would govern employment at defense construction sites and overrode some of the labor provisions of the new Constitution.[28] The Ministry of Labor's Resolution 583 dictated the exceptional legal regime that would govern employment at the Cayuga construction site.[29] The most dramatic difference between the labor provisions of the Cuban Constitution and those of Resolution 583 had to do with permissible work hours. While the Cuban Constitution stipulated limits of 44 hours per week, or 176 hours per month, Resolution 583 raised the monthly limit to 240 hours, with the possibility of extending that limit to 300 hours in the case of an emergency.[30] Those 240 monthly hours would be considered "ordinary hours," and only hours worked beyond that number would be compensated at overtime pay rates. US officials were also successful in avoiding the cost of severance pay for Cuban workers when they gained permission from the Ministry of Labor to employ Cuban workers on a day-by-day basis.[31]

Mario Lazo, Pan Am's attorney and frequent adviser to the US embassy, also served as Cayuga's attorney and guided them through this process, building on his experience with the ADP. He described Resolution 583 as "the most liberal labor ruling the Cuban government has issued in recent years" and predicted (albeit incorrectly) that it would "do away with virtually all labor problems."[32] Two weeks later, the Labor Ministry issued a second resolution, which extended the exceptional labor regime to construction work at Pan Am's ADP sites at Camagüey, Rancho Boyeros, and San Julián.[33]

The resolutions were not widely publicized, and workers continued to denounce Cayuga in *Hoy* and on the street.[34] A month after the new resolutions were announced, some 2,000 workers gathered to protest Cayuga's continued failure to abide by Cuban labor law.[35] The workers sent telegrams addressed to Fulgencio Batista and Franklin Roosevelt that read, "Thousands of workers of the San Antonio Air Base . . . protest the anti-democratic attitude of the Cayuga Construction Corporation, which refuses to recognize the construction worker syndicate and maintains labor conditions that are not in accordance with Cuban laws."[36]

CTC leaders tried to insert themselves as intermediaries between the protesting workers and the US and Cuban governments, leveraging their proclaimed dedication to the Allied cause to present themselves as sympathetic to US interests, while still critical of Cayuga's practices.[37] In a confidential letter to a senior official in charge of Latin American Affairs in the State Department, one CTC leader wrote, "Some of us who are Cuban labor leaders consider that neither the action of the unions nor political agitation should interfere with the completion of this work . . . a contribution to the interests of the war against Nazism and fascism, but this position of ours is rejected by a certain group of workers in light of the fact that the Cayuga Construction company has no regular wage scales, system of administration or hiring for these workers and employees." The letter went on to suggest that Cayuga officials meet with these more empathetic CTC leaders, who could help them work toward an agreement with base workers.

Other well-known political figures made further efforts to walk the fine line between denouncing the company's practices (and the Cuban government's support of them) and appearing to obstruct the war effort. Carlos Prío Socarrás, senator from the Auténtico opposition party who would go on to become president of Cuba in 1948, challenged the constitutionality of Resolution 583. He argued, unsuccessfully, on behalf of a group of Cayuga personnel department employees, that all work in excess of eight hours per day should be compensated with overtime pay as set forth in the Constitution.[38] According to Lazo, CTC leaders followed challenges to the constitutionality of Resolution 583, hoping that a favorable decision would provide an entry point for challenging the ministry's policies on labor rights at war projects more broadly, but such a decision never materialized.[39] Lazo himself noted in later years that he and his firm had always doubted the constitutionality of certain aspects of the Resolution but believed that "the urgent need" to build the bases "overcame any technical questions of legality." He noted that if not for the cover provided by the Resolutions, "the men would have worked at the Batista Airport in open and complete violation of the Cuban Labor laws."[40]

In September, the Cuban Minister of Labor, José Suarez Rivas, became the first senior official of the Batista administration to visit the base in San Antonio de los Baños. His visit would put an end to organizing for years to follow. After his tour of the grounds, Suarez Rivas held a press conference at which he publicly proclaimed the unity of the Cuban and US governments in the creation of the exceptional legal regime that governed base employment regulations. He announced, "Once the primordial necessity of the construction of the base was declared by the Ministry of Defense, work conditions compatible with the mutual benefit of both governments were established" and asserted that this was in accordance with Cuban workers' professed desire "to contribute effectively to the victory of the Allied nations."[41] "The defense of our coasts and waters," he continued, "requires the suppression of 'red tape.'"[42] These public declarations defeated workers' hopes that the Cuban government would intervene on their behalf.

Though collective organizing diminished in late 1942, workers continued to protest in the form of individual grievances filed against Cayuga with the Ministry of Labor for particular violations. But during this period, when a worker filed a complaint denouncing a labor violation, the protocol was for the Labor Ministry or local labor office to send an investigator who would determine if a violation had occurred. If the Labor inspector determined that the complaint had merit, the case could proceed to court. In the case of base labor complaints, that administrative step offered the Labor Ministry further opportunities to uphold the resolutions that the Labor Minister had issued, without involving the courts, which might raise questions about the resolutions' legality.

The resolutions proved enduring and successful in stifling individual claims. In the roughly one year of intense construction work between the initiation of the project and the transfer of control over the base to the Puerto Rico District of the Army Corps of Engineers in March 1943, not a single one of 1,500 complaints filed by workers against the Cayuga Construction Company was deemed legitimate. Yet in other industries at this time, according to Mario Lazo, 90 percent of claims were found in favor of workers.[43] Lazo attributed these outcomes to the US embassy's advocacy for Cayuga, declaring, "Unquestionably the principal reason for our success is the assistance given by the Embassy."[44]

By pursuing exemptions from social legislation through Cuban government agencies under the banner of wartime cooperation, the US government was able to intervene in the application of Cuban social legislation while shielding itself from accusations that it was infringing on national sovereignty. Whereas before Pearl Harbor, Pan American Airways had to seek exemptions from social legislation through backroom conversations, after the attack, "cooperation" provided an aboveboard way to intervene in the era of non-intervention.

WORKING FOR THE US ARMY

When the airbase at San Antonio de los Baños was completed and control of the base shifted from the Cayuga Construction Corporation to the US Army, the Army took over the employment of Cuban personnel who worked on the base. From this time on, US embassy officials offered a different rationale for refusing to apply Cuban labor law at the Batista Air Base. They argued that the US government could not be expected to apply foreign legislation in its own employment practices. In this sense, when the base became active, the central question regarding the jurisdiction of labor law at bases shifted from *whether* the law applied to *whose* law applied. The Cuban government agreed in principle that the United States should not be held to Cuban labor legislation.[45] But Cuban workers were quick to point out that employment practices at Batista Airfield did not align with US law either. It was a unique concoction, frequently void of the benefits of both countries' legislation.

When determining the applicability of Cuban law on US bases in Cuba, the obvious point of comparison was the base in Guantánamo Bay, where laws pertaining to employment were also undergoing analysis and clarification, as extensive construction on the base significantly increased the number of Cubans that visited its territory for work each day.[46] In June 1942, the Cuban Ministry of Labor issued an opinion that Cuban social laws did not apply in the territory of the Guantanamo Naval Base because the United States enjoyed full jurisdiction in that space. But such a legal interpretation regarding social law at the airbase at San Antonio, a space that officials were eager to portray as distinct from Guantanamo, would have been more problematic. By maintaining that the US government, as an employer, could not be held to a foreign nation's employment policy, US officials effectively established the same legal regime at the Batista Air Base as that which ruled in Guantanamo; they just grounded it in a different rationale.

To drive the point home with Cuban employees, the post engineers at the Batista Airfield drew up a waiver of rights that Cuban employees signed upon accepting employment or having their existing employment with Cayuga transferred to the US Army Corps of Engineers. Workers were first presented with the memoranda exchanged between the US and Cuban governments affirming that the US government would not be held to Cuban social legislation. Employees were then required to sign a waiver that stated:

> I have read and fully understand the contents of the Memoranda exchanged between the American Embassy, Havana, and the Ministry of State of the Republic of Cuba dated December 1, 1942 and December 5, 1942 respectively, to the effect that Cuban civilian personnel employed at said Airport by the United States government are not subject to the Labor and Social Laws of Cuba; that in consideration of such employment I hereby renounce any and all rights under the Labor and Social Laws of Cuba and accept in lieu thereof the rights, and obligations provided by the laws of the United States of America applicable to my employment at said Airport.[47]

Lawyer Mario Lazo cautioned US authorities that, legally, these waivers were illegitimate. He explained that diplomatic correspondence between the United States and Cuba did not have the force of law, and there was no provision of Cuban law that exempted employees of the US government. Moreover, the Cuban Constitution explicitly prohibited the renunciation of one's rights.[48] Employees' signed waivers would not hold up in court. In his final analysis, however, Lazo concluded that the Corps of Engineers had two options: they could comply with Cuban legislation or they could continue with the waivers, which, if illegitimate in a legal sense, could still serve as "a practical means of discouraging claims."[49] The Army took the latter course.

This improvised system did not go uncontested. After the war, workers rallied for the application of Cuban law at the base. Cuban communists were untethered from their allegiance to the Allied war effort and the "Pax Batistiana" was no longer relevant, as Batista left the presidency in 1944 at the conclusion of his term and was succeeded by a candidate from the opposition. That presidential election marked the first time in ten years that Batista's preferred candidate did not take office. In this context, workers gathered for a meeting at San Antonio's city hall in September 1945. They identified themselves as "workers, who know their rights acquired by their own effort and struggle, and know how to put up high the flag of our country, compelling the compliance of our social laws, rights accomplished by virtue of our Constitution." They acknowledged that they had made sacrifices during the war and sought "justice in peace-time."[50] On the topic of waivers, the organizers assured base workers that if they had signed a waiver, "there was no need to worry, since no one could make them renounce their social rights in their own country."[51]

At a hearing on the base, Commanding Officer Leigh Wade asserted yet another interpretation of jurisdiction over labor on US bases overseas. He announced that neither country's labor legislation applied but rather, US air and naval bases were ruled by special legislation created by US military authorities.[52] Facing renewed efforts at organizing on the base, he cited a US War Department directive that prohibited unionization on military bases and encouraged workers instead to consider forming a welfare organization and filing individual grievances with the proper base authorities.

Workers denounced this response as yet another infringement on Cuba's sovereignty. *Hoy* published an editorial declaring, "by virtue of our Constitution and the legal dispositions of our country all workers have the right to organize themselves and measures of social benefit protect them completely. There is no and cannot be any exception. Otherwise, the fundamental principles of our Republic would be ignored, creating a lamentable precedent and placing a piece of our own territory and a group of our citizens beyond the protection of our laws."[53] In other words, the Batista Base would become another Guantanamo, the very thing that Cuban leaders had sought to avoid from the outset.

When Colonel Wade fired three of the workers' chosen delegates, 700 workers went on strike. Cuban authorities detained several Cuban workers during the strike, and others traveled to the capital to demand that the Cuban government rectify the situation. Sympathy strikes in the tobacco industry broke out elsewhere in the state, but the successes of these efforts were circumscribed.[54] The strike lasted only four days. The fired organizers were never reinstated, but their status was changed from "dismissed" to "suspended." The detained Cuban workers were released. Though *Hoy* reported the resolution to the strike as a victory for workers, US officials saw the resolution as no less a victory for themselves.[55] The greatest triumph, from the embassy's perspective, was that the CTC officially agreed with the United States that Cuban laws did not apply on the base. CTC leaders assured Colonel Wade that they would subject the leader of the strike to disciplinary action. After the strike at San Antonio, labor agitation diminished.

EQUAL PAY FOR "COMPARABLE AMERICANS"

Cuban workers frustrated with US contractors, the US embassy, and the Cuban government ultimately staged one final, unusual maneuver in an effort to make demands on the Cayuga Construction Corporation. A year and a half after Cayuga completed the work in San Antonio de los Baños, a large group of former Cayuga employees took the company to task for violation of a Cuban right that had not been included in the exemptions granted by the Ministry of Labor: Article 62 of the Cuban Constitution, which guaranteed equal pay for equal work. The Cuban plaintiffs in the case insisted that a number of the 700 US citizens that Cayuga brought to Cuba when building the base occupied the same positions as many of their 11,000 Cuban counterparts—working as bricklayers, truck drivers, cooks, typists—but received far higher wages. With the rhetoric of Pan-American equality so pervasive during the war, and so central to inter-American co-operation in hemisphere defense, the premise of equal pay for equal work regardless of one's national citizenship had particular potency, and the merits of the case rested on whether Cuban employees did indeed carry out the same work as "comparable Americans," as the defense lawyers called them.[56]

What made this case unusual was that the workers filed their claims not in Cuban courts, but instead, in New York, beyond the reach of the State Department and the Pax Batistiana. Reminiscent of the old joke that there has never been a successful coup d'état in the United States because there is no US embassy there, it seemed to Cuban workers that perhaps a court in the United States could successfully uphold Cuban labor legislation for the very same reason. As one official put it, "realizing they would probably get soundly licked in the Cuban Courts, they took the case to New York for action."[57] In the context of the muddled relationship between sovereignty, jurisdiction, and space that prevailed in San Antonio de los Baños during the war, Cuban workers tested the limits of that ambiguity in search of new avenues of redress.

The case began on September 29, 1944, when 1,064 former Cayuga employees filed a suit against the Cayuga Construction Corporation in a New York City Court for claims in the amount of $1,473,252.54, the difference between the rates that the plaintiffs were paid compared to their US counterparts. Because the US government would be financially liable for any amount awarded to the plaintiffs, the US Office of the Attorney General handled Cayuga's defense in cooperation with the Judge Advocate General's Office. Mario Lazo, due to his intimate knowledge of Cuban labor law and Cayuga's employment policies, was brought in as a consultant.

The defense team immediately challenged the jurisdiction of the New York City Court to hear such a case. The motion to dismiss argued, "there is no factor or circumstance involved which would warrant or con-done the assumption by the courts of New York, or of any other State in the United States, of the function of interpreting Cuban law as applied to

Cuban nationals, under Cuban contracts, performed in Cuba."[58] The court denied this motion and, to the great alarm of the State Department, accepted jurisdiction over the case.[59] Cayuga appealed the decision, but the Appellate Division of the New York Supreme Court dismissed Cayuga's appeal.

The State Department reacted with grave concern. US officials had been critical of Cayuga's excessive hiring of US citizens.[60] But, when Cuban workers demanded in court that they be paid the same rates as Americans for the same work, Ambassador Braden called the lawsuit a "wholly unjustified raid on the US treasury."[61] Another official referred to the Cuban plaintiffs as a "crowd of scalpers."[62] More pressing, *Vigil et al v. Cayuga* might precipitate other, similar cases. The US attorney general argued that, if the court accepted jurisdiction, "the precedent thus established may be expected to lead to a flood of litigation in our courts by nationals of other countries asserting rights and seeking remedies here, to which they are not entitled and which they could not obtain in the courts of their own countries." He calculated that hundreds of thousands of nationals of other countries had worked for the US War and Navy departments on construction projects around the world during the war.[63] Lazo estimated that additional claims could by brought by 50,000 other workers from Cuba alone.[64]

Such concerns did not prove to be entirely misguided. Over the following two years, Cuban workers filed two additional suits against Cayuga in New York, increasing the number of plaintiffs to 2,048 and the amount of money requested to nearly $3 million. At first, the news of the suit traveled around Cuba by word of mouth but in 1945, the lawyer on the case began taking out ads in the newspaper in search of further plaintiffs; he stood to collect 50 percent of any sum awarded by the courts. One worker testified that the lawyer had been forced to hire a secretary just to handle the crowds of workers who showed up at his office to join the suit.[65]

Somewhat ironically, the defense's primary argument against New York's jurisdiction was that, to entertain these workers' claims in New York would violate Cuban sovereignty. Lazo insisted, "the Cuban Constitution need not be observed and enforced by the United States." He continued, "any attempt by the courts of the United States to interpret and apply Cuban labor and social measures . . . might be regarded by Cuba as an impairment of its sovereign rights. . . . Such a step would be inimical to the friendly relations existing between the two countries at the present time, the maintenance of which are of the utmost importance in furthering the joint war effort of the two nations."[66]

The State Department struggled with what role it could play in a domestic lawsuit. Lazo encouraged the State Department to intervene directly in the case by filing an *amicus curiae* brief presenting the US government's interests. The proposed brief would explain that it was the Cuban government, not Cayuga, that had established the employment procedures and working conditions at the airbase.[67] But the Department of Justice (DOJ) believed that a State Department intervention in New York would be inappropriate. Instead, the DOJ suggested a State Department intervention in Cuba could prove useful. Cooperation from the Cuban government might once more be the answer.

The DOJ and officials from the War Department made a series of suggestions. First, they requested that the State Department use ongoing negotiations surrounding the timing of the transfer of the Batista Airfield to the Cuban government to insist that the Cuban government agree to indemnify the United States for any payments that resulted from the lawsuit.[68] They reasoned that, had they known that the "equal pay for equal work" clause would be invoked against Cayuga, they would have sought exemption from that provision too.[69] The notion that it was the Cuban government's fault that the US embassy had not thought to ask for exemption from this particular aspect of Cuban law was hardly compelling and the State Department refused this course of action. The second suggestion was that the State Department obtain from the Cuban government a statement verifying that the Cayuga Construction Corporation had, in fact, followed Cuban law.[70] After some consideration, the State Department refused this course as well, in part, because the statement was false, but also because it anticipated Batista's successor would not wish to associate himself with Batista's labor policy.[71] What's more, Carlos Prío Socarrás, who had challenged the constitutionality of those policies, was now the minister of labor.

The only attempted intervention that the State Department did make in the case was to seek a statement from the Cuban minister of justice indicating US courts should not hear the case because, by skipping the "administrative step" of first filing claims with the Ministry of Labor in Cuba that was required before appealing to a court of law, the claimants had not followed proper procedure. The Cuban minister of justice refused to issue such a statement and simply replied that the American courts would be best suited to determine their own competence to hear the case.[72] Ultimately, the case was tried and lost in New York without intervention from the Cuban government or the US State Department. The proceedings stretched into the early 1950s, and the case was finally settled without further appeal in 1954 in favor of Cayuga. The judge found that the Cuban claimants were simply unable to prove that they had conducted the same work as their US counterparts, under identical conditions. Problems of scant documentation weakened the claimants' case, while the defense had the full force and resources of the US government behind it.

BASE LABOR IN BRAZIL

Labor strike suppressed by Cuban auth. Comparable case failed

When the War Department initiated base construction in Brazil in January 1941, several of the US government's broad concerns about labor legislation were the same as they were in Cuba. Brazil, like Cuba, had seen the development over the 1930s of labor protections that would make US defense construction more expensive and slower than US officials would have liked. US employers in Brazil found themselves, as they did in Cuba, operating in the midst of a pivotal moment in the history of social legislation and a sea change in the relationship between workers and the state. Vargas had instituted a series of labor laws in a piecemeal fashion over the course of the 1930s, and in 1943, the Consolidation of Labor Laws (CLT— Consolidacão das Leis do Trabalho) would amalgamate the new labor code and become Vargas's greatest legacy to the Brazilian legal system.[73]

The CLT, like the Cuban Constitution of 1940, was notoriously progressive but also notoriously idyllic and imperfectly applied. The myth that Vargas crafted around his paternalist relationship with the masses was one in which he "bestowed" social rights upon the people (in return for political support). One historian described Brazilian social legislation as "more akin to patronage than rights."[74] Though the older scholarship on labor in Brazil tended to dismiss labor justice as something of a façade crafted to coopt the labor sector, more recently historians have begun to take seriously the CLT as an ideal that workers sought to force into being through their actions in labor courts.[75] During the war, employment in US defense construction became an important site for that struggle in the Brazilian North and Northeast.

The scope and scale of US defense construction in Brazil was extensive. There, Pan Am built a chain of sea and land bases around the bulge of the Brazilian coastline, linking Amapá, Belém, São Luís, Fortaleza, Natal, Recife, Maceió, and Salvador through the Airport Development Program. The Corps of Engineers built further infrastructure in other parts of the country after Brazil joined the war. As in Cuba, defense construction presented welcome employment opportunities that Brazilians seeking work as blacksmiths, painters, truck drivers, machine operators, and manual laborers were eager to take advantage of. But the working conditions that they encountered sometimes tempered their enthusiasm.

Take for instance, the experience of João Ferreira, a twenty-five-year-old Brazilian carpenter who was living in Belém in 1942 when he was recruited to work on Pan Am's Airport Development project in Amapá. The Amapá ADP site was located in northern Amazonia, nearly 400 miles north of Belém and some six nearly impassable miles from the closest village. The offer that Ferreira accepted when he boarded the boat bound for Amapá was for a decent job offering a daily pay of 16 cruzeiros, housing, and food. The reality he encountered when he arrived at the remote labor camp was significantly less appealing. He discovered that workers were housed 100 men per barrack. When it rained, which it did daily, the floor of the barrack turned to a swamp. The camp's medical supplies had been completely exhausted, and the food supply was quickly running out. Ferreira abandoned the post soon after his arrival and when he returned to Belém, he went to the offices of the local newspaper and requested that they publish his complaint.[76]

Pan Am's own public relations material on the Amapá airfield's construction largely confirmed Ferreira's account of labor conditions, even if it framed them with a more romanticized frontier motif. One piece described the airport's construction as "a story of toil and sweat under the equatorial sun, nerves jangled by incessant rains, bodies racked with fever, tractors mired in steaming mud and mosquitos whose sting meant weeks of headaches, even delirium, on a camp cot."[77] Another opened with an anecdote highlighting the lack of medical care available locally, recounting a story about a Pan Am engineer working in Amapá who was bitten on the finger by a bushmaster snake. According to the story, "to save his life, the engineer promptly shot off the end of his finger with a revolver."[78] The lack of medical care was consequential, as workers in Amapá faced significant health risks. During one month, 400 of 711 workers on the job were incapacitated by malaria.[79] Basic nutrition was also lacking. The engineer of the shot-off finger reported, "in the technical or staff mess hall we have not had any bread, eggs, or a single item of fresh vegetables or fruit in the last three weeks. The men are breaking out with open sores."[80]

As in Cuba, US citizens traveled to Brazil to work for the ADP in supervisory positions, and the air of superiority that some of them exhibited could not have helped to advance a spirit of Pan-American fraternity and equality in the workplace. Nelson Lansdale, an office manager at the Natal ADP site, wrote an account of his time there in which he sets the scene in Natal for the reader with a biting description: "Even the majority of its inhabitants, who are as lazy as they are ignorant, do not seem particularly to like Natal." Lansdale credited the ADP's accomplishments in Natal, where Pan Am built the largest US airbase outside of US borders during World War II, as the work of "an incredible horde of Americans who were to convert the back-woods of Brazil into a world crossroads."[81] As for the Brazilians who executed the work, Lansdale described them in thoroughly racialized terms as being "languid, easy-going, even charming, but for the most part irresponsible and incredibly lazy."[82] His assessment of the more skilled Brazilian clerical workers was not much better, attributing to them an "instinctive lack of efficiency" and insisting that "native employees simply do not produce to the same extent as do Americans at home assigned to similar jobs."[83]

While João Ferreira appealed to the press to voice his complaints about his brief experience working for the ADP, many more ADP workers took their complaints instead to a newly created system of labor courts that were erected throughout Brazil in 1941. It was in those courtrooms that the major struggles over Brazilian labor rights at US defense sites would be waged. In contrast to the labor organizing that took place in San Antonio de los Baños, organized labor was not a significant factor in struggles over base labor in Brazil, but the thousands of labor court cases that Brazilian workers filed against Pan Am's Brazilian subsidiary, Panair do Brasil, had much of the same effect that labor organizing had in Cuba: they forced US and Brazilian officials to address the question of whether Brazilian social legislation would apply to workers at US defense sites.

EARLY DISPUTES IN THE BRAZILIAN LABOR JUSTICE SYSTEM

The early days of the Airport Development Program in Brazil were slow-going. Initial work began in January 1941 but the goal of completing all construction within one year quickly proved impossible.[84] The scope of construction in Brazil was unparalleled as the ADP initiated work at twelve locations at the program's outset and Panair do Brasil had no previous construction experience. Lack of available mechanical equipment at the construction sites led to improvisation in construction techniques. When no asphalt mixer was available, Brazilian workers were made to hand-mix the asphalt, or trample it with their feet.[85]

Soon after the ADP began, Panair do Brasil became a commonly heard name in the halls of the newly established labor courts across the regions of Brazil where the ADP was underway. When created, the Brazilian labor justice system consisted of a National Labor Board (Conselho Nacional do Trabalho—CNT) at the national level, eight Regional Labor Courts (Conselhos Regionais do Trabalho—CRT), and thirty-six local courts

Figure 3.1 Brazilian workers at Val de Cães Field, Belém, Brazil, April 1943. US National Archives, Photo no. 342-FH-3A00800-77498AC.

Figure 3.2 Brazilian workers mix concrete at Parnarmirim Field, Natal, Brazil, May 1943. US National Archives and Records Administration, Photo No. 342-FH-3A00799-77294AC.

(Juntas de Conciliacão e Julgamento—JCJ) distributed throughout the country. There were JCJs in all the towns in which the ADP initiated construction except for Amapá, and there were Regional Labor Courts in Belém, Recife, Fortaleza, and Salvador.[86] The court system placed the state in the position of mediator between employer and employee and, in this case, between Brazilian workers and the US government. Through the thousands of claims filed against Panair during the war, workers, lawyers, and judges near defense sites tested the efficacy of newly created courts to uphold recently drafted legislation in the face of encroaching US and Brazilian federal power.

Pan Am's corporate records show evidence of extensive labor complaints against Panair in all the towns in which the ADP undertook construction, but neither the company nor most of the labor courts preserved records of the cases. Only the tribunal in Belém preserved the bulk of the case records from the period and there, at least 655 claims were filed against Panair between 1941 and 1945. The ADP division of Panair appeared as the respondent (*reclamado*) in the Belém labor courts far more frequently than any other employer in the North at this time. These records, together with the correspondence of Panair's legal counsel and US Army Corps of Engineers investigations into Panair's labor policy, offer concrete insight into larger trends.

Belém was a midsize city near the mouth of the Amazon River in the North of Brazil, home to around 200,000 residents in 1940. It had once been a major hub of the Brazilian rubber industry, but the city declined when the rise of more efficient rubber plantations in Southeast Asia put an end to the Amazonian rubber boom in the 1910s. World War II marked something of a revival in Belém, as the ADP was just the first of a series of wartime initiatives that would energize the city and the region around it. The US and Brazilian governments partnered to create the Rubber Development Corporation (RDC), which revitalized the Amazonian rubber industry in order meet US defense needs when the Allies lost access to Southeast Asian rubber under Japanese occupation.

Throughout the war, the vast majority of the claims filed against Panair had to do with the terms on which workers were fired. It is unlikely that rights associated with dismissal were the only worker benefits that Panair failed to provide; more likely, workers were just less willing to challenge Panair on the company's observance of Brazilian labor legislation until after losing their jobs. Panair frequently dismissed workers without giving them the compensation to which they were legally entitled. According to a 1935 law, workers fired without just cause were entitled to four days' prior notice (*aviso previo*), and those who worked for a twelve-month consecutive period were entitled to severance pay.[87] The amount one was owed in severance increased proportionately beyond twelve months of service.

In Cuba, costs resulting from workers' rights to severance were avoided when the Cuban Minister of Labor granted US contractors permission to hire manual workers on a day-to-day basis. But the United States had a decidedly different relationship to Brazil and was not, in 1941, in a position to lobby the Brazilian government for the kinds of exemptions that US employers obtained in Cuba. For one thing, despite the language of sovereign equality of all American nations, US officials seemed to view Brazilian sovereignty as more formidable. Furthermore, Brazil did not formally join the war until August 1942. The tenuous nature of the alliance between the United States and Brazil precluded the State Department from seeking the Brazilian government's assistance in avoiding the costs encountered in the observance of certain labor rights until October 1943.

The workers who filed claims against Panair in Belém were not typically union members—in only 9 of 655 case records did workers specify a union membership on the *termo de reclamação* that they filled out when filing a complaint. However, the records of the JCJs do reflect coordination around workers' use of the labor justice system. The earliest claims were often one-offs filed sporadically by individual workers, but as construction progressed and word of favorable judgment by the JCJs circulated, workers descended on the courts to file claims in groups—sometimes as many as twenty-five on a given day, or groups adding up to forty or fifty over two to three days, generally with the same complaint. The type of work performed by those who made use of the courts ran the gamut from manual laborers to blacksmiths to foremen. They included in their ranks ninety-eight women, mostly hired in landscaping work, as well as one widow, who filed claims on behalf of her deceased husband.[88]

During the early years of base construction in Brazil, labor courts found in favor of ADP workers with somewhat surprising frequency, given the labor justice system's reputation for disempowering workers. Of the nearly 200 claims filed by workers against the ADP in Belém before October 1943, which was when the Corps of Engineers began to actively intervene in Panair's labor policy, workers were denied compensation in only fourteen cases.[89] Over half of these cases were settled through "conciliation," a process through which employers were incentivized to bargain for a settlement because the final sums owed through that process were sometimes lower than the employer would have to pay in the event of an adverse judgment with no attempt at conciliation. In the case of the JCJ in Belém, a gamble on conciliation was a worthy one. Of the sixty-nine cases in which Panair refused conciliation, the company lost fifty-four of them outright. But conciliation was not always a bargain. In the settlements reached through this process between Panair and ADP workers, workers frequently still received the exact sum that they originally requested.[90]

Data on labor cases in Bahia, though limited, allow for some regional comparison. In Bahia, during the one-month period from August 14 to September 15, 1943, Panair confronted 139 labor claims related to ADP work. The company lost seventy-eight of those cases outright, was able through conciliation to reduce the amount Panair owed in forty-two cases, and won the remaining nineteen.[91] The evidence confirms that the high incidence of claims against Panair do Brasil in the Belém labor court was not unique to ADP work in that location, nor were rulings favorable to workers.

Panair attorneys and the Corps of Engineers officials who later investigated the costs of Panair labor disputes had many theories about why Panair fared poorly in the labor courts. Their assorted theories offer insights into their perceptions of workers, labor court delegates, and the system in general. Part of the explanation for worker victories was attributed to workers' skill at exploiting Panair's poor record-keeping, leaving the company unable to disprove "false" claims in court.[92] As one ADP attorney put it, "our records, in most instances, are insufficient to refute any employee's statement that he has worked twelve consecutive months, when in reality he probably worked six months and then quit, returning to work some months later."[93] Others insisted that workers refused to sign a receipt indicating that they were given prior notice and then promptly reported to court falsely claiming that they had never received it, in order to be paid double what they were owed.[94] Such cynicism likely reflects derogatory views of Brazilian laborers as untrustworthy, but these theories also display the lawyers' and employers' perception of a distinct degree of savvy possessed by workers as they navigated new labor laws and their enforcement in the new courts.

Other Panair attorneys opined that the system was rigged against them. As one attorney claimed, "The courts here . . . were and are prone to favor the weaker side of the dispute, i.e. the laborer. Only when the employer has a very strong evidence on his side is he liable to win."[95] The early day-to-day operations of labor justice institutions were decentralized and heavily influenced by regional politics and the proclivities of local labor boards. From the perspective of Panair, this posed a significant obstacle to formulating a unified approach to navigating the labor justice system across regional jurisdictions. The social legislation was applied differently in different states according to the disposition of local courts and each state's Interventor, a political figure that one Panair attorney described as "a local dictator who could do what he pleased in every way."[96] Another lawyer agreed, insisting, "the different States and Courts have a habit of paying no attention to decisions of neighboring courts. . . . It takes 2 or 3 years for a local agency to recognize a Federal Decree."[97]

Another piece of the explanation for early worker victories, however, was simply that Panair did not fight them. Instead, through conciliation, the airline often readily settled claims and then requested reimbursement from the US government. Panair was a leading airline in Brazil and stood to grow as German, French, and Italian aviation companies were expelled during the war. Panair executives frequently lamented the damage that ADP work and the labor disputes it inspired were doing to the company's reputation. Maintaining Panair's prestige among Brazilians was, for Pan Am, a more pressing objective than keeping the US War Department's expenses to a minimum. And so, in these early months and years of the ADP work, the airline did not always push back.

PLEADING THEIR CASE OUTSIDE THE COURTROOMS

The tide of worker victories began to turn in 1943 when a couple of Panair's lawyers began to make the case that the ADP should be exempt from Law 62, which dictated rights to termination benefits. There was, in fact, a case to be made. As written, Law 62 only applied to workers engaged in work "of indefinite scope and duration."[98] As an airline, and not a construction company, Panair fit the description of an employer engaged in work of indefinite scope and, accordingly, Panair employees were entitled to the protections of Law 62. In the early years of the ADP, an internal assessment determined it was best not to split hairs on this question, because it seemed that the regulations concerning work of temporary duration were even more burdensome still, and the airline would be better off avoiding such a designation in court.[99] But in 1943, the Consolidation of Labor Laws clarified the differences between work of definite and indefinite scope, giving Panair's lawyers the vocabulary with which to differentiate between Panair's ADP workers and its other employees.[100] In short, Panair lawyers argued that Panair-ADP was a distinct unit engaged in work of definite scope within a company of indefinite scope; and therefore, Panair's ADP employees should be exempt from severance obligations even while Panair's other employees were not. This argument did not initially hold up in court. Presiding judges countered that it did not matter if workers were hired for temporary positions, if the workers did not know that they were being hired for temporary work. Unless Panair could produce signed contracts that showed workers were informed that they were being hired temporarily, the courts would not be sympathetic.[101]

After months of failed attempts at winning with this argument in court, Panair lawyers began pursuing a more successful strategy of lobbying, behind closed doors, personal friends who occupied seats on labor courts. The chief ADP counsel for Panair, Edson Valença, took credit for pioneering this strategy. As he described it, "We pleaded our case, first of all, outside of the courtrooms!"[102] In private conversations with a friend on the JCJ in Recife, he stressed that the work of the ADP division of Panair was in fact sponsored by the US and Brazilian governments in the name of hemisphere defense. As a wartime project, he argued, it was inherently temporary.[103] As in Cuba, the ADP commercial façade had helped to get the project started, but behind closed doors, the commercial front was disavowed to accelerate the work. This strategy of personal lobbying worked for Valença at the local level, and the Recife JCJ began finding in favor of Panair in such cases; but the regional labor court in Recife, where Valença held no personal sway, continued to reject his position on appeal.

In an effort to obtain favorable judgments higher up in the labor justice system, Valença counseled Ennio Lepage, a Panair lawyer handling cases in Belém, to take this approach with a Regional Court delegate with whom Lepage was friendly in Pará. Lepage's private lobbying of the Regional Court delegate proved decisive. In mid-1943, a tie-breaking vote partially overturned a lower court decision in Belém, denying ADP workers severance pay but granting them the far inferior prior notice pay. With this decision, Panair won exemption from severance obligations in a regional court for the first time.[104]

While Panair lawyers parsed the technicalities of Brazilian labor legislation and worked their personal relationships to influence the labor justice system, court delegates representing workers' interests within that system envisioned their mission as one that transcended the particularities of any one case; their objective was to defend a larger project of social welfare. Despite the shift in the CRT decisions, justices in the lower JCJ court refused to let Panair off the hook, and the lower court in Belém continued to find over 100 new cases involving almost identical claims in favor of workers over the following months. One by one, they were appealed and overturned at the regional level.[105]

In these moments, the debates surrounding individual claims turned into larger debates over the meaning, purpose, and character of the nascent labor justice system. In the opening proceedings of one regional court case, a court delegate declared: "Once more the appellant appears before this honorable court with the objective of robbing some thousands of workers . . . of the benefits of Social Legislation and the jurisdiction of Labor Justice."[106] Panair's attorney denounced the lower court as "intransigent" in its refusal to accept the interpretation of the CRT.[107] He complained, "we are always attacked with this astounding phrase: PANAIR IS TRYING TO REMOVE THOUSANDS OF WORKERS FROM THE PROTECTION OF LABOR LEGISLATION." Noting the common reference that delegates made to the sheer volume of claims against the company, the Panair lawyer contended that what mattered was the law, not the volume of complaints, insisting "this numerical detail should not have the least bit of importance."[108] But this difference of perspective cut to the heart of the popular political project to build social welfare through social rights. The president of the JCJ, Raymundo de Souza Moura, made the point well when countered that, in fact, that so-called numerical detail was "exceptionally important" in the labor justice system. Moura explained:

> The basis of labor law is social peace. . . . In a common court, the rights of one in-
> dividual and the rights of a group are the same because private law, as the name
> implies, is essentially individualistic. In the labor court, the rights of one worker
> and the rights of thousands of workers are not the same thing, because social
> rights are essentially public, they are more concerned with public order and so-
> cial peace than with one worker or employer. . . . To violate the rights of one
> worker is *grave*, but to violate the rights of thousands of workers is *gravíssimo*.[109]

In other words, the volume of claims again Panair was important because the extent of the threat that Panair's employment policies posed to Brazilian social peace correlated to the number of workers harmed.

THE CORPS OF ENGINEERS TAKES CONTROL AND THE VARGAS ADMINISTRATION STEPS IN

The debates within the labor courts took place in a broader context of war.[110] The growing unity of the United States and Brazil in the Allied war effort created tensions between Vargas's domestic and foreign policies. In mid-1943, when the fate of ADP workers' right to severance was still being determined, the US War Department became increasingly concerned about the cost of labor benefits for US defense construction projects across Latin America. Impending massive layoffs as construction wound down in Brazil in the last months of 1943 sparked a review of severance pay policy in the higher echelons of the War Department. Between August and November 1943, Panair anticipated laying off 30,000 Brazilian workers, and severance and prior notice payments would add up significantly.[111] Identifying the mild success that Panair lawyers in Recife and Belém had recently obtained in gaining exemption in labor court decisions, the War Department ordered Panair to cease making severance and prior notice payments to ADP workers across the board.[112] The legal interpretation that Panair lawyers had advanced in a spotty, experimental fashion became the grounds on which the US government would justify systematic withholding of such benefits. If inefficiency and incompetence had often been responsible for Panair's earlier failure to uphold labor laws on defense construction sites, when the Corps of Engineers took over Panair employment policy in 1943, War Department officials insisted on a more systematic and intentional withholding of certain worker benefits to minimize costs.

Of course, the War Department's hopeful adoption of the Panair lawyers' interpretation of Brazilian law did not matter as long as most Brazilian courts did not agree with that interpretation. There would simply be more orders, from more courts, to compensate more workers after their grievances were heard. For this reason, both Pan Am and the US War Department urged US embassy officials in Rio to seek formal exemptions from these benefits from the Brazilian government. Appealing to the State Department's concerns about the danger of wartime anti-US sentiment in the Americas, one Pan Am executive made the case that systematically withholding worker benefits would be bad for inter-American unity in the war effort. Alluding to the myriad programs of the Office of the Coordinator of Inter-American Affairs in Brazil, he argued that "the amount of money sought to be saved by the policy set forth in the directive [to withhold benefits] is indeed small as compared with that which the United States is spending through other agencies to foster good will and prestige under the good neighbor policy." He warned that such goodwill programs would be "sterilized by a program of close economy affecting large numbers of low paid Brazilian laborers."[113] For these reasons, he insisted that if Panair were to discontinue benefit payments that they be given explicit legal coverage in the form of a presidential decree, presumably framed in terms of the imperatives of wartime sacrifices by Allied nations. After all, he argued, "it would not be any proper justification for a Brasilian corporation's non-compliance with Brasilian law to show an order of a United States Army official forbidding compliance with the law."[114] The Corps of Engineers supported this reccomendation and went so far as to draft a suggested decree-law for Vargas to issue that would exempt all war agencies from paying severance payments upon firing of their employees.[115] The embassy yielded and approached the Brazilian government about obtaining formal exemptions, a strategy that worked well in Cuba.

By 1943, the strengthening of the US-Brazilian alliance in the war effort had brought US and Brazilian authorities much closer together than they had been when construction began. By this time, US hemisphere security strategies and Vargas's nation-building agenda had dovetailed in a vast array of wartime projects, including health and sanitation projects, nutrition and food supply programs, and training programs in related fields such as farming, nursing, and midwifery. Wartime cooperation fostered the revitalization of the rubber industry in the Amazon and made possible the new steel mill in Volta Redonda. Perhaps most dramatic of all, wartime cooperation came with extensive military aid.

In this context, when the US embassy sought its ally's assistance in obtaining exemption from certain costly provisions of Brazilian labor law at base sites, the request was hard to accept, but also hard to refuse. Vargas ultimately found a third way. He declined to grant Panair formal exemptions. Instead, through a series of informal maneuvers, his administration placed pressure on the labor courts to interpret existing law in the way that most suited US interests. First, US embassy officials were advised to craft a strictly confidential memorandum for the Minister of Labor, Industry, and Commerce. In the memo, the embassy would lay out the argument Panair attorneys had developed to justify ADP exemptions from Law 62. Now that the "sponsor" of the project was explicitly known by Brazilian authorities outside of Vargas's inner circle, the memo argued that the ADP should also be exempt because it was, in fact, a US agency.[116] Embassy officials wrote this memo with the assistance of a legal adviser from the Brazilian Ministry of Labor. Once formally submitted to the ministry, the same legal adviser who helped to write it issued an opinion in favor of its principles. A confidential circular was then issued to the regional courts in the North and Northeast instructing them to interpret the law in this particular way and to communicate this interpretation to local ADP workers.[117]

Pan Am was unsatisfied by this gesture and was quick to point out that a confidential opinion would be of questionable use given the reputation of the northern and northeastern labor courts for going their own way. One executive said of the labor delegates in the North, "they are not interested in any information contained in letters or radios. . . . The only way that they will dismiss any pending suits or future suits of any kind will be by decree-law signed and published by the President of Brazil."[118] Upon further prodding from the embassy, the Brazilian Ministry of Labor sent a member of the National Labor Council on a secret tour of the northern and northeastern labor courts to reinforce the ministry's position in personal conversations with regional delegates and labor court judges in Bahia,

Maceió, Recife, Natal, Fortaleza, São Luis, and Belém. In other words, the strategy of "pleading the case outside the courtrooms" was not only the purview of corporate attorneys, but was also embraced by government officials eager to informally shape the course of labor justice decisions without threatening the appearance of autonomy.

Finally, in January 1944, the highest labor court, the National Labor Council (CNT), passed a ruling reflecting the ministry's position on an ADP case emanating from Belém.[119] The court ruled unanimously that Panair was not obligated to pay severance or prior notice, further impressing upon the regional and local courts throughout the country how such cases should be handled. A ruling in favor of Panair in the CNT meant that any adverse lower court ruling against Panair could be appealed to the national level for a favorable one. For this reason, despite the continued absence of a formal decree-law granting ADP exemptions, the CNT calmed Panair executives' anxieties. Even so, Pan Am executives continued to point out that as an interpretation of existing law, the ruling was always subject to change.

All told, the Army Corps of Engineers calculated that Brazilian interventions on behalf of the US government with regard to these and other labor benefits saved the US government some $600,000.[120] They saw this savings as clear evidence of an enhanced relationship between the two nations working together in war, while others would more likely have characterized it as a negative byproduct of wartime cooperation.[121] Once the US government took over operations of the ADP airfields from Panair, Brazil shielded the US government as an employer of Brazilian workers from being subjected to claims in the labor courts, in a similarly quiet and informal manner. After further conferences between the Corps of Engineers, the embassy, and the Brazilian government, the president of the National Labor Council sent a confidential circular instruction to the presidents of the Regional Labor Councils in Recife, Bahia, Fortaleza, and Belém. In it, he stated that the Labor Courts would have no further jurisdiction over labor claims arising from US bases once the US government replaced Panair as the employer at the bases.[122]

The reach of the national government into the regional and local courts did have its limits. None of the actions taken by the government was binding. Many judges and workers persisted in their efforts to see the labor protections upheld. Many JCJs refused to abide by either the circulated instructions or the requests of the Labor official who toured the northern courts.[123] As late as July 1945, cases originating in Bahia and Fortaleza still had to proceed through appeals all the way to the CNT to achieve decisions in favor of Panair.[124] More than a year after the representative from the

Ministry of Labor toured the northern and northeastern courts, Panair still had 1,330 labor cases pending throughout the region.[125]

Panair workers hired toward the end of the war learned the legal rationale that Panair used to defeat claims related to Law 62 and tried to use that knowledge to make a case for their own claims in labor courts. When US authorities officially took over responsibility for maintenance of the bases from Pan Am on September 1, 1944, Panair dismissed another wave of workers.[126] This time the workers fired were not the construction workers, painters, and foremen employed by the ADP during the construction period. Rather, they were employees charged with vigilance, maintenance, and other base operations who had been hired by the airline, not by its "temporary" ADP division. These workers argued explicitly in court that, since they were not employed by the ADP, they were entitled to severance. In the first week of September alone, 105 workers filed new claims in the JCJ in Belém. In all but one of those cases, both the lower and regional courts found in favor of the workers' right to severance pay. Despite making a case that seemed to accept and account for the exemptions to Law 62 that Edson Valença and his colleagues had pioneered, every one of their cases was overturned when Panair appealed them to the national level.

At base sites across Latin America, US government officials and contractors tested the limits of inter-American alliances as they sought to evade provisions of labor legislation without dramatically sullying the project of Pan-American solidarity. Eager to create wartime bases that appeared to be aligned with the Good Neighbor policy and its flagship respect for territorial sovereignty, US officials sought ways to avoid costly provisions of local social legislation without simply declaring jurisdiction of US labor law over Latin American territories or flagrant indifference toward local labor rights. They assessed their attempts to sidestep labor law in terms of its impact on goodwill, on the one hand, and its legal and political defensibility, on the other. As the war progressed, the latter became more important than the former, as fear of Axis sympathies dissipated and alliances with Latin American leaders, strengthened by the war, afforded US actors greater legal and political coverage in their evasion of social benefits.

Throughout the war, Presidents Fulgencio Batista and Getúlio Vargas both walked the line between cooperation with the United States and maintenance of the support of the labor sector, whose rights were compromised in the process. Workers, meanwhile, sought to benefit from the employment opportunities that defense construction and base operations presented, without sacrificing social rights. While in some ways the least powerful of the actors in play, they were instrumental in forcing the issue of labor rights into the diplomatic realm through organizing and legal action, sometimes precipitating real victories.

In their work on law and society in Latin America, historians Carlos Aguirre and Ricardo Salvatore identify a common feature in legal cultures in the region that "attributes to law more elasticity than it is supposed to have," citing "an excessive amount of judicial discretion" and a certain "arbitrary" quality to the law's enforcement that has dramatically shaped power relations in Latin American societies.[127] In the communities surrounding World War II defense sites, that elasticity rendered law a dynamic terrain on which all manner of actors sought to manage US power as they engaged in wartime cooperation. It was also crucial in enabling Latin American leaders and their US counterparts to forge creative resolutions to those conflicts along the way.

Comparison of base labor struggles and their resolutions in Cuba and Brazil reveals just how advantageous the improvised nature of the governance arrangements surrounding military bases proved to be. The distinct labor histories and political contexts in each country shaped the divergent courses that the Cuban and Brazilian governments improvised to resolve the labor issues that arose at defense sites. Vargas refused to grant the United States the kinds of formal exemptions from Brazilian social and labor legislation that the Cuban government eventually offered, providing instead a different solution that had a similar effect. The Vargas administration's strategies for accommodating US interests by finessing the application of the law without changing the law fit seamlessly into the larger legal culture of Estado Novo Brazil. Though the War Department was never able to obtain formal exemptions from existing law, the ease with which labor rights could be imperfectly applied was in some ways more advantageous to both governments. The approach crafted in Brazil was less explicit and official than the approaches taken in Cuba—but as a result, it was also more porous, less conspicuous, and less contested. By refusing to make this aspect of his complicity with the US government visible, Vargas also inadvertently shielded the US government from the goodwill consequences of its own interventions.

While many would of course suspect machinations behind the scenes, the cooperation of US and Brazilian authorities in withholding labor rights was not transparent to all. This history reified a lesson that would arise in many different aspects of wartime cooperation again and again: not only did cooperation provide a means to intervene in a period of non-intervention, it also helped to obscure the infringements of international cooperation on national sovereignty and the consequences of those infringements in the daily lives of civilians. Though the Cuban and Brazilian histories of base labor took different paths, they ultimately arrived at the same practical outcome: popular leaders suspended certain labor provisions at the behest of US officials, and they did so in ways they hoped would shield them from popular backlash. Relying on the knowledge and savvy of local counterparts—lawyers, labor experts, and government officials—US officials were able to pursue strategies for advancing US interests that were uniquely suited to each context and therefore more likely to be successful than any rigid, one-size-fits-all solution devised in Washington. Side by side, these histories demonstrate the adaptability of US–Latin American security cooperation so essential to its success on the ground.

CHAPTER 4

Discrimination in the Canal Zone

In September 1941, a Colombian journalist reporting from Panama published an article titled "Bitter Race Rivalry in the Canal between Workers from Different Countries." The article listed the many offenses that Colombian workers who were recruited by US agencies to work on defense projects in Panama faced during the war. Underlying each of them was a system of segregation in the Canal Zone in which race was conflated with nationality and non-US citizens were placed on a separate payroll with access to separate housing, cafeterias, hospitals, and clubhouses. The gulf between the rhetoric of Pan-American fraternity and the system of segregation was vast. As the reporter put it, "We are under the tutelage of the country which is the standard-bearer of Democracy in these critical moments of the history of the world, yet, Latin American workers in the Panama Canal Zone have not any guarantees for the mere fact that they were not born with blue eyes in the land of Uncle Sam." Speculating about the costs of these conflicts for hemispheric unity, he asked, "Will this not be the antidote to what they preach all over the American Continent?"[1]

If the prevailing conflicts that arose on defense construction sites in Brazil and Cuba centered primarily on newly won labor rights, the labor conflicts that predominated in Panama revolved more fundamentally around questions of race- and nation-based discrimination. To be sure, US employers' condescending regard for local workers plagued labor relations at defense sites in Cuba, Brazil, and elsewhere in Latin America, but the practices of race- and nation-based discrimination in Panama were unique in that they were embedded in a formal system of segregation that predated the Good Neighbor policy and survived its ascent. Segregation

Cooperating with the Colossus. Rebecca Herman, Oxford University Press. © Oxford University Press 2022.
DOI: 10.1093/oso/9780197531860.003.0005

blatantly contradicted the message of Pan-American equality that the US government sought to disseminate in the region as it courted the loyalty of Latin Americans in the war effort. It harkened instead to the mode of inter-American relations that the purportedly new era was meant to replace, one heavily informed by varying notions of US superiority: Anglo over Iberian, Protestant over Catholic, white over racially "mixed."

Here, too, the conflicts that US basing precipitated became intertwined with ongoing social and political struggles otherwise largely unrelated to US power. The rise of mass politics in Latin America had prompted a reckoning with racial and ethnic hierarchy. Many countries across the region saw new articulations of nationalism that grounded national identity in particular imagined cocktails of racial mixture that made their societies unique. In countries with large Afro-descended populations, like Brazil, this meant embracing blackness (albeit in limited, conditional ways) as a component of the nation's makeup. In others, including Panama, the primary focus was on embracing a fusion of indigenous and Spanish blood.[2]

These more inclusive visions of national identity sometimes hardened the lines of exclusion as well. Nationalists in Panama celebrated a Spanish-speaking, Catholic mestizo nationalism that allowed for the inclusion of Spanish-speaking "colonial" black Panamanians while actively and forcefully rejecting black West Indians and their Panamanian-born children.[3] The US government's recruitment of workers from the British West Indies as well as from neighboring Spanish American republics for wartime defense construction in Panama drew the differences between how different people across the Americas thought about racial hierarchy in sharp relief. In the early years of the war, white and mestizo Spanish American workers did not protest the color line itself—rather, they protested their location on the wrong side of that line, resentful that US authorities placed them in a non-white category in the Good Neighbor era. Segregation was offensive to them both for what it suggested about Latin American inferiority to US Americans and for what it suggested about Latin American equivalence to black West Indians. In fact, the "bitter race rivalry" referenced in the Colombian newspaper article's title was not an allusion to the disdain of US Americans toward Colombians, but was inspired instead by a race riot that had erupted in a Canal Zone labor camp between white and mestizo Colombians and their black British Caribbean peers.

As these local battles played out, the war against fascism progressed and a global rhetorical repudiation of racism gained ever-greater moral weight. Along the way, the contours of the struggle over segregation at defense sites on the isthmus also shifted. Throughout, actors on every side of the issue—those eager to police racial hierarchy, those who sought merely to reform it, and those who fought to upend it entirely—all employed the language of the Good Neighbor policy and touted the stakes of hemispheric unity to advance their respective agendas.

THE GOOD NEIGHBOR POLICY IN GOLD AND SILVER

The scope of the United States' defense agenda on the isthmus created substantial defense construction labor needs. In addition to the 134 defense sites that it developed on Panamanian land outside of the Canal Zone, the US government also resolved to build a third, wider set of canal locks that could accommodate the passage of larger warships, as well as additional work to improve and enhance defense infrastructure within the Zone's borders. The work promised not only to create extensive employment opportunities for Panamanians; it would exhaust the available workforce within Panama and require employers to recruit workers from abroad.

Though diplomats endeavored to stay within the bounds of the new era of inter-American affairs as they negotiated their plans with the Panamanian government, the practical execution of those plans relied on a long-standing system of operations on the isthmus that had not significantly changed with the advent of the Good Neighbor policy. From its creation in the early twentieth century, Canal Zone labor policy was built on the scaffolding of intertwined racial and national hierarchies. When the canal was first built, a "gold roll" of US citizens carried out skilled work, while a "silver roll" of workers, the majority from the West Indies, undertook so-called semi-skilled and unskilled work under inferior conditions.[4] Besides determining wages and benefits, "gold" or "silver" status also determined access to housing and facilities. The gold and silver wage scales were purportedly designed to be competitive with the rates of pay available to the workers that Zone employers sought to attract: the silver pay scale was set to approximate the "local rate" for labor in the Caribbean, while the gold pay scale was meant to attract skilled workers from the United States.[5] The disparate quality of gold and silver facilities was justified along similar lines. The construction period left behind a system of segregation in the Canal Zone in which race was mapped onto nationality. With few exceptions, to be a non-US citizen was to be non-white. It was into this system that Latin American workers of all races would find themselves awkwardly slotted in wartime.

Canal Zone segregation exemplified the racist underpinnings of US policy in the region in the early twentieth century, when US officials had routinely justified interventions and occupations in Latin America with racialized convictions about Latin Americans' insufficient fitness for self-government. The Good Neighbor commitment to non-intervention was, in some sense, a repudiation of such manner of thinking. In the postwar period, a wave of decolonization across the globe would render anachronistic the idea of race as a barrier to sovereignty. To a certain extent, the Good Neighbor policy prefigured that shift, but there was one crucial difference: through the Good Neighbor policy, the United States extended fraternity and equality to Latin Americans not so much by renouncing racist ideas about fitness for self-government, but by expanding the boundaries of what constituted whiteness.[6] Wartime posters touting Pan-American unity often portrayed light-skinned "brothers in arms." To be sure, some U.S. efforts during the war specifically sought to combat German and Japanese propaganda in Latin America that criticized the United States' record on racial discrimination, for instance, by sending African American "goodwill ambassadors" to the region. But often, the media that the Coordinator's Office produced was whitewashed, appealing to a particular vision of mestizaje.[7]

Middle- and upper-class Panamanians eager to take advantage of some of the better wartime employment opportunities seized on this unspoken

Figure 4.1 Propaganda poster created by the Coordinator's Office of Inter-American Affairs, circulated in both Spanish and Portuguese, featuring a conspicuously light-skinned cast of characters. Poster reads: "The Americas United for Victory and Human Progress." US National Archives and Records Administration.

truth in making the case for Panamanians' eligibility to join the gold roll. In 1939, when the US government announced its intention to build the new canal locks, Panamanian ambassador Jorge Boyd appealed to Franklin Roosevelt on the question of US-Panamanian labor equality, with the interests of skilled Panamanians foremost in mind. As he advocated for Panamanians' right to occupy gold positions, Boyd reminded Roosevelt of the "principle of equality between Panamanians and Americans" that had become so important to relations between the two countries in recent years.[8] This was not the first time the topic had come up. When negotiating the Hull-Alfaro Treaty of 1936, the hallmark of the Good Neighbor turn in US-Panamanian relations, Panama had elicited and obtained a guarantee that Panamanian citizens would have the same opportunities of employment in the Canal Zone enjoyed by US citizens.[9]

But Roosevelt was constrained in his ability to guarantee gold roll employment for Panamanians. The US Congress exercised a greater degree of control over defense construction in Panama than it did elsewhere in Latin America because Congress was charged with the task of allocating funds to the Canal Zone (unlike ADP projects, which drew from Roosevelt's Emergency Funds). As Congress deliberated funding for the third set of canal locks, the American Federation of Labor successfully lobbied for an amendment to the bill that significantly limited employment opportunities for non-US citizens. The resulting McCarran Amendment to the third locks bill stipulated that skilled and technical positions would be reserved for US citizens.

The Panamanian government was outraged. The amendment distinctly violated the terms of the 1936 Treaty and the spirit of the Good Neighbor Policy. At the behest of the State Department, the amendment was expanded to allow Panamanians and West Indians with more than fifteen years of service to also assume skilled positions, but the number of workers from both groups was negligible compared to those who might otherwise seek gold roll opportunities. Roosevelt navigated contradictory domestic and international pressures: the bill passed with the amendment, but the amendment was suspended each year.[10] Even so, Panamanians occupied only a tiny fraction of gold positions during the war and the matter remained a point of contention throughout. To the great dismay of many, a white or mestizo Panamanian was still a silver Panamanian.

This is not to say that the battle over segregation was one waged between racist US Americans and Panamanian opponents of racism. In Panama outside of the Canal Zone, racial discrimination was also rampant, though it was maintained through different channels and informed by different prejudices. Tens of thousands of black Caribbean migrants had come to Panama to work on the canal during the early years of the Republic and the West Indian worker had become a symbol of "native" frustration with both US power and the unfulfilled promise of Panamanian modernity.[11] The economic turmoil of the 1920s and 1930s fed the articulation of an increasingly anti-black nationalism in Panama, as well as in other Spanish American republics in the circum-Caribbean with large populations of West Indians.[12] In Panama, mestizo nationalism would peak with the electoral victory of Arnulfo Arias in 1940 and his racially exclusive vision of "*panameñismo*."[13] Arias's campaign slogan, "Panama for the Panamanians," encapsulated not just the anti–US but also the anti–West Indian sentiment at the core of Panamanian nationalism at this moment.

In 1939, just as Ambassador Boyd had invoked the Good Neighbor policy to insist on more inclusive labor policies for some Panamanians, he also invoked it to insist on more exclusionary policies when it came to West Indians, whom US officials had again begun to recruit for construction work in Panama. Echoing sentiments then shared by many "Latin" Panamanians, Boyd impressed upon Roosevelt the "unlimited damages to Panama" that had resulted from past recruitment of this "undesirable race." Requesting that Zone officials hire white Spaniards instead of black Caribbeans, he explained, "Panama has been anxious to improve its race and considers this a very happy opportunity to do so." Panama would even pay the added costs of transportation from Europe on the condition that Spanish workers live in Panamanian cities instead of Canal Zone housing, "so that they would mix with our natives." From Boyd's perspective, foregoing black labor entirely would be the ultimate Good Neighbor gesture: "A better and more practical evidence of real cooperation to the welfare of our nation could not be offered by the United States."[14]

The Panamanian government further protested US labor recruitment in the West Indies on the grounds that it violated Panamanian immigration laws and, therefore, it violated Panamanian sovereignty. Panamanian immigration restrictions against non-Spanish-speaking black migrants were instituted in the mid-1920s and reached their zenith in the late 1930s.[15] The new Constitution in 1941 consecrated this trend, allowing immigration only by those "capable of contributing to the ethnic, economic and demographic improvement of the country," expressly forbidding immigration by those "of the black race whose mother tongue is not Spanish, the yellow race, and the races from India, Asia and North Africa," and stripping many Panamanian-born West Indians of their citizenship.[16]

The Panamanian migration ban specifically against non-Spanish-speaking black people encapsulates a key, if obvious, dimension of race and national identity in Panama and elsewhere in Latin America during this period: being black and being Latin American were not mutually exclusive. During this moment in which societies across the region were rethinking the relationship between race and citizenship, ethnic nationalist projects were routinely informed by an older Latin American interpretation of scientific racism that reconciled Latin American demographics with the desire to be taken seriously as a peer by other Western nations. While eugenicists in the United States and Europe gravitated toward hereditary determinist theories of race that viewed racial inferiority as immutable, many Latin American eugenicists had advanced scientific racist ideas that were less deterministic and allowed more room for environmental factors to shape populations.[17] This was a convenient interpretation for Latin American elites to embrace because it allowed for the "improvement" of national stock to take place through assimilation, public health and education initiatives, and miscegenation.[18] Black immigration was antithetical to this aspirational march toward whiteness.

When Boyd insisted on more inclusive policies for white and mixed-race Panamanians and more exclusive policies prohibiting West Indian immigration, he did so under pressure from nationalist groups in Panama identified with the Acción Comunal political party that was so instrumental in the political sea change in the country in the 1930s. The organization Afirmación Nacional called Arias's predecessor President Augusto Boyd out directly in a letter to the president that they published in a major Panamanian newspaper. In the letter, they insisted that Boyd halt US plans to recruit workers from the West Indies and demanded that, if the Panamanian population was insufficient to meet the labor requirements of defense construction, "Hispanic-American" workers who would not "denaturalize the ethnic physiognomy of our nationality" be sought instead.[19] In President Boyd's reply, also published in the papers, he expressed gratitude for "the wholehearted cooperation of patriotic organizations" such as Afirmación Nacional in this "arduous task" and reassured the organization's members that "the Panamanian people and government, always united in defense of our national interests, will see this danger which threatens our national security disappear in a definite and positive manner."[20] In other words, while the US government contemplated the stakes of their labor recruitment policy in terms of its potential impact on a wartime alliance with Panama, Panamanian leaders were forced to reckon with the domestic political implications of their acquiescence or resistance to US endeavors.

Scholars have noted that immigration restrictions during the interwar years were, for countries like Panama, a way of performing modernity to a global audience—testament to the fact that there was a superior body politic that needed protecting from undesirable elements.[21] Citizens of Panama wringing their hands over the coming deluge of black workers explicitly included concerns about Panama's global standing among their objections. Afirmación Nacional, for instance, insisted, West Indians "mixing with the daughters of this country is affecting the ethnic classification of our *pueblo*, with notable harm to our international prestige."[22]

It was in this context that racist professions to US authorities in a confraternal manner sometimes looked like a bridge across the divide of lingering US perceptions of Latin American inferiority. One West Indian Panamanian, reflecting on the years leading up to the war, reported a sense that as white and mestizo Panamanians became more racist, Canal Zone officials became more likely to "concede social equality" to them.[23] Panamanian diplomats were also attuned to the bridge of racism. In a memo back to the Panamanian Foreign Ministry after meeting with President Roosevelt, the Panamanian ambassador reported that the president had agreed that it was better if West Indian men bred (*"se enrazaran"*) with "their own women" and "not with our [Panamanian] women."[24] Assurances from canal authorities that West Indian workers would be restricted to the Canal Zone and repatriated after construction only provoked objections from Panamanian officials, who contended that Panama should reap the commercial benefits of US activities in the Zone, and if workers were confined, they would not spend money in Panama. At the suggestion that only men be brought so that they would not have children in Panama, the foreign minister argued that this would only encourage the men to have sex with and produce children with Panamanian women.[25]

In an effort to be accommodating to its wartime ally, Washington considered a number of alternative options. The cost of transporting Spanish workers and the risk of importing fascist sympathizers doomed that particular suggestion. As an alternative, the Panamanian government requested workers from elsewhere in Latin America. The Canal Zone governor rejected a proposal to find the workers in Puerto Rico, even though officials in Washington favored that plan for the extent to which it could ameliorate unemployment on the island. The governor's reservations foresaw some of the ways that Latin Americans would fit awkwardly into the prevailing system of segregation in the Zone when he remarked that Puerto Ricans "could not be treated in the same way as white employees and yet as American citizens they would doubtless resent being classed with West Indian Negroes. Puerto Ricans would accordingly have to be housed, fed and paid on a different standard from any kind of labor now existing in the Zone."[26] Ultimately, canal authorities brought around 22,000 workers to the isthmus during the war. Roughly 5,000 of them came from Jamaica, where they joined some 5,000 more workers of West Indian descent who remained in the Canal Zone from earlier periods of migration or were born there.[27] The rest of the foreign laborers were from other Latin American countries, including at least 12,773 Salvadorans, 2,248 Costa Ricans, and 2,244 Colombians.[28]

Of course, the choice between Latin American workers and black workers was a false one. Records from early recruitment efforts in Costa Rica noted that the workers being recruited there were, in fact, primarily West Indians and West Indian–descended Costa Ricans working on United Fruit plantations. Similar issues were encountered in Colombia, a nation whose racial diversity resulted not just from migrant labor but from the legacy of slavery. There, Panamanian consular officials carried explicit instructions to only stamp the passports of recruited workers who appeared white or mestizo. When the Canal Zone governor urged the Panamanian president to ease the racial restrictions on the border because it was preventing enough workers from coming through, he agreed to do so on the condition that black workers be kept inside the Canal Zone upon arrival.[29]

RACISMS COLLIDE

The arrival of tens of thousands of workers who brought with them ideas about racial hierarchy that did not suit the binary color line in the Canal Zone further strained the system.[30] Canal Zone officials relied increasingly on "foreign" versus "US" classifications to police the separation of gold and silver workers in a way that could sidestep the troublesome gap between workers' own racial identities and Canal Zone officials' perceptions of their race. Responding to an inquiry about the number of black employees in the Canal Zone, the Canal Zone governor explained that he could not supply precise numbers except to say that of the nearly 40,000 people working for the Panama Canal and Panama Railroad Company, "between 8,000 and 10,000 of these employees are indisputably white. The remainder constitute for the greater portion a mixture of races. This is the reason for our primary classification of employees on the basis of nationality rather than of race or color."[31] African Americans, who posed an obvious challenge to this classification scheme, were no longer hired beginning in 1941.[32]

Initially, the economics of wartime scarcity threatened to upend the system. Because several US government agencies present in Panama initiated construction projects simultaneously, competition between contractors for the limited labor supply led to rapid wage inflation, pushing many workers considered non-white by Canal authorities above the pay threshold that entitled them to access gold facilities. In January 1941, in order to stem wage inflation and to keep the system of formal economic segregation more in line with the racial segregation that canal authorities desired, contractors operating in Panama agreed to a policy that stabilized wages and all hiring agencies adopted the silver-gold payroll system. At the same time, the racial aspect of segregation was made more explicit than it had been before the war. The Central Labor Office began physically screening individuals to determine which facilities they would be permitted to use. A memo from February 1943 quoted an earlier published guideline that limited access of black workers to gold facilities: "When Negroes, other than silver employees of that unit, colored messengers, and colored maids, enter gold Clubhouses and Restaurants, they should be informed that gold units are for white gold employees; and they should be asked to leave in a courteous manner explaining that colored people are accommodated in the silver Clubhouses provided for them."[33]

Tensions within silver housing and facilities between Latin American and West Indian workers festered until erupting in violence. As early as the summer of 1940, police officers had to be stationed during mealtime in a silver mess hall in Gatún, where fights ensued when Panamanians demanded that they receive their meals before West Indians.[34] A memo to the chief of police on the matter noted that this case illustrated the difficulties they might anticipate "between various classes of silver labor."[35] Tensions peaked in the summer of 1941, when riots broke out at labor camps across the Canal Zone, and continued into 1942.[36] Some incidents lasted days and grew to involve as many as 3,000 workers at a time, who fought with knives, rocks, bottles, and sticks.[37] Most frequently, fights that broke out were not confined to workers originated from one particular Latin American nation, but rather, they took place between West Indian workers on the one hand and Latin Americans of varied nationalities on the other. After an incident at the Cocolí labor camp in which a friendly game of arm wrestling got out of hand and turned into a fight involving the hurling of stones, ten men were arrested who included citizens of El Salvador, Colombia, Costa Rica, Panama, and Ecuador.[38]

US employers in Central America had long used racial animosity and linguistic divisions as a labor management strategy in other settings, but Canal Zone employers during World War II were tasked with mediating such tensions to prevent them from inhibiting defense construction.[39] To prevent fights between Latin American and West Indian workers, officials began to informally segregate housing facilities and mess halls further.[40] When it came to placing Spanish-American-born "offsprings of West Indians," Canal Zone officials improvised: "they are placed where they get along best."[41] White and mestizo silver workers further policed these divides, with many reportedly referring to any mess hall attendant whose skin was "darker than brown" as "Jamaican," even if they spoke Spanish and were born in Spanish America.[42]

INVOKING THE "MORAL FORCE THAT THE AXIS LACKS"

Even as they jockeyed to rearrange the racial hierarchy of Canal Zone labor camps, workers in Panama began to use rhetoric of equality and anti-racism to protest discrimination, repurposing the language that was ubiquitous in wartime propaganda across the region. Good Neighbor messaging espoused the common heritage of "Americans" from across the region as pioneers of republicanism and therefore natural allies in the war for democracy. This language, which sought to flatten racial difference in the Americas in favor of fraternal bonds, was circulated alongside the familiar tracts of Allied leaders—the Four Freedoms, the Atlantic Charter, and the UN Declaration—that spelled out the moral imperatives of war. Some US efforts specifically sought to combat German and Japanese propaganda in Latin America that criticized the United States' record on racial discrimination in order to drive a wedge in the inter-American alliance.

Silver workers from Panama and surrounding Latin American countries routinely protested discrimination by invoking the threat it posed to hemispheric unity, just as the 1941 "Bitter Race Rivalry" newspaper article had. Seizing on the rising currency of anti-racism in the war against Nazism, they increasingly framed their case against discrimination in a more rhetorically powerful way. Rather than quibble with the particulars of the racial hierarchy in the canal, they instead began to denounce the hierarchy's existence altogether.

In September 1943, Victor Urrutia, the Panamanian president of an organization called the Society of Panamanians in the Service of the Government of the United States, authored a memo denouncing Canal Zone segregation on behalf of eighteen Panamanian labor, youth, community, and political organizations. As the title of the memo, "Inter-American Relations in the Canal Zone," suggests, the memo framed Canal Zone labor issues in foreign policy terms.[43] Over the course of seventeen pages, Urrutia employed the familiar motifs of the Good Neighbor policy in making his case against labor practices in the Canal Zone and put the integrity of the Allied cause on the line. To Roosevelt he declared, "Your Excellency will not fail to understand that the present situation is harmful to your great country's democratic prestige" and demanded that in Panama "there should be a practical application of the principles of racial equality and non-discrimination on the basis of nationality, which constitute the most noble features of democracies and which furnish them with the moral force that the Axis lacks."[44]

The memo argued that US policy in the Canal Zone should be taken as an opportunity to convince Latin Americans of the righteousness of the Allied cause, noting Latin American workers would "support the Allies with more or less fervor according to the degree to which they see clearly the difference between totalitarianism and democracy." US defense projects across the region had created contact zones in which the idea of Pan-American solidarity could thrive or perish. Underscoring the great consequences of contact on this scale, Urrutia argued, "the conditions of treatment and pay of these non-American laborers employed on defense projects outside the territory of the United States, are important from two points of view: that of the welfare of the workers, and that of continental *solidarity*, the latter a factor of the greatest importance for effective defense of our Hemisphere."[45] He asserted the same argument that Pan Am executives in Brazil had made there, that anything short of fair treatment would counteract the ongoing efforts to engineer hemispheric solidarity: "What is happening in the Canal Zone, affecting families spread all over the Continent, *nullifies completely all the efforts of the Government in Washington and of the other Governments of America for the purpose of creating a true continental solidarity*."[46]

Urrutia's evocation of the entire region of Latin America was not overblown. In fact, the cause of segregation was taken up during this period by the Confederation of Latin American Workers (CTAL), a pan-Latin-American labor federation founded by Mexican labor leader Vicente Lombardo Toledano.[47] In fact, it was Lombardo Toledano who delivered Urrutia's memo to US government officials. Lombardo's rising star among Latin American workers, combined with his pro-Soviet political stance, made the prospect that this issue might gain traction across the region more concerning for those US officials who stayed abreast of the issue. State Department officials worried that Lombardo Toledano might "attain the dominant control of labor in the Canal Zone, permitting him thereby to acquire a powerful and dangerous weapon for use not only locally but throughout the hemisphere."[48]

Anticipating the argument that labor organizing could impede the war effort and must therefore be temporarily suspended, Urrutia explained, "We would advocate that the settlement of the grievances of Latin American workers be postponed if it interfered with the defense of the Continent. Fortunately, however, *entirely the contrary is true*. The immediate improvement of working conditions of the non-American workers would result in the strengthening of the natural and artificial defenses of the Continent."

He then cautioned, "Inversely, the postponement of these improvements would weaken these same defenses to such a degree that . . . it might prove fatal."[49]

In contrast to Brazilian and Cuban workers who demanded that US employers observe local legislation, Urrutia did not question whether US law applied in the Canal Zone; instead, he pushed for its application. The memo quoted Roosevelt's own Executive Order 8802, issued in June 1941, which banned discrimination against workers in defense industries on the basis of race, creed, color, or national origin.[50] Though the failed application of Executive Order 8802 in the Canal Zone was hardly shocking given the persistence of Jim Crow in the US South, the memo proclaimed, "If subject to criticism and blame in the United States itself, the color line becomes doubly condemnable and stupid when put into practice in the name of the United States Government in the heart of Latin America."[51]

In denouncing racism in all its forms, the memo appeared to represent the plight of all non-US citizen workers in the Zone, but the fissures of domestic race and class divides were evident when the contents of the memo turned toward particular demands whose substance was geared toward the concerns of skilled middle-class workers who believed their rightful place was alongside US technicians. Urrutia was an assistant engineer hired by the US Army and trained in the United States. In this sense, he was a prototypical upper-middle-class Panamanian. According to personnel reports, his organization only accepted members who stood some chance of joining the limited number of Panamanians already on the gold roll, who tended to be "lighter-colored members of the better families in Panama."[52] No self-identified West Indian organizations were among the signatories of the memo, though several of the signatories, including Urrutia, were affiliated with the opposition political party, the Partido Liberal Renovador, that had begun to court West Indian political support. The Canal Zone governor speculated that Urrutia was motivated by such political ambitions. Whether Urrutia was a "true believer" in the principles he preached or not is difficult to discern, but what is indisputable is that he recognized the currency of an international anti-racist message during World War II and sought to use it to shape the course of US-Panamanian cooperation.

West Indian contract workers in the Zone, as subjects rather than citizens, were in quite a different position from that of their Latin American peers. The alliance between Britain and the United States was hardly vulnerable to the weight of their grievances, and British representatives in Panama were generally of little assistance in advancing West Indian interests. The British ambassador to Panama opined that Anglo-American relations "should only be put to the strain . . . for matters of higher importance" than West Indian labor objections and impressed upon a vice consul sympathetic to the silver cause that "the British West Indians here are a continual potential menace to the smoothness of our diplomatic waters, and we must do our utmost to prevent it from invading them."[53] The Jamaican government sent a labor representative to the British consulate in Panama to address the labor unrest of the early war years, but rather than advocate on behalf of workers, his mission was to ameliorate the disruption that such grievances caused. Notably, when he returned to Jamaica at the conclusion of his term, Canal Zone authorities thanked him for his service.[54]

West Indians who had been in Panama for decades by this time and their Panamanian-born children who were coming of age also seized on the rhetorical rise of anti-racism as a powerful tool and deployed it to combat both of the racial hierarchies that subjugated them: Jim Crow in the Canal Zone and mestizo nationalism in the Republic. Many from this community were active adherents to black internationalism in the first three decades of the twentieth century and had, accordingly, long been convinced that racism was a transnational phenomenon requiring a transnational solution. They had openly balked at "Latin" Panamanians' adoption of scientific racism, which denigrated mixed-race Panamanians even as they embraced it. The internationalist anti-racist sensibility on the rise during World War II appeared to create a space in which to redefine the contours of Panamanian nationalism away from the exclusionary terms of *panameñismo*. An editorial in the West Indian Panamanian newspaper the *Panama Tribune* insisted in 1944, "true Panamanianism" should be based on "the principle of a square deal for all, irrespective of race or color."[55]

George Westerman, a prominent West Indian Panamanian journalist, emerged as a leader in the effort to redefine Panamanian nationalism in more inclusive terms. Born in Colón in 1910 to West Indian parents, Westerman was of the *"criollo"* generation of Panamanian-born West Indians who grew during this time to outnumber the generation of their island-born parents. He and like-minded leaders encouraged their constituents to embrace Panamanian national identity as an effective means of improving their lot. If *panameñismo* relied on cultural arguments for exclusion, assimilation would render such arguments null.[56] This approach entailed identifying allies in the Republic and building bridges with them. Together with West Indian Panamanian lawyer Pedro Rhodes, Westerman founded the National Civic League in 1944, which mobilized West Indian Panamanians and "Latin" Panamanians together to fight discriminatory Panamanian legislation and identify and bolster supportive politicians.[57] Westerman also founded an Isthmian Negro Youth Congress (INYC), which collaborated with Panamanian labor leaders with socialist ties as well as Lombardo Toledano's CTAL to host high-profile events, including a Panamanian Independence Day event held symbolically in the Canal Zone.[58]

Westerman and his allies successfully asserted West Indian Panamanians as a visible and growing political bloc, shifting the terrain of race and politics within the Panamanian Republic. The opposition Renovador Party began to seek out West Indian support, giving interviews and taking out ads in the *Panama Tribune*.[59] In 1944, the Renovador Party's presidential candidate campaigned against anti-black legislation in Panama, forcing the ruling party to also shift toward inclusion, however begrudgingly. In December 1944, de la Guardia's administration suspended the discriminatory 1941 Constitution. The nature and source of popular pressure on the Panamanian government when it came to issues of race and citizenship shifted under the feet of the Panamanian political elite. The evolution of these local politics had implications for Panamanian dealings with the United States on the topic of labor segregation as the war wore on.

The Panamanian government endeavored to walk a fine line between harnessing worker discontent with US policies, on the one hand, and remaining a stalwart US ally, on the other. In fact, politicians discovered that the anti-racist rhetoric of wartime could prove useful to them in the same way it did to white and mestizo silver workers: it allowed them to press old grievances in newly resonant moral rhetoric. This balancing act was especially important for the administration of Ricardo de la Guardia, who was mindful of his reputation as a US lackey. For the de la Guardia government, discrimination against Panamanian workers in the Canal Zone was a productively symbolic cause. It succinctly captured a litany of broader injustices against Panama. Repudiation of Canal Zone discrimination signified a broader rejection of US condescension.

In a stark departure in tone from the Boyd administration's appeal to President Roosevelt at the outset of the war, the Panamanian government began to employ the language of anti-racist internationalism to fight continued labor discrimination against Panamanians. At the International Labor Organization (ILO) meeting in Philadelphia in 1944, the Panamanian representatives appealed to a global audience for solidarity. The government delegate presented a petition signed by 5,000 workers requesting "the immediate abolition of all labor policies inspired or enforced through racial discrimination or segregation in the Canal Zone." The petition noted that discrimination ran "in frank contradiction to the principles of fraternity and racial equality that President Roosevelt extols in the name of the Good Neighbor policy and that have been incorporated in a general sense in the Atlantic Charter and the pact of the United Nations."[60] In a speech before the ILO, the government delegate highlighted the irony that the United States would treat an important ally in this manner in a war that was largely begun by pernicious theories of racial hierarchy. "I can testify to the profound resentment, bitterness and doubt felt by every one of these men when they hear appeals to their solidarity in the fight for democracy," the delegate affirmed.[61]

West Indians in Panama were skeptical of the Panamanian government's pivot on the issue of race, even as they sought to encourage it. When the ILO speech was delivered, the suspension of the 1941 Constitution was still half a year away, and Panama's most racially explicit discrimination laws remained on the books. The ILO delegation purported to denounce racism, but a *Panama Tribune* editorial called out persisting racism against West Indians and their descendants in Panama as "the weak spot in [the ILO delegation's] otherwise impregnable armor" and condemned Panamanian officials and labor leaders as "bigots, blinded by the prejudice and narrow nationalism that have been the cause of all the distress and horror in the world today."[62] Indeed, even as de la Guardia's administration took up the mantle of anti-racism at the ILO, it constrained space for organizing against racism at home. When a group applied to the mayor of Panama City for a permit to hold a large meeting on the topic of discrimination, President de la Guardia instructed the mayor not to issue it.[63]

THE US RESPONSE

Urrutia's memo and de la Guardia's public protests gained the attention of some officials in Washington. Some within the administration seemed convinced by the messaging that workers and politicians had so skillfully cultivated. Roosevelt's assistant drafted a letter to the acting governor of the Canal Zone stating, "The Canal Zone is not merely a military installation but the chief place in Latin America where the United States as a nation resides as a friend and welcome guest among its neighbors. As such, it constitutes a continuing and dramatic demonstration of the American attitude in Latin America to the peoples of all races and nationalities in those countries." The letter concluded, "It is my desire that there be nothing in our employment or other policies in the Canal Zone which might serve as justifiable basis for any charge that the United States of America deals with its neighbors of any race or nation in anything less than the fairest and most neighborly spirit."[64]

But for such a potentially explosive foreign policy issue, the State Department was in a poor position to intervene. The Canal Zone was a

US defense site uniquely situated beyond the reach of the US diplomatic corps, falling instead under the purview of the War Department. For his part, the Canal Zone governor disavowed all allegations of discrimination based on race and nation. He made the case that, while he agreed that equal work should be compensated with equal pay, US citizens and the citizens of other nations did not conduct equal work: "The white American is almost invariably far superior in quality and quantity of productivity to the other races employed. . . . This might give the misleading appearance of racial and nationalistic discrimination."[65] On only one point did the governor admit to racial segregation, but this he justified with its acceptability in the continental United States. He admitted that the canal schools were segregated, but this, he said, aligned with "the same distinctions that are in effect in the public school systems of many parts of the United States."[66]

In conversation with Panamanian officials, the State Department lamented the War Department's failure to correct the situation despite repeated complaints.[67] Some State Department and White House officials saw the Fair Employment Practices Commission (FEPC) as one potential avenue for penetrating the conservative walls of Canal Zone governance, but others were staunchly opposed, noting that the FEPC committee functioned only through public hearings, and publicizing the very issues that most antagonized US–Latin American relations hardly seemed desirable.[68] Others worried that if EO8802 were applied in the Canal Zone, it would also have to be applied in other places where the US government was "carrying out foreign projects with mixed personnel" and they were not prepared to commit to that.[69] Finally, Roosevelt was reportedly reluctant to be vocal on the topic of discrimination in the Canal Zone during an election year.[70] Instead, a small commission was appointed to quietly investigate.[71]

Ultimately, officials in Washington balanced the critiques coming from workers against their own skepticism that the Panamanian government was sincerely moved by the issue. Though de la Guardia as a politician was less personally committed to the xenophobic nationalism of the Arias administration, his cohort of elites was comfortably supported by the racial hierarchy of Panamanian society and he was certainly no champion of West Indian rights. If the embassy's foremost goal was to maintain a positive relationship with the Panamanian government (as it had proven to be in Cuba and Brazil by the end of the war), then in some sense, the discontent of the silver workers was only as important as the Panamanian government appeared to think it was. Indeed, for most of the war, bilateral entreaties by the Panamanian government on the subject of Canal Zone labor made no mention of the broader issue of segregation except to protest Panamanian exclusion from the gold roll. When the Panamanian foreign minister did attack the premise of the entire dual payroll system in late 1944 (the same month that the 1941 Constitution was suspended), the US ambassador to Panama suspected political opportunism, just as the Canal Zone governor had suspected of Urrutia. He calculated that ruling elites simply recognized that they would have to make concessions to Panama's black population in order to stay in power.[72] One US embassy official charged, "the ruling element of Panama, a small white group, [is] hopelessly outnumbered by the negroes and mestizos" and would not wish for policies which might threaten their supremacy.[73] He thought that in fact, the elimination of the gold and silver roll distinctions would be an "unsatisfactory development" from the Panamanian government's perspective.[74]

In this context, Washington focused on instituting reforms that would alleviate the frustration of more elite Panamanians. As one official noted dismissively, "It is as these [skilled white Panamanians] become bitter and join in the chorus of protest now being sung by more or less professional agitators, who are relatively less powerful and less influential, that such a danger will become particularly acute."[75] Accordingly, the most substantive concessions met the concerns of skilled Panamanian workers.

Such policies would not only curb the concerns of the Panamanian government, they could undermine the nascent unity of silver roll workers from varying nations and skill levels. Officials framed their endeavors around the terms of the 1936 treaty between the United States and Panama that forbade discrimination against Panamanians, rather than framing it around Executive Order 8802, which forbade discrimination based on race. In other words, they partially addressed the problem of nation-based discrimination, separating it from the problem of race-based discrimination. These policies reinforced the divisions that had begun to fade by appeasing some members of the silver community while ignoring the complaints of others. Two boards were established in September 1944 in the Zone to consider and investigate claims of discrimination made by Panamanian employees who claimed to be doing identical work as US employees but receiving different wages or benefits.[76] These boards were not concerned with complaints arising from citizens of countries other than Panama. The Army issued new regulations that granted vacation to employees on an equal basis regardless of nationality—but only for those on the gold roll.[77] Silver employees did see some improvement in their circumstances as well, even if they were not top priority. Through conferences between the Panamanian foreign minister and the commanding general of the Zone, it was agreed that silver workers would receive vacation benefits after thirty days of sick leave had been accumulated and overtime pay for work in excess of eight hours rather than ten.[78]

The wartime embrace of anti-racist internationalism in the Zone did, however, set the stage for a struggle that would continue beyond the war's conclusion. It opened the doors for the first time to interracial and international cooperation in fighting Canal Zone discrimination. In 1945, silver workers organized in a single union across racial and national lines for the first time. "Latin" workers and West Indian Panamanians in the Canal Zone joined together to apply for a CIO charter, ultimately establishing Local 713 of the United Public Workers of America (UPWA).[79] The Local launched a newspaper, cleverly titled *Ac-CIÓ-n*, and announced the union's mission in the first edition in no uncertain terms: "we are united for the expressed purpose of replacing the Hitlerian condition that now exists in the Canal Zone."[80] Their mission remained productive for the Panamanian government, and the first edition of *Ac-CIÓ-n* included a letter from the president of Panama declaring his government's "decided and enthusiastic support" for the CIO's "just mission to eradicate racial discrimination, which has no possible justification in a true Democracy."[81]

The collision of the binary color line with the variety of racial logics held by workers that migrated to the Canal Zone for defense construction from elsewhere in Panama and neighboring Spanish American countries made racial discrimination a problem of inter-American politics and, by extension, a threat to hemispheric security. No matter the camaraderie touted incessantly on the international stage at Pan-American Conferences and grand proclamations of a new day in inter-American affairs, the reality of enduring segregation on the ground told a different story. All that highfalutin rhetoric, however, created new frameworks for combating old problems, and the vocabulary of war and Pan-Americanism made its way into the ongoing struggle over the relationship between race and citizenship. The United States' goodwill security imperative, it turned out, could be wielded as a rationale for enforcing racial exclusion, for rearranging its contours, or for abolishing it altogether. The productive possibility of that language resonated through the labor camps and diplomatic channels alike, as workers effectively weaponized the rhetoric of the Good Neighbor policy and the Allied cause to demand change on the ground, while Panamanian politicians did the same in dealings with Washington. As the war wore on, the politics of race on the ground and around the globe changed, and so, of course, did the interplay between the two. "Latin" workers eschewed quibbles over racial hierarchy in favor of a more resonant message of anti-racist internationalism, West Indian Panamanians asserted new political strength in the Republic, and Panamanian politicians cashed in on the rising currency of anti-racist rhetoric on the global stage.

The gold-silver system continued intact until 1955, and the motifs that Canal Zone workers and the Panamanian government began to employ during World War II continued to dominate in discussions of the matter in the 1950s, when the Cold War and the early stirrings of decolonization provided new global backdrops against which to insist that ending segregation in the Canal Zone was an urgent matter of US national security.[82] The Panamanian delegation to the ILO meeting in 1954 declared "racial discrimination continues in the Panama Canal Zone in violation of all principles of human dignity and of continental solidarity," but was careful to add, "this attitude is not in conformity with the eminently democratic spirit of our great North American neighbor, which is the keystone and the hope of free men throughout the world."[83]

CHAPTER 5

Sex, Honor, and Moral Hygiene

Rui Moreira Lima, a Brazilian fighter pilot who served in Italy in World War II, recalled many years later an illuminating moment in his family's experience of the war in the northeastern Brazilian town where he grew up. His family lived not far from the US base in São Luis, Maranhão. His father, a judge, was such an avid supporter of the Allied cause and of the US-Brazilian alliance that he had a bust of Franklin Roosevelt in the family's home. But when a young US soldier appeared on their doorstep to invite Moreira Lima's sister to a dance at the new USO club in town, his father grew so offended that he smashed the bust of Roosevelt into pieces.[1]

When US personnel fanned out across the defense sites in Latin America, nearby residents encountered US power in the intimate spaces of everyday life, beyond the labor camps and construction sites, bringing inter-American relations squarely into the realm of the interpersonal. Many Brazilians look back on the US military presence in the North and Northeast during World War II nostalgically, as part of Brazil's proud contribution to the war effort. But records from the era reveal a portrait of US-Brazilian relations consonant with what Brazilian writer Blanchard Girão described as "allies in the larger struggle, but adversaries in private battles."[2] The newcomers forged new spaces and modes of sociability—at USO clubs, hotels, movie theaters, and beaches—that upset existing practices. Their arrival also fueled the growth of local sex industries, and US officials improvised new systems for regulating prostitution. The scope of the upheaval that the US presence precipitated varied from site to site, and country to country, but across these spaces, the influx of US personnel sparked concerns among local residents about the impact that the

Cooperating with the Colossus. Rebecca Herman, Oxford University Press. © Oxford University Press 2022.
DOI: 10.1093/oso/9780197531860.003.0006

US presence would have on the social norms and moral health of their communities.[3]

The tumult that surrounded gender relations, as with labor rights and racial discrimination, was all the more significant for the extent to which it was tangled up with social, economic, and political change in this era. As in Europe and the United States, "modern women" in the 1920s and 1930s broke with tradition across Latin America and created new spaces for themselves in politics, family, the workplace, and the public eye. Where popular governments consolidated power, they often conceded to demands for female suffrage—as in Brazil in 1932, Cuba in 1933, and Panama in 1941—but these new political rights materialized alongside new gendered moral codes.[4] By the time the war began, years of economic and political turmoil had produced widespread anxieties around the loss of sexual boundaries, the transgressions of modern youth, and broader fears of societal moral degradation that US basing would only exacerbate.[5] Political projects in the 1930s staked their legitimacy, in part, on gendered prescriptions intended to instill modern society with order and ran the gamut from fascists' radical Catholic conservativism, to leftist campaigns to modernize working-class families, to populists' state-led paternalism. Prostitution featured prominently in these debates as well. As a growing cadre of public health professionals, doctors, and other "experts" jockeyed with one another to create a roadmap for national progress, how and whether to manage prostitution was a recurring question.

US diplomats monitoring local conflicts surrounding sex worried about the damage they might cause to the broader goodwill security project, and military officials at the new US bases were concerned about what harm soldiers' sexual behavior might cause to their own physical and moral health. But US efforts to control sexual relationships in the areas surrounding defense sites in order to mitigate these concerns often only created further basis for local protest. US influence, no matter how restrained in Good Neighbor rhetoric and military accords, seemed poised to intervene in broader contentious questions of sex as a matter of sovereignty and state formation.

FRATERNITY AND ANTAGONISM IN THE "TIME OF THE COCA-COLAS"

Brazilian writer Blanchard Girão titled his book about life near the US base in Fortaleza *The Invasion of the Golden-Haired Men: From the USO to Abuse in the Time of the Coca-Colas*. The invasion in his title referred to both an encroachment on Brazilian territory and a trespassing on the bodies of Brazilian women, presented at times as two equally egregious affronts to the institution of Brazilian sovereignty. "There were the Americans," he wrote, "with their khaki Army uniforms and white Navy uniforms, fighting over space and women with the natives of the land."[6] When Girão calls the era the "Time of the Coca-Colas," he refers not only to the beverage, which became a symbol of the purported Americanization of Brazil that transpired during World War II, but also the disparaging nickname, "Coca-Cola," that Brazilian men gave Brazilian women who transgressed local norms to attend dances at USO clubs, go on dates with US servicemen, and walk in one-piece bathing suits down Iracema beach, where soldiers spent much of their leisure time.[7] The term referred to the fact that women who attended USO dances were served Coca-Cola there, but it was also reproachful and dismissive, rendering the women objects of foreign male consumption, alienated from their own Brazilian-ness by virtue of their behavior. Girão asserted a commonly held view about the corrupting nature of the US military presence when he contended that the arrival of US troops ushered in a "sexual revolution" through which Brazilian women "lost their fear of sin or hell."[8]

Anxieties about the behaviors of Brazilian women during this era were not confined to the towns and cities hosting US defense sites, nor did they originate with the arrival of US troops. Female honor had been an essential component of social order in Brazil since the colonial era and remained a central pillar of social hierarchy after independence. The Penal Code of 1890, drafted at the dawn of Brazil's First Republic, had enshrined certain norms regarding comportment and respectability in law, and proclaimed the state responsible for defending honor and public morality.

By the 1920s and 1930s, the 1890 Penal Code appeared increasingly antiquated as women's presence in the public sphere expanded.[9] Particularly in the large cities of Rio, São Paulo, and Belo Horizonte, middle- and upper-class women increasingly occupied white-collar jobs and socialized in public spaces, leading lives beyond the watchful eyes of chaperones, while feminists lobbied for greater political rights. Growing numbers of jurists thought Brazil ought to modernize its gendered edicts, but worried at the same time about the demise of family values that seemed an inherent feature of modern life and a potential hindrance to the nation's progress. Getúlio Vargas found his administration tasked with renewing the state's efforts at sowing and enforcing public morality, but in a way that would project modernity on the world stage. A new penal code issued in 1940 as part of the social, political, and legal revolution that marked Vargas's consolidation of power updated criminal laws around honor and morality, and the state's role in protecting it.[10]

In the religious and conservative towns and cities of the North and Northeast, the vast changes wrought by World War II basing accelerated the social changes evident and ongoing elsewhere in the nation.[11] The US military presence incensed those who opposed these social changes and provided a foreign interloper to blame. For all the talk of "sexual revolution," local discourse also frequently depicted sexual transgression as the result of the predatory behavior of US men. For instance, a distasteful joke circulating in Belém during the war was that a virgin in Belém could be defined as "a girl under eight years old who could outrun the ADP."[12]

The portrait of competition over women portrayed in Girão's book fits within a broader context of US Americans' conspicuous consumption of wartime resources that became out of reach for local elites during the war and incited resentment. Merchants, taking advantage of their new dollar-bearing patrons, raised prices on their goods at the same time that disruptions to trans-Atlantic trade and travel from southern Brazil limited supplies. Competition was particularly acute for middle- and upper-class residents. While rice and beans, dietary staples for the working class, remained relatively plentiful throughout the war, it was high-quality meats, vegetables, and fruits that residents competed for with US personnel. While Brazilians' cars sat idle as gasoline was rationed, uniformed US soldiers and sailors continued to gallivant around town in Army vehicles. Per one report, a US private earned a higher salary than the prefect of Natal.[13] In Belém, the cost of a haircut quintupled.[14]

Feelings of displacement among the middle and upper classes were further exacerbated by the fact that US personnel occupied social spaces where well-off residents used to gather. One report on relations in Recife noted that the city's best hotel was "entirely taken over by our enlisted men daily from 4 p.m. onwards," which left "no place for Brazilians to meet their friends as had been their habit."[15] Another, from Belém, described the feeling among upper-class Brazilians as one of being "compressed."[16] Adding insult to injury, elites looked on in disgust as US men degraded these spaces and the standards they represented by flouting local customs with their informal dress and behavior, such as failing to don ties and coats when eating meals at nice restaurants.[17] The entire social hierarchy seemed under assault.

The picture in Cuba and Panama was somewhat different from what it was in Brazil. US diplomatic officials recognized that US servicemen and civilian workers were likely the first North Americans that most residents of northern and northeastern Brazil had ever met in person, and worried about the harm that soldiers and sailors might cause while essentially "playing the part of an Ambassador."[18] But if the novelty of the US soldier in Brazil seemed cause for concern, locals' familiarity with the figure of the US soldier in Cuba and Panama hardly did the United States' good-will initiative in the region any favors. Instead, when the behaviors of US servicemen provoked conflict in those countries, they summoned decades of prior insult.

In Panama, the US soldier had become, by the late 1930s, a symbol onto which nationalists like Arnulfo Arias inscribed their particular anti-imperialist brand of politics. Criticism of US soldiers often revolved around their perceived moral failings and their transgressions with women. A weekly paper put out in 1940 by Arias supporters declared, "We all know perfectly well what is the social and moral condition of the American soldier. He belongs to a legion of human beasts without . . . the most elemental morals." Demonstrating the Catholic moralism undergirding Acción Comunal's vision for the nation and attendant gender politics, the paper declared that these "alcoholized, demoralized, cocainized soldiers" did not "respect here the authority, the law, the women, the children, nor even God."[19]

As in other countries, Panamanian women had begun to occupy new spaces in public life earlier in the century, and the Panamanian state sought to modernize laws governing gender relations in limited ways.[20] A new Código Nacional in 1917 had introduced coeducation, divorce, and compulsory civil marriage. But as in Brazil and elsewhere, even the architects of these shifts observed them with caution. By the time Arias rose to power, the apparent loss of traditional values often linked to the rise of modern womanhood was caught up with other changes, like rapid urbanization and high unemployment, that fed a generalized anxiety about the nation's decline. Panamanian politicians endeavored to concede greater autonomy to women while preserving Panamanian patriarchy, and to regulate prostitution while containing its ill effects.

A broad project of moral regeneration suited the nationalist agenda of Arias's Acción Comunal, which tended to portray social ills as exogenous, heaping the blame on West Indian migrants and the US military. As a historically global crossroads, commerce, recreation, and entertainment in the major cities on the isthmus had long catered to the demands of the foreign clientele that those institutions relied upon. The periods of railroad construction, and then of French and US canal construction, had been instrumental in shaping the entertainment sector in Panama's major cities. In the 1920s and 1930s, many cantinas and brothels relied upon US sailors who took leave while passing through the canal. The Panamanian state benefited from taxes on those establishments, but as always, the economic benefit was measured against a moral cost, and the moral cost did not appear justifiable to everyone.

While a US military presence was not novel on the isthmus when World War II began, it grew by an order of magnitude during the war. The number of US military personnel stationed in the Canal Zone grew from 13,000 before the war to 67,000 at its peak.[21] The 134 defense sites outside of the Canal Zone brought men in uniform deeper into the interior of the Republic, into very different settings from the urban hubs of Panama City and Colón. The population of the isthmus expanded further with the tens of thousands of US personnel who stopped in Panama while passing through the Canal on warships, and the roughly 20,000 workers from Central America and the Caribbean who migrated to the area for work on defense construction.

The notion that US soldiers and their hosts during World War II were "allies in the larger struggle but adversaries in private battles" resonated no less in Panama than it did in Brazil. In fact, the language of battle was common in contemporary accounts of interpersonal conflicts on the isthmus. On one May afternoon in 1942, for instance, a newspaper reported on a fight that broke out in a plaza in Panama City between US soldiers and Panamanian police and bystanders, "transforming [the plaza] into a real battlefield." The fight centered on the kind of battle over patriarchal authority seen elsewhere. It began when a Panamanian police officer chided a Panamanian woman who was out drinking with a group of US soldiers for "publicly misbehaving." When he approached the group to "call [the woman] to order," a fight between the men ensued that quickly grew into a free-for-all, with the soldiers wielding their chairs as weapons and Panamanian bystanders joining the fight on behalf of the Panamanian police.[22]

In contrast to Brazil, where formal allegations of sexual assault were conspicuously absent from the archives, the archive of the Panamanian Foreign Ministry revealed three instances in which US soldiers were accused of rape during World War II.[23] Significantly, all three allegations were against black US soldiers. If the prospect of US servicemen sullying the honor of Panamanian women was intolerable, it was doubly so on occasions in which the soldier was black, given the racial politics of Panamanian nationalism at the time.[24]

Even when tensions around gender relations did not boil over, they simmered. During the war, the pages of Acción Comunal's self-titled newspaper reflected the sort of crusading patriarchal values that the party's politics espoused, articulating concerns about the threat that the US presence posed to women and families, and indirectly suggesting that de la Guardia's liberal government was not up to the task of protecting public morality. For instance, in July 1943, *Acción Comunal* exposed an apparent scandal at the Hospital San Tomás. The hospital director had been allowing dances to be held in the cafeteria, attended by US soldiers and Panamanian nursing students. The paper described the young women, dancing the foxtrot until midnight, as "providing a bit of respite to the Good Neighbor muchachos." The honor of the women's families was on the line, the article insisted, and invited readers to imagine the "displeasure of the parents and relatives who find out that their daughters are attending dances without their permission . . . inviting slander against them from all sides."[25] Like the Coca-Colas, Panamanian women who dated US soldiers acquired an identifying epithet, "Gate Girls," which was intended to evoke an image of undignified desperation: women hanging around the gates of the Canal Zone waiting for soldiers to emerge.[26]

A further source of concern about the corrupting moral influence of the US military presence related to the growth of sex commerce during the war. As the population of US servicemen in Panama grew, so too did the number of women exchanging sex for money. The bustling bars in the terminal cities and, more significant, in the towns near defense sites further from the Zone, contributed to the atmosphere of moral anxiety. While the largest and most frequented red light districts were located in Panama City and Colón, smaller red light districts cropped up in David and Chorrera. In the smaller towns and villages where US defense sites appeared, houses of prostitution were established in thatched-roof huts.[27] And in the most remote locations, women referred to as "mechanized" prostitutes took to the road and circulated among far-removed encampments.[28]

The boundaries between sex and sex commerce were not always clear. While some women worked full time in the industry and possessed formal identification cards, other women who worked primarily as washerwomen or domestic workers would sometimes supplement their income with sex work. Still others established ongoing relationships with one or a few US soldiers in a way that sustained them financially, but did not fit the picture of prostitution that fell under the state's regulatory regime.[29] As a result of these various links between sex and money, Panamanian women who pursued romantic relationships of any kind with US soldiers risked being stigmatized as sex workers.

Cuba, like Panama, had a long and tense history with US military and civilian personnel in matters of love and sex. The towns of Caimanera and Guantánamo, where US servicemen most often recreated while on leave from the Guantanamo Naval Base, had evolved economically in direct relation to US military clientele since the base was established in 1903.[30] Elsewhere in the country, between the periodic US military occupations and, more recently, the booming tourism industry, the sexual appetites of US citizens had come to shape certain aspects of the nation's urban landscapes as well. In the 1920s, Cuba became the most popular overseas destination for US travelers escaping the puritanical proscriptions of the Prohibition era, and the boom in tourism contributed to flourishing sex and gambling industries in Havana. The US military presence during World War II, while far smaller in scope and more contained than it was in Brazil or Panama, would provoke many of the same kinds of conflicts that it did elsewhere, intersecting in similar ways with gender, family, honor, and morality as contested terrain of Cuban nation-building.

With US influence only a peripheral concern, issues of gender and family had preoccupied Cuban legislators since independence, as the nation's founders sought to eradicate what they viewed as the backward traditional ways of Spanish colonialism and chart a course befitting the modern republic that revolutionaries had spent decades bringing into being. The separation of Church and State began immediately after independence, during the first US occupation, and in the years that followed, legislators endeavored to further distance Cuban civil law, still rooted in the Spanish colonial Civil Code of 1889, from the dictates of Catholic tradition—for instance, by granting married women property rights in 1917 and legalizing no-fault divorce the following year. The United States occupied an odd position in matters of legal reform. On the one hand, Cubans deeply resented the Platt Amendment, which circumscribed the Cuban government's authority to legislate in myriad ways during the first three decades of Cuban independence, and valued the extent to which laws governing matters of family and honor remained the exclusive domain of the Cuban state.[31] On the other hand, many jurists who sought to turn Cuba into a modern, secular nation looked at the United States as a worthy example when considering legislative possibilities.

In the 1920s, Cuban women became increasingly politically active and were instrumental in pushing for some of the social and legal reforms that would become the signature accomplishments of the 1933 revolution.[32] When the Constituent Assembly finally convened to draft the Constitution of 1940, they created a new section in it titled "Family and Culture," which became the latest site of debate over whether the remaking of the Cuban nation required social reform in addition to political reform.[33] As was the case everywhere else, the volatility of revolutionary change and the entry of women into politics provoked some unease even among those men who advocated for it, and across the island citizens surveyed the moral health of their communities with anxious vigilance. In this context, US defense contractors, and later soldiers, began to arrive in the name of hemisphere defense at bases in Camagüey, San Julián, La Fé, and San Antonio de los Baños, while their numbers swelled beyond previous measure in Guantánamo as well, introducing a new set of actors and factors into those communities' own reflections on these broader national debates.

If US civilian and military personnel were a familiar sight in the towns nearest the Guantanamo base in eastern Cuba, in the small town of San Antonio de los Baños, they were not. Home to only around 13,000 residents in 1940, San Antonio de los Baños was transformed by the construction of the US airbase during World War II. The most comprehensive account of the war years that I have been able to find from a contemporary observer is a university thesis written by Orestes Robledo Reyes, who was eighteen years old when Cayuga built the base. In his thesis, he described the base as "an economic blessing, but a true moral disgrace."[34] The language of "allies in the larger struggle but adversaries in private battles" so common in depictions of inter-American relations near bases in Panama and Brazil resonated with Robledo's description of the war years in San Antonio. Describing the transformation of the town, he wrote, "a population of the highest moral customs, with a grand concept of respect for others . . . a place of mild-mannered, cordial, pleasant people, saw itself suddenly invaded by military men and *forasteros* (outsiders)."[35] Describing the transformation of the city's public spaces, he lamented the "terrain lost in the battle over decency and morality."[36]

In San Antonio, the trouble began with the influx of workers for the Cayuga project—both US civilians and migrants from surrounding areas of Cuba (some portion of whom were West Indian immigrants) whose numbers overwhelmed the town's infrastructure. The town experienced a housing crisis, with landlords evicting long-standing tenants in order to rent to US workers at higher prices, while hundreds of Cuban and West Indian migrants slept on the ground in doorways, the parks, and the plazas. To feed themselves, many went from house to house begging for food.[37] Some homeowners converted their homes into boarding houses for Cayuga workers, with twenty men to a room, in what Robledo describes as "the worst conditions of moral hygiene imaginable."[38] Things only worsened when the soldiers arrived. Seemingly overnight, marijuana cigarettes became available for purchase on street corners, and gambling and alcoholism seemed endemic. Prostitution flourished in seven newly opened cabarets, three new brothels, and in the streets and parks. According to Robledo's account, "the prostitute flaunted her sins on the most central streets."[39] As he described it, one encountered "miscreants, thugs . . . pickpockets, thieves, cheats, pimps and addicts at every step." "Young women," he explained, "could not even walk on the street alone, and when they went out with a chaperone they were still exposed to the corrupting and perverse influence" of what they witnessed.[40] Townspeople worried about the long-term consequences that this wartime accommodation might have for San Antonio as "young people from the town's most respectable families mixed promiscuously" with delinquents in the street.[41]

As in Belém, US personnel in San Antonio de los Baños showed little regard for conservative social customs regarding proper attire. One US official expressed concern that he saw US civilian employees of Cayuga "running around San Antonio with no shirts or undershirts, which is distinctly against the social code of a small country town such as this."[42] US personnel did not "understand the Cuban customs and Cuban viewpoints on dating and chaperoning," the report continued, and as a result, they had "made a nuisances of themselves."[43]

Benito González, the director of San Antonio's local newspaper *La Tribuna*, denounced US personnel for similar behaviors, decrying how they "shamelessly" walked around the center of town wearing only pants, "as though they were living in the middle of the jungle, with manifest dishonor and incalculable disdain for our customs and our laws."[44] He connected the disrespectful comportment of US personnel directly to the broader history of US imperialism in Cuba. "The accelerated march of the US government, building airbases . . . under the guise of cooperation with Cuba in the battle for Democracy, has overwhelmingly destroyed the illusion that we created when we eliminated that appendix to the 1901 Constitution," González wrote, referring to the Platt Amendment. Even if Cubans had formally succeeded in abrogating the Platt Amendment in 1934, he continued, the *ariguabense* community's experience made plain that Cuba's subjugation to the United States persisted "in a tacit manner."[45]

Though González and Robledo agreed about the ultimate impact of moral degradation that resulted from the US military presence, embedded in each of their critiques were opposing viewpoints in the broader ongoing national debate about the proper strategies for and state role in ensuring the moral health of the Cuban nation. González, with echoes of those Cubans who welcomed political reform while resisting social reform, described traditional family values as "the one good thing that we inherited from the colonizing metropolis," and explained that local protests regarding US behaviors were born of the "passionate patriotic feeling nestled in the hearts of those Cubans who still love Cuba and her magnificent traditions."[46] By contrast, Robledo, who was younger and writing a few years later, reflected the views of a growing cadre of doctors, psychologists, and other "experts" who believed that modern approaches to education were required in order to create modern Cuban citizens. Robledo criticized the San Antonio government for failing to offer the town's youth a proper sexual education, which he contended was vital for "instilling sexual morality during adolescence."[47] The implication was that, in the absence of such an education, the town's defenses were down and the town's youth were poorly equipped to withstand the corrosive influence of the wartime boom and the social ills of modern life.

Both men vehemently criticized the national government and local officials for failing to protect the community from this moral decline. According to Robledo, national and municipal authorities stood by and watched the moral degeneration of the town "with arms crossed, which was just as good as cheering it on."[48] When Grau San Martín won the presidency in 1944, defeating Batista's chosen successor in part by pushing a platform of restoring decency in Cuban life and customs, he replaced chiefs of police across the country.[49] The new chief of police in San Antonio, Narciso Ravelo, worked with local community leaders on a project of moral regeneration. In a span of twenty-four hours, they shut down the cabarets, taverns, gambling dens, and brothels and began policing illegal activity in the streets, garnering widespread support from local residents. Grau's action in San Antonio aligned with other efforts his administration implemented after coming to power to maintain Cuba's alliance with the United States in the war effort while reorienting the nation's footing in that relationship in a way that displayed greater autonomy than Batista's government had by this time. In these instances, foreign and domestic policies intersected again.

INTERPERSONAL ENCOUNTERS AND
INTERNATIONAL GOODWILL

US officials were acutely concerned with the interpersonal encounters of military and civilian personnel near bases in Latin America for a number of reasons. State Department and Coordinator's Office officials worried primarily about the impact that social tensions might have on the project of Pan-American unity and goodwill in the defense effort. By November 1942, Brazilians had begun to use the term "invasion" colloquially to refer to the large numbers of US military and civilian personnel pouring into the country.[50] US ambassador Jefferson Caffery cautioned, "Unless something is done about this, trouble looms ahead."[51] US military and public health officials, meanwhile, were fixated on US personnel behavior in the areas surrounding bases, but not for the same reasons that preoccupied the State Department. They were concerned with the sexual health of US soldiers as a feature of military readiness and also with the consequences that the diminished moral health of US soldiers might have on US society when soldiers returned home after the war's conclusion.[52] These varied concerns precipitated a host of initiatives to manage US personnel's encounters with locals and to manage locals' impressions of the United States, in ways that penetrated all aspects of quotidian life.

During the war, the US government invested a great deal of resources in the public relations messaging of wartime unity across the hemisphere. Since its creation in 1940, one of the Coordinator's Office of Inter-American Affairs' (OIAA) primary tasks was to counter Axis sympathies and inspire goodwill toward the United States through the circulation of news, film, television, and radio programming in Latin America that cast a positive light on the United States and its culture. Much of the material aimed to promote the ideals of the Four Freedoms and the Atlantic Charter, often presented in ways that portrayed the American Republics as natural allies in this fight, having together formed the vanguard of representative democracy since throwing off the shackles of European imperialism. But while the government poured money into all sorts of programs intended to facilitate greater understanding between the people of the Americas, the haphazard encounters between US personnel and residents near base sites ironically seemed to leave these fellow Americans feeling less comprehensible to one another than ever before.

Some OIAA materials were designed to change public perceptions of the United States in Latin America in ways that directly countered the conclusions that many local residents in the military base borderlands were drawing from living with their wartime guests. For instance, one objective of wartime propaganda was to persuade elites in South America, where European culture and fashion had always been held in high regard, that the United States was not devoid of sophisticated culture. They also attempted to persuade Catholics that Americans in the United States were not spiritually bereft.[53]

But, while some material was meant to portray US religious integrity to a Catholic audience, other materials presented modern visions of American womanhood that, for conservative Catholics, had the opposite effect. A common trope in OIAA radio programming that targeted female audiences were tales of romantic relationships between Latin American leading ladies and handsome US soldiers, offering women in Latin America what one historian has described as "the fantasy of female autonomy," even as those storylines endeavored not to stray too far from acceptable social practices, by including guardrail characters such as a chaperoning-sister figure or the specter of a disapproving aunt.[54] The magazine *Em/En Guardia* that the Coordinator's Office circulated across the Americas often featured US women engaged in war-related activities on the cover. And Hollywood films circulated all sorts of tropes about women in the United States that appealed to some and repelled others. One conservative newspaper article in Fortaleza described such materials as conduits of "paganizing Americanism."[55]

In an effort to confront tensions on the ground at base sites, the US government put the infrastructure of the Coordinator's Office of Inter-American Affairs to use in more targeted ways near bases. Across Latin America, the Coordinator's Office created local "Coordination Committees." These were volunteer groups, usually led by US businessmen who resided abroad, but in northern and northeastern Brazil, Brazilians often ran them for lack of an expatriate community to draw from. The idea was that these committees could help to promote inter-American understanding and friendship by mobilizing their existing contacts and familiarity with the local area. By 1943 there were regional subcommittees in most of the cities with a large US troop presence in Brazil, including Belém, Fortaleza, Natal, Recife, and Salvador. They held local film screenings about US-Brazilian wartime accomplishments, including one about the airbase in Natal and another about the rubber campaign in the Amazon, in addition to hosting puppet shows, window displays, and picture boards.[56] Tailoring OIAA propaganda work to local contexts, they tried to seize the "public relations" opportunities afforded by cooperative wartime work near base sites, like a large dike that the United States and Brazil collaborated on in Belém.[57]

At the same time, the Coordination Committees also sought to combat the air of superiority with which US soldiers carried themselves by introducing servicemen to Brazilian culture and customs, supplying bases with local music and English-language literature about Brazil.[58] As one OIAA official put it, "we cannot of course hope to bring every fighting man to a high state of culture but at least we can show him the advantages that would come through proper deportment while in this country."[59] The War Department became more proactive in educating US soldiers as well, and before long, men who were going to be stationed in Brazil were cautioned in an informational booklet ahead of time, "it may be surprising . . . to discover that many Brazilians think that we in the United States are among the world's most immoral people."[60] Enlisted men just passing through Belém were similarly given instructions upon arrival that urged them to be "particularly careful of their dress and conduct" during their stay, "due to the delicate international feeling of Brazil toward the US."[61] Similar programs were suggested in Cuba, where one official advocated a series of educational talks on Cuban customs at the base in San Antonio, to teach the men "what they can and what they cannot do here." In Panama, organization commanders often lectured their men on occasions that were expected to be particularly vice-ridden, such as payday or on the eve of troops' departure.[62]

Finally, there were efforts to mitigate tensions by simply reducing the visibility of US personnel. Suggestions in this vein included simple steps like having officers wear plain clothes when working jobs off base; insisting that ADP workers (who were rumored to be particularly contemptible in their behavior) refrain from wearing their own uniforms, which might be confused for official military uniforms; and making efforts to pare back the number of US personnel in the region more broadly.[63] More creative suggestions included reducing or withholding soldiers' pay to mitigate the competition with locals that was driving up the price of scarce goods, limiting the number of servicemen who could circulate together in public spaces to groups of three or four, and setting a maximum threshold for the number of uniformed men who would be permitted to gather in any public bar or restaurant.

The most systematic measures that US officials took to mitigate the consequences of interpersonal encounters in the communities around military bases centered on the management of sex. They pursued three different, overlapping strategies. First, they tried to provide US personnel with recreation options that might divert their attention and keep them away from vice. Second, they created spaces where men could socialize with the "right" kind of women, perceived for a number of racist and classist reasons to be less likely to carry venereal disease. And finally, base officials and military police improvised systems for regulating prostitution in the red light districts near the bases in an effort to reduce contagion.

The first of these efforts formed part of a larger, global initiative to provide US servicemen with "wholesome" recreation options overseas. Here, the interests of US diplomats coincided with those of the military, since boredom and a lack of alternative options seemed responsible for the behavior that both generated ill will in local communities (the diplomats' concern) and threatened US personnel's moral and physical health (the military's concern).[64] Healthy recreation, the logic went, could go some way in keeping men away from vice-ridden activities by occupying their time and energy with other things.

Recreation opportunities available at bases in Latin America in the early years consisted mainly of athletics and movie screenings. The base in Belém had a baseball diamond and there were plans to build handball, basketball, and volleyball courts, and a variety of track and field facilities. Movies on base were popular throughout Latin America, but conditions and supplies frequently got in the way. In Belém, the ubiquity of mosquitos posed such a challenge to outdoor movie viewing that base officials attempted to improve a screened-in area made from cheesecloth.[65] A venereal disease specialist visiting Panama summed up the thinking of those who believed that wholesome recreation options would tamp down on promiscuous sexual behavior when he declared, "one has only to see the deserted cantinas and hungry prostitutes on nights when some good entertainment is offered at camp to appreciate its significance."[66]

The project of creating recreation options on base to entertain US personnel intended to reduce sexual encounters, but the architects of these programs never expected to eliminate sex entirely. The War and Navy departments officially advocated abstinence for US troops as the best means of protecting their moral and physical health, and the United States passed legislation forbidding prostitution near domestic US military bases. But prevailing assumptions regarding military masculinity led officials on the ground in Latin America to reject abstinence as a realistic goal. OIAA official Morris Berg, who toured the Latin American base sites to determine recreational needs at different posts, concluded, "we must face the facts realistically: men will indulge despite home, background, training, lectures, and educational advantages, or the extreme danger of venereal infection in the locality."[67] Sexual virility was, in Berg's view, a natural feature of a strong military, kept alive by the culture of the barracks. He observed members of the armed forces "disparaging the fighting ability of sexual abstainers" and noted that men were prone to boast about invented conquests and even feign the use of prophylaxis to "convince his pals" of his masculinity.[68] Berg expressed sympathy for troops stationed at the US base in the Galápagos Islands, where there was no nearby population and therefore, no women, and echoed a not uncommon sentiment at the time that "extreme restriction" in some instances could precipitate rape.[69] A responsible approach at military posts abroad would accept the necessity of sexual outlets, and work to make them as safe as possible. Accordingly, the second and third strategies for managing servicemen's sexual encounters were geared more toward management than suppression.

The notion that creating spaces where men could socialize with the women from elite families would provide an effective means of combating physical and moral decline was rooted in racist and classist beliefs about promiscuity and disease. Conrad Van Hyning, an official from the Community War Services, alleged after a tour of the Caribbean that a central problem he and others faced as they sought to address the threat posed by venereal disease was that promiscuous sexual behavior was not taboo in Caribbean societies among poorer women. "There is no moral pressure upon women except those of the highest social class which provides any inhibitions," he explained.[70] O. C. Wenger, a senior surgeon at the US Public Health Service charged with developing a new venereal disease control program in the Canal Zone, attributed the flourishing sex industry on the isthmus not to US servicemen, but to the black migrant workers engaged in defense construction. Wenger alleged that in truth, Canal Zone authorities were responsible for the situation they found themselves in "because they import thousands of unattached negro males from various points in the Caribbean whose sex standards are on par with those of our southern negroes." "This," he explained, "creates a demand for frequent and promiscuous sex relations which can be satisfied through no other media than commercial prostitution."[71]

Overwhelmingly racist pronouncements decrying the undesirability of non-white Latin American prostitutes were commonly deployed to illustrate the corrosive impact of alcohol consumption on US soldiers, by purportedly illustrating the extent to which alcohol clouded judgment. One official who toured Panama during the war argued that US troops, "regardless of their feelings of isolation or boredom would not, in full possession of their faculties, have anything to do with the type of women available. . . . Most of the women with whom they associate show evidence of a preponderance of Negro and some Indian blood. . . . They are unattractive by any standard."[72] Wenger asserted that, "if the 474 men who claimed they were sober when they exposed themselves to the type of women we see in Panama and Colón were really sober and in their right minds, they should be sent before a psychiatric board."[73] He similarly viewed the fact that white servicemen shared sex partners with black men working in the Canal Zone as a sign that they were not acting rationally.[74]

These assumptions about sex and venereal disease contagion in Latin America—that promiscuity and disease were endemic among the non-white poor but that upper-class (usually whiter) women were honorable and chaste—lent support to an increasingly common conventional wisdom among US officials that one avenue toward limiting the spread of venereal disease while still permitting soldiers necessary contact with women was to facilitate greater opportunities for soldiers to socialize with women from upper-class families.[75] USO and Red Cross clubs seemed to pose optimal venues for such an initiative.

The United Service Organizations (USO) was created in 1941 when the War and Navy departments and six civilian organizations—the YMCA, YWCA, the National Catholic Community Service, the Salvation Army, the

Jewish Welfare Board, and the National Travelers Aid Association—joined forces to create programming that would boost troop morale. Remarking on the poverty of off-base recreational options, the preliminary program of the USO noted, "the homesick boy is often easy prey for the vicious elements which promote questionable recreation and even vice."[76] Club services would include counsel, religious services, group activities, and social events.[77] USO clubs opened across the United States and the more densely populated defense sites in Latin America, and the organization also sent camp shows to perform at Red Cross clubs operating in other parts of the world. As civilian undertakings rather than official military facilities, USO and Red Cross clubs opened in towns adjacent to bases rather than on the bases themselves.

Some officials imagined that supervision of the socialization that occurred within the clubs, and the fact that the clubs would not serve alcohol, might put concerned parents at ease and as a result, USO clubs might not only improve the morale of US soldiers but also foster goodwill in local communities. Paul Van Orden Shaw, the manager of the USO club in Belém, contended that, by creating a new, supervised venue for social interaction with upper-class Brazilians, the club would build a bridge to local families who otherwise felt hemmed in by the military presence. The club indeed proved popular among servicemen from the time of its opening. Its facilities grew to include a snack bar, ping-pong tables, pool tables, basketball and handball courts, and a reading room. The club hosted two weekly dances, weekly basketball tournaments, and weekly concerts by local artists.[78] But a major attraction was, simply, the women. As Van Hyning put it bluntly, USO clubs were "the only place where servicemen can . . . meet girls who are not prostitutes."[79]

The soldiers enjoyed the clubs, but the clubs did little to improve local relations at locations in Brazil and in some cases exacerbated already simmering tensions. The broad objectives of improving locals' impressions of US personnel and managing US personnel's sexual behavior were meant to be complementary, but sometimes worked at cross purposes. Unsurprisingly, the idea that the chastity of women from respectable families in Brazil could provide a form of venereal disease control for the US military did not go over well with patriarchal guardians of family honor, even if it was never explicitly stated. USO clubs, rather than settle tensions, sometimes became a symbol of them.

Those US officials more familiar with local customs were unsurprised. The US consul general in Belém wrote to the State Department to express his concern about the fact that the man sent to open the club had no experience in Brazil, no familiarity with local customs, and no interest in the

Figure 5.1 Dance at a USO Club in Brazil during World War II, precise location uncertain. Photo taken by Billie Goodell. Courtesy of Fred Nicolau.

Figure 5.2 Dance at a USO Club in Brazil during World War II, precise location uncertain. Photo taken by Billie Goodell. Courtesy of Fred Nicolau.

counsel of those, like himself, who were better informed. "Social life in Brazil is conducted on an entirely different plane than in the United States," he explained. "I am concerned that the commendable initiative shown by [the USO director] may bring violent Brazilian reaction to the operation of the USO unless local social practices are more faithfully observed."[80]

The consul's statements of fear of violent reaction were not hyperbolic. Just two weeks after the club's opening in Belém, male students gathered at the doors of the USO to protest the fact that Brazilian women were permitted entry while Brazilian men were not. The club was forced to close and call the police, who resolved the disturbance.[81] As the consul general put it, "the young Brazilian boys dislike the idea of their sisters and sweethearts dancing with the American enlisted men."[82]

The central locations of USO clubs in communities adjacent to bases compounded these problems. New clubs were frequently opened in hotels and social clubs, which increased their visibility and put the conflicts that they generated on public display. As such conflicts developed, many Army and embassy officials recommended that USO locations be transferred to more peripheral locations or onto the bases themselves. Besides creating conflicts with local communities, some argued that the USO inadvertently fostered the very behaviors they sought to dissuade, speculating that the clubs acted as a "drawing card to induce [servicemen] to go to town where sooner or later they ended up in a house of prostitution."[83] Other Army officials who similarly linked USO attendance with visits to brothels requested that USO clubs start selling beer in order to reduce the need for troops to visit bars and clubs where prostitutes solicited clients. But USO directors countered that it was difficult enough to maintain order among sober servicemen at the USO and that drunkenness would only make things worse. Besides, it was already challenging to attract upper class women to club events at all and would only become more difficult if alcohol were served.[84]

After these initial disturbances, club operators made efforts to enhance relations with local men by including them in USO events. Local men were occasionally invited to play basketball and volleyball against teams of US servicemen. USO operators also appealed to local parents by hosting "open houses" to which the club invited women and their families to visit and learn about the recreation program in hopes of changing their impressions of the club.[85] Eventually, the admission of the parents and relatives of young women as chaperones at dances diminished some families' concerns, and attendance picked up.[86] And some officials in Brazil did ultimately credit the recreational clubs with reducing venereal disease among US soldiers.[87]

While many sources offer insights into US and Brazilian men's reactions to the USO, there are unfortunately far fewer that speak to Brazilian women's responses to them. The limited glimpses of women's engagement with the USO and other social opportunities that the US military presence facilitated in Brazil show women from middle- and upper-class families who broke with custom and exerted forms of autonomy not commonly accepted, at the risk of ostracism. Besides inviting them to attend the dances, the USO clubs hired local women as hostesses to staff the clubs. Brazilian women further assisted in USO activities as volunteers, serving on committees that managed food, decorations, shopping, and hostess duties. Red Cross Clubs similarly relied on female volunteers, some for tasks that took them far from home. The Belém Red Cross Club took dance parties up to the Amapá base monthly, which required flying a group of women, usually a mix of US and Brazilian volunteers, to the remote base.[88] Women also participated in maintaining victory gardens and other civil defense efforts, making claims on autonomy, public space, and full citizenship through their contributions to the war effort. By framing their actions as evidence of their devotion to the war effort, women from upper- and middle-class homes gained greater leeway in extending their lives outside of their homes than they were permitted for non-war-related causes.[89]

While high society permitted some engagement with civil defense efforts on the part of Brazilian women, they were less forgiving of transgressive social behavior. Just as US officials used the tools at their disposal to try to shape social practices, local communities did the same. Their tools, of course, were different. One of the most powerful tools that men possessed was shame. Men in Fortaleza compiled the names of "Coca-Colas" in lists that circulated throughout the community. Later in the war, they formed a Carnaval block called the "Cordão das Coca-Colas," in which men dressed in drag and wore sashes and hats that bore the names of the women they sought to disgrace as they paraded through town during annual Carnaval festivities.[90] One resident looking back recalled that men were especially keen to target the women from well-to-do families who dated US soldiers and mostly spared the lower-class women, viewing them less as deviants than as victims. According to his account, elite women who became identified as Coca-Colas were so stigmatized by the war's conclusion that they were forced to leave town to secure romantic futures for themselves elsewhere.[91]

Local officials endeavored to tamp down on impropriety through assorted "morality campaigns." Though Brazilian newspapers, under strict censorship during the war, rarely covered the misbehavior of US personnel, a brief article called "Moralizing the Cinemas" snuck past the censors to

Figure 5.3 Brazilian women participate in a Victory Garden program developed by the Comisão Brasileiro-Americana, c. 1943. US National Archives and Records Administration.

denounce an incident that took place in the Olimpia Theater in the center of Belém in April 1944. "It is getting truly scandalous what one sees in the movie theaters of Belém," the article began, "scenes of repugnant debauchery by shameless couples that shrewdly take advantage of the darkness in the room." At the center of the story were two US soldiers and two Brazilian women whom local authorities detained for what Brazilian documents called "moral offense," and the newspaper described as "libidinous acts."[92] Though the article did not call out the women by name, it noted that they were from light-skinned, well-off families and described the women as "slender and elegant, wearing light patterned dresses."[93] When the women's parents came to get them from the police station, according to the paper, the arresting officer "made [the parents] see their daughters' lack of decency, and sent them away after making severe recommendations."[94]

The USO was less problematic as an institution in Panama than it was in Brazil. While scandal and talk of moral degradation abounded in Panama, the USO was not the same symbol of these concerns that it was in Brazil.

Figure 5.4 The "Cordão das Coca-Colas" with the composer Lauro Maia in 1944. Courtesy of Miguel Ângelo de Azevedo, Arquivo Nirez, Fortaleza, Ceará, Brazil.

The robust Canal Zone infrastructure and community presence there that predated World War II meant that there was preexisting recreational activity to build on. The US residents of the Canal Zone had long enjoyed access to clubhouses, and several of the civilian agencies that partnered to form the USO already had a local presence there. Furthermore, given the peculiar nature of the Canal Zone, which was not a base itself but rather a larger territory where several bases were located, USO clubs could be opened within the Zone's borders and not smack in the middle of Panamanian towns and cities. And, because the population of US civilians was so large, the US military could rally US women to socialize with the men in a "wholesome" way, rather than rely on Panamanian women from elite families. Van Hyning hinted at the power that US officials believed the mere sight of a US woman might have on soldiers when he noted, as US officials grappled with how to slow VD contagion in Panama, that "there were many suggestions that the USO bring in a number of attractive American girls," not for sex, but rather, "just so the boys could see what they still looked like, even though they were only present as samples."[95] This kind of logic prevailed on occasion, as when a group of US women flew to a remote US base in Panama to put on a "full dress jungle fashion show" for the men stationed at a coast artillery position.[96]

Ultimately, USO clubs in Panama were more successful in fulfilling their imagined purpose as sites that promoted cultural exchange and mutual understanding. Panamanian cultural acts routinely performed at USO clubs, introducing US soldiers to local dances, costumes, and traditions, albeit in a theatrical manner. A Pan American Day celebration at the Bolivar Avenue USO Club honored the theme "Toward Hemispheric Solidarity and Good Will," and the Star-Spangled Banner played back to back with the Panamanian national anthem.[97] The Cristobal USO Club organized a "Panama Night," where over 2,000 members of the US armed forces, alongside members of the Panamanian and US communities on the isthmus, were given "the opportunity to taste and appreciate a sampling of the culture of Panama."[98] Guest lists at the most high-profile events included important Panamanian politicians, like the mayors of Panama City and Colón and, on some occasions, the President of the Republic and members of his Cabinet.[99]

Even as USO clubs in Panama served a useful purpose in promoting cultural exchange and engaging US servicemen in healthy activities, many officials soberly recognized the limitations of such facilities. As Mo Berg put it, "no matter how attractive the day-room, club or recreational facilities are made on the post, or ship, the soldier and sailor seek respite away from

Figure 5.5 Eleanor Roosevelt views the prize-winning *polleras* during a dance at the Tivoli USO Club in Ancón, Panama. US National Archives and Records Administration, FDR Presidential Library.

the usual milieu for native attractions, usually feminine."[100] On-base recreation might engage soldiers' attentions some of the time and boost morale, but it would not be enough to keep them abstinent. The USO and Red
Cross recreation options remained relatively buttoned up, and residents,
soldiers, and workers within the Canal Zone continued to flood into the
Republic to frequent the bars, cantinas, and brothels in search of alcohol,
drugs, and sex. As a result, US officials embarked upon another mission to
shape sex around the bases that would further rile local communities. That
mission was to make the sex industry safer by regulating it.

REGULATING PROSTITUTION

The question of whether and how US officials would respond to prostitution near overseas bases was not just one of moral hygiene and public
health, but also of legislative and police power. To intervene in local sex
industries, whether through policies of suppression or regulation, US
officials would have to exert extraterritorial authority over the domestic
policies of their Latin American allies at this most crucial moment in which
non-intervention in the domestic affairs of the other American Republics
was a cornerstone of US foreign policy and a central tenet of wartime Pan-
Americanism. The US military's official policy regarding prostitution in general was one of suppression. The May Act of 1941 banned prostitution
near military bases inside the United States with this objective in mind.
But since the United States did not have the authority to mandate laws
regarding sex work in foreign countries, the project of suppressing prostitution near overseas bases would have been a more complicated endeavor.
And, despite the order from Washington that officials overseas should do
as much as they could to restrict prostitution, US base commanders in
Latin America chose instead to try to regulate it.[101]

The necessity of regulating prostitution seemed straightforward enough
to US officials on the ground, as they considered prostitution a necessary
evil that could, at best, be sanitized. But the practical matter of how to
go about doing it was a bit more complicated. Brazilians, Cubans, and
Panamanians had been engaged in debates common in countries around
the world between the mid-nineteenth and the mid-twentieth centuries
over whether to regulate prostitution as a public health measure that
might protect their societies' moral and physical hygiene, or to follow the
course of other "modern" countries and abolish the practice instead. At
the time of the war, they had settled on varying answers to that question,
and the legal and political contexts in which prostitution operated differed

between countries and also within them. In Panama, prostitution was legal and regulated, though unregulated clandestine prostitution flourished and the official system of state regulation was universally criticized as ineffective. In Cuba, prostitution was very intentionally neither regulated nor criminalized, making it difficult to seek Cuban assistance in a program of regulation *or* suppression. And in Brazil, the national government was officially antiregulatory, but in practice, in cities across the nation, local police enjoyed a great deal of discretionary power to deal with the issue as a matter of public order, and forged haphazard systems for both the suppression and regulation of prostitution that were inconsistent from place to place. Notably, in none of these countries was prostitution wholly criminalized, meaning that even if military officials on the ground had been inclined to follow the War Department's official policy of suppression, any efforts to suppress an activity on foreign soil that was not prohibited by the laws of that country could have raised questions about jurisdiction and sovereignty.

Ultimately, US officials tailored improvised systems for regulating prostitution to the particularities of each setting. In Panama, where prostitution was both legal and formally regulated, if US officials tried to take regulation into their own hands, they would be assuming a responsibility that was the official purview of the Panamanian state. This proposition was potentially explosive, and loaded with historical significance, as public health had been one of the many areas of state governance over which the United States had assumed authority in Panama in the early twentieth century after the nation became independent. The Treaty of 1903 between the United States and Panama granted the chief health officer of the Canal Zone control over sanitary measures in the terminal cities of Colón and Panama City, even though those cities were located outside of the Zone, where Panamanian jurisdiction was undisputed.

US officials had periodically condemned the legality of prostitution in Panama over the years. When moral reformers pressing for abolition in the United States sought to combat the prostitution of North American women on the isthmus in the 1910s, the acting governor of the Canal Zone declared the Panamanian port cities "off limits" in order to pressure Panama economically into abolishing prostitution altogether. The uproar that this effort provoked quickly proved the attempt imprudent. Panamanians, protective of their nation's right to regulate its own social policies, resented the United States' attempt at coercion.[102] The income that sex commerce generated for the Panamanian state, and a sense that prostitution was required to keep foreigners away from honorable Panamanian women, together made abolition a losing proposition. To be sure, economic incentives to maintain the sex industry always existed in tension with concerns about the corrosive effects that prostitution and vice might have on Panamanian society. But while other countries saw abolition as a marker of modernity and moral health, Panamanian reformers, attuned to the particular problems that inevitably accompanied the nation's status as a global entrepôt, aspired instead to create a modern regulatory system that could protect the moral health of the Panamanian population. Their approach mirrored what is sometimes referred to as the "French system"—sex workers were segregated into a designated tolerance zone and underwent regular medical inspections to prevent the spread of disease.

As experts saw it, the chief obstacles to an effective, modern regulatory system in Panama were clandestine prostitution (instances in which women worked outside of red light districts and beyond the reach of official regulatory channels), as well as the corruption that allowed clandestine prostitution to thrive. The owners of bars where clandestine sex workers sought clients had an obvious stake in protecting their anonymity, as did the police officers and politicians who were bribed to look the other way. High-level politicians were reportedly in on schemes that facilitated the importation of sex workers from abroad, which some advocated as a means of meeting the demand for sex workers while preventing Panamanian women from falling into the trade.[103] Alluding to politicians' complicity in facilitating the immigration of sex workers, the Canal Zone health officer snidely remarked, "[prostitutes] seemingly get priority on planes over me."[104] The practice of regulation itself was also corrupt. In some places, women could pay for clean health certificates without undergoing examinations. A rumor circulating during the war indicated that Arnulfo Arias himself was a silent partner with the chief prostitute inspector in one such scam.[105] Other women reported having to pay $50 in order to buy their release from a quarantine hospital.[106]

The financial incentives for women who chose to exchange sex for money were significant. By one calculation, foreign women netted $500 to $1,000 per month, which they often sent back to their home countries. Panamanian sex workers did nearly as well. When a married mother of two who worked as a prostitute, earning around $300 per month, was asked why she engaged in sex work, she replied, "I am educating my children."[107] An eighteen-year-old who came from a family in which she was one of five siblings responded to the same question, "I am making more money and helping my family a great deal more than my father."[108] Sex workers themselves were among the most active in trying to mold the regulation system in ways that best protected their interests.[109]

A series of letters that Juan Perdomo, a Panamanian prostitute inspector working in Panama City during the war, wrote in protest to the president of Panama reveal that those civil servants not prone to corruption were not exactly set up for success in their role as regulators. Perdomo protested that he was deprived of an official vehicle as a result of gasoline curtailment during the war, despite what he perceived as the vital importance of his job to the war effort. He proclaimed, with a flourish, "it is up to us to defend our fatherland and democracy, for this reason, I invest all my energy, working on my feet until exhaustion overwhelms me. . . . I hunt venereal disease like you cannot imagine."[110] Without a car, he had to transport women suspected of clandestine prostitution to the police station by taxi or bus, and he had been paying their fares out of pocket. Furthermore, he complained that the mayor had recently prohibited him from removing women from cantinas for inspection, making his job impossible.[111]

US officials surveying the high prevalence of venereal disease among soldiers stationed in Panama were wholly unimpressed by the existing system of regulation. Under the prevailing system, US health officials had the authority to inspect houses of prostitution for sanitary conditions like running water, but the examination of sex workers themselves and the issuance of health certificates were the responsibility of Panamanian authorities. In the late 1930s, some US military commanders had advocated for creating Army-sanctioned brothels inside the Canal Zone so that they would have complete control over the governance of those venues and would not have to rely on cooperation or coordination with the Panamanian government, though the suggestion never went anywhere.[112] The idea of placing entire cities "off limits" to combat venereal disease also arose from time to time, but the tactic had provoked outrage during World War I and might well be seen as an especially egregious offense in the Good Neighbor era.[113]

The dismissiveness with which US officials viewed Panama's system did not help relations between the two governments, perhaps in part due to the extent to which this dismissiveness evoked decades of doubt regarding Panamanians' competence to manage all manner of governmental affairs. US officials did little to hide the fact that they looked upon Panamanian regulation with suspicion and condescension, creating tension where collaboration was desired. One episode escalated into an international incident when a US military police officer tore up several women's health certificates declaring that they were meaningless. The US ambassador issued an official apology.[114]

Army officials experimented with using Panamanian legislation on the books to try to make inroads in the fight against venereal disease by starting a campaign to hold women accountable in Panamanian courts for the crime of "venereal contagion."[115] A Panamanian law from 1930 made it a crime to knowingly infect someone with venereal disease and World War II saw a relative boom in such cases in the Panamanian city of Colón, where a number of US military personnel pressed charges against the women that they believed had infected them. Court cases listed individual US servicemen as plaintiffs in the case, but historian Jeffrey Walker has argued that the cases represented part of a concerted effort by US Army doctors to use the legislation to combat the prevalence of venereal disease in men stationed at bases near Colón. When servicemen were diagnosed, Army officials encouraged them to return to Colón to initiate proceedings against the women they had sexual encounters with most recently. This did not prove a particularly winning strategy, as the available evidence does not reveal a single case that resulted in conviction. Women who worked within the regulatory system could point to their health certificates as evidence that they could not knowingly have transmitted a venereal disease, even if medical inspections prompted by the case turned up infection, because their weekly exams by Panamanian officials had led them to believe that they were healthy. Clandestine sex workers brought to court in these cases were often pressured by the Panamanian state to register, but judges proved hesitant to convict them.[116]

In this context in which US officials lacked the authority to regulate prostitution themselves, they pursued a new solution under the banner of international cooperation. US officials designed a regulatory system that suited their objectives and then called on Panamanian authorities, as allies, to implement the aspects of the system that US officials could not legally execute themselves without violating both War Department policy and Panamanian sovereignty.

In January 1942, the Canal Zone health officer proposed the plan to President de la Guardia, who agreed in principle on the need to cooperate; but he recognized a certain imperative in avoiding the appearance that his government was relinquishing authority over domestic policy to Canal Zone officials, and he declined to formally consent to the proposed plan for some time.[117] As the Canal Zone health officer put it, "that is a political football, as you know, and they will never put themselves on paper in such a manner that the opposition can make a point of it."[118] In short, the regulation of sex work became yet another area where Panamanian leaders were hesitant to formally concede control, at least in part because of how politically damaging it could be to do so.

Ultimately, de la Guardia announced a program that simultaneously addressed US military officials' concerns about venereal health and the

Panamanian public's concerns about moral health, while foregrounding the latter in order to effectively obscure US interests in the whole affair. He agreed to cooperate with US officials' plan to combat the spread of venereal disease, which included greatly expanding treatment clinics both in the nation's largest cities and in the interior, as well as revamping Panama's approach to regulation.[119] The Panamanian government would eliminate the position of prostitute inspector and cease issuing health cards that purported to certify a clean bill of health. Instead, they would examine all sex workers and send those infected to quarantine hospitals.[120] To this end, the Panamanian government would pass legislation that the Canal Zone health officer himself had drafted. The Venereal Disease Public Health Act consecrated the new framework through which Panamanian officials would execute their responsibilities under the cooperative program.[121] US authorities had recognized that their inability to legislate in Panama was a major obstacle to their efforts to combat the spread of venereal disease there, but through this cooperative program, they did in fact find a way to craft Panamanian legislation.

President de la Guardia, however, framed the initiative to his cabinet and to the Panamanian public at large as a Panamanian "campaign of moral sanitation," described in starkly nationalist terms, in which the United States would only provide a supporting role. Announcing its "Pro-Public Morality" campaign in Panamanian newspapers, the administration listed the many ways that the government intended to counter the moral degradation that so preoccupied the Panamanian public. These included sanctioning foreigners who were caught engaging in vice, immediately deporting foreigners who violated public morality, imprisoning Panamanians guilty of the same, prosecuting clandestine sex workers, and intensifying police surveillance of clandestine prostitution. Additionally, the plan would ensure the "protection of peasant women and their families," by returning those women who had ventured to the cities during the war to engage in prostitution to their homes in the countryside with a police escort after being cured of any disease they carried.[122]

Newspapers enlisted the Panamanian public to join the campaign. Asserting that venereal disease and alcoholism "saps the vitality of present and future generations," one paper urged every citizen of Panama to consider themselves "a soldier of the army of Social Hygiene."[123] By framing US involvement as auxiliary to a nationalist public morality campaign, de la Guardia was able to put US security concerns to the service of a popular national agenda while obscuring the extent to which his administration had engaged in old patterns with the United States by permitting US interests to alter domestic policy.

At the same time that the US and Panamanian governments found ways to navigate difficult politics in pursuit of their respective interests, the growth of prostitution during the war and the advent of the new morality campaign amplified public discourse among civilians over how best to protect the moral hygiene of Panamanian communities, and prompted citizens to make new demands on the state. Some seventy residents of a neighborhood adjacent to a red light district in the western Panamanian city of David, where a US defense site was established during the war, submitted an impassioned petition to the minister of government and justice just one month after the new morality campaign was announced, requesting that the tolerance zone that they lived beside be relocated. Denouncing the "*mujeres de mala vida* and US soldiers," they insisted that their own low economic status should not condemn them and their children to bear witness daily to "the most reprehensible and intolerable immoralities" that took place in their midst. "The fact that we are poor and humble does not diminish our respectability," the petition read, "nor is it reason to treat us with scorn."[124] Similarly, the chamber of commerce of Colón petitioned the same month to move a red light district in that city, in light of the fact that over 500 "HONORABLE PERSONS" lived inside the existing tolerance zone.[125] The petitioners insisted that the problems associated with prostitution on the isthmus required not just chemical prophylaxis, but a "social moral prophylaxis."[126] Children, symbols of the nation's future, were featured prominently in such complaints. The petition noted that of the 533 honorable residents in Colón's red light district, 267 were children, "the men of tomorrow."[127]

In Brazil and Cuba, the legal landscape was quite different. Both governments were antiregulatory but in neither country was prostitution itself criminalized. This put Cuban and Brazilian national authorities in awkward positions when US officials sought formal collaboration in confronting problems related to prostitution near US defense sites in those countries. The antiregulatory positions in Brazil and Cuba dated to pivotal shifts toward republican rule near the turn of the century—the birth of the Brazilian First Republic and the advent of Cuban independence—as politicians, legislators, doctors, eugenicists, and others concerned with public health and moral hygiene grappled with how to cultivate citizens as capable participants in democratic governance. Their embrace of antiregulatory policy also reflected some concern for international posturing. Abolition was considered by many to be the stance of the more "enlightened" Western nations in the twentieth century, and Cuba and Brazil, finally free of the antiquated institutions of slavery and monarchy, both sought to claim their rightful place among peer democracies on the global stage. When military police openly flouted each country's antiregulatory position by mounting their own systems of regulation, they demonstrated little awareness of or regard for such history.

In Brazil, red light districts grew across the North and Northeast during the war; their English-language nicknames in some towns, such as "Wall Street" in Recife and "Skid Row" in Natal, reflected that their main clientele were US servicemen.[128] Top US military leaders in Brazil appealed early on in the war to Brazilian national authorities for assistance in suppressing prostitution, seeking, in particular, assistance from Vargas in convincing state authorities to cooperate with them on the matter. It was not the case that prostitution in Brazil went completely uncontrolled. Rather, while the government remained officially opposed to regulation, Brazilian jurists and public officials granted local police extensive discretionary power to police prostitution in the name of moral sanitation and urban cleanup, relying on laws against pimping and vagrancy even as prostitution itself was not prohibited.[129] The Brazilian Ministry of Health, while agreeable in principle, does not appear to have given US appeals for wartime cooperation much attention or resources.[130]

Brazilian state government officials, for their part, resisted control from Rio, preferring to manage their own local systems. As in Panama, US officials were largely dismissive of local regulatory systems, which, they contended, did not work—women failed report for mandatory medical examinations and were permitted to work even when found to be infected.[131] Belém had developed a functional regulatory system in the early 1920s along the lines of the French system.[132] But when US Navy and Army officials began regulating prostitution in Belém in the early 1940s, they did so on their own, supplanting the authority of local officials.

The nature of US-improvised regulation systems differed across Brazilian defense sites, usually including elements of the French system in addition to concerted efforts to police the movement of US servicemen and compelling them to use prophylaxis. In Belém, the geography of the tolerance zone, located on one side of the city, made entrance to the district by US servicemen easier for US military police to control. Base officials set up a prophylaxis station, or "pro station," at the entrance to the red light district. When servicemen arrived at the district, they were required to leave their base-issued leave pass at the pro station and were given a separate pass to enter the district. Upon leaving the district, servicemen would turn in the pass and retrieve their leave pass after receiving a post-exposure prophylaxis.[133] The men were encouraged to only seek paid sex from women working in the segregated area, so that their use of prophylaxis could be monitored.[134]

Figure 5.6 US Navy VP-83 crew member with Queenie, a sex worker in Belém during the war. Courtesy of Fred Nicolau.

Local medical and police authorities did not participate in this system in Belém, but at other base sites in Brazil, US military officials did forge collaborative protocols for monitoring prostitution with local help. In Natal, for instance, local doctors examined sex workers working in clubs within the red light district every two weeks. They issued the women a health card containing their photograph and stamped the card to indicate disease status on the day of each medical visit.[135] US authorities instructed servicemen to only patronize sex workers who displayed their cards. Men received medical exams upon entering and exiting the district, and the pass that each man was issued upon entering the district had to be signed and dated by the sex worker that he visited before he returned to collect his ID. If he became infected, authorities undertook a system of contact tracing whereby the women he visited and their recent customers were all examined to check for contagion.[136] This system incentivized sex workers to take precautions, as a record of clean health was good for business.[137]

In Cuba, US military authorities encountered yet another set of politically and socially laden circumstances surrounding prostitution. Cuban legislators in the early twentieth century had inherited a system of prostitution regulation from Spanish colonialism, and many associated it with the backwardness of empire, unbefitting a modern republic.[138] Linking the project of Cuban nation-building to one of moral regeneration, advocates of abolition prescribed a robust national public health system that would attend to the health and moral hygiene of the Cuban population in a more holistic manner. The Cuban state abolished the regulation of prostitution in 1913, but did not criminalize it. In this way, prostitution came to occupy an ambiguous legal state, in which it was neither illegal nor legally regulated.

As in Brazil, US military officials made efforts to partner with Cuban authorities early on in the war. During a visit to the island, Dr. Joseph Earle Moore, a US Public Health Service official, attended a luncheon with several Cuban health officials, including the Cuban minister of public health, Sergio García Marruz, a leading Cuban specialist in venereal disease, Vicente Pardo Castello, as well as the chiefs of the Cuban Army Medical Corps and Navy Medical Corps. Dr. Moore inquired whether the Cuban government could take steps to suppress the practice of prostitution in Caimanera, a town near the Guantanamo Naval Base. Dr. Pardo Castello explained that, since prostitution was not illegal, "no official measures" could be taken to close prostitution houses, but perhaps something might be done "unofficially."[139] In the end, US officials in Cuba, as in Brazil, improvised unofficial systems.

Though there is less available information on how prostitution was managed in San Antonio de los Baños, documentation on the issue in eastern Cuba, near the Guantanamo Naval Base, offers some clues about the various methods that US authorities experimented with in Cuba. During the year and a half following Moore's failed appeal for inter-governmental collaboration in controlling prostitution, US Navy officials improvised a system for regulating and monitoring prostitution in Caimanera that Conrad Van Hyning described as "the most friendly and completely-organized prostitution area I have yet seen."[140] In order to travel to Caimanera, US servicemen had to be transported from the base by boat, so the coming and going of US military personnel was easily regulated. The ship of enlisted men arrived in town just after 6 P.M. and left at 10 P.M. each night, with officers arriving at 10 P.M. and departing at midnight. Women were treated and inspected by a private Cuban doctor whom the women themselves paid, but who reported to the Navy when an infection was discovered. The pro station in town doubled as a clinic for the women. They registered in the doctor's notebook and their regular examinations were recorded there. When a woman did not report for an examination, she was reported to the police. Infected women were permitted to return to their rooms as long as they did not work until they were cured. If they did not comply, they were run out of town.[141]

Army and Navy officials also turned their ability to declare particular businesses "off limits" into a tool for regulating sex work. After inspecting a bar or restaurant where a US serviceman believed he was infected, a military official could declare the venue off limits to US personnel. Such a move could be economically devastating for the venue if the status were prolonged, so the venue owner was incentivized to do anything necessary to become "on limits" again.[142] After ensuring that any women infected with venereal disease were treated, the owner could request a reinspection. This practice put the burden of ensuring prostitutes' health on the venue owners, who revealed themselves to be yet another ally in the United States' improvised arrangements. Their interests aligned—as one official reported, "when word gets out that their girls are clean, business booms."[143]

In 1943 a committee on venereal disease created in the Community War Services office considered pursuing formal programs for cooperation in venereal disease control with Caribbean and South American countries. But their abandonment of the idea betrays the utility of the more informal approaches already established at each site. After tours of the region and assessments of the ad hoc solutions already in place, the program's officers deemed that attempting anything more than what they had cobbled together informally would create trouble.[144] "We cannot expect foreign governments to change their customs and their laws to conform to the customs and laws of the United States for the benefit of the members of our armed forces who are stationed temporarily in their countries," the report explained.[145] What US officials had been able to cobble together on the ground was good enough, and it avoided raising questions of systematic US extraterritorial authority on a larger scale.

Near US defense sites, sex became another subject of governance that drew attention to the uncomfortable relationship between national sovereignty and international cooperation. Even those in the areas surrounding base sites who were proud to embrace international cooperation in the Allied war effort sometimes resented the extent to which US power threatened to intervene in local matters concerning women. When US defense sites opened, they did so in the midst of ongoing revisions of expectations surrounding female autonomy, social etiquette, and the proper state response to prostitution. No one position on any of these matters singularly represented some unified Brazilian or Panamanian or Cuban position that US officials could either respect or violate and, in so doing, demonstrate their deference for or mockery of national sovereignty. With the advent of basing, new sets of foreign interests simply entered the fray.

Those who had a stake in such debates often did what they could with the US presence to advance their own agendas. Some women seized opportunities presented by the war effort to assert greater autonomy and break with more conservative social norms. Men defending conservative norms found, in the US presence, a new rhetorical framework with which to claim their own moral tenets as authentic and legitimate and to condemn alternatives as inherently exogenous by linking them to US soldiers. Still others found in State Department officials' belief in goodwill as a wartime imperative a language for pushing back against some of the more overwhelming features of the US military presence and seeking a kind of cultural exchange that they found to be desirable.

Just as "national" interests in these matters were not uniform, neither was there uniformity in US officials' perspectives on sex as something to be managed. While State Department officials worried about the ill will generated by US servicemen's poor behavior, US military officials were far more preoccupied with servicemen's physical and moral health, and less attuned to the outcry of those who lamented moral degradation in their communities.

The various ad hoc systems that US officials devised for regulating prostitution illustrate better than any other feature of sex management around bases the extent to which ambiguity in law and its enforcement inadvertently facilitated US extraterritorial rule. In Cuba, the official antiregulatory stance of the national government posed no discernible challenge to local regulatory schemes. In Brazil, a significant gap existed between official national policy and ground-level practice, and systems for policing prostitution varied significantly from location to location well before the US military arrived. In Panama, where the national government did endorse regulation in principle, clandestine prostitution flourished in practice, often with the buy-in of those officials responsible for regulation. In these settings, the new regulatory arrangements that

US officials mounted went remarkably uncontested, at least as far as the archives reveal.

As with the improvised solutions to the "problem" of labor law, adaptability to local circumstances was essential to these schemes' "success." Despite the official War Department policy of prostitution suppression, local base authorities found themselves able to exercise enormous discretion in addressing the problem of prostitution locally, eschewing suppression in favor of regulation. They pursued whatever system might best suit the circumstances in which they found themselves, sometimes in defiance of local law, sometimes in collaboration with local authorities. Though the counterfactual cannot be tested, it's hard to imagine that any uniform policy of prostitution regulation, issued from and sanctioned by the War Department, could have enjoyed the same degree of success in settings as diverse as the larger cities of northern Brazil and the smaller towns of rural Cuba.

CHAPTER 6
Criminal Jurisdiction

No issue proved a greater sticking point as US officials negotiated the terms of wartime basing with their allies in Latin America than the matter of criminal jurisdiction over US military personnel stationed in the region. US military leaders insisted that jurisdiction over their troops overseas was necessary to ensure discipline and order within the armed forces, but many in Latin America regarded the right to enforce national law within national borders as a defining feature of sovereignty. Manifest in this one issue were so many of the tensions between cooperation and sovereignty that overseas basing surfaced. The jurisdiction question seemed an explicit test of the United States' recent commitment to respect the territorial sovereignty of the other American Republics and of Latin American nationalists' commitment to defend that sovereignty in the face of US power. Those who opposed extraterritorial authority viewed the US government's desire for it as evidence of continued condescension in US policy toward the region; if all Americans were equally fit to govern, then Latin American laws, courts, judges, and police officers should be trusted to do the job. Moreover, it was not just a matter of international law or politics; like so many of the governance issues that arose on the ground, it was socially significant. To community leaders lamenting the descent of their cities and villages into moral disrepair, the right to police the behavior of US troops in their midst and to enforce not just the laws, but the social norms encapsulated in the law's prohibitions, all seemed a moral imperative to which they, as allies, were entitled.

After World War II, Status of Forces Agreements (SOFAs) dictating the terms of governance over criminal actions by US troops would become a

Cooperating with the Colossus. Rebecca Herman, Oxford University Press. © Oxford University Press 2022.
DOI: 10.1093/oso/9780197531860.003.0007

standard feature of US basing overseas.[1] But during World War II, no such template yet existed. US officials managed to successfully negotiate jurisdiction over US troops in many parts of the world during World War II, including in "peer" nations of Western Europe, but in Latin America, with the specter of past politics and the fervor of nationalism hovering over the wartime alliance, foreign ministers across the region consistently declined to formally surrender jurisdiction over US servicemen as a matter of principle. Even if they had been able to manage it, the arrival of US soldiers at the new defense sites predated the conclusion of the military agreements that sanctioned their stay. In places where precedent offered loose guidelines for managing jurisdiction, as was the case in Panama, the protocol for implementing agreed-upon principles proved a source of great conflict as well. Where diplomats could not reach an agreement at all, US officials simply moved forward without one, content to rely on claims that their right to jurisdiction was vested in "accepted principles of international law," while sparing their Latin American allies the political costs of conceding the point. In this context, protocol for managing criminal actions by US personnel in Latin America, like the diverse systems for regulating prostitution or managing the demands of labor legislation, were simply forged on the ground, improvised according to the circumstances encountered at each site. While Latin American authorities typically defended their right to exercise jurisdiction in principle, they often surrendered it in practice. And in the confusion between principle and practice, a host of revealing conflicts ensued.

FRIENDLY FORCES, INTERNATIONAL LAW, AND "CIVILIZED" NATIONS

In May 1944, US Navy Lieutenant Charles McBratnie hit and killed a child in a car accident near the US base in Natal. Brazilian police arrested McBratnie and ordered that he be placed at the disposition of Brazilian courts to be tried for first-degree manslaughter. US Vice Consul Harold Sims attempted to intervene on McBratnie's behalf. In a letter to the chief of the state police, Sims set forth the position that the US government had maintained throughout the war when matters of criminal jurisdiction over US troops arose. According to international law, he explained, a member of the US armed forces stationed in a friendly country was not subject to local jurisdiction, but rather to that of the higher authorities of his own command. Perhaps anticipating the likely objections to this assertion, which US officials had by this time fielded across the region, Sims continued, "It is my understanding that this exemption from local jurisdiction is recognized by all civilized nations; and is not considered a diminution of their sovereignty or independence."[2]

The statement was loaded, whether Sims meant it to be or not. Though he perhaps only intended to reassure Brazilian officials that this principle of extraterritorial authority applied equally to all peer nations and was therefore in line with the principle of sovereign equality so important to inter-American relations in the Good Neighbor era, the insinuation that Brazil, by refusing to surrender jurisdiction in the case, was not behaving as a civilized nation struck a chord. A Brazilian officer responding to Sims's letter retorted, "I believe that he is mistaken when he affirms that this is in accordance with international law and adopted by civilized nations, along with which, I have not the slightest doubt in affirming, Brazil has always been included, and that without asking favors of anyone."[3]

When US authorities couched their right to extraterritorial authority over US personnel overseas in "accepted principles of international law," the proposition was far from neutral. To be sure, international law had evolved, in part, to manage relations between territorially exclusive sovereign nations and would seem, therefore, a proper mechanism for resolving some of the inherent contradictions between overseas basing and territorial sovereignty that so plagued defense sites across the Americas during World War II. But international law had also come to serve another purpose: it not only structured the relationships between the powerful nations of the North Atlantic, it was also a tool for legitimizing those nations' violation of the sovereignty of states that they perceived as inferior.[4]

Since the mid-nineteenth century, the US government, like European powers, had asserted extraterritorial authority over its citizens in those countries it regarded as "uncivilized" or "semi-civilized" across the Asia-Pacific, including in China, Borneo, Siam, Japan, Korea, and Tonga.[5] To dispel the perception that the United States' request for extraterritorial authority over US personnel in Latin America during World War II was rooted in similar logic, US officials emphasized that the principle of extraterritoriality, as it pertained to friendly forces stationed in other countries, applied equally to peer, "civilized" nations. But there was really only one example that US officials could point to as precedent for this practice in peer nations when the war began: the successful assertion of jurisdiction over US soldiers in France during World War I.[6]

As Christian countries born of European settler colonialism, Latin American republics were generally recognized as civilized nations in the realm of international law. But foreigners' nineteenth-century assertions of extraterritoriality in Latin America, and the perpetual violation of the territorial sovereignty of Latin American countries in a variety of other ways into the twentieth century, placed those nations in yet another category that, if rhetorically different from the "barbarous" countries where Europeans and North Americans asserted extraterritoriality on the basis of civilization, was otherwise functionally quite similar. When foreign countries asserted authority over their citizens in nineteenth-century Latin America, they justified that authority with the same rationale that they used in China and the Ottoman Empire at the same time, highlighting purported deficiencies of local law and legal institutions.[7]

Practices of extraterritorial authority and intervention in Latin America had fit naturally within the broader landscape of US foreign policymaking toward the region in the late nineteenth and early twentieth centuries when US officials made little effort to conceal their sense of superiority over their neighbors. Rather than invoke barbarism to justify US infringements on sovereignty in Latin America, however, officials more often cited the similarly racialized attribute of incompetence. Theodore Roosevelt's 1904 pronouncement that "chronic wrongdoing" in Latin America might "require intervention by some civilized nation," for instance, illustrated the point. Under the terms of the Roosevelt Corollary, Latin American republics would not enjoy the full privileges of territorial sovereignty accorded to civilized nations in instances in which Roosevelt's government deemed US tutelage necessary.[8] As Europeans during the same period cast colonialism in Asia and Africa as a civilizing mission, Theodore Roosevelt's paternalism toward Latin America assumed a similar tone.

To be sure, assessments of civilization and competence across and within Latin America were not uniform. In the late nineteenth and early twentieth centuries, Washington regarded the larger nations of South America as a class apart from the smaller republics of the circum-Caribbean. And, for that matter, plenty of jurists and statesmen from the region held their own thoroughly racialized beliefs about race and incompetence that were quite similar to those of their counterparts in the United States. These beliefs inspired all manner of domestic policies designed to "improve" national demographics in Latin American countries as a matter of nation-building. But even those in the region who subscribed to scientific racist beliefs defensively guarded Latin American nations' position as civilized nations on the global stage. Latin American lawyers asserted their own conceptions of international law that would defend territorial sovereignty in Latin America from the encroachments of US and European overreach.[9] In that broader mission, the integrity of local courts had featured prominently at least as far back as Carlos Calvo's assertion in the 1860s that domestic courts should resolve the disputes of foreigners.[10]

US efforts during World War II to formally establish US extraterritorial authority over US military personnel in Latin America dredged up this deeper history. The imperial underpinnings of extraterritorial authority simply did not accord with the spirit and rhetoric of the Good Neighbor era. Though the proposal for jurisdiction over US military personnel was far narrower than the extraterritorial authority that the US government exercised across Asia, nationalists in Latin America connected the two. A Brazilian military commander in Belém, protesting the presumption of US jurisdiction over servicemen in Brazil, asserted how detrimental it would be to US-Brazilian relations "if Americans had special privileges here like those they've had in China."[11]

When US military personnel fanned out far beyond the Americas during World War II, the United States did successfully assert jurisdiction over US troops in Europe, albeit through hotly contested, drawn-out negotiations, as well as in Australia, New Zealand, and Canada.[12] Such agreements added to the pile of evidence that US diplomats presented in support of their assertions regarding their right to jurisdiction over US troops in Latin America. But the contexts did not prove comparable in the eyes of Latin American leaders and, perhaps surprisingly, the United States was able to obtain concessions from more powerful allies elsewhere that its comparably weaker allies in Latin America refused to yield. Leaders wary of backsliding in inter-American affairs, and of the nationalist backlash that might accompany concessions regarding jurisdiction, resisted US calls for formal agreement on the matter. Like so many other features of governance in the areas surrounding bases, the matter of jurisdiction was sorted out on the ground along the way.

PANAMA

As one of the few sovereign nations that hosted large numbers of US military personnel over a prolonged period before World War II outside the context of an occupation, Panama had experience with disputes over criminal jurisdiction. There, the United States had long asserted its right under international law to exert extraterritorial authority over US military personnel, and the Panamanian Supreme Court had proven sympathetic to that interpretation. In 1925, after a dispute between US and Panamanian authorities regarding who held jurisdiction over a case in which a US soldier hit and killed a Panamanian civilian while driving an ambulance, the case rose to the Supreme Court, which ultimately determined that Panama did not have jurisdiction over the case.[13] The crime had occurred outside of the

Canal Zone, on soil under Panamanian jurisdiction, but because the soldier in question was acting in an official capacity when the incident occurred, the court ruled that he was subject to the authority of his own command rather than the Panamanian justice system. The general understanding of jurisdiction that was applied in this case would more or less hold for the duration of the war, when the US military presence grew: crimes committed on base or on duty fell to US authorities to adjudicate, while crimes occurring off base and off duty were the purview of the Panamanian justice system.

Despite this precedent, the issue was politically delicate. When the United States began soliciting defense sites beyond the borders of the Canal Zone, the commanding general of the Canal Zone suggested that Washington try to simply extend the Zone's justice system into the new territories so that cases involving US military personnel that arose at the new defense sites would be decided in Canal Zone military courts, while any case involving civilians would go to the civil courts in the Zone.[14] But the sea change in Panamanian politics and the Good Neighbor recalibration in US-Panamanian relations in the 1930s made that proposal a nonstarter. Consistently, from the nationalist administration of Arnulfo Arias into the more US-friendly administration of Ricardo de la Guardia, the Panamanian government maintained an explicit desire to avoid the creation of "little Canal Zones" throughout the country.[15] The question of jurisdiction over the new spaces and the people who would be stationed at them seemed one of the clearest indicators of how different these new sites really were from the 553 square mile territory that the nation had already relinquished to US control.

When US personnel began arriving at the new sites in Panama in March 1941, no agreement on the matter had yet been reached. It would be two more years before the Panamanian National Assembly would approve of a formal lease agreement, and the agreement itself only specified the terms of US jurisdiction within the leased sites, not over US personnel when venturing beyond them. In the meantime, local officials hashed out a protocol for managing criminal actions by US servicemen as necessary, through conflict after conflict.

A pivotal episode in the process of determining proper protocol was what officials came to refer to as the "Breeden Case." On the night of February 3, 1942, a US private, referred to in records only by the last name Breeden, went drinking at a cantina in the small village of Paso Blanco near the US encampment where he was stationed. Later that night, he walked around the village with two other soldiers, harassing some of the women who lived there. One woman reported that he tried to force her into a bedroom, but

Figure 6.1 The members of the Castillo family, who escaped with their lives when a US private set fire to their home, are photographed in the space where their home used to stand. Courtesy of the Archivo del Ministerio de Relaciones Exteriores de Panamá.

her grandson intervened on her behalf.[16] The man then appeared at another house, inquiring where he might find a prostitute.[17] Lingering, unwelcome, Breeden became fixated on a woman named Leonidas Castillo who was there visiting her neighbor. Uncomfortable, Castillo left her neighbor's home and sought refuge in her grandfather's house nearby. Breeden followed her. Shortly after entering her grandfather's home, Castillo heard the strike of a match. That sound was the soldier setting the straw house on fire, and flames soon engulfed the thatched roof.[18]

Inside the house, five adults and twelve children asleep in their beds awoke to Castillo's screams. They all managed to escape the house safely before it burned to the ground, leaving behind only a pile of ash, three twisted iron bed frames, and fragments of dishes.[19] As they tried to make sense of what they were witnessing, Leonidas's uncle spotted Breeden attempting to set fire to a separate structure that housed their kitchen. He chased the man and knocked him to the ground.[20] Paso Blanco had no local police force to call on, so the family waved down a passing US Army vehicle, which carried them all to the nearby base.[21] The officer in charge at the base took Breeden into custody, told the family that the US government would pay for the damages, and provided them with two US Army tents to use as temporary shelter.[22]

The incident might have ended there. Base officials did not alert the US embassy in Panama City. Although the criminal act was committed by a

Figure 6.2 The tent that the US Army provided to the Castillo family for temporary housing stands among the burnt remains of their belongings. Courtesy of the Archivo del Ministerio de Relaciones Exteriores de Panamá.

US soldier off base and off duty and therefore would typically fall under the jurisdiction of Panamanian authorities, the Army did not contact the Panamanian police or government. But three days after the incident, Leonidas Castillo's uncle, Eric Gilkes, traveled twenty-five miles to a police station in Panama City. After describing the incident in a statement, he requested that the authorities undertake an investigation.[23] Gilkes's journey to Panama City set off a chain of events that turned this local conflict into an international one: the district attorney who received his complaint alerted the attorney general, who in turn contacted the minister of justice and government, who related the incident to the minister of foreign relations, who then protested to the US ambassador.

Luis Carrasco, the district attorney who reported on the case, described reports from local residents of a broader landscape of abuse and moral degradation in Paso Blanco that the US military presence had precipitated. The village was reportedly besieged by problems with drunken servicemen from the neighboring encampment who "tormented" the community. Entrepreneurial locals had opened several cantinas after the arrival of the US troops, but there was no stable police force in the village to monitor the actions of drunken soldiers. Fatefully, there was no local fire station to respond to arson. Carrasco couched his observations in patriotic terms, noting that the base must remain, "for continental solidarity," but he also observed the contradiction between the US alliance with Panama, on the one hand, and the disorder that the US military presence had brought to this village, on the other. He warned that if this was happening in Paso Blanco, it was likely happening elsewhere in the country. His own unsolicited suggestion was that the two countries should forge a mixed police force of Panamanian police and US military police that could, together, preserve order.[24]

Foreign Minister Octavio Fábrega contacted the US embassy and formally requested that Private Breeden be turned over to Panamanian custody so that he could be tried for his crimes in Panamanian courts.[25] In making his request, he underscored, as the district attorney had, the damage that incidents like the Breeden Case could cause to the project of Pan-American unity, noting that the Panamanian public had learned of this case with "great indignation." He stressed how difficult it was to explain "deeds of this nature" by a member of the US Army, when he had been allowed onto to Panamanian territory "in a generous act of solidarity with a friendly and Allied nation." In closing, Fábrega cautioned that if abuses by US servicemen did not stop, the Panamanian government would be forced take "drastic measures."[26]

Fábrega's letter, three months after the fire occurred, appeared to have been the first that the US embassy had heard of the affair.[27] Just as protocol between the US and Panamanian governments was lacking, protocol for communication between US military and diplomatic officials in Panama was also deficient. By the time the Panamanian Ministry of Foreign Relations formally requested that Breeden be turned over to Panamanian authorities, the US armed forces had already administered their own justice. Breeden had been court-martialed, found guilty of arson, dishonorably discharged from the military, and sentenced to twenty years in prison, later reduced to five.[28] At the time of Fábrega's request, Breeden was imprisoned in a guardhouse in the Canal Zone, awaiting transfer to the United States to serve out his prison term at Fort Leavenworth. The Foreign Ministry's request that Breeden be turned over to Panamanian authorities was denied.

Anticipating objections from Panamanian authorities, US Major General William Shedd explained that, since an arson charge in Panama would ordinarily result in a sentence of three to six years, he thought that the five-year sentence awarded by the court-martial should prove satisfactory to the Panamanian courts. He noted that the policy of the War Department was to bring offenders to trial as quickly as possible so that, if they were found not guilty, they could be made available for service again as soon as possible. By the time that the Panamanian government requested that the military authorities turn Breeden over for trial, the court-martial proceedings against Breeden had concluded.[29]

Fábrega was outraged. He viewed this episode as a "violation of Panama's territorial jurisdiction by US military authorities," and believed his perspective was supported both by international law and by precedent.[30] He did not find Shedd's suggestion that the five-year sentence should be satisfactory since it was comparable to what the Panamanian justice system might have ordered the least bit compelling, since it was not the job of the US Army to interpret Panamanian law.[31]

Conflict over the Breeden Case precipitated discussions about protocol. If the principles upon which jurisdiction rested in different kinds of cases were more or less agreed upon, what procedures could be put in place to ensure that those principles would be upheld in practice? Canal Zone authorities established a new regulation that any case involving certain major violations—including murder, rape, manslaughter and arson—while off duty outside of the Canal Zone would not be brought to trial until it was determined, in writing, whether the Panamanian government wished that the soldier be turned over for trial in Panamanian courts.[32] The Panamanian government was satisfied with this policy and, without pursuing further right to try Private Breeden, declared the incident over.[33]

However, with subsequent incidents, new questions over protocol arose. Most common was conflict over who could determine whether a soldier accused of a crime was on or off duty when the crime occurred. This detail was significant because it determined which country should exercise jurisdiction. Fábrega conceded that a detained soldier's superiors would be in the best position to determine whether the offense was committed while on duty or off duty, but he maintained that the Panamanian government could not, "without renouncing essential attributes of Panamanian sovereignty," concede that the military's determination would be taken as definitive.[34] US Army officials countered that, while they accepted Panamanian authorities' right to investigate whether the offense occurred on or off duty, the right to officially determine that fact rested with the US armed forces.

This was not a trivial issue, because the claim that a soldier was in fact on duty when an incident occurred became a common and effective means by which US authorities retained jurisdiction in instances where they were likely not entitled to it. For example, in one episode, a US soldier named Martin Olson stationed at Rio Hato got behind the wheel of a car after drinking five rum and Cokes and caused an accident that resulted in the death of a five-year-old boy and left two women in critical condition. He was released on bail and, once he took refuge on the base at Rio Hato, his superiors refused to turn him back over to Panamanian authorities, insisting that he had been on an official mission when the accident occurred.[35] In defiance of US claims, Fábrega circulated instructions to all judges, district attorneys, and other concerned parties in Panama decreeing that, though the opinion of an offender's superiors as to whether the offender was acting within the purview of his duties was valuable, it should not be considered definitive, and the functionary should conduct his own investigation to arrive at his own conclusion.[36]

Panamanian officials tried to hold the upper hand where they could, leaving US officials frustrated with the system at times. Traffic accidents proved to be a particularly common category of incident in which US officials found themselves articulating their own protests over Panama's procedures.[37] Panamanian police were often the first on the scene at a traffic accident and in those instances would sometimes take US soldiers into custody while conducting their own investigation about whether the soldier was on or off duty. Panamanian authorities were often reluctant to relinquish authority quickly when they had a soldier in custody, given the challenges in getting him back if and when they wanted to. This meant that they frequently detained men longer than necessary even when the facts indicated that the offense fell outside of their jurisdiction.[38] Panamanian judges also angered US officials by fining the detained men. Canal authorities argued that fines should be levied against the US government and that the men were being taken advantage of.[39]

Police, judges, and prosecutors were not the only actors who engaged in battles over criminal jurisdiction. A diverse cross-section of Panamanian civilians, like Erik Gilkes, also participated. Though often ineffective, their efforts demonstrate that residents on the isthmus, especially women, appeared to view criminal justice as a potential tool for pushing back against the impunity of US personnel. On one occasion, a Colombian sex worker named Flor Maria Jaramillo pressed charges against a US seaman who pushed her in a cantina, causing her to hit her head and suffer a cranial fracture that left her incapacitated for months. The soldier was arrested but released on bail. A judge sentenced him to eight months of jail time, but when he was ordered to report to begin his sentence, US authorities conveyed that he had been transferred elsewhere and was no longer on the isthmus.[40] A similar outcome occurred in a case in which Beatriz Castillo, a woman who ran a clandestine brothel, pressed charges against four US servicemen for breaking and entering. In this case, the defendants attempted to turn the proceedings around on the plaintiff by accusing Castillo of the crime of "venereal contagion" for allegedly having given them gonorrhea.[41] Some time into the proceedings against the men, the case came to a standstill when the men failed to appear, and US authorities confirmed that they had been transferred and were no longer in Panama. The court continued the proceedings with the men in absentia.[42]

Records of failed efforts by Panamanian officials to exert authority over US personnel who were black demonstrate that Panamanian racial anxieties compounded perceptions that Panamanian communities were threatened by the military presence. On one occasion, the mayor of Bejuco appealed to the governor of his province for advice after two black soldiers allegedly attempted to rape a woman at gunpoint, as well as a pair of sisters—fifteen and twelve years old—on their way home from school. "These black American soldiers constitute a threat to our community but are protected by the cloak of the US military and the extraterritoriality that it enjoys," the letter read. "What can be done about these soldiers that treat us like a conquered country? They do whatever they want—they are an Army at war, and don't want to pay any mind to the civil authorities of our country."[43] On another occasion, the foreign minister wrote to the US ambassador about a "soldier of color" from the US Army who had committed the most "reprehensible bestiality" in assaulting and attempting to rape a Panamanian woman in the small village of Pueblo Chiquito, in the province of Veraguas. "This action has caused intense disgust . . . among the hamlet's residents and my government cannot be made an accomplice to such acts."[44]

Of course, US officials' own racial anxieties about the residents of the towns where bases were built shaped the extent to which they were willing to submit US personnel to local systems of justice. Historian Steven High has shown a revealing pattern at US bases on British colonies. While US servicemen were regularly tried in local courts in Newfoundland, where the majority of the civilian population was white, "virtually no" US troops were tried before local courts in any of the predominantly black British Caribbean territories, likely due to the racial makeup of prospective juries, even though the same agreements regarding shared jurisdiction applied to the US military presence across these spaces.[45]

CUBA

In Cuba, the issue of jurisdiction over US troops in the 1940s was also heavily burdened by the past. The treaty that created the Guantanamo Naval Base in 1903 contained what had come to be viewed as an irreconcilable contradiction: it both preserved Cuban sovereignty over the territory

that the US military occupied, and it granted the United States full jurisdiction over the same space.[46] The fiction of "sovereignty without jurisdiction" was, by the time of the war, an embarrassment not to be repeated.
There was also precedent for general agreement regarding the US interpretation of international law as it pertained to extraterritorial authority over
military personnel. During World War I, the Cuban Supreme Court had
recognized the principle that territorial sovereignty was subject to exception, and one such exception was jurisdiction over friendly forces in a time
of war. But the 1910s were hardly a period that Cubans in the 1940s were
eager to recreate, particularly as it related to US power.[47] As with other
features of wartime basing, precedent was more of a liability than an asset.

When US and Cuban officials negotiated the proposed expansion of the
Guantanamo Naval Base in the early 1940s, arguments over jurisdiction
in the expanded territory stalled the initiative until fed-up US officials
abandoned the project and instead turned their sights to a new base in
nearby Jamaica, where rights to jurisdiction were more easily secured.[48]
A murder case in Guantánamo in 1940 thrust the issue into the public
eye. In December of that year, a twenty-seven-year-old Cuban named Lino
Rodríguez was killed while trying to board a US Navy ship.[49] The ship had
docked in the town of Guantánamo to recruit workers for construction on
the base, and when Rodríguez was not selected among the recruits, he leapt
aboard the ship anyway in a desperate attempt to secure a day's work. On
the ship, US Lieutenant Kenneth M. West struck Rodríguez, sending him
overboard, and Rodríguez died.

As protests erupted in the days and weeks following the incident,
Cubans demanded that the US marine responsible be tried in Cuban
courts. Whether West would face Cuban courts or a US court-martial
hinged on a question of territory: was Rodríguez killed by the trauma
suffered when he was hit on board the ship under US jurisdiction? Or, did
he drown after being knocked overboard, in which case he was in water
under Cuban jurisdiction? Investigations ensued to determine the precise
location of the man's death. Was there water in his lungs to indicate that
he was still breathing when he landed in the sea? Cuban authorities ultimately conceded that the jurisdiction of the foreign-owned ship prevailed,
and Lieutenant West and two accomplices were tried by US courts-martial
and found not guilty.[50] The process of determining jurisdiction in the case,
however, demonstrated how even jurisdictional arrangements that seemed
quite clear-cut in their distribution of authority still relied on subjective
assessments, in which US authority often prevailed.

Though the project of expanding Guantanamo was ultimately abandoned,
the question of jurisdiction plagued negotiations over the cooperative

military agreement that the US and Cuba signed in the summer of 1942. In the agreement, Cuba granted the United States military jurisdiction within the limits of the new base under construction in San Antonio de los Baños, but made no mention of Camagüey or San Julián, and refused to formally concede jurisdiction over US troops on Cuban soil beyond the limits of the base. Eager to conclude the agreement but unable to reach a consensus, officials from both sides agreed to omit any explicit guidelines regarding jurisdiction over US soldiers beyond the bases. Though the agreement included protocol for how to handle fugitives of justice who sought refuge within or beyond the base, other matters of jurisdiction would simply be settled "through consultation" between the Cuban Foreign Ministry and the US embassy in Havana.[51]

As a result, arrangements for managing the behavior of US personnel were improvised in different ways in the different locations throughout the country where US troops were stationed. Similar to the mechanisms devised for policing sex work in the areas surrounding defense sites, US officials and local actors negotiated arrangements for policing US troops that responded to local circumstances and tweaked those arrangements along the way. These systems required the buy-in of an array of actors— Cuban judges and police, US and Cuban military officials, and local residents. Their cooperation was overseen, from a distance, by the Cuban Foreign Ministry, which acted both as the most vocal defender of Cuban sovereignty on the issue of jurisdiction in principle and an active facilitator of the diminution of sovereignty in practice.

In Camagüey, the relatively small number of US troops stationed in that city during the war impacted the nature of policing and jurisdiction. The original plan was fairly deferential. The chief of police in Camagüey ordered his men not to arrest US servicemen and instructed them instead to inform the US provost marshal of any problems. But this created an atmosphere in which US servicemen enjoyed "practical immunity."[52] Cubans soon began to complain, as Panamanians and Brazilians did, that US forces acted more like occupiers than allies. In a local news bulletin, a lieutenant colonel in the Cuban Army lamented, "they say that soldiers from the US are very disciplined but it's not true, their discipline is based on doing what they feel like, without taking into consideration that they are in a free and sovereign country and their stay in Cuba is governed by pacts between governments."[53]

As elsewhere, authority for authority's sake was not the bottom line. Also in play were the broader social conflicts surrounding the US military presence. Cuban police resented not only their inability to police the behavior of servicemen but also US officials' high wages and popularity among

Cuban women. Tensions ultimately erupted at a dance hall on the night of June 27, 1943, when twenty Cuban police officers and thirteen US officers and enlisted men brawled at the Club Riverside. Though witness accounts differed over who threw the first punch, at the center of the fight was a conflict between a Cuban police officer and a US soldier who was at the club that night with the Cuban officer's former girlfriend. The US troops who joined the brawl were outnumbered and unarmed. They were beaten with police clubs, and at least one Cuban officer fired his gun. Several of the soldiers were badly injured and four of them had to be airlifted out of Camagüey for further medical treatment. One of the men never regained full cognitive abilities as a result of a clubbing to the head. According to witness reports, a Cuban police captain clubbed the US officers and enlisted men as they entered his police wagon, and then declared before the crowd of onlookers that, even though he might lose his job as a result of his actions, he was glad to have beaten the "American dogs."[54]

US and Cuban officials became convinced that a new arrangement had to be reached in order to reduce tensions in Camagüey. Worried about a subsequent backlash, US officials declared the town temporarily off limits to US troops stationed at the airfield. The soldiers, humiliated by the experience, were said to be "cleaning their rifles" for a chance at revenge.[55] US authorities worried that once US personnel were able to resume their outings in town, they might carry concealed weapons so that they would not be caught unprepared again.[56] A joint US-Cuban committee that included the commanding officer of the Batista Air Base and representatives from the Cuban National Police and the Cuban Air Force conducted a joint investigation of the incident.

The commanding officer of Batista Air Base ultimately suggested that officials in Camagüey try an arrangement similar to that which he had helped to create in San Antonio de los Baños.[57] There, the Cuban police and the US military police worked together to monitor the areas on and surrounding the base, and military authorities viewed this as an effective model for governing US troops in the absence of formal protocol regarding jurisdiction. The expectation was that, when US military police detained Cubans on the base, they would be turned over to Cuban authorities, and when Cuban police detained US servicemen in town, those men would be turned over to US military authorities.

Though the arrangement was certainly more successful than the one devised in Camagüey and worked smoothly for the most part, it too generated tension. US military officials were sometimes less than satisfied with the Cuban police force's execution of their end of the bargain. For example, base authorities grew frustrated with the ubiquity of Cuban vendors who, seeking to take advantage of the economic opportunities offered by the US military presence, set up shop on the Batista Air Base to sell goods illegally to US troops and construction workers, usually foodstuffs like meat, cheese, and bread. Base officials viewed such activity as a nuisance and a potential public health hazard and posted hundreds of notices in English and Spanish around the base declaring the practice illegal. Initially, military police protocol was to escort illegal vendors from the base and turn them over to Cuban police.[58] But they quickly became dissatisfied with how Cuban police handled matters, as the same vendors repeatedly reappeared on the base, apparently insufficiently disincentivized by local police. Wresting some control back from Cuban police, US military police began to experiment with other forms of discipline. When MPs caught illegal vendors more than once on the base, they began burning the vendors' stock in the base incinerator and detaining them in the guard house for as long as six hours. The only parameters on their actions in disciplining Cuban civilians, according to the commanding official on the base, were "to do bodily harm to no one and to lock no one up longer than necessary." No official record was kept of the disciplinary measures.[59]

The cooperation of Cuban police was required for these informal arrangements to work, and it was often offered begrudgingly. As for judicial actors, the responses of different judges to the arrangements in Cuba were varied and relied largely on their individual interpretations of international law and its relationship to Cuban law. Some judges were predisposed to accept the United States' interpretation of international law around jurisdiction over troops in friendly countries. In October 1942, the Cuban solicitor general sent a copy of the 1918 Supreme Court opinion to all prosecuting attorneys suggesting that, in the absence of a formal agreement, the same protocol should be followed during World War II. The opinion was reprinted in newspapers nationwide. However, two months later, the Cuban foreign minister declared that the opinion was unconstitutional, holding fast to the Cuban government's broader claim to safeguard Cuban sovereignty by reserving Cuba's right to jurisdiction over US troops stationed there.[60]

In the context of this ambiguity, local courts sometimes proceeded to try to exercise jurisdiction over US servicemen. A fight over a laundry bill in San Antonio de los Baños is illustrative. One December day in 1943, thirty-four-year-old US Corporal Willie Weaver, twenty-two-year-old Private Douglas Alston, and twenty-one-year-old Private Eugene Whitehead went to a laundromat near the base to collect their uniforms after being cleaned and pressed. Before they left the shop, a fight broke out between the three men and the laundromat owner, Julio Barton, a sixty-three-year-old native of Jamaica, who insisted that the men still owed him two dollars on their bill.[61] Barton emerged from the fight with bruises on his face, contusions on his arm, and a busted lip. A Cuban firefighter passing by during the brawl tried to intervene and he too was injured. Witnesses reported that the US troops attacked both the laundryman and the firefighter. The three soldiers countered that in fact it was the laundryman who attacked them, and his injuries were incurred in their efforts to simply restrain him. According to prevailing informal protocol, Cuban police turned the three servicemen over to base authorities.[62]

Ordinarily, base authorities would then be left to discipline the men on their own, but on this occasion, the three men were instead summoned to appear before the 7th Circuit Court. The US State Department did not learn of the altercation until the day before the men were due to appear in court. When embassy officials reached out to the Cuban minister of justice and pointed to the informal protocol ordinarily followed, the ministry assured them that this incident would not deviate from the norm. A few months later, however, base authorities received another court summons for the three men. By this time, the men had been tried by courts-martial and were found guilty of acting disorderly in uniform in a public place. All three were fined and one was demoted. The commanding officer in Cuba requested that the State Department share this information with the judge who sent the summons, hoping that the punishment would satisfy him.[63] In the meantime, to prevent US troops from unknowingly allowing themselves to be held accountable to the Cuban justice system, US officials issued an order prohibiting all military personnel from appearing before Cuban courts without the express permission of headquarters.[64]

The Cuban Foreign Ministry's response to this incident illustrated the grand maneuver that the Cuban government tried to make in regard to jurisdiction. Having publicly renounced as unconstitutional the notion that Cuban courts lacked jurisdiction over US servicemen, and having refused to formally concede jurisdiction to the US government in written agreements, in practice, the Cuban Foreign Ministry actively worked to facilitate US jurisdiction over US troops. Ambassador Spruille Braden discussed the laundry bill incident with Foreign Minister Jorge Mañach, seeking assistance on the matter. Braden reminded Mañach of the ad hoc governance arrangement that, "although not provided for by written agreement between our two countries," had been "the accepted practice during the present war."[65] Mañach agreed to discuss the matter with the judge in question and encourage him to observe the ad hoc arrangement, but even as he agreed, Mañach reasserted for the record, "I wish to inform you that the Government of Cuba retains the full right to its jurisdiction over the delinquencies and infractions of the law which occur within national territory."[66] He insisted that, regardless of how things had played out in practice, "the position of the Ministry of State has never changed from the maintenance of outright jurisdiction over all acts committed by the United States military."[67]

Conflicts over jurisdiction were not just legal matters, but also cultural ones, connected to the common fears of moral degeneration. Many residents in San Antonio de los Baños perceived local police as complicit in permitting the town to descend into vice. By allowing the proliferation of new brothels, cantinas, and cabarets in town, as well as all manner of illicit behavior exhibited on the streets and city parks, residents alleged, the police were complicit in the corruption of women from "decent" families.[68] Orestes Robledo Reyes reported that this state of affairs changed when Grau San Martín appointed a new chief of police in 1944 who systematically cracked down on drug sales and other vices. But, even after shutting down the venues that encouraged moral degradation, as Robledo put it, "that still left the problem of the North Americans."[69]

There was one episode that Robledo recounted with all the flourish of local legend in which local authorities refused to accept their lack of jurisdiction over US servicemen and tried instead to find a way around the existing arrangement. One night, when the Central Plaza in San Antonio was at its busiest, a local judge, Francisco Alonso Echeguren, was out at a bar with friends when he observed a US soldier committing an unspecified "moral offense" and ordered the police to quickly apprehend the man. They did, and took the man straight to the courthouse. The police then quickly tracked down the court clerk, who was out at the theater, and he too was rushed to the courthouse. "Within seconds," they convened an extraordinary court session that Robledo described as a "trial for the morality of the community." The soldier was sentenced to six months in prison, and the judge "paid from his own pocket" for a car that drove the man to a Havana jail where he would begin serving his time. "By the time the North Americans began to mobilize their powerful resources," Robledo wrote, "it was too late; their compatriot was already sleeping at the Castillo del Principe prison." The tale became lore: "that night, in a few minutes, an honorable judge won the greatest battle for the morality of his people."[70]

Through the end of the war, authorities in Washington occasionally raised the prospect of revisiting the issue of jurisdiction to obtain a formal agreement on the matter. In November 1942, War Department officials drafted a proposed agreement for jurisdiction over the additional 5,000 US troops who would soon depart for San Julián, Camagüey, and San Antonio de los Baños. The draft agreement stipulated that the United States would enjoy exclusive jurisdiction over its personnel on Cuban territory regardless of the nature or location of the crime committed. It highlighted the World War I agreement between the US and France, as well as the Visiting Forces Act recently approved by the British parliament. The draft outlined procedures for the arrest and prosecution of US troops, as well as protocol for the use of US troops as witnesses in Cuban courts and for the temporary confinement of troops.[71] According to the proposed agreement, Cuban authorities would have the right to arrest US troops while outside of the boundaries of leased defense sites, but would have to promptly turn them over to US military authorities. Within the limits of the military posts, US officials reserved the right to arrest, try, and discipline anyone, regardless of nationality, if there were reasonable grounds to believe the person guilty of any crime against the security of the United States.[72]

The proposed agreement was never presented to the Cuban government. US embassy officials opposed broaching the matter because the improvised systems for dealing with criminal acts by US servicemen devised on the ground more or less aligned with the formal arrangement that US officials wanted, without requiring the Cuban government to make a formal commitment that, politically, it never could. Embassy officials worried that to raise the issue again in search of formality would simply rock the boat. The establishment of a formal agreement regarding jurisdiction would perhaps have led to greater uniformity in the practices observed at different defense sites across the country, and may have ensured consistency over time, but State Department officials ultimately determined that any risk that the informality of the existing arrangements involved was less than the risk that pursuing formality seemed to pose. If publicized, such a formal agreement could prove so unpopular as to threaten the stability of the Cuban government and, by extension, the US-Cuban alliance. This position remained consistent throughout the war. When the State Department inquired with the US ambassador in Cuba again a year later about the desirability of including a formal clause about jurisdiction in a supplementary military agreement that the two countries were negotiating, all parties agreed that matter was better left alone.[73]

BRAZIL

In Brazil, as in Cuba, the question of jurisdiction over US troops proved too problematic to resolve in the diplomatic realm when US soldiers began to populate defense sites across the North and Northeast, so it was sorted locally instead. In Brazil, US officials preoccupied with asserting authority over US personnel were eager to prevent the misbehavior of US citizens from sullying the project of Pan-American unity or inspiring sympathy among Brazilians toward the Axis powers. The sheer scale of the US presence in Brazil made this a tall order. And US officials' efforts to police the behavior of US personnel in Brazil in order to minimize tensions had the opposite effect when those efforts seemed to violate Brazilian sovereignty.

Not all US strategies required jurisdiction. In Belém, the commanding officer of the US Army Forces, Colonel Leo Post, hoped that a focus on discipline and education would help to decrease the number of disruptive incidents between US servicemen and local residents. To that end, he issued an instructional memo to his men on how servicemen should behave in Belém and threatened to declare the entire city off limits if they did not act accordingly.[74] Post was also among those US officials who advocated moving the USO club away from the center of town, to a less conspicuous location. But the US military presence in Belém was not confined to Army personnel, and Post decried a lack of discipline within the Navy. The claim was not unsubstantiated. One report calculated that 90 percent of all police cases involving US personnel in Belém involved Navy or merchant seamen and only 10 percent involved men from the Army.[75]

What's more, civilian personnel were present in large numbers throughout the North, working on projects like the Airport Development Program, the Rubber Development Corporation, and assorted cooperative programs run through the Office of the Coordinator of Inter-American Affairs, most notably, the Serviço Especial de Saúde Público (Public Health Special Service—SESP). Colonel Post observed that Belenenses did not differentiate between the uniforms worn by the Army, Navy, SESP, or even the ADP. Complicating matters further, though SESP was a civilian organization, it frequently hired medical professionals from the Army, and those men sometimes wore their military uniforms even though they were not under Post's command. US authorities in the consulate worried that the Army would get a bad reputation for behavior exhibited by US personnel beyond its ranks, to the detriment of the alliance.[76]

The large, multifaceted US presence in Brazil meant that the question of who should police the behavior of US citizens in wartime became one that transcended military personnel to include civilians, whom the State Department viewed as inadvertent ambassadors on the ground. The matter of policing civilians first arose as a diplomatic concern in Belém in September 1942. A fight broke out at the Grande Hotel in the center of town, where Pan Am had established an office in the early days of the ADP. The fight involved a number of drunken ADP employees, and became a conspicuous affair. According to a report of the incident, "a large amount of hotel glassware was broken" and "mattresses and pillows were thrown out of the hotel windows."[77] The US consul in Belém, Edward McLaughlin, received a phone call from the Pan American Airways office at the hotel as the fighting escalated, asking him who should be called to restore order. The consul advised the Pan Am officials to call the US military police. No arrests were made, as the fight had subsided by the time the military police arrived on the scene. However, the provost marshal in Belém advised the US consul in the wake of the incident that he was not authorized to arrest US civilians.

In the wake of that incident, the consul took the lead in creating a new governance arrangement that he thought would suit Belém's wartime circumstances. McLaughlin insisted that it was imperative that some authority from the United States take charge of maintaining order among all US citizens, and it seemed good sense to him to work out an arrangement between the US military police and the local police. Together, the consul and the commanding officer at the Val de Cães base devised an arrangement through which US military police would detain US civilians caught disturbing the peace and turn them over to Brazilian police at a predetermined location, ideally the police station in Belém, to minimize "embarrassment"—presumably to the US government. Though disciplinary action would be left to Brazilian police to execute, the consul advised the Brazilian police chief of his views regarding adequate punishment, and reserved the right to reclaim custody of detained civilians.[78]

In crafting this arrangement, little consultation was made with higher authorities in the Brazilian government, the US State Department, or the US War or Navy departments. Rather, McLaughlin simply informed the embassy in Rio of the solution he had improvised.[79] The arrangement did receive official sanction when Brigadier General Roland Walsh and Vice Admiral Jonas Ingram, the commanding officers of the US Army and Navy Forces in the South Atlantic, issued a joint order granting the provost marshal in Belém responsibility for "the good conduct, good order and discipline of all US citizens" in the interest of maintaining "the peace and security of the Belém area."[80] This arrangement functioned for a short while, but it had no legal standing, and the authority granted to the provost marshal was rescinded when the judge advocate's office in Recife issued an opinion in June 1944 that denied the US military police any authority over US civilians.[81]

As for policing the behavior of US servicemen, the model largely followed the practice in Cuba: Brazilian police released detained US soldiers into US custody. The practice of informally permitting US jurisdiction over US servicemen worked fairly well in Brazil for the first few years of the defense effort. In Belém, the US military police had an office in town in the Army's prophylactic station, which they also used as a detention center. One officer manned the office and the others operated as roving patrols around the city and its outskirts. They had one Brazilian plainclothesman on payroll who acted mainly as an interpreter. Otherwise, cooperation was informal. All agreed that US servicemen were subject to Brazilian laws and regulations, but offending servicemen detained by Brazilian police were to be turned over to US military police for further action. Sometimes Brazilian police would collect a fine from the detained serviceman, but otherwise there was little friction in the process.

By the middle of the war period, however, as concerns about moral degradation grew, local comfort with prevailing arrangements began to falter, prompting new conversations about jurisdiction. By this time, early reports of positive relations between US personnel and Brazilian civilians had given way to more common reports of resentment and strain. One incident that occurred in Belém in 1944 is particularly illuminating. On April 13, local police arrested two US soldiers and two Brazilian women as they exited the Olimpia Theater in the center of town. They were charged with the crime of "moral offense," but the precise nature of the offensive behavior was unclear. In Brazilian documents, the four were accused of "*onanismo*," while the local paper more diplomatically described them as guilty of "libidinous acts."[82] US records were more dismissive of the behavior. Among themselves, US officials confided that they believed that "the actual offense was necking" or merely "putting [an] arm around a girl's shoulder" and chalked it up to the "childish practice of two soldiers."[83]

When the US military police learned of the arrest, they immediately contested Brazilian officers' authority on the matter. For years, the informal arrangement in Belém was that detained US soldiers were turned over to US military police for further action. The "theater incident" threatened to upend this system. Though Brazilian police ultimately relented and released the men with a fine, the episode did not end there. The flurry of local and international correspondence drafted in the wake of this incident dwarfed that which followed seemingly graver crimes such as murder and vehicular manslaughter that also resulted from the US military presence. US officials could not make sense of the import of the event. The vice consul assured the State Department that, "although this immoral conduct was never specifically defined, it does not appear that any actions of a really seriously immoral nature were involved."[84] But this begged the question at the heart of debates around law and crime as they intersected with culture surrounding the military bases of World War II Latin America—immoral according to whom? After years of relatively little conflict over the policing of US troops in Belém, the theater incident reignited debates over sovereignty and jurisdiction that had never been formally settled.

The disruption to the usual practice on this occasion also revealed that some of the key actors in the arrangement devised to govern troop behavior in the region did not know whether it was based on any legal grounding. In the weeks following the theater incident, the US vice consul in Pará wrote to the State Department requesting information about whether US jurisdiction was explicitly included in the military agreements between the United States and Brazil, which were secret, noting, "it is thought that reference to such an agreement would be more effective than any discussions of international law with the Belém authorities."[85] By way of reply, the State Department explained, "While there is at present no agreement between the United States and Brazil recognizing this principle, it is understood that such jurisdiction has usually been recognized in practice."[86]

A series of additional incidents that occurred in the months following the theater incident further inflamed sensitivity around the issue of jurisdiction. Some formal agreement regarding jurisdiction over US servicemen became increasingly desirable from the perspective of the US government. But rather than obtain jurisdiction through a diplomatic agreement, it was obtained through a Brazilian Supreme Court ruling that was made with input that Vargas's government provided under pressure from the US State Department.

The Supreme Court case involved the death of a Brazilian civilian named José Domingues Ramos who attempted to enter the US base in Recife to collect a fine that was owed to him by an American sailor. When Ramos attempted to force his way onto the base, Arthur James Gilbert, a US Navy seaman on guard at the time, shot him. Ramos died a few days later. In the days and weeks following the shooting, the question arose of what kind of court should hear the case. The civil criminal court in the state of Pernambuco declared itself incompetent on the grounds that the crime was a military offense. However, when the case was then passed on to the auditor of the 7th Military Region, he declared Brazilian military courts incompetent to hear the case, because the victim was a civilian and the offender was not a member of the Brazilian armed forces.[87] In effect, the driving question in this case when it began was not whether the United States or Brazil had jurisdiction, but which court in Brazil had jurisdiction. The case eventually rose to the Supreme Court in late 1944, and the court decided that neither Brazilian civil nor military courts were competent to hear cases against US servicemen, and that such cases should be left to US military courts.[88]

As with the question of the applicability of labor law, the US embassy actively sought to influence the highest court's decision on the matter of criminal jurisdiction. Embassy officials discussed the case informally with the minister of foreign affairs, the minister of war, the minister of navy, and the minister of aeronautics. According to embassy officials, "they were all in agreement that the policy which had been followed up to the present time—i.e., that it is both correct and practical to turn over our soldiers and sailors to American military courts—should be continued." The Supreme Court justice who wrote the opinion in the case consulted with those officials.[89] Whether or not their influence was pivotal, embassy officials took credit for the outcome. One official stated bluntly, "the Embassy paved the way for this very satisfactory decision."

Despite Brazilian leaders' support for this outcome behind the scenes, Vargas's administration did not wish for the case or its implications to be widely publicized in Brazil, nor was the government willing to openly endorse the court's opinion. When an Army official in Natal inquired with the State Department as to whether the United States might ask that a directive on the matter be issued, affirming the Supreme Court decision as a matter of official policy, the State Department explained that the embassy had counseled them "to avoid any publicity on the Supreme Court decision in question, because while the Brazilian Government is perfectly willing in practice to allow US armed forces to have jurisdiction for offenses committed by their personnel in Brazil, it did not wish to establish the practice as a matter of right, due to Brazil's well known sensitivity about her sovereignty."[90] Several cases in the years following the Supreme Court ruling showed that that ruling was enough, as judges consistently declared themselves incompetent to hear such cases, even when police detained US servicemen. The ruling did not, of course, make the US military presence any less disruptive in Brazilian cities.

In this sense, in Brazil, the evolution of the government's policy surrounding the question of criminal jurisdiction was similar to the evolution of the government's policy regarding the jurisdiction of labor legislation over base employment. In both cases, as the US-Brazilian alliance strengthened over the course of the war, the Brazilian government proved increasingly willing to assist the US government in pursuit of its unpopular objectives. In both instances, however, rather than issue formal decrees or agreements from the executive office, the Brazilian government leaned on the justice system to issue court rulings that provided US authorities with the concessions they sought, thereby distancing Vargas from the concessions themselves, which ran counter to his nationalist persona.

Like so many other features of governance around these military bases, the story of criminal jurisdiction at defense sites lays bare the various creative ways that US officials and their Latin American counterparts struggled over and reconciled the inherent tensions between international cooperation and national sovereignty. Arrogant assertions of international legal principles, passionate defenses of sovereignty, informal protocol hashed out on the ground, and imaginative interpretations of that protocol once put into practice all allowed for the loose coexistence of two seemingly contradictory things: sovereign equality and indisputable hierarchy.

For the most part, officials and residents in the military base borderlands at each defense site settled into systems for governing the behavior of US personnel that more or less "worked." To be sure, with no legal grounding for the improvised arrangements, each disputed arrest threatened to become an international affair. But informality had its perks. It permitted US authorities to exercise jurisdiction over servicemen in practice, while also allowing Latin American leaders to go on championing the sanctity of sovereignty in principle. If it appeared that the Panamanian government surrendered a greater degree of sovereignty than the governments of the other Latin American republics by consenting to a system of shared jurisdiction, the contrary proved true in practice. The arrangement that the United States negotiated with Panama gave Panamanians a framework with which to assert their authority in clear terms, albeit with mixed results, giving them jurisdiction over some cases some of the time. In Cuba and Brazil, where leaders seemingly resisted US calls for jurisdiction, the US armed forces proved able to assert jurisdiction over all offenses all of the time.

Despite the relatively smooth operation of US extraterritorial authority over servicemen in practice throughout the war, formal agreements over jurisdiction in the diplomatic realm remained unreachable. And when the US government attempted to extend its stay at many Latin American defense sites beyond the war's conclusion, the matter of jurisdiction proved no less problematic during negotiations for postwar basing than it had been before. The issue so plagued diplomatic negotiations over new base leases that one US official seeking extended basing rights in Ecuador proclaimed of the word "jurisdiction": "I think we should resolve never to use it again."[91]

From the interpersonal to the international, the management of crime was yet another arena in which the rhetoric of inter-American equality and the reality of inter-American hierarchy collided in real time. The improvised arrangements were not sustainable beyond the war's end. If being "allies in the larger struggle" gave residents reason to tolerate their "private battles" with US personnel for the duration of the war, the end of the war eliminated such rationale and prompted actors on all sides to reconsider practices of inter-American cooperation moving forward.

CHAPTER 7

Cooperation at the War's End

In the stacks of the Panamanian National Archives is a batch of letters written by citizens of Panama to the president and his minister of finance on the heels of the Allied victory in World War II. After US soldiers slowly withdrew from some of the 134 defense sites that the United States built and occupied throughout Panama during the war, residents of towns and villages near abandoned encampments sought to reappropriate the land and lay claim to the equipment and facilities that were left behind. "Dear Mr. President," one letter read, "I am writing to ask that you grant me one of the houses that the North American armed forces have left at the disposition of the Panamanian government. . . . I am, Mr. President, a poor man, scraping by on a salary that is hardly enough to take care of my wife, three children, and elderly parents."[1] In another letter, a truckers' union requested use of a building from a nearby base for training exercises.[2] An entrepreneur inquired if he might transform military barracks into dairy barns.[3] Firefighters sought lumber to build a new floor in their station; a governor requested toilets and sinks for a nursing home; a mayor requested a water tank for his townspeople.[4] Still others proposed to turn military buildings into cultural centers, libraries, health clinics, schools, sports clubs, and jailhouses.[5]

Other, less deferential appeals to the Panamanian government were made on the street. These went beyond polite requests for property transfers, demanding instead something the president was less prepared to facilitate: the restoration of territorial sovereignty. While the US armed forces willingly withdrew from most of the defense sites leased during the war—leaving priests, truckers, and the downtrodden to lay claim to

Cooperating with the Colossus. Rebecca Herman, Oxford University Press. © Oxford University Press 2022.
DOI: 10.1093/oso/9780197531860.003.0008

abandoned buildings—US troops lingered at other sites, stalling while US and Panamanian diplomats tried to negotiate a new base agreement that would extend their leases and allow them to stay. President Enrique Jiménez tried, as Arnulfo Arias and Ricardo de la Guardia had before him, to turn the US desire for defense infrastructure into quid pro quo material benefits for Panama, while minimizing the encroachment on Panamanian sovereignty that a new lease would permit. But across the country, Panamanian civilians fed up with the wartime abuses committed by US troops on Panamanian soil took to the streets. Carrying signs proclaiming "Not One More Inch of Panamanian Territory," the protestors insisted on the expulsion of the remaining servicemen.[6]

The months and years following the end of World War II witnessed all sorts of assertions —personal, political, and economic—by people across the Americas endeavoring to shape what would follow the extraordinary period of wartime experimentation in inter-American cooperation. In the name of cooperation, the United States had built over 200 defense sites in Latin America; distributed nearly half a billion dollars of lend-lease aid; launched military missions in every country in the region; invested heavily in raw material extraction; developed roads, railways, and public health infrastructure; and opened new avenues for inter-American educational exchanges ranging from modern art to military training. Despite the fact that ample work remained to effectively hold Washington accountable to the principles of non-intervention and sovereign equality, people across the political spectrum welcomed the unprecedented US investment in the Americas during the war. Those resources, properly channeled, could be a crucial first step in realizing the commitment declared at the Third Foreign Ministers meeting in 1942 to work together toward "the solution of the outstanding problems of the Continent."[7] But this grand experiment was born of a number of contingencies: the particular security concerns of this particular war had made US officials more preoccupied with Latin American interests and goodwill than ever before. What would cooperation with the Colossus look like in a time of peace?

Latin American activists, leaders, and diplomats confronted this question in a world remade. US national security, just recently reimagined as a hemispheric project, was reconceived again during the war as a global undertaking. Amid shifting US conceptions of national security, foreign policy concerns, and budgetary constraints, Latin American heads of state and their foreign policymakers contemplated the domestic and international politics of continued cooperation with the United States and the forms it might take in the postwar period. As people across the region asserted their own visions for postwar inter-American relations, everywhere from

Bretton Woods to basing protests, the prospect of hemispheric cooperation held promise. The question was what kind, and at what cost. In the struggle to properly answer that question, the long-standing project to invite beneficial engagement with the United States while containing US overreach continued, and debates over the nature of the compromises required to reconcile national sovereignty and international cooperation in the Americas remained front and center.

VISIONS FOR INTER-AMERICAN COOPERATION IN THE POSTWAR WORLD

The reorientation in US strategic thought regarding national security that took place in the final months of 1938 was already dated by the war's end. No longer solely focused on deflecting an extra-hemispheric attack or preventing enemy inroads within the nations of the Western Hemisphere, defense officials sought to maintain order and military readiness throughout the world. These designs for global defense suited the ambitions of an emboldened cadre of foreign policy makers and public intellectuals who insisted that the only possible future world peace was one in which the United States led the way.[8]

US plans for global leadership when the war ended greatly resembled the particular kind of hemispheric leadership that the nation had pursued in the Americas when the war began. US security would rely on two broad projects: a system of international cooperation and collective security rooted in multilateral institutions on the one hand, and a far-reaching network of overseas military bases on the other. These multilateral and unilateral initiatives would be stitched together by an ever-expanding number of transactional bilateral agreements dressed up with ideological flourish.

As the contours of a future world order became the subject of ever-greater discussion in 1944, Latin American diplomats were eager to shape the conversation. Though some differences distinguished their various proposals, there was a remarkable degree of consensus among foreign policy makers in Latin America who worked to formalize the inter-American system, preserve a place for regionalism within the new United Nations, and ensure that both regional and international multilateral organizations would respect and respond to the interests of less powerful members.[9]

A number of snubs sustained early on in the process made clear that the new United Nations would likely reify the hierarchy in international politics among sovereign states that had long structured Latin America's relationship to Europe and the United States. No Latin American country was invited to the meeting at Dumbarton Oaks, where the initial plan for the United Nations was discussed. Disappointment deepened further still when it became clear that no Latin American nation would receive a permanent seat on the UN Security Council, a point of particular frustration for Brazil.[10]

Nonetheless, Latin American representatives coordinated among themselves to apply pressure where they could to encourage rules and norms that would protect the interests of less powerful nations within this flawed system. At the meeting in Bretton Woods, where representatives from the Allied nations worked to establish the rules for a future international monetary system, Latin American delegates lobbied for a greater focus on economic development.[11] In the months between Dumbarton Oaks and the subsequent meeting in San Francisco where the UN Charter was drafted, suggestions for amendments and alternative proposals poured in from Mexico, Brazil, Uruguay, Venezuela, Costa Rica, and Guatemala. The most common critique of the existing proposal was that the envisioned structure of the United Nations granted too much power to the "Big Four" relative to the rest of the UN's future membership, and Latin American delegates worked as a bloc to try and increase Latin American representation on the Security Council and to strengthen the power of the General Assembly.[12]

In the meantime, Latin American leaders called for an inter-American consultative meeting to discuss regional plans for the postwar period within the Western Hemisphere. The Inter-American Conference on Problems of War and Peace convened at the Chapultepec Castle in Mexico City in February and March 1945. Argentina, which had not yet declared war, did not attend. By and large, the Latin American diplomats present favored the creation of a strong, autonomous regional system, even as international multilateral institutions took shape, as the best way to build on the strides made in inter-American cooperation in the 1930s and early 1940s and maintain a privileged relationship with the United States. The United States, by contrast, was reluctant to make any binding commitments to regionalism that might conflict with the final form that the United Nations would assume, and it generally worked to delay firm commitments to the American system until after the meeting that was scheduled to take place in San Francisco.

As the delegates at Chapultepec deliberated the formalization of the inter-American system that had been cobbled together since the 1890s, they contemplated the fate and prioritization of two, overlapping features of inter-American wartime cooperation: economic collaboration and mutual security. Perhaps unsurprisingly, the US delegation and Latin American delegations diverged in terms of which of these features they believed to be more important moving forward. The United States largely sought to maintain a security alliance at as low an economic price tag as possible, while Latin American delegations were focused far more on the economic and social problems facing the continent.

Economic development was at the top of postwar agendas across Latin America, as inflation surged in the region during the war. Desire to avoid the postwar economic depression that the region experienced after World War I inspired a concerted effort to think carefully about postwar economics in the hemisphere. Latin American leaders during this period commonly supported active state involvement in economic growth, and popular support for social welfare-oriented political and economic agendas continued to rise, bolstered by a wave of democratization underway. In the spirit of confronting the "outstanding problems of the continent," folks leading the charge at Chapultepec, like Mexican Foreign Minister Ezequiel Padilla, advanced a vision of a planned international economy. Mexico, Chile, Peru, and Brazil all shared their own ideas about various forms of future economic cooperation that would improve the standard of living in Latin America and aid Latin American economic growth.[13]

An essential requirement of this vision for postwar economic cooperation was that the US government remain committed to the social welfare of Latin American people after the war's conclusion. Concern early in the war that poverty and inequality in Latin America created breeding grounds for fascism had made Latin Americans' economic well-being a security interest for the United States and helped to justify unprecedented US spending on development programs in the region. Laurence Duggan, head of the American Republics desk at the State Department, anticipated difficulties would ensue if and when the United States abandoned the wartime projects. He remarked in 1943 that "the people of the other American republics by no means are yet convinced that this country desires to help them improve their standard of life. Many believe that war considerations are alone responsible for our overnight courtship and that once the emergency has passed the United States will return to its former indifference, leaving them to stew in their own juice."[14]

Nonetheless, the skeptics were largely proven right. At Chapultepec, Washington's position quickly became evident: rather than provide continued development aid and join forces in coordinated planning, US officials preferred for governments to step back and allow "the markets" to do the work. The US delegation condemned what they described as economic nationalism in the Americas and made their preference for free trade and limited intervention clear. The US delegation's stance elicited widespread criticism from across the political spectrum in Latin America—from relatively conservative elites to leftist labor organizers, who were all watching for signs of US support for state-led growth. The push and pull between these various viewpoints played out as representatives batted around an Economic Charter for the Americas. The charter's final text ambiguously committed the American Republics to economic coordination, while delaying discussion of the more controversial details of that coordination until later.

The second pending matter as the war drew to a close was the future of military cooperation and of the budding inter-American military system. If the social well-being of people in Latin America was less of an urgent security concern for US officials in 1945 than it had been in 1940, Latin America remained an important region in US defense officials' understanding of national security, and they were eager to lock in the gains that the United States had made in enhancing US–Latin American military relations during the war.[15] Even if Latin America appeared safely ensconced in the United States' sphere of influence at the war's end, defense officials wanted to ensure that Latin America remained a "stable, secure, and friendly flank to the South," as US Secretary of War Robert Patterson put it.[16]

While the delegates at Chapultepec did discuss, in broad terms, the future of inter-American security cooperation, US military officials pursued their more concrete goals in this realm bilaterally in a new round of Staff Conversations with their counterparts in each Latin American country in 1944 and 1945. These Staff Conversations were already underway at the time of the Chapultepec Conference. In those conversations, the United States sought continued basing rights in specific places, the continued flow of strategic resources from Latin America to the United States, and Latin American support for a program of military standardization in the Americas—that is, a program through which Latin American military establishments would adopt US military training, doctrine, and weapons. Standardization, US officials reasoned, would prevent the return of European military missions and the dumping of surplus weapons from Europe and the Pacific in Latin America in the postwar period, and it would foster goodwill toward the United States among top military officials in the region.[17] Given the contentious nature of some of the facets of military cooperation—especially basing, but increasingly, weapons transfers as well—US military officials preferred for the details of these matters to be worked out bilaterally and urged the US delegation at Chapultepec to avoid the topic of bases in particular.[18]

As in the first round of Staff Conversations held in 1940, US officials' ability to obtain acquiescence hinged on their ability to provide weapons to their Latin American partners. This presented a challenge because the

Lend Lease Act, which had enabled military aid to Latin American countries during the war, was due to expire in June 1945. Military leaders would need a new legal means for facilitating weapons transfers to the region. The War and Navy departments advocated for a proposed Inter-American Military Cooperation Bill, which would facilitate further military aid to Latin American countries, and an interim program was established that permitted some continued assistance in the meantime, but the bill would ultimately stall due to internal fighting between US government agencies and shifting strategic priorities.[19]

By this time, the orientation within Washington toward inter-American military relations had begun to shift. At the outset of the war, it had been the State Department that advocated military cooperation for the diplomatic value of such initiatives, while the War and Navy departments had been reluctant. But by the end of the war, it was the Navy and War departments that were most convinced of the utility of continuing to build strong relationships with Latin American security forces, and it was leaders in those departments who pushed, in particular, for the continuation of military aid to support their vision of standardization, while the State Department expressed reservations. The matter became embroiled in a broader turf war between the State Department and the War and Navy departments over the making of US policy in Latin America, as the State Department expressed concern that military objectives were beginning to outweigh diplomatic priorities in shaping US efforts in the region.[20]

Though the Joint Chiefs of Staff preferred to keep the specific details surrounding basing and weapons provisions confined to the bilateral realm, Chapultepec Conference participants did address the question of a future security alliance. Latin American delegations broadly supported continued inter-American military cooperation at this time (though protests over military aid to anti-democratic governments would grow at the war's conclusion). The Mexican delegation proposed replacing the temporary Inter-American Defense Board with a permanent organ that would be made up of the General Staffs of each American Republic.[21] A second proposal, this one jointly offered by Brazil, Colombia, and Uruguay, also sought to create a strong collective security system.[22] The State Department and US military leaders were divided on the proposals. The US Joint Chiefs of Staff, represented at the Chapultepec Conference by Lieutenant General Stanley Embick (the chairman of the Inter-American Defense Board), were eager to move ahead with a regional security alliance despite the State Department's preference to await the outcome of the San Francisco conference before making regional commitments.[23] In the end, the State Department's preference won out, and the United States and Mexico reached a compromise that watered down the Mexican proposal into a recommendation that, when the war concluded, a permanent organ would be considered. In the meantime, the Inter-American Defense Board would continue to operate as it had.[24]

Ultimately, the conference proved only a way station between the existing ad hoc system of inter-American cooperation and a more institutionalized system that would come into being by the end of the decade. The concluding Act of Chapultepec dictated next steps by calling for the future drafting of a permanent treaty for an inter-American defense alliance and a permanent charter for the inter-American political system. Though all present imagined that those agreements would be drafted within the year, ongoing tensions between the United States and Argentina caused recurring delays, and another two years passed before representatives of the American Republics gathered again to make good on the Act of Chapultepec's concluding recommendations. In the meantime, the question of whether and when US military personnel would evacuate the wartime bases became an urgent matter that could not be postponed and, like so many of the fights over basing, demonstrated the constraints that domestic politics could place on international relations.

THE FATE OF BASES

While US and Latin American leaders worked to lock in those aspects of wartime cooperation that they wanted to see continued into the postwar era, the question of basing only became more delicate. As had been true in 1939, the territoriality of basing made it different from other sorts of cooperation. The encounters with US power that Latin American civilians experienced on the ground, the struggles over authority, and the perception of moral degradation fostered disillusionment with the broad proclamations of Good Neighborliness and equality on which the wartime alliance otherwise rested. While Latin American leaders eagerly sought to institutionalize several aspects of the wartime alliance in the postwar period, basing was not among those practices of inter-American cooperation that they hoped to continue. But US visions for postwar security called for a long-term global network of overseas bases, including the retention of many of the bases acquired in wartime in Latin America.

In November 1943, the US Joint Chiefs of Staff began contemplating postwar basing requirements in concrete terms. Strategists envisioned "a widespread system of bases beyond which lies a region which may be considered as constituting the United States' strategic frontier."[25]

In the new landscape, bases would provide essential infrastructure for intercepting attacks against the United States well before they penetrated US borders, and they would enable the United States to quickly and efficiently project US power against an adversary anywhere in the world.[26] In addition to bases, defense officials sought the air and transit rights that would permit them to move seamlessly between the nodes of the basing network. Though the grand plans devised during the war years would meet budgetary and political constraints after the war ended and the United States would relinquish many of the bases acquired in wartime, the broader vision of a global military presence persisted.[27]

According to the projected basing needs that the JCS outlined, the United States required extensive basing rights in the Western Hemisphere and the Far East.[28] In the Americas, the plans called for exclusive military rights at bases in Cuba, Panama, Guatemala, and the Galápagos Islands and further rights on a "participating and, if necessary, a reciprocal basis" at desired sites in Mexico and Brazil.[29] Subsequent planning in the spring of 1945 further refined US basing plans. The new proposal relied on a system of "primary bases" in locations of compromised sovereignty like the Philippines, the Canal Zone, the Hawaiian Islands, and Puerto Rico. "Secondary base areas" in sovereign territory, including in the Republic of Panama and the Brazilian Northeast, would provide access to and protection of the primary base areas. Following these were "subsidiary base areas" that would make the system more flexible, including the base in Belém, and "minor base areas," including the Cuban bases in San Antonio de los Baños and San Julián.[30]

In January 1944, Roosevelt instructed the State Department to initiate the necessary negotiations to obtain the base rights and facilities specified in these designs.[31] When US officials began seeking extended basing rights, they had to contend with long-standing fears, strengthened by Axis propaganda, that wartime bases would turn into a permanent US military presence. In August 1941, still months before the attack on Pearl Harbor but nearly a year after the Pan American Airways' Airport Development Program began covertly building airfields, German news outlets had claimed that the Roosevelt administration was attempting to develop a network of bases across Latin America. Calling the United States the "American thumbscrew," the report described these maneuvers as blatant acts of imperialism.[32] After the attack on Pearl Harbor and the official establishment of US bases, Axis propaganda on the subject continued to inflame regional fears about what this meant for the future. A Portuguese-language broadcast from Germany to Brazil asserted, "instead of a Nazi invasion there will be a Yankee invasion."[33] Japanese broadcasts meanwhile taunted that the United States "never does anything for nothing. She expects a full return for everything she does."[34]

The US government made some efforts to assuage Latin American concerns about long-term basing over the course of the war. Under Secretary of State Sumner Welles held a press conference in March 1943 in which he made a blanket statement that the US would not try to retain bases in Latin America beyond the war's conclusion.[35] But the assurances did not last long. As a US vice consul in Ecuador described the problem, "no sooner is the specter laid to rest of indefinite occupation of military bases acquired in Latin-America by the United States in the post-war period than the indiscreet remarks of some individual prominent in the public life of the United States again revivifies the apparition."[36] When a resolution was introduced in the US Senate calling for the acquisition of permanent bases off the coast of South America, Brazilian journalist Francisco de Assis Chateaubriand likened the resolution to "the language Hitler used to support his expansionist politics in Central Europe."[37]

The prompt return of the wartime bases was often tied to the integrity of the Good Neighbor policy by contemporary observers. As one US journalist reporting on the matter wrote, "The United States for a period tried the strong-arm formula inherited from Europe in dealing with some of our neighbors and we reaped trouble out of it everywhere. We have led a parade toward cooperation during the past 10 years and we found quick need for friends to the south when we were attacked from Asia and Europe. We are the last Nation that would want to change a trend that has worked so successfully, even if we could."[38] Latin Americans challenged the United States on the same grounds, posing the prompt devolution of bases as a test of the survival of the Good Neighbor policy. An editorial in one Peruvian newspaper, responding to statements made by the subcommittee on Naval Affairs in the House of Representatives about the desirability of long-term bases in Latin America, stated:

> An emergency situation was involved in which there predominated the spirit of friendly inter-American cooperation in the war effort which the great republic of the north is carrying on . . . but, once the world has returned to normal conditions, there will no longer exist the necessity to maintain military installations outside the control of a given country and thought should be given only to the idea that there should govern in America peace, solidarity, and respect for the sovereignty of each one of the nations of this hemisphere. . . . We are sure that such is the thought of the government and the people of the United States, who understand that this policy of good neighbors, which contrasts with the mistaken policy of force which sometimes was followed in the past, is that

which truly attracts the sympathy and friendship of the Latin American peoples, jealous of their independence and of their sovereignty.[39]

Assis Chateaubriand in Brazil similarly commented that "the miracle of the new American order" would be jeopardized by any US effort to retain permanent bases in Latin America.[40]

By 1944, however, US officials, rather than categorically deny the possibility of long-term basing in Latin America, began to simply insist that Latin Americans need not worry about the prospect of US basing, as any basing rights they sought would be negotiated in the Good Neighbor spirit of inter-American cooperation. At a news conference in June 1944, Secretary of State Cordell Hull was asked whether the US planned to retain its bases in Latin America after the war. In his reply, he outlined the cooperative basis on which all wartime security cooperation with Latin American countries had been carried out, and insisted that the retention of defense sites in the future would only be done with consent.[41] Of course, the consent of an ally in office did not always reflect the consent of the general public.

Other State Department officials were attuned to the potential divergence between official and popular positions on continued US basing. A former State Department official cautioned President Harry Truman that Latin Americans were "in a position to go either violently pro-American or violently anti-American after the war. Which way they go depends almost entirely on one question. . . . The retention of bases." In jest, he continued, "The argument of those who desire to keep troops permanently in South America is that next time we may be attacked from the south. If we do not respect our contract and return the bases, I believe I can assure you that the next time we will be attacked from the south."[42] Given the delicacy of the issue, as US officials endeavored to secure consent for postwar basing, they did so in quiet bilateral discussions with each country, one by one, just as they had in their earlier efforts to acquire the bases to begin with.

BRAZIL

In Brazil, US officials sought to conclude an agreement that would allow the United States to retain wartime bases for another ten years. The State Department approached the Brazilian government on the topic in January 1944. The War Department had expressed a desire for long-term leases of the most important airfields Pan Am had built in the North and Northeast, but noted that, if that were not feasible, it would be acceptable to negotiate joint command of the bases by the Brazilian Air Force and US Army Air Forces, as well as full rights for the use of the fields by US military aircraft, and rights to install certain radio and communications installations.[43] Getúlio Vargas agreed to a joint command arrangement, but bases remained the ultimate bargaining chip. In return, Vargas demanded a continuing supply of armaments and a guarantee of assistance in the event of an attack on Brazil, not only by a non-American power but also by an American one (with Argentina in mind).[44]

The two countries signed the Military Aviation Agreement in Rio de Janeiro on June 14, 1944, which US officials hoped would become a model for agreements with other countries in Latin America.[45] But the agreement would not survive Brazil's transition to democracy in 1945. The agreement was framed in terms of mutual defense and reciprocity and proclaimed to protect Brazilian sovereignty. It provided for the continued maintenance of strategic airbases while explicitly stating that this agreement would be concluded, "without in any manner implying the permanency of the armed forces of the United States of America at the air bases in question."[46] During the ten-year duration of the agreement, US and Brazilian military aircraft and personnel could freely use the bases included in the agreement. A Technical Commission for the Conservation of Airports, composed of an equal number of representatives from the United States and Brazil, would determine the boundaries of the airfields, the necessary installations required at each airport, and the most equitable manner of dividing the cost of maintenance of the bases between the two countries. The agreement also allowed both the US and Brazil to station personnel at the sites. The arrangement gave the US armed forces access and options, while reducing the costs and manpower required to maintain the airfields and the public relations problem of extending unilateral basing rights.

Vargas was aware of the likelihood of popular backlash against a continued US military presence and sought to diffuse it by keeping continued collaboration as inconspicuous as possible. He insisted that the agreement be kept secret and stipulated that the US personnel stationed at the bases after the war should dress as civilians.[47] But these measures were not enough to prevent popular protest from precipitating the complete withdrawal of US military personnel from base sites in Brazil, as the shifting political landscape on the ground made these basing plans untenable. Vargas was among the dictators to lose power in the Democratic Spring. The elected government of Eurico Dutra, Vargas's former minister of war, was no more eager for the Secret Base Agreement to be made public, given Dutra's complicity in finalizing it.

Celebrations were held to mark the transfer of bases from US to Brazilian control, but in the months and years following the "transfer" of US bases back to Brazilian authorities, the continued presence of US personnel suggested to passersby that this was an illusion. In January 1946, the *New York Times* published an article that observed that Brazilians were "beginning to chafe under the presence of so many United States uniforms, jeeps, trucks and other motor transport." Highlighting the fodder this sort of resentment would provide for those opposed to US predominance in the region, the article noted, "our enemies are talking about the 'forces of occupation' and are getting slight, but increasing credence."[48] US officials in Brazil echoed these concerns. The US vice consul in Recife noted, "the people of Recife as a whole are rather tired of seeing uniforms on the streets."[49] According to him, US servicemen were also tired of being there and the situation was deteriorating. Discipline among the ranks was breaking down. Theft of equipment and materials during the transfer of installations and equipment to the local armed forces became a common occurrence in the confusion of the postwar wind-down in Latin America. According to the Recife consulate, it was common knowledge that amid this confusion, US troops were participating in the theft, alongside Brazilian servicemen and civilians. The vice consul echoed the recommendations of others that US personnel wear civilian clothing when off the base and went a step further to suggest that the reduced number of US military technicians that would stay on to collaborate with the Brazilian Air Force be put under the command of the Brazilian military.[50]

More problematic, the lingering presence of US troops became a powerful talking point for the Communist Party in Brazil. Across Latin America, the Allied victory had given a boost to Communist Party membership, and in the spirit of the Democratic Spring, Communist parties were briefly legalized in most countries in the region. Communists eagerly attacked the continued US presence as evidence of imperialism. One Brazilian Communist Party member, Diógenes Arruda, reflecting on the postwar period recalled, "we launched a mass campaign to force the Americans to deliver the military and naval bases that were still being occupied by them since the war. We said: Get out, Americans! Get out of the bases in our country!" The Communist Party held a series of rallies on the issue in Rio, Natal, and Recife, at which Arruda claimed there were hundreds of thousands of attendants.[51] The leftist newspaper *Tribuna Popular* published articles with titles like "Soldiers of Imperialism on Our Soil—Not One Minute More!" and "Only One Flag Must Fly!"[52] The Soviet Union accused the United States of maintaining bases in Brazil at a meeting of the United Nations Security Council. The Brazilian ambassador denied this charge, frustrating Brazilians at home in Recife, Natal, and elsewhere who witnessed firsthand that, in fact, US troops did continue to walk among them.[53]

The pressure did not come from Communists alone. Telegrams poured in to members of Congress from Brazilian civilians of various ideological stripes, demanding that US troops leave at once.[54] Many called on the government to insist on the evacuation of US troops in order to prevent Communists from gaining any ground with this issue. As Assis Chateaubriand put it, "there can be no continental solidarity with occupation. . . . We must not give the Communists ammunition."[55] To counter these accusations, some US officials suggested that the agreement be made public in order to prove to those in doubt that the US troops were stationed in Brazil with the consent of the Brazilian government and that limits on the duration of their presence did exist. However, US embassy officials cautioned that the agreement should not be given publicity until the details of its implementation were worked out.[56] To expose the agreement could make the newly democratic Brazilian government more vulnerable to Communist criticism.

The Right, meanwhile, defended the bases as having been beneficial for the country. Carlos Lacerda, for instance, followed a visit to the naval base in Recife by commenting on the hundreds of millions of cruzeiros worth of equipment he had seen there. "Who left behind all that capital to the Brazilian Navy? Our invaders, our enemies the Americans," he commented sarcastically. Lacerda further praised what he seemed to perceive as the civilizing effects of the US military presence in the North and Northeast, noting that he found at the bases "machines and installations where there used to be deserted huts, a hospital where there were palm-trees before." Despite his praise for the legacies of wartime cooperation, he maintained a nationalist stance regarding rumors of a permanent US presence, insisting that Brazilian military leaders would never agree to such an arrangement.[57] With left, right, and center all championing, in their own way, the ultimate withdrawal of US troops, there was no viable path forward for a continued US basing presence, even under the terms of the 1944 agreement.

In March 1947, the US and Brazilian governments exchanged notes recognizing the formal withdrawal of all US troops from the Brazilian bases. The Brazilian foreign minister released his note to the Brazilian press to dissuade further rumors.[58] Anti-communist press coverage called this a victory, arguing, "the detractors of Pan-Americanism yesterday had an irrefutable reply to one of their most persistent calumnies—that of the imperialistic intentions of the United States, that they would remain at the military bases . . . located in our territory."[59] To the contrary, Communists perceived the transfer as a triumph of their campaigning. Communist leader Luiz Carlos Prestes sent a telegram to the foreign minister in which he stated, "The Brazilian Communist Party, which consequently fought against the extended stay of foreign troops in our land after the military collapse of Nazi-fascism, fulfills the patriotic duty of sending you at this moment warm congratulations and trusts in Your Excellency for a continued force in defense of the sovereignty and of the interests of Brazil against the improper intentions of the agents of North American monopolistic capital . . . and against the Truman plan of colonization in Brazil."[60]

CUBA

Efforts to negotiate extended base agreements in Cuba failed completely. There too the biggest constraints on US efforts were matters of domestic politics. The US government sought extended rights in San Antonio and San Julián, but Ramón Grau San Martín, who defeated Batista's preferred successor in the 1944 presidential election, had staked his legitimacy in part on restoring Cuban sovereignty.[61] As one editorial put it, Batista had negotiated the terms of US basing on Cuban soil in secret, "behind the backs of the people," and Grau's government, "the government of the Revolution, which carries the slogan 'Cuba for the Cubans,' could not permit that portions of national territory remain under the control of a foreign power even one minute more than necessary, no matter how friendly or fraternal it might be."[62] With Grau in office, the evacuation of US troops after the war was a political imperative.

US officials soon recognized the political difficulty that any Cuban administration would face in extending a lease to the US, no matter how agreeable the alliance had been during the war.[63] US ambassador Spruille Braden believed there was a solution akin to many wartime arrangements; he suggested that perhaps a formal agreement, which would be difficult to obtain, would not be necessary.[64] Citing the "principle versus practice" framework that had guided much of the US wartime strategy in Cuba, he asserted that the United States "shall probably be able to obtain, in practice, much of what we desire although it will be difficult, if not impossible to get this or any other government of Cuba to sign a treaty or other agreement granting these special privileges."[65] In other words, they did not need formal rights if they could count on getting what they needed in the event that they needed it. Army officials chimed in with their own opinion that the Cuban economy was sufficiently tied to the United States that they would not worry about their ability to gain Cuban cooperation in the event of an emergency.[66] Cognizant of the value of bases as a bargaining chip, Braden further noted that it was possible that the United States still might secure the basing privileges it sought in the event that "the Cuban Government, in its anxiety to obtain some special favor from us, will be willing to meet our desires on this and/or other matters in return."[67]

US officials revisited the matter on the eve of the Japanese surrender. Article VIII of the Military Agreement between the United States and Cuba indicated that the United States could occupy the San Antonio de los Baños base "during the present war and up to six months after the restoration of peace between the United States and all of the foreign powers at war."[68] Cuban authorities argued that "the restoration of peace" meant the Japanese surrender, while some US authorities seeking to hold on to Cuban bases in hopes of negotiating extended rights prior to evacuating insisted that "the restoration of peace" would only be official with the signing of a peace treaty, which could take years.[69] This semantic maneuvering permitted the US military to linger while trying to secure additional basing rights.

Some US officials insisted that the Batista Airfield was the best of its kind in the Caribbean, and it would be uniquely capable of accommodating the stationing of heavy bombers, which could only be done with a formal lease. Braden's successor Henry Norweb suggested a bit of horse trading was in order: basing requests "must be offset through the presentation of overwhelming counter-inducements."[70] He suggested that the State Department emphasize the financial benefits of maintaining an active base on the United States' dime. The United States would cover the estimated $600,000 annual price tag of keeping the base operational, and Norweb argued that in the postwar period, the base would pay Cuban wages in the amount of one to two million pesos per year and would provide the primary economic activity for surrounding towns. But these incentives were not sufficiently enticing to Grau when faced with immense domestic opposition, and he held the line.

May 20, 1946, marked the forty-fourth anniversary of Cuban independence and the end of the United States' first occupation of Cuba. On that symbolic date, the US flag was lowered on the Batista Airbase as the Star-Spangled Banner played. After a short speech by the head of the Cuban Army, the Cuban anthem began and the Cuban flag was raised, signaling the official transfer of the Batista Airbase from the US to the Cuban armed forces. The remaining US troops stationed at the base ceremoniously boarded aircraft awaiting them on the tarmac and departed the site, bound for Puerto Rico. Shortly after the transfer ceremony concluded, President Grau arrived at the base to commence official Cuban Independence Day festivities. These events were traditionally held in front of the Cuban Capitol building each year, but in 1946 they were celebrated instead at the newly Cuban airbase.

Onlookers employed different narratives to describe the symbolism of the base transfer, just as they had in Brazil. For some, the transfer demonstrated the endurance of the Good Neighbor era of inter-American cooperation between juridically equal, sovereign nations. One Cuban paper called the transfer "proof of how democratic nations fulfill their agreements in a plan of harmonious collaboration."[71] The leftist newspaper *Hoy*, by contrast, depicted the transfer as "the culmination of an energetic, just and patriotic campaign by the Cuban people in defense of their legitimate sovereignty."[72] In either case, for those residents of San Antonio de los Baños who lamented the corrosive impact of the military presence on the town's culture but welcomed the economic benefits, the soldiers' departure seemed to offer a new opportunity to enjoy the latter without the former.

PANAMA

The most extensive efforts to extend US basing rights and the most extreme anti-basing protests both occurred in Panama. There, the United States relinquished many defense sites early and voluntarily, with no fanfare, but they held on to fourteen of them while negotiating a new lease agreement with the Panamanian Foreign Ministry that they hoped would extend their hold on the sites over the long term.[73] Violent protests would finally compel the Panamanian National Assembly to unanimously reject the treaty that US and Panamanian diplomats concluded, and the United States withdrew in 1947. The US failure to extend the leases at the fourteen sites was a watershed in US-Panamanian relations that some view as a starting point for the popular movements that forced an agreement in 1977 to eliminate the Canal Zone and turn the canal over to Panamanian control by the end of the century.[74]

By the end of World War II, the strategic importance of the Panama Canal was on the decline as the United States transformed from a regional power with moderate military resources to a global power with immense military capacity. The Navy now possessed carriers that were too large to pass through the existing canal locks. The abandonment of the project to build a third set of locks midway through the war diminished the future utility of the canal. Further advances in weapons technology made during the war, in particular, the invention of the atomic bomb, made canal defense a more challenging objective than ever before.[75] But despite its declining value, the canal continued to be a key asset and, as the war drew to a close, the Joint Chiefs of Staff thought it necessary to maintain a network of airbases outside of the Canal Zone that could be used to spot and interdict any approaching hostile aircraft. Given that there was no Panamanian military at the time, there was no possibility of establishing postwar basing along lines that were reciprocal or cooperative, nor was it possible to decrease the visibility of the US military presence by relying on the collaboration of the local armed forces—both techniques that were applied to the deal struck with Brazil.

Though US and Panamanian diplomats would ultimately conclude a treaty, the path to an agreement was tense. The original base agreement indicated that US troops would withdraw from all defense sites within one year of signing the peace treaty that ended the war.[76] Panamanian Foreign Minister Ricardo Alfaro insisted that the Japanese surrender should count as that war-ending peace treaty, and he set a September 1, 1946, deadline for US evacuation of the leased sites. The vague phrasing of the lease agreement had been intentional in order to give the United States a delay between the war and the evacuation as protracted as five or six years.[77] Army officials were reluctant to pull out of the sites that they sought to keep in the postwar period, but Panamanian officials insisted they would not discuss new leases until the United States had withdrawn.[78]

In the course of negotiations for the new base agreement, at two opposite extremes were Foreign Minister Alfaro and the US commanding officer of the Caribbean Defense Command, Willis Crittenberger. Alfaro sought joint US-Panamanian control over the new sites, significantly increased rent payments, and a very limited lease term. Crittenberger advocated for a plan that would territorially expand the Rio Hato airbase, the United States' most important base outside of the canal, and a ninety-nine-year lease term. He also sought permission for US troops to move freely throughout the country and US control of Panamanian roads, telecommunications, and airways. Crittenberger remained convinced that Latin American nations' best means of contributing to hemisphere defense was in making territory available to the United States.[79]

At the United Nations General Assembly meeting in New York in November, Alfaro raised the issue of US base occupation. Reminiscent of the strategy of Canal Zone workers during the war, Alfaro proclaimed that the only weapon that Panama had in dealing with the United States was that of "protest before the world."[80] Egypt had denounced Britain's right to keep bases on Egyptian soil after the war, and strategists in Washington worried that Alfaro would do the same. The State Department and the War Department were divided on how to manage this. The State Department, more concerned with the political costs of basing terms that offended Panamanian nationalists, sought to temper the War Department's requests. They were willing to provide economic inducements to Panama, but thought that such matters should be handled separately, rather than framed as a naked quid pro quo.[81] This was still unacceptable to Foreign Minister Alfaro, who resigned in protest. Before his departure, Alfaro told President Jiménez that if he did not get the US to commit to economic assistance before signing the agreement, "he could whistle for it after." The State Department worried, rightfully, about giving the impression that they were taking Panamanians for fools.[82] The United States finally agreed to bring the terms of US requests more in line with the preferences of the Panamanian government, dropping the request for the lease on the Rio Hato base from a ninety-nine-year term to a ten-year term and reducing the leases of the other bases to five-year terms.[83]

The day after Alfaro's resignation, US Ambassador Frank Hines and new Panamanian Foreign Minister Francisco Filós signed the Filós-Hines Agreement. Panamanian President Jiménez sought to avoid popular rejection of the agreement by emphasizing that it "stipulated in clear and precise terms two principles: assurance of our national sovereignty and the temporary character of the agreement."[84] During the twelve days between the conclusion of the treaty and the vote on whether to approve it in the National Assembly, however, massive demonstrations broke out across the country.

The first protest began with just over 100 students from the National Institute, carrying posters denouncing US imperialism. As they processed from the Institute to the National Assembly, they were joined by hundreds more demonstrators. They arrived at a historic plaza in the old district of Panama City numbering in the thousands, and violence erupted there. The Panamanian National Police brutally repressed the gathering using clubs, guns, and tear gas. By one count, sixty protestors were wounded.[85] The following day, perturbed by news coverage of the repression, people across the country joined the fight against the Filós-Hines Treaty. The protests were no longer just anti-US but now also anti-Jiménez. Panamanian officials sought to delegitimize the protests by dismissing them as communist agitation, but the ever-growing volume of the protests made the claim ineffective. Demonstrations continued to develop across the country over the following days, incorporating new groups and cropping up in new cities. On December 15 there was a general walkout, and on December 16, 10,000 women marched on the National Assembly. On December 20 after protestors stabbed a US soldier in Colón, both terminal cities were declared off limits to US troops.

Years later, one of the student activists who participated in the protests, David Acosta, collected a series of interviews with individuals who participated in the anti-basing protests and published them in a book titled *The Decisive Influence of Public Opinion in the Rejection of the Filós-Hines Treaty*, alongside a number of other historical sources documenting the events of December 1947.[86] Across the wide-ranging explanations that the documents and interviews offered for people's decision to participate in the anti-basing movement, the legal, cultural, gendered, and racial conflicts that structured Panamanian encounters with US soldiers throughout the war years were salient. One columnist explained, "The contact we had with the gringos, their expressions of contempt for us, the humiliating way they treated us, the constant mockery they made of our laws, our customs, and our social and moral principles have created, little by little, a national consciousness."[87] Acosta himself recalled the catalyzing effect of the US prejudice he witnessed and experienced when he worked on the silver roll in the Canal Zone during his school vacations. "The impact of the racial discrimination imposed by the Americans against Panamanian, Latin and workers of other races was immense," he explained.[88] Communist student leader Cleto Sousa, who was fifteen years old at the time of the protests, framed the dichotomy between those who supported and opposed the treaty as "those who proposed to sell our dignity," on the one hand, and "those who defended the dignity of our mothers, sisters, and daughters," on the other, invoking both the gendered dimensions of patriarchal battles against the US presence and the grand bargain that the political economy of security cooperation seemed to represent to many on the ground.[89]

Of course, women also drove the protest movement forward, not as subjects of male protection but as key political protagonists. Renowned labor organizer Marta Matamoros recalled how, when the struggle over Filós-Hines began, "Women said, *Presente!*" Thousands of women of all ages, from neighborhoods across Panama City and its outskirts, joined together in a women's march. After descending on the Plaza de Francia, Matamoros and four of her *compañeras* gave speeches on the courthouse stairs, "so that the officials of the National Assembly would hear the protest and patriotic sentiment of Panamanian women."[90] Matamoros connected these protests to a broader global struggle against the racist paternalism embedded in international relations. The successful movement against Filós-Hines, she said, "was a lesson for Panamanians to continue the struggle until eliminating all traces of imperialist tutelage."[91]

As the protest unfurled, a committee within the National Assembly was convened to consider the agreement. That committee summoned not only the acting foreign minister but also the recently resigned foreign minister Ricardo Alfaro, former president Harmodio Arias, and representatives from civic organizations who were involved in the ongoing protests.[92] The commission's greatest objection was the ten-year renewable lease term of the Rio Hato airbase. They tried to convince officials to reduce the term in a bid to pass the treaty with some sign of concession from the United States that might turn popular opinion. But such minimal efforts were too little, too late. On the morning of December 22, the National Assembly voted unanimously, 51–0, to reject the base agreement. Accepting defeat, the United States evacuated the remaining defense sites within three months.[93]

Significantly, the interviews in David Acosta's book were mostly conducted in July 1977, just a few months prior to the signing of the Carter-Torrijos Treaties, through which the United States agreed to relinquish control of the Panama Canal and to leave the Canal Zone. Their memories of the protests against Filós-Hines and the meaning that they attributed to them were surely influenced by this longer history of Panamanian protests against the continued US territorial occupation of Panama. The 1947 protests, from the perspective of 1977, stood out as the crucial first step toward a more complete US evacuation of the isthmus. Those protests, they believed, put the Panamanian government on notice that popular opinion would henceforth constrain the Panamanian government's options in dealing with the United States. As Camilo Pérez, another student participant in the anti-basing movement, put it, the protests "demonstrated that in our country, power comes from the people, and that the government would not be able to go over the heads of the people again."[94]

By the late 1940s, US basing priorities and budgetary constraints had continued to shift in ways that diminished the importance of some of the bases that the Joint Chiefs had initially sought to retain in postwar Latin America. The continued US military presence in the few places where the United States managed to hang on to wartime defense sites, like those in Guatemala, continued to be deeply unpopular and to spark incidents that brought simmering tensions to a periodic boil. By the end of the decade, calculations in Washington had shifted. Those bases, like the occupations of the early twentieth century, no longer seemed to warrant the trouble that they created.[95] Even so, while bases were, one by one, formally transferred to Latin American governments through boisterous ceremonies, replete with speeches that upheld the timely base transfers as evidence that the Good Neighbor policy was alive and well, US military personnel were regularly left behind at former defense sites in plain clothes, often in a training capacity, leading one Latin American newspaper to decry base evacuation with the headline, "¡*Viva la farsa!*" (Long Live the Farce!)[96]

Meanwhile, in the multilateral realm, the Joint Chiefs of Staff advocated folding the United States' basing needs in Latin America into the plan for a postwar inter-American Military System. The Act of Chapultepec had called for an inter-American mutual security treaty, and the Joint Chiefs wanted to include access to bases in the Americas in the terms of that agreement. In January 1946, the Joint Chiefs presented suggestions for the kinds of arrangements they would like to see incorporated. They envisioned a "suitable, integrated over-all hemispheric system of air bases," whose scope and specifications would be determined by the future Inter-American Military Council, the permanent organ for military cooperation that the Mexican delegation had suggested at the Chapultepec Conference.[97] The reciprocal defense treaty would include an agreement that the military bases and facilities of all countries would be made available to all other signatory nations when military forces were acting in accordance with the treaty's provisions, and military transit privileges at all air and naval facilities would be provided on a reciprocal basis. Each American Republic would assume responsibility for developing and maintaining the desired defense sites.[98] This seemed like a plausible solution to the United States' infrastructure needs in Latin America, as it would give the United States a basing network without the political and economic costs of operating the bases—that is, access without occupation.

"SKELETONS WITH AN ARMOR OF IRON": THE RIO TREATY, THE OAS, AND POSTWAR DISILLUSIONMENT

Two years passed between the Chapultepec Conference and the meeting in Brazil where the Inter-American Treaty of Reciprocal Assistance, more commonly known as the Rio Treaty, was finalized. A conference in Bogotá followed six months later where the Organization of American States (OAS) was formally created. In the meantime, the gulf between the US government's primary focus on security and Latin American governments' primary focus on economic and social issues only widened, and enthusiasm for the postwar promise of inter-American cooperation waned. Commenting on the lopsided attention that US officials gave to military cooperation over economic and social concerns, Mexican Foreign Minister Jaime Torres Bodet commented that by investing in military defense but not social and economic matters, the Latin American republics would become "skeletons with an armor of iron."[99]

By the time the American Republics convened in August and September 1947, the United States was already growing disillusioned with the United Nations and was more eager to create a strong regional security alliance than the US delegation to Chapultepec had been, while Latin American delegations had lost enthusiasm for security cooperation. The Mexican delegation in 1945 had been a chief advocate for the creation of a permanent inter-American military organ, but by 1947 the country had turned away from the prospect and was outmatched only by Argentina in its efforts to water down the degree of power that such an organ would possess. Popular opposition to US military aid in Latin America had grown since the war, as people across the region expressed concern that the weapons given to Latin American militaries were being used to buttress anti-democratic agendas.[100] Latin American delegations continued to be more fixated on economic problems facing the region and hoped that the United States' renewed embrace of regionalism might yet allow the American Republics to create an inter-American system that would concern itself with such matters. To this end, they hoped to tie the security arrangement to be debated at the Rio conference to an economic plan. The US delegation, however, anticipating such bargaining techniques, successfully insisted that the Rio Conference only concern itself with questions of defense and that the American Republics defer deliberations over the economic troubles facing the continent to a subsequent conference to be held in Bogotá.[101]

The meeting concluded with the signing of the Rio Treaty, the United States' first regional security alliance, which was later upheld as a possible model for NATO. The treaty formalized the principle that the American Republics had embraced in the early days of World War II: that an attack on any one American state would be treated as an attack against all of them. It also formalized the protocol for consultation to be pursued in the event of an aggression, largely following the protocol used for the three meetings of foreign ministers that had convened in response to major crises during World War II. The treaty included no mention of the basing network that the Joint Chiefs of Staff had envisioned, nor did it create a permanent organ like the Inter-American Military Council discussed in Mexico City; those details were punted to the conference that would convene in Bogotá the following year.

Six months later, representatives of the American Republics gathered in the Colombian capital. Latin Americans' gamble that, if they signed the Rio Treaty in Brazil, economic aid would follow in Bogotá, proved a poor one.[102] Reminiscent of Ricardo Alfaro's words of caution to Enrique Jiménez that if he did not secure economic assistance before committing to US basing requests, he could "whistle for it later," Latin American delegations in

Bogotá found themselves with little leverage when the US delegation once more deferred concrete plans for economic assistance.

US military officials also left the conference in Bogotá unsatisfied. The now united US Defense Department wanted to address the matter of base access, but the State Department successfully resisted, insisting that the matter was too delicate politically and would distract from the primary goal of the conference, which was to formalize the Organization of American States.[103] Instead, the State Department suggested, as it had before, that basing should be considered on a bilateral basis, with less publicity. The project of creating an Inter-American Defense Council also fell flat. The compromise that the Argentine and Mexican delegations forced was to permit the toothless Inter-American Defense Board to continue to function in its existing form.

The Bogotá conference did accomplish the central task, however, of formalizing the Organization of American States. The OAS's organizational structure and charter reflected many of the features that Latin American delegates advocated for in trying to craft international organizations that counterbalanced rather than reinforced the international hierarchies created by military and economic inequality between nations. The OAS was designed to be more democratic than the United Nations: each state had one vote, and a two-thirds quorum was required for binding decisions.[104] The OAS Charter reflected those principles that had provided the underpinnings for wartime cooperation: it affirmed the juridical equality of all states regardless of military or economic power, it reiterated the principle of nonintervention, and it avowed that "the territory of the State is inviolable."[105] On paper, the OAS seemed to realize the promise of inter-American cooperation that Latin American politicians and activists had envisioned for decades.

But instead of euphoria, a period of disillusionment ensued. Latin Americans watched as the security logic that had once moved resources south from the United States instead pushed them east and west. The manner of thinking that had inspired development aid in Latin America during World War II—that an investment in the economic stability of a region was an investment in security because sites of poverty were breeding grounds for anti-liberal ideologies—lived on in the Marshall Plan to rebuild Europe and in Truman's Point IV Program, a technical assistance program for countries "resisting" communism.[106] As US officials eagerly confronted economic devastation and the social upheaval it engendered in order to ensure a favorable geopolitical balance of power in Asia and Europe, they considered the American Republics safe. In some targeted countries in Latin America where the goodwill security imperative still appeared vital, like Panama, development aid continued to flow through bilateral arrangements. But a Marshall Plan for Latin America never materialized. The institutions were there and the rhetoric remained, but none of it could facilitate the kinds of beneficial engagement with the United States that Latin Americans sought without the infusion of US resources. And the money followed the threats.

CODA: THE COLD WAR

On April 23, 1961, the US State Department invoked the Rio Treaty to solicit regional support against a purported new threat to hemispheric peace and security: the Cuban Revolution. A telegram to all US embassies in Latin America instructed embassy officials to inquire with the "highest authorities available" about the prospect of taking collective action against the Cuban government. "Dominance [of] Castro regime by Sino-Soviet bloc established beyond . . . reasonable doubt," the telegram proclaimed, "US now considers situation that of intrusion of extra-continental power into Hemisphere."[107] Given the inter-American system's central principle of non-intervention, the Rio Treaty was an improper tool for interfering in domestic politics in Cuba, but a case for collective action could be made for using it to fight international subversion. Aware that this was a difficult needle to thread, the State Department telegram noted that as US officials approached their counterparts in Latin America, "[the] distinction between 'intervention' in internal affairs of another State and defense against widening area of domination by extra-hemispheric powers is [a] vital one."[108]

Had Cuban officials been aware of the telegram, they might have found the irony laughable. After all, the Rio Treaty had been created to "prevent and repel acts of aggression against any of the countries of America" and, just six days earlier, nearly 1,300 paramilitaries trained and armed by the United States' CIA had disembarked on the Cuban shores of the Bay of Pigs intending to overthrow the Cuban government.[109] The invasion, modeled on a successful coup that the CIA had orchestrated against the democratically elected president of Guatemala seven years earlier, was just the latest in a string of unsuccessful initiatives to unseat the new Cuban government. If there were a grave threat to sovereignty in the Americas, it would seem to many in the region that the threat was seated in Washington.

In a manner reminiscent of World War II basing negotiations, in 1961 leaders across the ideological spectrum cautiously seized the opportunity presented by increased US security concerns in the region to renew requests for US support for Latin American development. Such assistance, they reasoned, would bolster US security objectives in two ways: it would help leaders in Latin America to combat communism by raising the standard of living of the region's poor, and it would enhance the United States' profile in the region, making it easier for Latin American leaders to greet US calls for solidarity affirmatively. The Colombian administration of Alberto Lleras Camargo was particularly savvy in making the point, insisting that if the United States wanted to strengthen the inter-American system, it could do so "by demonstrating [the OAS's] ability to deal with problems of underdevelopment as well as security."[110] Lleras Camargo proposed a plan of action by which an inter-American conference on economic and social problems would convene first, to establish firm commitments to Latin American development and mitigate the popular revulsion that the Bay of Pigs invasion had provoked across the hemisphere, before convening a meeting of consultation of the American foreign ministers to consider the Cuba question specifically.[111]

The Cuban Revolution reinvigorated the framework of US-Latin American security cooperation, which had remained active, if diminished, since the late 1940s. The Korean War and the apex of the Guatemalan Revolution in the early 1950s were both earlier flashpoints in which US officials revived military aid and discussions of economic assistance, and by the end of the 1950s, US officials became alarmed once more about the anti-US sentiment that seemed endemic in the region, but the Cuban Revolution brought Latin America back to the foreground of US national security planning in a more sustained and comprehensive manner.[112] Military and police training and weapons transfers resumed more intensely, reoriented now around counter-insurgency, and a resuscitated goodwill security imperative prompted John F. Kennedy to announce the "Alliance for Progress" in 1961. Building directly on a Brazilian proposal advanced two years earlier and sometimes dubbed a Marshall Plan for Latin America in the press, the United States declared a commitment to invest as much as $10 billion in Latin American development initiatives.

Cuban leaders, facing alienation in the inter-American system, called out the extent to which an international system shaped too dramatically by the United States' agenda and resources simply reified the hierarchy that Latin American architects of multilateralism had hoped to eliminate. On the eve of the vote that would oust Cuba from the OAS in January 1962, Cuban president Osvaldo Dorticós cautioned Latin American delegates that the OAS must tolerate a diversity of political and social systems in the Americas or else consider itself the United States' "Ministry of Colonies."[113] Indeed the most consequential difference between World War II and the Cold War was that the shift from hemisphere defense to counter-insurgency as the central objective of US–Latin American cooperation rendered many domestic political struggles targets of US–Latin American security cooperation, rather than casualties of it. The intertwined hierarchies of domestic and international politics in the Americas contorted in new ways as the Cold War infused cooperation with the Colossus with a new set of promises and perils.

Conclusion

In David Acosta's book documenting the anti-basing protests that led to the rejection of the Filós-Hines Treaty, he offers a timeline of US interventions in Latin America over the nineteenth and twentieth centuries. Beginning in 1832, the list goes on for four pages before arriving at the period under consideration in this book, which Acosta flags as the "Good Neighbor Parentheses," before resuming the list of interventions with an entry for 1948.[1] This list reflects a popular narrative of the history of US–Latin American relations in which intervention is a constant apart from this one curious period of time. This book has endeavored to remove the parentheses from the Good Neighbor era—not merely by demonstrating, as other scholars have, that the period itself was riddled with intervention after all (though it was) or that the United States simply innovated new tools for sustaining hegemony during this period (though it did), but by taking a wider-angle lens to the history of the region that views intervention as one feature of a broader, dynamic contest over US power and resources in the Americas.

Could there be cooperation without *entreguismo*? An affirmative answer to that question never appeared more plausible to popular nationalists in Latin America than during World War II. For decades prior to the war, diplomats and jurists in Latin America had pursued cooperation with the United States as an avenue for productively channeling US resources while restraining US power. By the 1930s, officials in Washington recognized cooperation with Latin American countries as the United States' best bet for protecting and advancing its interests in the region. When war appeared imminent, the US State Department doubled down on its recent

Cooperating with the Colossus. Rebecca Herman, Oxford University Press. © Oxford University Press 2022.
DOI: 10.1093/oso/9780197531860.003.0009

affirmations of non-intervention and sovereign equality as central principles of inter-American affairs. But when US strategists clamored for a network of defense installations across the Americas, the rhetoric and practice
of US–Latin American partnerships could not be so easily reconciled.

In the end, World War II cooperation accomplished a bit of each of the
things that its various architects intended: it constrained US power in
certain ways and advanced it in others. Latin American leaders leveraged
basing rights into unprecedented military and economic assistance while
circumscribing US power at defense sites by insisting on clear term limits
and declining to concede to US extraterritorial authority. But even as foreign policy makers in the United States and Latin America agreed upon
mutually beneficial plans of action under the broad rubric of hemisphere
defense, conflicts over governance at defense sites demonstrated that
trade-offs between cooperation and sovereignty would have to be made.

On the ground, the international prerogatives of hemisphere defense
collided with a number of social and political contests that were underway
before the bases opened and would continue after they were gone. Struggles
over labor rights at US bases were not only about the finer points of severance pay, but about the endurance of a broader vision of social rights tenuously obtained through mass political projects in the 1930s. Segregation
in the Canal Zone collided awkwardly with a broad reimagining of the relationship between race and citizenship within Latin American countries
and in international society. And battles over leisure practices, prostitution, and crime all intersected with contests to stake out the proper role of
women in family and social life.

Local residents engaged in those projects made the most of the wartime
circumstances. The language of the Good Neighbor and the Allied cause
proved powerful rhetoric—reframing racial equality or social welfare, for
instance, as projects essential to international peace and security. In other
cases, the foreign presence could make for a productive straw man, as when
defenders of conservative patriarchal values presented their own positions
in newly nationalist garb by contrasting their values with the degrading
libertinism of the foreign interloper.

But of course, US officials' primary concern was with the smooth and efficient advance of the US basing project rather than with any one side of the
various local contests in which US personnel found themselves enmeshed.
And when conflicts arose that obstructed that mission, US officials appealed
to their wartime partners for assistance in resolving them. Latin American
leaders, benefiting from wartime aid, strived to settle local conflicts in ways
amenable to US interests, without damaging their own popular legitimacy.
The successful execution of the wartime basing agenda relied, in many

instances, upon the elasticity of Latin American legal cultures, as when Brazil's Labor Ministry pressured labor court judges to interpret Brazilian labor law in a particular manner, or when Cuba's Foreign Ministry implored criminal and civil courts to dismiss charges against US personnel.[2] It also relied on a certain elasticity in US imperialism. US actors on the ground overseas improvised systems for regulating sex work, exerting extraterritorial authority and evading labor legislation that were contoured to fit the particular circumstances encountered in each location, and sometimes in defiance of official US policy. It was precisely the informality of local arrangements that made the whole endeavor work as well as it did.

As it turned out, a lot about the "new" way of doing things in the Americas was old. But differentiating the new from the old was a politically and socially consequential imperative. Put simply, the leaders of the Americas were so invested in the premise of sovereign equality that they had the good sense to undermine it quietly. US officials pursued US interests in ways that were palatable to Latin Americans when possible—and when not possible, they pursued them instead in ways that were discreet. Latin American leaders, for their part, worked to constrain US power when possible—and when not possible, they sought simply to obscure its intrusions.

And yet, there were limits. Even where leaders in the region were willing to extend US basing rights in return for aid in the postwar period, the political costs in the postwar era proved too great. Bolstered by the Allied victory and freed by the war's conclusion to resume criticism of US imperialism, the Left in Latin America mobilized against continued US basing endeavors. If it was plainly apparent that international politics could constrain the scope of the possible in domestic political contests around defense sites, the postwar fate of basing was a reminder that domestic politics could demarcate the scope of the possible in international relations as well.

The closure and transfer of the bases in the years following the war continued a trend toward the deterritorialization of US power in Latin America begun in the 1920s. By contrast, those aspects of US–Latin American security cooperation developed during World War II whose direct consequences on domestic politics were more difficult to discern (military and police training, weapons provisions, and economic aid), and aligned more fully with visions of nation-building, proved more enduring. These practices, as a foundation for US–Latin American alliances, became all the more important when US strategists relied on access to, rather than occupation of, military installations in the region.

The US basing network in Latin America never returned to its wartime size. Further advances in aviation technology, the political costs of territorial manifestations of US power, and the shift from hemispheric defense to counterinsurgency as the primary objective of US–Latin American security cooperation all diminished the likelihood that the United States would ever again seek such ubiquitous military infrastructure on Latin American soil. There were occasional moments during the Cold War when the United States sought new bases, and in those instances, basing negotiations were once again used to drive hard bargains.[3] But more often, the United States met the territorial demands of its power projection in the Western Hemisphere by relying on its unincorporated territories and the bases obtained during World War II in British colonies in the Caribbean, until decolonization in the British Caribbean changed the basing map once again.

Those two prewar exceptions—the naval base in Guantánamo Bay and the Panama Canal Zone—remained under US control in the decades following the war and only became more powerful targets of nationalist ire and symbols of US imperialism. In 1960, after the Cuban Revolution, the Cuban government stopped cashing the checks that the United States paid in rent for the Guantanamo base, and Cuba maintains to the present day that the United States' continued occupation of the base is illegal. When the United States opened its now infamous prison on the base in 2002, the Bush administration relied on the ambiguous legal status of the place to justify the lack of US constitutional protections afforded to prisoners held there. In Panama, the anti-basing protests that thwarted the Filós-Hines Treaty marked the beginning of a decades-long struggle against the continued US presence on the isthmus that culminated in the 1977 signing of the Carter-Torrijos Treaties that paved the way for the transfer of the canal to Panamanian control at the end of the century.[4] A portion of the former Canal Zone is now a public space, tellingly called the Parque Nacional Soberanía, Sovereignty National Park.

At the end of the twentieth century, the United States' continued "War on Drugs" and the loss of the military bases that the United States had operated inside the Canal Zone revived US interest in obtaining basing rights elsewhere in Latin America. During the late 1990s and early 2000s, the United States sought bases in Colombia, Bolivia, Ecuador, and Brazil. But US basing remained problematic, all the more so with the "pink tide" that swept the region in the early 2000s. Popular left-leaning leaders who rose to power during this period saw greater advantage in rejecting US overtures for bases than they did in leveraging them in requests for quid pro quo benefits.[5] The more typical modern-day US bases in Latin America are what one scholar calls "quasi bases" that operate informally. In Guatemala, Costa Rica, Honduras, and Colombia, the United States does not formally lease bases, but the US armed forces use and partially control parts of national bases through unofficial or secretive agreements with national governments, reminiscent of the World War II arrangements.[6]

Global basing was not an invention of World War II; overseas bases have been a key feature of imperial power for centuries. But prior to the war, overseas bases were not often located on territory that the basing nation professed to recognize as sovereign and equal. The problem of basing on the soil of purportedly sovereign peers is a distinctly modern one. While in some ways a peculiar element of international relations, bases tell a broader story about the persistence of hierarchy in an international order that, if composed of nations that are juridically equal before international law, are unequal when measured by just about every other metric.

When Ecuadorian president Rafael Correa declined to renew a US lease for a base in Ecuador in 2009, he quipped that the United States could keep its base in Manta just as soon as it permitted him to open an Ecuadorian base in Miami.[7] The comment recalled Ricardo Alfaro's lament in a conversation with Sumner Welles in the late 1930s: "Your cooperation is not at the expense of your sovereignty . . . and ours is."[8] A critical assessment of how cooperation has both facilitated and inhibited the operation of US power in Latin America over time and across space, how it has brought foreign interests to bear on domestic political projects, and how it has empowered those who engaged it on US terms and disempowered others, can help to explain things that are difficult to account for when narratives of US–Latin American relations are sorted primarily into stories of oppression from above or resistance from below. It can help to account for the endurance of US power in the region despite the centuries-old consensus in Latin America that US power must be guarded against. And it can help explain how cooperation, envisioned by some in Latin America as an avenue for collapsing international hierarchy, in practice helps to preserve it. In this broader story of US–Latin American relations, World War II is not an inconsequential blip, but a transformative crucible.

NOTES

INTRODUCTION

1. I use the words "sovereignty" and "bases" routinely over the course of this book and some definitions are in order. I find Stephen Krasner's typology of various kinds of sovereignty in the modern era to be useful. Stephen D. Krasner, *Sovereignty: Organized Hypocrisy* (Princeton, NJ: Princeton University Press, 1999), 3–4. In my own analysis, when I use the term "sovereignty" I am referring to Westphalian sovereignty, "political organization based on the exclusion of external actors from authority structures within a given territory." When the actors in this book invoke sovereignty, the meanings and stakes vary, but typically, they are also referring to a conception of Westphalian sovereignty— that is, the exclusion of US actors from the authority structures within their nations. As the following chapters demonstrate, however, the authority structures that defenders of sovereignty had in mind were not always political institutions; some of the most powerful conflicts conceived as fights over sovereignty played out in the social and cultural arena.

   As for the term "military base," over the last eighty years, the US military has developed an extensive typology to describe different kinds of military installations. This extensive vocabulary did not yet exist during World War II. I use the terms "bases" and "airfields" interchangeably in this book, as the historical actors of the period did, to describe the facilities that the US military built or enhanced for use by its military aircraft in hemisphere defense during World War II, and staffed with US military personnel. The number of personnel stationed at these bases differed sometimes quite dramatically from site to site. The more inclusive terms "defense sites" and "defense installations" include airfields as well as those sites where the US military built and operated equipment for use in hemisphere defense that were not necessarily large enough or intended to accommodate aircraft. This distinction is significant particularly for understanding the nature of US military infrastructure in Panama, where the US formally leased 134 "defense sites," but only a subset of them could reasonably be described as bases.

2. Important exceptions include Max Paul Friedman, who argues that World War II marked the end of the Good Neighbor era rather than its high point in *Nazis and Good Neighbors: The United States Campaign against the Germans of Latin America in World War II* (New York: Cambridge University Press, 2003), and military historians attentive to the World War II origins of the inter-American security system, e.g., John Childs, *Unequal Alliance: The Inter-American Military System,*

1938–1979 (Boulder, CO: Westview Press, 1980); and Servando Valdés Sánchez, *Cuba y Estados Unidos: relaciones militares, 1933–1958* (La Habana: Editora Política, 2005). Though not primarily concerned with the war itself, scholarship on Latin American innovations in multilateralism often signals the enduring importance of developments in the 1930s and 1940s. See, e.g., Greg Grandin, "The Liberal Traditions in the Americas: Rights, Sovereignty and the Origins of Liberal Multilateralism," *American Historical Review* 117, no. 1 (February 2012): 68–91, and "Your Americanism and Mine: Americanism and Anti-Americanism in the Americas," *American Historical Review* 111, no. 4 (October 2006): 1042–1066. David Green asserts a story of continuity between Good Neighbor politics and US support for right-wing dictators during the Cold War in *The Containment of Latin America: A History of the Myths and Realities of the Good Neighbor Policy* (Chicago: Quadrangle Books, 1971). Eric Zolov writes about the "afterlife" of the Good Neighbor in Mexico in the 1960s in *The Last Good Neighbor: Mexico in the Global Sixties* (Durham, NC: Duke University Press, 2020).

3. "Se anunció el retiro de agregados militares estadounidenses" *Portal del Sur*, April 30, 2014.

4. On this trend see Max Paul Friedman, "Retiring the Puppets: Bringing Latin American Back In: Recent Scholarship on United States–Latin American Relations," *Diplomatic History* 27, no. 5 (November 2003): 621–636. A flood of scholarship in this vein has come out since, but some salient examples include Tanya Harmer, "Brazil's Cold War in the Southern Cone, 1970–1975," *Cold War History* 12, no. 4 (2012): 659–681, and "Fractious Allies: Chile, the United States and the Cold War, 1973–76," *Diplomatic History* 37, no. 1 (2013): 109–143; Molly Avery, "Promoting a 'Pinochetazo': The Chilean Dictatorship's Foreign Policy in El Salvador during the Carter Years, 1977–81," *Journal of Latin American Studies* 52, no. 4 (November 2020): 759–784.

5. This is such a burgeoning trend it would be impossible to provide a comprehensive list, but what follows is a sampling of scholarship in various areas in which such work is happening. For examples of work on Latin American innovations in global economic governance, see Christy Thornton, *Revolution in Development: Mexico and the Governance of the Global Economy* (Oakland: University of California Press, 2021); and Margarita Fajardo, *The World that Latin America Created: The United Nations Economic Commission for Latin America in the Development Era* (Cambridge: Harvard University Press, 2022). For examples where collaboration was a formative dynamic in economic development in the Americas see Amy Offner, *Sorting Out the Mixed Economy: The Rise and Fall of Welfare and Developmental States in the Americas* (Princeton, NJ: Princeton University Press, 2019); and Tore Olsson, *Agrarian Crossings: Reformers and the Remaking of the US and Mexican Countryside* (Princeton, NJ: Princeton University Press, 2017). On regional security pacts, see Tom Long, "Historical Antecedents and Post–World War II Regionalism in the Americas," *World Politics* 72, no. 2 (April 2020): 214–253. On international law, see Juan Pablo Scarfi, *The Hidden History of International Law in the Americas* (New York: Oxford University Press, 2017); and Kathryn Sikkink, "Latin America's Protagonist Role in Human Rights: How the Region Shaped Human Rights Norms post WWII and What It Means for the Field Today," *Sur: International Journal on Human Rights* 12, no. 22 (December 2015): 207–219. On international labor organizing, Patricio Herrera González and Juan Carlos Yáñez Andrade, "Saberes compartidos entre América Latina y la Organización

Internacional del Trabajo: un recuento historiográfico contemporáneo," *Anos 90* 27 (2020): 1–14. On multilateralism and other attempted innovations in international order, see Grandin, "The Liberal Traditions in the Americas" and "Your Americanism and Mine"; Tom Long and Carsten-Andreas Schulz, "Republican Internationalism: The Nineteenth-Century Roots of Latin American Contributions to International Order," *Cambridge Review of International Affairs* (July 2021), DOI: 10.1080/09557571.2021.1944983; Carsten-Andreas Schulz, "Civilisation, Barbarism and the Making of Latin America's Place in 19th-Century International Society," *Millennium: Journal of International Studies* 42, no. 3 (2014): 837–859; Alan McPherson and Yannick Wehrli, eds., *Beyond Geopolitics: New Histories of Latin America at the League of Nations* (Albuquerque: University of New Mexico Press, 2015); Thornton, *Revolution in Development*; Corinne Pernet, "Shifting Position to the Global South: Latin America's Initiatives in the Early Years at the United Nations," in *Latin America, 1810–2010: Dreams and Legacies*, ed. Claude Auroi and Aline Helg (London: Imperial College Press, 2012), 83–100; Zolov, *The Last Good Neighbor*. Two edited volumes that feature cooperation as an important current in US–Latin American relations, including contemplations of several of the themes described above, are Juan Pablo Scarfi and Andrew Tillman, eds., *Cooperation and Hegemony in US–Latin American Relations: Revisiting the Western Hemisphere Idea* (New York: Palgrave Macmillan, 2016); and David Sheinin, ed., *Beyond the Ideal: Pan Americanism in Inter-American Affairs* (Westport, CT: Praeger, 2000).

6. See the influential volume *Close Encounters of Empire: Writing the Cultural History of US–Latin American Relations*, ed. Gilbert M. Joseph, Catherine LeGrand, and Ricardo D. Salvatore (Durham, NC: Duke University Press, 1998). This approach has not been confined to work on marginalized historical actors; Michel Gobat's book *Confronting the American Dream* offers a rich and nuanced perspective on Nicaraguan elites' engagement with US power on the ground; see Gobat, *Confronting the American Dream: Nicaragua under US Imperial Rule* (Durham, NC: Duke University Press, 2005). Patrick Iber demonstrates the ways that Latin American artists and intellectuals engaged foreign cultural diplomacy initiatives in an effort to advance their own visions of social democracy in *Neither Peace nor Freedom: The Cultural Cold War in Latin America* (Cambridge: Harvard University Press, 2015).

7. For examples see Frank Andre Guridy, *Forging Diaspora: Afro-Cubans and African Americans in a World of Empire and Jim Crow* (Chapel Hill: University of North Carolina Press, 2010); Katherine M. Marino, *Feminism for the Americas: The Making of an International Human Rights Movement* (Chapel Hill: University of North Carolina Press, 2019); Jocelyn Olcott, *International Women's Year: The Greatest Consciousness-Raising Event in History* (New York: Oxford University Press, 2017).

8. Fernando Coronil, "Foreword," in *Close Encounters of Empire: Writing the Cultural History of US–Latin American Relations*, ed. Gilbert M. Joseph, Catherine LeGrand, and Ricardo D. Salvatore, (Durham, NC: Duke University Press, 1998), xi. The scholarship on US basing tends to be divided along similar lines, focusing either on the network or "empire" of bases, or on bottom-up histories of specific base sites. For examples of the former approach, see Robert E. Harkavy, *Bases Abroad: The Global Foreign Military Presence* (New York: Oxford University Press, 1989); David Vine, *Base Nation: How US Military Bases Abroad Harm America and the World* (New York: Metropolitan Books, 2015); Alexander

Cooley, *Base Politics: Democratic Change and the US Military Overseas* (Ithaca, NY: Cornell University Press, 2008); James R. Blaker, *United States Overseas Basing: An Anatomy of the Dilemma* (New York: Praeger, 1990); Chalmers Johnson, *Dismantling Empire: America's Last Best Hope* (New York: Metropolitan Books, 2010); C. T. Sandars, *America's Overseas Garrisons: The Leasehold Empire* (New York: Oxford University Press, 2000); Anni P. Baker, *American Soldiers Overseas: The Global Military Presence* (Westport, CT: Praeger, 2004). Examples of the latter approach include David Vine, *Island of Shame: The Secret History of the US Military Base on Diego Garcia* (Princeton, NJ: Princeton University Press, 1999); Harvey R. Neptune, *Caliban and the Yankees: Trinidad and the United States Occupation* (Chapel Hill: University of North Carolina Press, 2007); Masamichi S. Inoue, *Okinawa and the US Military: Identity Making in the Age of Globalization* (New York: Columbia University Press, 2007); Katherine T. McCaffrey, *Military Power and Popular Protest: The US Navy in Vieques, Puerto Rico* (New Brunswick, NJ: Rutgers University Press, 2002); Jana Lipman, *Guantánamo: A Working Class History between Empire and Revolution* (Oakland: University of California Press, 2009); Catherine Lutz, ed., *The Bases of Empire: The Global Struggle against US Military Posts* (New York: New York University Press, 2009).

CHAPTER 1

1. On Cubans' engagement with ideas about race and fitness for self-rule, see Ada Ferrer, "Cuba 1898: Rethinking Race, Nation and Empire," *Radical History Review*, no. 73 (January 1999): 22–46. On the US framing of occupation as benevolent tutelage, see Louis A. Pérez Jr., "Incurring a Debt of Gratitude: 1898 and the Moral Sources United States Hegemony in Cuba," *American Historical Review* 104, no. 2 (April 1999): 356–398, and *The War of 1898: The United States and Cuba in History and Historiography* (Chapel Hill: University of North Carolina Press, 1999).
2. Treaty Between the United States and the Republic of Cuba Embodying the Provisions Defining Their Future Relations as Contained in the Act of Congress Approved March 2, 1901, signed May 22, 1903. General Records of the United States Government, 1778–2006, RG 11, National Archives.
3. "Agreement Between the United States and Cuba for the Lease of Lands for Coaling and Naval Stations," February 23, 1903.
4. República de Cuba, *Constitución política de 1940*, July 1, 1940.
5. "Convention on the Rights and Duties of States," signed at the Seventh International Conference of American States in Montevideo, Uruguay, December 26, 1933.
6. Laurence Duggan to Sumner Welles, September 17, 1940, Box 1, Classified General Records of the United States Embassy in Havana, 1940–1961, Record Group 84: Records of the Foreign Service Posts of the Department of State (hereafter RG 84), US National Archives and Records Administration, College Park, MD (hereafter NARA).
7. Catherine Lutz, "Introduction: Bases, Empire and Global Response," in *The Bases of Empire: The Global Struggle against US Military Outposts*, ed. Catherine Lutz (London: Pluto Press, 2009), 10. Though the exact number of overseas bases today is unknown, and one's definition of what counts as a base moves the needle, 800 is a recently cited estimate. See David Vine, *Base Nation: How US Military Bases Abroad Harm America and the World* (New York: Metropolitan Books, 2015), 3. Overseas bases were not the mere product of US imperial

expansion, they had also been an essential infrastructure facilitating that expansion. The United States' first "international" bases were those outposts located in territories home to Native nations in what would become the US West. On this longer history, see Brooke L. Blower, "Nation of Outposts: Forts, Factories, Bases and the Making of American Power," *Diplomatic History* 41, no. 3 (June 2017): 439–459.

8. Convention for the Construction of a Ship Canal (Hay–Bunau-Varilla Treaty), November 18, 1903, Article III. Katherine A. Zien describes this as "subjunctive sovereignty" in *Sovereign Acts: Performing Race, Space and Belonging in Panama and the Canal Zone* (New Brunswick, NJ: Rutgers University Press, 2017)

9. Theodore Roosevelt to Cecil Arthur Spring-Rice, British Foreign Office, January 18, 1904. Theodore Roosevelt Papers Library of Congress Manuscript Division. Theodore Roosevelt Digital Library Dickinson State University.

10. Alfred Thayer Mahan, *The Interest of America in Sea Power, Present and Future* (Boston: Little, Brown and Company, 1897).

11. The US relinquished the lease at Bahía Honda in 1912.

12. Theodore Roosevelt, Annual Message to Congress, December 6, 1904.

13. These interventions did not result in the establishment of formal military bases, but the strategic advantage of having a military presence in Haiti, the Dominican Republic, and Nicaragua during World War I added a further layer of justification to the prolonged US occupations of those countries for the war's duration. Alan L. McPherson, "World War I and US Empire in the Americas," in *Empires in World War I: Shifting Frontiers and Imperial Dynamics in a Global Conflict*, ed. Andrew Tait Jarboe and Richard Standish Fogerty (New York: I. B. Tauris, 2014).

14. Carlos Gustavo Poggio Teixeira argues that when speaking of international relations, it would be more productive to talk about South and North American regional subsystems, rather than a singular "Latin America," in *Brazil, the United States and the South American Subsystem: Regional Politics and the Absent Empire* (Lanham, MD: Lexington Books, 2012).

15. Michel Gobat, "The Invention of Latin America: A Transnational History of Anti-Imperialism, Democracy and Race," *American Historical Review* 118, no. 5 (December 2013): 1345–1375.

16. Carlos Calvo, *Derecho internacional teórico y práctico de Europa y América* (Paris: D'Amyot, 1868).

17. For a nuts-and-bolts overview of the inter-American system see G. Pope Atkins, *Encyclopedia of the Inter-American System* (Westport, CT: Greenwood Press, 1997). On Latin American challenges to US overreach at these conferences, see Max Paul Friedman and Tom Long, "Soft Balancing in the Americas: Latin American Opposition to US Intervention, 1898–1936," *International Security* 40, no. 1 (Summer 2015): 120–156; and Leandro Morgenfeld, *Vecinos en conflicto: Argentina y Estados Unidos en las Conferencias Panamericanas, 1880–1955* (Buenos Aires: Ediciones Continente, 2011).

18. Stetson Conn and Byron Fairchild, *The Framework of Hemisphere Defense* (Washington, DC: Government Printing Office, 1960), 4–5.

19. Franklin D. Roosevelt, The Five Hundredth Press Conference, November 13, 1938, *The Public Papers and Addresses of Franklin D. Roosevelt, 1938 Volume*, 598–599.

20. While the initial desire for bases contemplated the requirements to deflect a foreign attack, the bases later proved useful for submarine patrols and they were vital for moving US resources to the Allies across the South Atlantic.

21. Stetson Conn, Rose C. Engelman, and Byron Fairchild, *Guarding the United States and Its Outposts* (Washington, DC: Office of the Chief of Military History, Department of the Army, 1964), 305.

22. Bonsal to Messersmith, July 11, 1941, Box 135, General Records of the United States Embassy in Havana, RG 84, NARA; Knox to Hull, April 6, 1942, Box 169, General Records of the United States Embassy in Havana, RG 84, NARA. To say that the United States could more easily advance its basing agenda in colonial territories is not to say that they were welcomed or proceeded unimpeded. Importantly, in the British Caribbean islands and in Puerto Rico, the United States' basing agenda faced significant local opposition, which was made more powerful by the social, political, and economic turmoil ongoing in each place in the years leading up to the war. This local resistance created similar dynamics to those in play in Latin American Republics, whereby US officials eager to keep the peace (in part because instability threatened US interests) attempted to accommodate some local demands or otherwise take steps to make their efforts mildly more palatable. In other words, the international dimension of the basing story in the American Republics was quite different, but the local stories were often markedly similar. On basing in Puerto Rico during World War II, see Gerardo Piñero Cádiz, *Puerto Rico: El Gibraltar del Caribe: Intereses estratégicos estadounidenses y la base aeronaval Roosevelt Roads* (San Juan: Editorial Isla Negra, 2008); Jorge Nieves Rivera, "De Puerto Rico a Puerto Guerra; Las alteraciones al paisaje puertorriqueño con fines militares entre el 1939–1945," *Diálogos* 22, no. 1 (June 2021): 134–155; Jorge Rodríguez Beruff, *Strategy as Politics: Puerto Rico on the Eve of the Second World War* (San Juan: Editorial Universidad de Puerto Rico, 2007), ch. 8; Jorge Rodríguez Beruff and José L. Bolívar, eds, *Puerto Rico en la Segunda Guerra Mundial: Baluarte del Caribe* (San Juan: Ediciones Callejon Inc., 2012). On US bases in the Caribbean, see Steven High, *Base Colonies in the Western Hemisphere, 1940–1967* (New York: Palgrave Macmillan, 2009); Harvey Neptune, *Caliban and the Yankees: Trinidad and the United States Occupation* (Chapel Hill: University of North Carolina Press, 2007); and Conn, Engelman, and Fairchild, *Guarding the United States and Its Outposts*, chap. XIV.

23. Lieutenant Colonel Robert Olds, Air Corps, Memorandum for Special Inter-Department Committee, May 21, 1940, Subject: Airways Facilities Required by Military Aviation Beyond Continental Limits of the United States, 810.20 DEFENSE/9-1/2 Central Decimal Files (hereafter CDF) 1940–1944, Record Group 59: General Records of the Department of State (hereafter RG 59), NARA. Lieutenant Colonel Robert Olds, Draft of "Report of Sub-Committee on Caribbean Airways," May 23, 1940, 810.20 DEFENSE/10-1/2, CDF 1940–1944, RG 59, NARA.

24. Memorandum: Meeting to Discuss Air Navigation Facilities in the Western Hemisphere between representatives of the War Department, Civil Aeronautics Authority, State Department, and Pan American Airways, May 27, 1940, 810.20 DEFENSE/12-1/2, CDF 1940–1944, RG 59, NARA.

25. Conn and Fairchild, *The Framework of Hemisphere Defense*, 6. On the German threat in Latin America, see Max Paul Friedman, *Nazis and Good Neighbors: The United States Campaign against the Germans of Latin America in World War II* (New York: Cambridge University Press, 2003); David G. Haglund, *Latin America and the Transformation of US Strategic Thought, 1936–1940* (Albuquerque: University of Mexico Press, 1984), chap. 9; Stanley Hilton,

Suástica sobre o Brasil: a história da espionagem alemã no Brasil, 1939–1944 (Rio de Janeiro: Civilização Brasileira, 1977); Leslie B. Rout Jr. and John F. Bratzel, *The Shadow War: German Espionage and United States Counterespionage in Latin America during World War II* (Fredrick, MD: University Publications of America, 1986).

26. During World War I, the United States had wanted a united American front against the Central Powers, but only eight Latin American states declared war and most of the region's largest nations (Argentina, Mexico, Chile, Colombia) remained neutral.

27. Under Secretary of State Sumner Welles to Secretary of War Henry L. Stimson, October 24, 1940, 810.20 DEFENSE/323-1/2, CDF 1940–1944, RG 59, NARA; Julius H. Amberg, Special Assistant to the Secretary of War to Hugh Fulton, Chief Counsel, Truman Committee, August 13, 1943, 810.79611 PAN AMERICAN AIRWAYS/3429, CDF 1940-1944, RG 59, NARA.

28. Roosevelt, The Five Hundredth Press Conference, November 13, 1938, *The Public Papers and Addresses of Franklin D. Roosevelt, 1938 Volume*, 598–599.

29. Resolution XV, "Declaration of Panama" of the "Final Act of the Meeting of the Foreign Ministers of the American Republics for Consultation under the Inter-American Agreements of Buenos Aires and Lima," concluded October 3, 1939.

30. Resolution XV, "Reciprocal Assistance and Cooperation for the Defense of the Nations of the Americas," states that "any attempt on the part of a non-American State against the integrity or inviolability of the territory, the sovereignty or the political independence of an American state shall be considered as an act of aggression against the States which sign this declaration." "Final Act of the Second Meeting of Ministers of Foreign Affairs of the American Republics," signed July 30, 1940.

31. Juan Pablo Scarfi, "In the Name of the Americas: The Pan-American Redefinition of the Monroe Doctrine and the Emerging Language of American International Law in the Western Hemisphere, 1898–1933," *Diplomatic History* 40, no. 2 (2016): 189–218.

32. Suggestions for Political-Economic Warfare to Prevent Nazification of Latin America, Vincenzo Petrullo, June 4, 1941. NAR, RG 4, Series O, Subseries 1, Box 1, Folder 2, Rockefeller Archive Center, Tarrytown, NY (hereafter RAC).

33. Franklin D. Roosevelt, Executive Order 8840, July 30, 1941.

34. See Gisela Cramer and Ursula Prutsch, eds, *¡Américas Unidas!: Nelson A. Rockefeller's Office of Inter-American Affairs, 1940–1946* (Madrid: Iberoamericana Vervuert, 2012); and Darlene J. Sadlier, *Americans All!: Good Neighbor Cultural Diplomacy in World War II* (Austin: University of Texas Press, 2013).

35. These programs were carried out following a cooperative model borrowed from the Rockefeller Foundation, through which a binational committee called a *"servicio"* or *"serviço"* initiated the work and, over time, the amount of US involvement and funding would diminish, while local funding and control increased, until the *servicio* ultimately became embedded in a government agency. United States Office of Inter-American Affairs, *History of the Office of the Coordinator of Inter-American Affairs* (Washington, DC: Government Printing Office, 1947).

36. Final Act of the Third Meeting of Ministers of Foreign Affairs of the American Republics, *The American Journal of International Law* 6, no. 2 (April 1942): 83.

37. Final Act of the Third Meeting of Ministers of Foreign Affairs of the American Republics, 61–95.

38. Atkins, *Encyclopedia of the Inter-American System*, 2.

39. Katherine M. Marino, *Feminism for the Americas: The Making of an International Human Rights Movement* (Chapel Hill: University of North Carolina Press, 2019). Notably, leading feminists from Panama and Cuba likened women's subordination to the subordination of Panama and Cuba on the international stage and the project of women's sovereignty to that of Latin American sovereignty. Marino describes the major military interventions of the early twentieth century as "feminist incubators," 9–10.

40. On these efforts, see Christy Thornton, *Revolution in Development: Mexico and the Governance of the Global Economy* (Oakland: University of California Press, 2021), chap. 2 and 3.

41. Lieutenant Colonel Robert Olds, Army Air Corps, Draft of "Report of Sub-Committee on Caribbean Airways," May 23, 1940, 810.20 DEFENSE/10-1/2, CDF 1940–1944, RG 59, NARA.

42. Meeting with Army, Navy, and Civil Aeronautics Authority to Discuss Airway Aids in Cuba and Haiti, May 15, 1940, 810.20 DEFENSE/8-1/2, CDF 1940–1944, RG 59, NARA.

43. Welles to Stimson, October 24, 1940.

44. Noel F. Busch, "Juan Trippe: Pan American Airway's Young Chief Helps Run a Branch of U.S. Defense," *Time*, October 20, 1941, 111. Pan American Airways was a salient example of what Emily Rosenberg described as a "chosen instrument" of the US government—private actors that carried out policies in the national interest overseas. Emily Rosenberg, *Spreading the American Dream: American Economic and Cultural Expansion, 1890–1945* (New York: Hill and Wang, 1982), 59.

45. The original contract was concluded November 2, 1940, with twelve subsequent supplemental contracts. See Pan American World Airways, Inc. Records (hereafter Pan Am Records), University of Miami Special Collections (hereafter UM). Jenifer Van Vleck discusses the extent to which the Airport Development Program contributed to the expansion of Pan Am's commercial air routes as well as inter-American integration in *Empire of the Air: Aviation and the American Ascendency* (Cambridge, MA: Harvard University Press, 2013). Other work on the Airport Development Program has appeared in aviation histories such as R. E. G. Davies, *Airlines of Latin America since 1919* (Washington, DC: Smithsonian Institution Press, 1984); Robert Daley, *An American Saga: Juan Trippe and His Pan Am Empire* (New York: Random House, 1980); and Dan Hagedorn, *Conquistadores of the Sky: A History of Aviation in Latin America* (Washington, DC: Smithsonian National Air and Space Museum, 2008). A nuts-and-bolts account of the Airport Development Program is outlined in an unpublished master's thesis, Deborah Ray, "The Airport Development Program of World War II: Latin America and the Caribbean" (M.A. thesis, New York University, 1964).

46. War Department Army Service Forces, Office of the Chief of Engineers, Secret Synopsis of Airport Development Program, November 1, 1945, Box 2009, Entry 433: Correspondence and Reports Relating to the Central and South American Airport Development Program, Record Group 165: Records of the War Department General and Special Staffs (hereafter RG 165), NARA. In addition to

the twelve Latin American countries where the ADP operated, Pan Am also built ADP sites in Dutch Guiana, French Guiana, and Liberia.

47. Confidential Memorandum from Chief of Naval Operations Harold Rainsford Stark to Under Secretary of State Sumner Welles, May 18, 1940, Subject: Cooperation of American Republics in Hemisphere Defense, 810.20 Defense/7-1/2, CDF 1940–1944, RG 59, NARA. Under Secretary of State Sumner Welles to US Ambassador George Messersmith, May 29, 1940, 810.20 DEFENSE/ 13-1/2, CDF 1940–1944, RG 59, NARA.

48. Welles to Messersmith, May 29, 1940.

49. For a recent detailed study on US-Uruguayan relations during the Good Neighbor era, including the basing scandal, see Pedro M. Cameselle-Pesce, "Forgotten Neighbors: The Challenge of Uruguay–United States Relations during the Era of Franklin D. Roosevelt, 1929–1945" (PhD diss., Fordham University, 2016).

50. "Terminamos hoy el gran discurso del Senador Haedo," *El Debate*, September 23, 1940.

51. "Es necesario defender nuestra independencia integral: No debe cederse ni arrendarse ni un sólo palmo del territorio nacional," *La Tribuna Popular*, August 28, 1940.

52. "Es necesario defender nuestra independencia integral."

53. "La nación no quiere bases," *El Debate*, November 20, 1940.

54. "Discurso del Doctor Herrera," *El Debate*, November 22, 1940.

55. "Las dos mociones aprobadas por la cámara de senadores," *El Debate*, November 23, 1940; "Confidencial: Bases navais e aéreas no Uruguai," Oswaldo Furst, Brazilian chargé d'affaires in Uruguay to Brazilian Foreign Minister Oswaldo Aranha, November 27, 1940, Caixa 3, Estante 8, Prateleira 6, Archive of the Brazilian Foreign Ministry (Itamaraty), Brasília, Brazil (hereafter Itamaraty Brasília).

56. "El senado se pronunció ayer categóricamente sobre las bases militares," *La Tribuna Popular*, November 22, 1940.

57. "Una lección para los colombianos," *El Siglo*, November 23, 1940. Not insignificantly, I discovered a clipping of this news story in the archive of the Brazilian Foreign Ministry.

58. "Una lección para los colombianos."

59. Lester D. Langley, *America and the Americas: The United States in the Western Hemisphere* (Athens: University of Georgia Press, 1989), 152.

CHAPTER 2

1. "Nuestra cooperación con los Estados Unidos," *Acción Comunal*, June 11, 1941, emphasis original.

2. See Thomas L. Pearcy, "Panama's Generation of '31: Patriots, Praetorians, and a Decade of Discord," *Hispanic American Historical Review* 76, no. 4 (1996): 691–719; José Conte-Porras, *Panameños ilustres* (Panama City: Litho-Impresora Panamá, 1978), 204–215; Isidro A. Beluche Mora, *Acción Comunal: surgimiento y estructuración del nacionalismo panameño* (Panama City: Condor, 1981).

3. Quoted in Lester D. Langley, "Negotiating New Treaties with Panama: 1936," *Hispanic American Historical Review* 48, no. 2 (May 1968): 232.

4. Article X of 1936 Treaty and Conventions between the United States and the Republic of Panama (also known as the Hull-Alfaro Treaty) signed in March 1936, not ratified by the United States until July 1939.

5. Sitios de Defensa: Negociaciones de los Convenios de 1942, Vol. 1, Archivo del Ministerio de Relaciones Exteriores de Panamá, Panama City, Panama (hereafter MRE Panama).

6. On the complicated figure and legacy of Arnulfo Arias, see J. Conte Porras, *Arnulfo Arias Madrid* (Panamá: J. Conte Porras, 1980); and William Francis Robinson, "Panama for the Panamanians: The Populism of Arnulfo Arias Madrid," in *Populism in Latin America*, ed. Michael Conniff (Tuscaloosa: University of Alabama Press, 2012). On the rise of *panameñismo*, see Alberto McKay, "Las primeras crisis políticas," in *Historia general de Panamá, Vol III, Tomo II*, ed. Alfredo Castillero Calvo (Panamá: Comité Nacional del Centenario de la República, 2004).

7. Aide Memoire, January 7, 1941, Sitios de Defensa—Negociaciones de los Convenios de 1942, Vol. 1, MRE Panama.

8. Dawson to State, February 13, 1941, 711F.1914/182, *Foreign Relations of the United States*, 1941, The American Republics Vol. VII, 427.

9. Acta Confidencial de una Conversación Tenida por el Excelentísimo Señor Presidente de la Republica con el Embajador de los Estados Unidos de Panamá, Sr. William Dawson, el 7 de enero de 1941.

10. MID-R, "A Strategic Study of Panama," February 8, 1940, quoted in John Major, *Prize Possession: The United States Government and the Panama Canal 1903–1979* (New York: Cambridge University Press, 1993), 261.

11. Acta Confidencial de una Conversación Tenida por el Excelentísimo Señor Presidente de la República con el Embajador de los Estados Unidos de Panamá, Sr. William Dawson, el 7 de enero de 1941.

12. He later conceded to US jurisdiction over US military personnel, but not civilian. *Memorias que el Ministro de Relaciones Exteriores Presenta a la Asamblea Nacional en sus Sesiones Ordinarias* (Panamá: Ministerio de Relaciones Exteriores, 1943), 159–393; Memorandum of Conversation, by the Ambassador in Panama (Dawson), November 9, 1940, 711F.1914/156, *Foreign Relations of the United States*, 1940, The American Republics, Vol. V, 1076; Aire Memoire (*sic*) January 7, 1941, Sitios de Defensa—Negociaciones de los Convenios de 1942, Vol. 1, MRE Panama.

13. Foreign Minister Raul de Roux to Ambassador Dawson, December 3, 1940, Sitios de Defensa—Negociaciones de los Convenios de 1942, Vol. 1, MRE Panama.

14. Almon R. Wright, "Defense Sites Negotiations between the United States and Panama, 1936–1948," *Department of State Bulletin* 27, part 1 (1952): 214.

15. Aire Memoire (*sic*), January 7, 1941.

16. Memorandum of Conversation between President Arias and Ambassador Dawson, December 7, 1940, enclosed in Dawson to Hull, December 9, 1940, 819.51/1165, *Foreign Relations of the United States*, 1940, The American Republics, Vol. V, 1098–1099. Memorandum of Conversation, by the Under Secretary of State (Welles) January 31, 1941, 711F.1914/227, *Foreign Relations of the United States*, 1941, The American Republics Vol. VII, 422.

17. The Panamanian Ambassador (Brin) to President Roosevelt, February 18, 1941, 711F.1914/189, *Foreign Relations of the United States*, 1941, The American Republics Vol. VII, 430; *Memorias que el Ministro de Relaciones Exteriores Presenta a la Asamblea Nacional en sus Sesiones Ordinarias* 1943, 159–393. Memorandum of Conversation, by the Ambassador in Panama (Dawson), November 9, 1940, 1076; Memorandum of Conversation, by the Under Secretary of State (Welles), January 24, 1941, 711F.1914/228, *Foreign Relations of the United States*, 1941, The

American Republics Vol. VII, 420; Acta Confidencial de una Conversación Tenida por el Excelentísimo Señor Presidente de la República con el Embajador de los Estados Unidos de Panamá, Sr. William Dawson, el 7 de enero de 1941.

18. "Memorandum para el Excelentísimo Señor Presidente, Demandas Principales que el Gobierno de Panamá Vería con Especial Agrado que Acogiera Favorablemente el Gobierno de Estados Unidos," Sitios de Defensa—Negociaciones de los Convenios de 1942, Vol. 1, MRE Panama.

19. Hull to Dawson, February 8, 1941.711F.1914/179, *Foreign Relations of the United States*, 1941, The American Republics Vol. VII, 425. The Department of State to the Panamanian Embassy, Memorandum, 711F.1914/189, *Foreign Relations of the United States*, 1941, The American Republics Vol. VII, 446. Ambassador Carlos Brin to Foreign Minister de Roux, April 4, 1941, Sitios de Defensa—Negociaciones de los Convenios de 1942, Vol. 1, MRE Panama. Ambassador Carlos Brin to Foreign Minister de Roux, July 9, 1941, Sitios de Defensa—Negociaciones de los Convenios de 1942, Vol. 1, MRE Panama. Memorandum of Conversation, by the Under Secretary of State (Welles) January 31, 1941. Brin to De Roux, January 31, 1941, Sitios de Defensa—Negociaciones de los Convenios de 1942, Vol. 1, MRE Panama.

20. Welles to Roosevelt, June 19, 1941, 711F.1914/3011, *Foreign Relations of the United States*, 1941, The American Republics Vol. VII, 453.

21. The Ambassador in Panama (Dawson) to the Secretary of State, December 9, 1940, 711F.1914/161, *Foreign Relations of the United States*, 1940, The American Republics, Vol. V, 1083.

22. Arnulfo Arias a la Nación, Press Release, March 5, 1941, Sitios de Defensa—Negociaciones de los Convenios de 1942, Vol 1, MRE Panama.

23. *Memorias que el Ministro de Relaciones Exteriores Presenta a la Asamblea Nacional en sus Sesiones Ordinarias* 1943, 159–393. Memorandum of Conversation, by the Ambassador in Panama (Dawson), November 9, 1940, 1076.

24. Secretary of State to the Ambassador of Panama (William Dawson), December 28, 1940, 711F.1914/162: Telegram in *Foreign Relations of the United States*, 1940, The American Republics, Vol. V, 1085.

25. Dawson to Hull, December 30, 1940, 711F.1914/165, *Foreign Relations of the United States*, 1940, The American Republics, Vol. V, 1089.

26. "Nuestra cooperación con los Estados Unidos," *Acción Comunal*, June 11, 1941.

27. In May 1941, an Office of Naval Intelligence report had determined that "a local revolution to throw out the crooked pro-Axis officialdom would be preference to intervention by the US," Thomas L. Pearcy, *We Answer Only to God: Politics and the Military in Panama, 1903–1947* (Albuquerque: University of New Mexico Press, 1998), 93. On US complicity in the coup, see Orlando Pérez, "Panama: Nationalism and the Challenge to Canal Security," in *Latin America during World War II*, ed. John F. Bratzel and Thomas M. Leonard (Lanham, MD: Rowman & Littlefield, 2006).

28. Acta de la Sesión del Consejo de Gabinete Celebrada el 13 de Agosto e 1941, Sitios de Defensa—Negociaciones de los Convenios de 1942, Vol 1, MRE Panama.

29. The Ambassador in Panama (Wilson) to the Secretary of State, March 16, 1942, 711F.1914/435, *Foreign Relations of the United States*, 1942, The American Republics, Vol. VI, 598.

30. Presbítero Ceferino Arrue y Broce to President Ricardo de la Guardia, April 12, 1942, Expediente 282, Caja 91, Fondo Presidencial, Archivo Nacional de Panamá, Panama City (hereafter ANP); Presbítero Ceferino Arrue y Broce to

President Ricardo de la Guardia, April 20, 1942, Expediente 282, Caja 91, Fondo Presidencial, ANP.

31. Governor Guillermo Espino to President Ricardo de la Guardia, April 20, 1942, Fondo Presidencial, Expediente 282, Caja 91, ANP.

32. Secretary General Agustín to Minister of Foreign Relations Octavio Fábrega, September 23, 1942, Expediente 282, Caja 91, Fondo Presidencial, ANP. On the depopulation of the Canal Zone in the 1910s, see Marixa Lasso, *Erased: The Untold Story of the Panama Canal* (Cambridge, MA: Harvard University Press, 2019).

33. Pérez, "Panama: Nationalism and the Challenge to Canal Security."

34. This platform included land reform, free schooling, a housing program for the elderly, paid national holidays, credits for building homes, health insurance for working mothers, and a larger role for the state in the economy. On this earlier period in Batista's political career, see Frank Argote-Freyre, *Fulgencio Batista: From Revolutionary to Strongman* (New Brunswick, NJ: Rutgers University Press, 2006); Robert Whitney, *State and Revolution in Cuba: Mass Mobilization and Political Change, 1920–1940* (Chapel Hill: University of North Carolina Press, 2001); Gillian McGillivray, "Cuba: Depression, Imperialism, and Revolution, 1920–1940," in *The Great Depression in Latin America*, ed. Paulo Drinot and Alan Knight (Durham, NC: Duke University Press, 2014), 246–275.

35. Dr. Mario Lazo to Pan Am's Eastern Division Manager in Miami W. O. Snyder, December 28, 1940, Camagüey Chronology, Folder 5, Box 505, Accession I, Pan American World Airways Records (hereafter Pan Am Records), University of Miami Special Collections (hereafter UM).

36. On an ultimately fruitless plot led by Army Chief Colonel José Pedraza in 1941 and the importance of the US embassy's support for Batista in preventing it, see Louis A. Pérez Jr., *Army Politics in Cuba, 1898–1958* (Pittsburgh: University of Pittsburgh Press, 1976), 116–121.

37. "Exposición de Plan de Obras Relativo al Empréstito de Cincuenta Millones," October 19, 1940, Box 1, Fondo EEUU-Cuba, Archivo del Ministerio de Relaciones Exteriores de Cuba (hereafter MRE Cuba).

38. República de Cuba, *Constitución Política de 1940*, July 1, 1940.

39. Captain George L. Weyler, Commandant Guantanamo Naval Base to Willard L. Beaulac, Chargé d'Affaires ad interim US Embassy, Havana, October 7, 1940, Box 1, Classified General Records of the United States Embassy, Havana, 1940–1961, RG 84, NARA; SOD to Messersmith, October 23, 1940, Box 1, Classified General Records of the United States Embassy, Havana, 1940–1961, RG 84, NARA. Though the water supply was never sabotaged during World War II, Fidel Castro would cut off the supply after the Bay of Pigs invasion twenty years later.

40. Weyler to Beaulac, October 7, 1940.

41. Ambassador George S. Messersmith to Philip W. Bonsal, Assistant Chief, Division of American Republics, State Department, October 25, 1940; George Messersmith to Secretary of State Cordell Hull, October 25, 1940, Box 1, Classified General Records of the United States Embassy, Havana, 1940–1961, RG 84, NARA.

42. SOD to Ambassador George Messersmith, October 23, 1940, Box 1, Classified General Records of the United States Embassy, Havana, 1940–1961, RG 84, NARA.

43. Navy Department Memorandum, Subject: US Naval Reservations Guantanamo Bay, Cuba, August 13, 1940, Box 1, Classified General Records of the United States Embassy, Havana, 1940–1961, RG 84, NARA.

44. Ambassador George Messersmith to Undersecretary of State Sumner Welles, December 2, 1940, Box 1, Classified General Records of the United States Embassy, Havana, 1940–1961, RG 84, NARA.

45. Undersecretary of State Sumner Welles to Ambassador George Messersmith, November 4, 1940, Box 1, Classified General Records of the United States Embassy, Havana, 1940–1961, RG 84, NARA.

46. Messersmith to Bonsal, July 15, 1941, Box 135, General Records of the United States Embassy in Havana, RG 84, NARA.

47. José Manuel Cortina, *Ideales internacionales de Cuba* (La Habana: Imprenta del Siglo XX, 1926).

48. Cortina, *Ideales internacionales de Cuba*, 16.

49. Messersmith to Weyler, July 15, 1941, Box 135, General Records of the United States Embassy in Havana, RG 84, NARA.

50. Ambassador George Messersmith to Philip Bonsal, December 13, 1940, Box 1, Classified General Records of the United States Embassy, Havana, 1940–1961, RG 84, NARA.

51. Messersmith to Weyler, July 15, 1941. Messersmith to Briggs, August 14, 1941. Briggs to Secretary of State, November 12, 1941, Box 135, General Records of the United States Embassy in Havana, RG 84, NARA. Messersmith to Orme Wilson, Liaison Officer, Department of State, November 29, 1941, Box 135, General Records of the United States Embassy in Havana, RG 84, NARA.

52. Knox to Hull, April 6, 1942, Box 169, General Records of the United States Embassy in Havana, RG 84, NARA.

53. Welles to Messersmith, July 25, 1941, General Records of the United States Embassy in Havana, RG 84, NARA; Knox to State, July 25, 1941, General Records of the United States Embassy in Havana, RG 84, NARA; Welles to Knox, August 7, 1941.

54. Ellis O. Briggs to Walter M. Walmsley Jr., Assistant Chief, Division of the American Republics, State Department, September 16, 1941, Box 135, General Records of the United States Embassy in Havana, RG 84, NARA.

55. Messersmith to Weyler, July 15, 1941.

56. Messersmith to Briggs, August 14, 1941.

57. Messersmith to Weyler, July 15, 1941.

58. Messersmith to Wilson, November 29, 1941.

59. Welles to Briggs, April 24, 1942, Box 169, General Records of the United States Embassy in Havana, RG 84, NARA. Knox to Hull, April 6, 1942, Box 169, General Records of the United States Embassy in Havana, RG 84, NARA.

60. Mary Ellene Chenevey McCoy, "Guantanamo Bay: The United States Naval Base and Its Relationship with Cuba" (PhD diss., University of Akron, 1995), 123.

61. Mario Lazo to Pan American Airways Vice President Evan E. Young, December 13, 1940, Camagüey Chronological Record, Folder 5, Box 505, Accession I, Pan Am Records, UM.

62. Memo from Mario Lazo, December 13, 1940, Folder 5, Box 505, Accession I, Pan Am Records, UM.

63. Mario Lazo to Division Manager Snyder, Miami, December 28, 1940, Camagüey Chronological Record, Folder 5, Box 505, Accession I, Pan Am Records, UM.

64. Lazo to Snyder, February 24, 1941, Camagüey Chronological Record, Folder 5, Box 505, Accession I, Pan Am Records, UM.

65. Lazo to Young, December 13, 1940.

66. Messersmith to State, June 19, 1941, Box 131, General Records of the United States Embassy in Havana, RG 84, NARA.

67. Cortina to Braden, July 17, 1942, Box 168, General Records of the United States Embassy in Havana, RG 84, NARA.

68. Untitled, December 13, 1940, Camagüey Chronological Record, Folder 5, Box 505, Accession I, Pan Am Records, UM.

69. American Vice Consul Milton Patterson Thomson to Messersmith, January 27, 1942, 810.20 DEFENSE/2377, Central Decimal Files (hereafter CDF) 1940–1944, Record Group 59: General Records of the Department of State (hereafter RG 59), NARA. Further detachments arrived in Havana (at Rancho Boyeros) and La Fe at this time.

70. Evan Young to Eastern Division, December 18, 1940, Camagüey Chronological Record, Folder 5, Box 505, Accession I, Pan Am Records, UM.

71. Final Lend Lease Agreement with Cuba signed November 7, 1941. For further details of US-Cuban military collaboration before, during, and after the war, see Servando Valdés Sanchéz, *Cuba y Estados Unidos: relaciones militares, 1933–1958* (La Habana: Editora Política, 2005).

72. Messersmith to State, January 8, 1941, 837.51/2762, *Foreign Relations of the United States*, 1941, The American Republics Vol. VII, 131–132. Ultimately, the two governments agreed on a $25 million credit from the Export-Import Bank for public works and agricultural diversification projects; in addition to technical assistance, Cuba also negotiated more favorable terms under the Second Supplementary Reciprocal Trade Agreement (signed December 23, 1941) and the Export Import Bank offered another credit to finance additional sugar production in 1941.

73. On the "special relationship" see Joseph Smith, *Brazil and the United States: Convergence and Divergences* (Athens: University of Georgia Press, 2010); E. Bradford Burns, *The Unwritten Alliance: Rio-Branco and Brazilian American Relations* (New York: Columbia University Press, 1966).

74. For example, see Eduardo Prado, *A ilusão americana* (São Paulo, 1893); and Manuel Oliveira Lima, *Panamericanismo (Monroe, Bolivar, Roosevelt)* (Paris, 1907). For broader discussions of Brazilian intellectuals and policymakers' support for and opposition to Pan-Americanism, see Kátia Gerab Baggio, "A 'outra' América: a América Latina na visão dos intelectuais brasileiros das primeiras décadas republicanas" (PhD diss., Universidade de São Paulo, 1998); and Leslie Bethell, "Brazil and 'Latin America,'" *Journal of Latin American Studies* 42 (August 2010): 457–485.

75. Frank McCann, *Brazil and the United States during World War II and Its Aftermath: Negotiating Alliance and Balancing Giants* (New York: Palgrave Macmillan, 2018), 30.

76. On US-Brazilian relations and Brazilian foreign policy in World War II, see Vágner Camilo Alves, *O Brasil e a Segunda Guerra* (Rio de Janeiro: Editora PUC-Rio, 2002); Roberto Gambini, *O duplo jogo de Getúlio Vargas: influência americana e alemã no Estado Novo* (São Paulo: Edições Símbolo, 1977); Jessica Lynn Graham, *Shifting the Meaning of Democracy: Race, Politics, and Culture in the United States and Brazil* (Oakland: University of California Press, 2019); Frank McCann, *The Brazilian-American Alliance, 1937–1945* (Princeton, NJ: Princeton

University Press, 1973), and *Brazil and the United States during World War II*; Gerson Moura, *Autonomia na dependência: a política externa brasileira de 1935 a 1942* (Rio de Janeiro: Editora Nova Fronteira, 1980), and *Sucessos e ilusões: relações internacionais do Brasil durante e após da Segunda Guerra Mundial* (Rio de Janeiro: Fundação Getúlio Vargas, 1991); Ricardo Antônio Silva Seitenfus, *O Brasil de Getúlio Vargas e a formação dos blocos 1930–1942: o processo do envolvimento brasileiro na II Guerra Mundial* (São Paulo: Companhia Editora Nacional, 1985).

77. Joseph Smith, "Brazil: Benefits of Cooperation," in *Latin America during World War II*, ed. Thomas M. Leonard and John F. Bratzel (Lanham, MD: Rowman & Littlefield, 2006), 146.

78. McCann, *Brazil and the United States during World War II*, 22.

79. Army General Chief of Staff Góes Monteiro to President Getúlio Vargas, July 7, 1939, GV c1939.07.07 Microfilm Roll 6, Photo 0347 a0348, Centro de Pesquisa e Documentação, Fundação Getúlio Vargas, Rio de Janeiro, Brazil (hereafter CPDOC-FGV).

80. Upon returning to Brazil and discussing the path forward with Vargas and other members of the National Security Council, he informed General Marshall that Brazil would commit to the "preparation of bases in the N.E. of the country, in accordance with our conversations . . . to this end the Brazilian government needs to know with certainty to what point and under what conditions it can count on the US government to furnish the most urgent indispensible material, listed in the note I left in your possession." He insisted that the terms of weapons transfers must be no less advantageous than those that Brazil received from Germany. His insistence about the terms would prove problematic, as US manufacturers were unwilling to offer terms as good as those offered by Krupp, and the US government was legally unable to supply the weapons itself. Góes Monteiro to US Army Chief of Staff George Marshall, August 8, 1939, GV c 1939.08.08, Microfilm roll 6, Photo 0383a038, CPDOC-FGV.

81. Stetson Conn and Byron Fairchild, *The Framework of Hemisphere Defense* (Washington, DC: Government Printing Office, 1960), 282.

82. Brazilian Army officials indicated that they believed no leader could survive the blowback of allowing such an arrangement, which included sending 9,300 US troops, including an infantry regiment. Conn and Fairchild, *The Framework for Hemisphere Defense*, 287.

83. Minister of War Eurico Dutra to Getúlio Vargas, June 5, 1941, in *Marechal Eurico Gaspar Dutra: dever da verdade*, ed. Mauro Renault Leite and Novelli Junior, 418–424.

84. Getúlio Vargas, August 19, 1941, *Diário Vol 2, 1937–1942*, ed. Lede Saraiva Soares (Rio de Janeiro: Fundação Getúlio Vargas, 1995), 416.

85. My sincere thanks to Frank McCann for sharing notes from his 1965 interview with Cauby Araújo, the only documentation I was able to find about this meeting. McCann discusses this exchange in his book *Brazil and the United States during World War II*, 63. For additional scholarship on the ADP in Brazil, see Paul Clemans, "Unwilling Tools of Empire: Pan American Airways, Brazil and the Quest for Air Hegemony, 1929–1945" (PhD diss., Florida State University, 2019); and Theresa L. Kraus, "The Establishment of United States Army Air Corps Bases in Brazil, 1938–1945" (PhD diss., University of Maryland, 1986).

86. For a rich history of the region as a focal point of US-Brazilian relations during World War II due to the United States' strategic need for rubber, see Seth

Garfield, *The Search for the Amazon: Brazil, the United States, and the Nature of a Region* (Durham, NC: Duke University Press, 2013).

87. Decreto-Lei n. 3.462. *Diario Oficial*, July 25, 1941, 620.6 (20) Defesa da América Assuntos Gerais 8.3.2, Arquivo do Ministério de Relações Exteriores (Itamaraty), Brasília, Brazil (hereafter Itamaraty—Brasília).

88. Aranha to Vargas, November 9, 1942, 620.6 (20), Defesa da América Assuntos Gerais 8.3.2, Itamaraty—Brasília.

89. "Ficarão para o Brasil todas as instalações americanas do Nordeste," *O Globo*, November 11, 1943, 620.6 (20), Defesa da América Assuntos Gerais 8.3.2, Itamaraty—Brasília.

90. Minister of War Eurico Dutra to Foreign Minister Oswaldo Aranha, May 9, 1942, 620.6 (20), Defesa da America, Assuntos Gerais. 8.3.2, Itamaraty—Brasília.

91. Projeto de Convenção Militar entre o Brasil e os EE. UU., 620.6 (20), Defesa da América Assuntos Gerais 8.3.2., Itamaraty—Brasília; General Eurico G. Dutra e Brigadeiro General Lehman W. Miller, "Termo de Ajuste—Regula as atividades da Comissão Mista Brasileira-Americana de Oficiais de Estado Maior," July 24, 1941, 620.6 (20), Comissão Militar Mista Brasil—EUA 07.04.03, Itamaraty—Brasília. The same month that Vargas issued the decree agreeing to Panair's construction, Brazil and the United States agreed to establish a mixed US-Brazilian commission that would survey the military requirements of northeastern Brazil and determine what each nation would contribute to the defense of the region, but the agreement also asserted that bases in Brazil would be commanded by the Brazilian armed forces and the US forces would only be allowed to use them when invited by Brazil for reinforcement.

92. They arrived in Belém December 19, 1941, and Natal and Recife December 20.

93. The agreement wouldn't be signed until May 28, but the major tenets were established at this moment.

94. Confidential instructions issued to Brazilian press by Department of Press and Propaganda, prohibiting publication of news or comment on establishment of air bases, etc., by United States in Brazil or any other Latin American country. 832.918/22 CDF, 1940–1944, RG 59, NARA.

95. Vargas, *Diários Vol. 2*, 415.

96. For instance, "Ficarão para o Brasil todas as instalações americanas do Nordeste."

97. For first-person accounts of Brazilians who joined the FEB, see Rui Moreira Lima, *Senta a pua!* (Rio de Janeiro: Biblioteca do Exécito Editora, 1980); and João Falcão, *O Brasil e a Segunda Guerra Mundial: Testemunho e depoimento de um soldado convocado* (Brasília: Editora UnB, 1998).

98. McCann, *The Brazilian-American Alliance*, 269.

99. The original offer of $100 million increased when Brazil broke diplomatic ties with the Axis powers and increased once more after declaring war, rising to nearly $350 million. Smith, "Brazil," 150.

100. On rubber, see, among others, Seth Garfield, *In Search of the Amazon: Brazil, the United States, and the Nature of a Region* (Durham, NC: Duke University Press, 2013); and María Veronica Secreto, *Soldados de borracha: trabalhadores entre o sertão e a Amazônia no governo Vargas* (São Paulo: Editora Perseu Abramo, 2007). On Volta Redonda, see Oliver Dinius, *Brazil's Steel City: Developmentalism, Strategic Power, and Industrial Relations in Volta Redonda, 1941–1964* (Stanford, CA: Stanford University Press, 2010).

101. See Morris Llewellyn Cooke, *Brazil on the March, a Study in International Cooperation: Reflections on the Report of the American Technical Mission to Brazil* (New York: Whittlesey House, 1944).

102. André Campos, *Políticas internacionais de saúde na Era Vargas: o Serviço Especial de Saúde Pública, 1942–1960* (Rio de Janeiro: Editora Fiocruz, 2006).

103. Smith, "Brazil," 153.

104. McCann, *The Brazilian-American Alliance*, 108.

105. Lars Schoultz, *Beneath the United States: A History of US Policy toward Latin America* (Cambridge, MA: Harvard University Press, 310). Conn and Fairchild, *Framework for Hemisphere Defense*, 173.

106. On US police training in Latin America, see Martha Huggins, *Political Policing: The United States and Latin America* (Durham, NC: Duke University Press, 1998). On US overseas police training programs and their consequences in the US, see Stuart Schrader, *Badges without Borders: How Global Counterinsurgency Transformed American Policing* (Oakland: University of California Press, 2019).

107. On the deportation of Germans, see Max Paul Friedman, *Nazis and Good Neighbors: The United States Campaign against the Germans of Latin America in World War II* (New York: Cambridge University Press, 2003).

108. Marc Becker, *The FBI in Latin America: The Ecuador Files* (Durham, N C: Duke University Press, 2017); and Huggins, *Political Policing*.

109. On the longer history of cultural exchange in the Americas, including both government-sponsored and private initiatives, see Richard Cándida Smith, *Improvised Continent: Pan-Americanism and Cultural Exchange* (Philadelphia: University of Pennsylvania Press, 2017).

110. Gisela Cramer and Ursula Prutsch, eds, *¡Américas Unidas!: Nelson A. Rockefeller's Office of Inter-American Affairs, 1940–1946* (Madrid: Iberoamericana Vervuert, 2012); and Darlene J. Sadlier, *Americans All!: Good Neighbor Cultural Diplomacy in World War II* (Austin: University of Texas Press, 2013).

111. Though these networks were initiated and justified in the name of the war against fascism, in many places SIS agents began to focus their intelligence gathering more closely on other non-war-related threats to US interests in the region, particularly Communists and labor organizing, to an ever greater degree after the Nazi threat subsided in 1943. Marc Becker, *The FBI in Latin America*.

CHAPTER 3

1. Base Legal Officer H. Pandolfi-de-Rinaldis to Headquarters Commanding Officer, March 9, 1945, Box 339, General Records of the United States Embassy in Havana, Record Group 84: Records of the Foreign Service Posts of the United States (hereafter RG 84), National Archives College Park, College Park, MD (hereafter NARA).

2. "San Antonio de los Baños Según el Censo de 1943," *Boletín Oficial de la Cámara de Comercio e Industriales*, August 1945, Archivo del Museo de San Antonio de los Baños, San Antonio de los Baños, Cuba (hereafter MSAB).

3. "La Construcción de la Base Aérea," *Boletín Oficial de la Cámara de Comercio e Industriales de San Antonio de los Baños*, August 1942, MSAB.

4. "El Centro Escolar," *Boletín Oficial de la Cámara de Comercio e Industriales de San Antonio de los Baños*, November 1945; Florenciano Villareal, "Comentarios sobre la Cayuga," *Boletín Oficial de la Cámara de Comercio e Industriales de San Antonio de los Baños*, November 1942; "Seriedad y Sanidad," *Boletín Oficial de la Cámara de Comercio e Industriales de San Antonio de los Baños*, June 1943; "El Banco

'Garrigo,'" *Boletín Oficial de la Cámara de Comercio e Industriales de San Antonio de los Baños*, October 1943; "Comentarios," *La Tribuna: Periódico político y de interés general San Antonio de los Baños*, February 15, 1943, MSAB.

5. "Párrafos del director," *La Tribuna: Periódico Político y de Interés General San Antonio de los Baños*, October 23, 1942, and October 18, 1943, MSAB. "Incalificable abuso," *La Tribuna: Periódico político y de interés general San Antonio de los Baños*, September 18, 1942; "Parrafos del director," *La Tribuna*, October 23, 1942; "¡Esto de la Muerte!" *La Tribuna*, April 16, 1943; "Parrafos del director," *La Tribuna*, June 18, 1943; "¡Adios prosperidad!" *La Tribuna*, September 15, 1944, MSAB.

6. For an overview of the rise of labor legislation across Latin America, see Juan Manuel Palacio, "From Social Legislation to Labor Justice," in *Labor Justice across the Americas*, ed. Leon Fink and Juan Palacio (Champaign: University of Illinois Press, 2017).

7. "Camagüey Cuba," Camagüey Chronology, Folder 5, Box 505, Accession I, Pan American World Airways, Inc. Records (hereafter Pan Am Records), University of Miami Special Collections (hereafter UM).

8. Digest of letter from F. J. Gelhaus, Construction Engineer, Miami to Division Manager Snyder, Miami, January 22, 1941, Camagüey Chronology, Folder 5, Box 505, Accession I, Pan Am Records, UM.

9. Confidential memorandum from Law Firm Lazo y Cubas, "Labor Law Violations in Camagüey, Cuba," November 13, 1941, Folder 5, Box 505, Accession I, Pan Am Records, UM.

10. Memorandum from Mario Lazo, "ADP—Labor Law Violations at Camagüey, Cuba," November 1, 1941, Camagüey Chronology. Folder 5, Box 505, Accession I, Pan Am Records, UM.

11. Memorandum from Mario Lazo, "ADP—Labor Law Violations at Camagüey, Cuba," November 1, 1941, Camagüey Chronology, Folder 5, Box 505, Accession I, Pan Am Records, UM.

12. Memorandum from Mario Lazo, "ADP—Labor Law Violations at Camagüey, Cuba," November 1, 1941.

13. Confidential memorandum from Lazo y Cubas, "Labor Law Violations in Camagüey, Cuba," November 13, 1941.

14. Letter from Mario Lazo to VP Young, January 8, 1942, Folder 5, Box 505, Accession I, Pan Am Records, UM.

15. Memorandum to FBI Director J. Edgar Hoover, May 23, 1950, I.C. Memo #46-12745. Records released through author's FBI Freedom of Information Act Request #1471928-000.

16. Spruille Braden to the Secretary of State, June 25, 1942, Central Decimal Files 1940–1944 (hereafter CDF 1940-44), 810.20 DEFENSE/2898, Record Group 59: General Records of the Department of State (hereafter RG 59), NARA.

17. "Enérgico pronunciamiento hace la Central Sindical del Proletariado contra la actuación de ese organismo que ha levantado grandes protestas entre los obreros," *Hoy*, July 29, 1942. The fact that the war placed constraints on labor organizing was of course not unique to Cuba. For an examination of constraints on labor organizing in the United States during the war, see Nelson Lichtenstein, *Labor's War at Home: the CIO in World War II* (New York: Cambridge University Press, 1982).

18. "Piden los obreros se les emplee en obras de San A. de los Baños," *Hoy*, July 15, 1942.

19. Eduardo Torriente to the President of the Cayuga Construction Company, Memorandum, August 1, 1942, enclosure to Lazo to Briggs, August 6, 1942, Box 268, General Records of the United States Embassy in Havana, RG 84, NARA; "Presentarán los obreros de la Cayuga, convenio colectivo de trabajo," *Hoy*, July 22, 1942; handbill titled *Ahora o Nunca! Comienzan los trabajos de la Base Aérea*, Box 168, General Records of the United States Embassy in Havana, RG 84, NARA.

20. "Presentarán los obreros de la Cayuga, ," *Hoy*, July 22, 1942; handbill titled *Ahora o Nunca! Comienzan los Trabajos de la Base Aérea*.

21. "Convocan un mitin para denunciar los abusos de la Cayuga," *Hoy*, July 30, 1942.

22. "Jefes de la Cayuga vejen y maltratan a los trabajadores para demorar las obras," *Hoy*, August 27, 1942.

23. Comité Pro-Trabajadores de la Base Aérea San Antonio de los Baños handbill, July 27, 1942, enclosed in letter from Loustalot to Braden, July 31, 1942, Box 168, General Records of the United States Embassy in Havana, RG 84, NARA.

24. For example, Cayuga wanted permission from the Cuban Ministry of Labor to work its employees 310 hours per month without eligibility for overtime pay. The most the State Department was willing to request was 260 hours, and ultimately the Minister of Labor approved 240, with provisions for increasing that limit if necessary. Briggs to Braden, June 24, 1942, Box 168, General Records of the United States Embassy in Havana, RG 84, NARA.

25. Briggs to Braden, June 24, 1942.

26. Ellis Briggs, Memorandum: Progress of Work at San Antonio de los Baños Airport, September 11, 1942, Box 168, General Records of the United States Embassy in Havana, RG 84, NARA; Ackerson to Ambassador, May 5, 1943, Box 207, General Records of the United States Embassy in Havana, RG 84, NARA.

27. Braden to Messersmith, May 8, 1943, enclosure 3 to dispatch No. 3056 of May 11, 1943, from Embassy, Box 207, General Records of the United States Embassy in Havana, RG 84, NARA.

28. This resolution built on a law that the Cuban government passed that granted the executive branch the power to declare the uninterrupted operation of essential industries during wartime (Acuerdo-Ley no. 5 of 1942). Then, the Cuban Ministry of Defense passed Resolution 111, declaring that the construction projects undertaken as a result of military agreements between the US and Cuba were essential to national defense. Dr. Aristides Sosa de Quesada, Ministro de Defensa Nacional, Resolución No. 111, June 25, 1942, Box 168, General Records of the United States Embassy in Havana, RG 84, NARA.

29. Dr. José Suárez Rivas, Ministro de Trabajo, Resolución No. 583, enclosure to despatch no. 409, July 13, 1942, from Embassy, 810.20 DEFENSE/2981, CDF 1940–1944, RG 59, NARA. Office workers were hired on a monthly basis.

30. Article 66 of the Cuban Constitution of 1940.

31. Briggs to Braden, June 24, 1942.

32. Lazo to Briggs, July 11, 1942, enclosure to despatch no. 409, July 13, 1942, from Embassy, 810.20 DEFENSE/2981, CDF 1940–1944, RG 59, NARA.

33. Resolution No. 584 of the Ministry of Labor, enclosed in letter from Ellis O. Briggs to Secretary of State, July 14, 1942, Box 168, General Records of the United States Embassy in Havana, RG 84, NARA.

34. "Protesta del sindicato de la construcción por numerosos atropellos," *Hoy*, August 14, 1942.

35. "Celebran los obreros de la construcción un acto contra atropellos," *Hoy*, August 23, 1942.
36. "Envían una protesta al Presidente Batista contra la Cayuga Co.," *Hoy*, August 26, 1942.
37. Juan Arévalo to Laurence Duggan, September 25, 1942, Box 168, General Records of the United States Embassy in Havana, RG 84, NARA.
38. Mario Lazo to Ellis O. Briggs, December 29, 1942, Box 168, General Records of the United States Embassy in Havana, RG 84, NARA.
39. Lazo to Ackerson, July 28, 1943, Box 168, General Records of the United States Embassy in Havana, RG 84, NARA.
40. Lazo to John F. Sonnett, Assistant Attorney General, Department of Justice, August 14, 1947, Record Group 60: Department of Justice (hereafter RG 60), NARA.
41. "Visitó Suárez Rivas la Base Aérea de San Antonio de los Baños," *Hoy*, September 12, 1942.
42. "Visitó Suárez Rivas la Base Aérea de San Antonio de los Baños."
43. Lazo to Ackerson, July 28, 1943.
44. Lazo to Ackerson, July 28, 1943.
45. The embassy sent a memo to the Cuban Ministry of State stating, "As all persons employed at the airport, regardless of nationality, will be employees of the United States Government, they will of course not be subject to Cuban labor and social legislation." A few days later, the Cuban Minister of State replied in agreement on this point. US Embassy Havana Memorandum, December 1, 1942, enclosed in letter from Ackerson to Lazo, August 4, 1943, Box 207, General Records of the United States Embassy in Havana, RG 84, NARA. Cuban Ministry of State, Memorandum No. 1938, December 5, 1942, enclosed in letter from Ackerson to Lazo, August 4, 1943, Box 207, General Records of the United States Embassy in Havana, RG 84, NARA.
46. For a discussion of the changing landscape for labor on the Guantanamo Naval Base, see Jana Lipman, *Guantánamo: A Working Class History between Empire and Revolution* (Oakland: University of California Press, 2008).
47. Civilian Personnel Branch, Base Headquarters, Box 277, March 18, 1943, General Records of the United States Embassy in Havana, RG 84, NARA.
48. Lazo to Ackerson, April 20, 1945, Box 339, General Records of the United States Embassy in Havana, RG 84, NARA.
49. Lazo to Ackerson, August 12, 1943, Box 207, General Records of the United States Embassy in Havana, RG 84, NARA.
50. Memorandum to the Officer in Charge, October 5, 1945, Box 339, General Records of the United States Embassy in Havana, RG 84, NARA.
51. Memorandum to the Officer in Charge, October 5, 1945.
52. "Denuncia a los jefes de la Base de San Antonio," *Hoy*, September 21, 1945.
53. "La Base Aérea de San Antonio de los Baños," *Hoy*, September 26, 1945.
54. "Grave situación se ha creado a los obreros de la Base Aérea de S. Antonio de los Baños," *Hoy*, October 5, 1945; "Se agrava la situación de los trabajadores de la Base Aérea de San Antonio de los Baños por la intransigencia de autoridades yanquis," *Hoy*, October 6, 1945; Memorandum to the Officer in Charge, October 5, 1945.
55. "Movilízanse los obreros de la base naval de Caimanera para hacer cumplir las leyes," *Hoy*, October 16, 1945.

56. Assistant Attorney General John F. Sonnett, Memorandum for FBI Director J Edgar Hoover, February 20, 1947. Records released through author's FBI Freedom of Information Act Request #1471928-000.

57. James H. Wright to Willard Barber, September 26, 1945, Box 339, General Records of the United States Embassy in Havana, RG 84, NARA.

58. John McGohey, US Attorney for the Southern District of New York, Defendant's Memorandum in Support of Application for Dismissal of the Complaint; Lorenzo Vigil et al., Plaintiff v. Cayuga Construction Corporation, Defendant, delivered to State Department January 11, 1945, 837.5041/1-1145, CDF 1945–1949, RG 59, NARA.

59. Quoted in Mario Lazo, Memorandum Re: Vigil et al v. Cayuga Construction Corporation, March 28, 1945, Box 339, General Records of the United States Embassy in Havana, RG 84, NARA.

60. Spruille Braden had noted that a "scandalously large proportion" of the cost of construction was being paid in wages to American employees and that "much of the work done by the latter could have been as effectively accomplished by Cuban employees at much lower wage rates." Spruille Braden to Secretary of State, May 11, 1943, Airmail no. 3056, Box 207, General Records of the United States Embassy in Havana, RG 84, NARA.

61. Spruille Braden to Secretary of State, Subject: Rulings handed down in the Case of Vigil et al. vs. Cayuga Construction Corporation, April 5, 1945, Box 339, General Records of the United States Embassy in Havana, RG 84, NARA.

62. Wright to Barber, September 26, 1945.

63. McGohey, Defendant's Memorandum in Support of Application for Dismissal of the Complaint.

64. Mario Lazo, Memorandum, Undated, RG 59, 837.504 (missing exact decimal), Box 5587, RG 59, NARA.

65. Testimony of Milton Young, Box 277 Enclosure no. 145-158-1183, Class 145 Enclosures, Enclosures to Classified Subject Files, 1930–1987, Civil Division, RG 60, NARA.

66. Mario Lazo, Memorandum, December 1944, Box 278, Enclosure no. 145-158-1183, Class 145 Enclosures, Enclosures to Classified Subject Files, 1930–1987, Civil Division, RG 60, NARA.

67. Mario Lazo to State Department, January 11, 1945, 837.5041/1-1145, CDF 1945–1949, RG 59, NARA.

68. Sonnett to Yingling, May 3, 1946; William J. Bacon, Assistant Judge Advocate General, to John F. Sonnett, April 29, 1946; C. L. Hall, Division Engineer of the Army Corps of Engineers to Chief of Engineers, 837.5041/5-346, CDF 1945–1949, RG 59, NARA.

69. C. L. Hall, Division Engineer of the Army Corps of Engineers, to Chief of Engineers, enclosed in letter from Sonnett to Yingling, State Department Legal Adviser, May 3, 1946, 837.5041/5-346, CDF 1945–1949, RG 59, NARA.

70. The embassy was provided with a draft of the statement that the attorney general sought. It read: "Cuban workers of all classifications are not entitled to wages equal to, or based upon a comparison with, wages paid to non-Cuban workers brought from the United States of America to Cuba by contractors of the United States of America." Enclosure #485675 to letter from Sonnett to Yingling, May 16, 1946, 837.5041/5-1646, RG59, NARA. State Department Memorandum of Conversation re: Claims of Cuban Workers Against the Cayuga

Construction Corporation, Participants Briggs, Yingling, Walker, Sonnett, Hayden, Corben, Cox, Tribbe, May 15, 1946, 837.5041/5-1546, RG 59, NARA.

71. Telegram from Norweb to Secretary of State, May 17, 1946, 837.5041/5-1746, CDF 1945–1949, RG 59, NARA.

72. Woodward to Secretary of State, June 14, 1946, 837.5041/6-1446, CDF 1945–1949, RG 59, NARA.

73. For a rich analysis of the origins and the origin stories of the CLT, see French, *Drowning in Laws*.

74. Brodwyn Fischer, *A Poverty of Rights: Citizenship and Inequality in Twentieth-Century Brazil* (Stanford, CA: Stanford University Press, 2008), 116.

75. There is a rich and extensive historiography on Brazilian labor; for an overview of major trends see Paulo Fontes and Alexandre Fortes, "Brazilian Labour History: Recent Trends and Perspectives: An Introduction," *Moving the Social* 49 (2014): 5–10; and on the growing body of scholarship on labor justice specifically, see Ângela de Castro Gomes and Fernando Teixeira da Silva, eds., *A Justiça do trabalho e sua história: os direitos dos trabalhadores no Brasil* (Campinas: Editora Unicamp, 2013).

76. "Queixou-se da Panair," *Folha Vespertina*, July 2, 1942.

77. "Two-Year Jungle Battle to Build Strategic Airport," News Reference Files, Folder 10, Box 259, Accession I, Pan Am Records, UM.

78. Samples, newspaper "fillers" from Amapá, without identifying project by name or location. Undated. News Reference Files, Folder 10, Box 259, Accession I, Pan Am Records, UM.

79. Chronological Record of Building Amapá Airport, November 12 and November 26, 1942, p. 34, Folder 10, Box 259, Accession I, Pan Am Records, UM.

80. Mario de la Torre, Excerpt from Report, May 21, 1942, Chronological Record of Building Amapá Airport, p. 16, Folder 10, Box 259, Accession I, Pan Am Records, UM.

81. Nelson Lansdale, "Birth of a World Crossroads: An Informal Narrative History of the Development of the Natal, Brasil Land and Sea Bases," p. 1, Folder 10, Box 259, Series I, Pan Am Archives, UM.

82. Lansdale, "Birth of a World Crossroads," 6.

83. Lansdale, "Birth of a World Crossroads," 34.

84. When the United States entered the war in December 1941, no more than 40 percent of any one ADP site in Brazil was complete. Stetson Conn and Byron Fairchild, *The Framework of Hemisphere Defense* (Washington, DC: Center of Military History, US Army, 1989 [1947]), 254.

85. Lansdale, "Birth of a World Crossroads," 12.

86. Many labor complaints regarding work on the ADP project in Amapá were filed in Belém. Early cases were heard there, though later in the war, the JCJ in Belém determined that the county court of Macapá was the appropriate venue for such complaints.

87. Lei N. 62 de 5 de junho de 1935, Câmara dos Deputados, Centro de Documentação.

88. Processo 618/43: Albaniza Feirreira Cipriano v. Panair do Brasil filed November 22, 1943; Processo 503 e outras/43: Raymunda Silva dos Santos v. Panair do Brasil filed November 9, 1943; Processo 561 e outras/43: Maria de Lourdes do Espirito Santo v. Panair do Brasil, filed November 16, 1943; Processos 597-604/43: filed November 17, 1943; Processo 605 e outros/43: filed November 18, 1943; Processo 663 e outras, filed November 26, 1943; Processo 644 e outros

filed November 24, 1943; Processo 47/42: Luzia Costa Silva v Panair do Brasil filed January 21, 1942, Arquivo do Tribunal Regional do Trabalho—Região 8, Ananindeua, Pará, Brasil (hereafter TRT-8).

89. Twenty-seven of those cases never reached the stage of resolution due to either a withdrawal of complaint or a failure on the part of the worker to appear. In other instances, the outcome is unclear due to illegible or missing documentation.

90. This outcome was more likely when the complaint involved relatively minor sums, such as "prior notice" claims worth only four days' salary. In cases involving larger sums, the outcome of conciliation was frequently somewhat less than the claimant sought.

91. Edson Valença to Francis J. Crosson, July 4, 1945, Exhibit V-3 of Pan American Airways' Response to Ross and Condra Second Report, Folder 20, Box 61, Accession II, Pan Am Records, UM.

92. Robert Condra and J. N. Ross, "Investigation of Administration of ADP and USED Activities in South America," Folder 5, Box 53, Record Group 77: Records of the Office of the Chief of Engineers (hereafter RG 77), NARA.

93. Maurice Robinson to Executive Assistant, Memo: Termination—Labor Contracts under Brazilian Law, October 25, 1943, 1, Folder 9, Box 953, Accession II, Pan Am Records, UM.

94. Processo 47/43: Mauricio Vicente do Couto e outros v. Panair do Brasil, filed February 9, 1943, TRT-8. Lieutenant Colonel Robert M. Wold of the Office of the Inspector General, Special Inspection of the Administration of the Cost-Plus-a-Fixed-Fee Contracts at Cal de Caes Airport, Belém, Brazil, Entry 26E, Box 276, General January 1, 1943, Record Group 159: Office of the Inspector General (hereafter RG 159), NARA.

95. Valença to Crosson, July 4, 1945.

96. Valença to Crosson, July 4, 1945.

97. Robinson to Executive Assistant, Memo: Termination—Labor Contracts under Brazilian Law.

98. Lei N. 62 de 5 de junho de 1935, Câmara dos Deputados, Centro de Documentação.

99. Employees of such companies could only be dismissed "with just cause" upon the *completion* of the project for which they were hired. Since the ADP was in constant flux, with new contracts added and others abandoned and workers hired and fired without the larger ADP project coming to an end, there was plenty of room to dispute when dismissals could be carried out with just cause. In the event that a temporary employee was fired without just cause, they were entitled to damages in the amount of half the total that the worker would have been paid if he or she had stayed until the project was completed—the "end" of the ADP could be interpreted as the end of the war. In that light, most ADP lawyers determined that they were best off simply making the severance payments required of permanent organizations rather than risking claims that "temporary" workers were fired before the ADP's completion, which could prove more expensive. Valença to Crosson, July 4, 1945.

100. Artigo 443, *Consolidação das Leis do Trabalho*, Decreto-Lei No. 5,452, May 1, 1943.

101. Processo 47 e outros/43, Mauricio Vicente do Couto e outros v. Panair do Brasil, filed February 9, 1943, TRT-8.

102. Valença to Crosson, July 4, 1945.

103. Valença to. Crosson, July 4, 1945.

104. CRT Processo 87/43 Firmo Diaz (JCJ Processo 206/43) and Joaquim Marco da Costa (JCJ Processo 209/43) v. Panair do Brasil—ADP and previous, unidentified claim against Panair cited in court proceedings. Filed in JCJ July 7 and 9, 1943. Ruled in CRT September 29, 1943, TRT-8.

105. Ennio Lepage to Regional Labor Board, October 18, 1943, Processo CRT 107/43 (JCJ 319/43, 333/43, 334/43), TRT-8.

106. Jose Marques Soares, CRT Processo 87/43 Firmo Diaz e Joaquim Marco da Costa v Panair do Brasil (JCJ 206/43), TRT-8.

107. Lepage to Regional Labor Board, October 18, 1943.

108. Lepage to Regional Labor Board, October 18, 1943. Emphasis original.

109. Raymundo de Souza Moura, President of the JCJ, December 13, 1943, Processo CRT 107/43 (JCJ 319/43, 333/43, 334/43), TRT-8. Emphasis original.

110. On Brazilian labor history in the context of World War II, see the work of Alexandre Fortes, most recently, "Trabalho, raça e política: o olhar norte-americano sobre o Brasil no contexto da Segunda Guerra Mundial," in *Trabalho & Labor: histórias compartilhadas, Brasil e Estados Unidos, século XX*, ed. Alexandre Fortes and Fernando Teixeira da Silva (Salvador: Sagga, 2020), 135–162; and "A Segunda Guerra Mundial e a Sociedade Brasileira," in *A Era Vargas 1930–1945, Volume II* (Porto Alegre: EDIPUCRS, 2021), 146–175.

111. Valença to Crosson, July 4, 1945.

112. After a conference with embassy officials in Rio, from which Pan Am officials were excluded, District Engineer Colonel Haner issued a directive ordering Panair to cease payments in all three contentious areas of Brazilian social legislation—severance, draftee salaries, and pension funds.

113. Rihl to Pryor, January 11, 1944, Folder 3, Box 132, Accession II, Pan Am Records, UM.

114. Rihl to Pryor, January 11, 1944.

115. Robinson to Executive Assistant, Memo: Termination—Labor Contracts under Brazilian Law.

116. Xanthaky to Minister of Labor, Industry and Commerce Enclosure to Caffery to State, Subject: Resolving Labor Legislation Difficulties for the Airport Development Program, December 3, 1943, CDF 1940–1944, 832.7962/101, RG 59, NARA.

117. Xanthaky to Minister of Labor, Industry and Commerce, December 3, 1943, , NARA; Robinson to Executive Assistant, Memo: Termination—Labor Contracts under Brazilian Law, 1. University of Miami Special Collections, Pan American Airways Archive. Series 2, Box 953, Folder 9; Oscar Saraiva, Legal Advisor, Ministry of Labor, Industry and Commerce to Ambassador of the United States, November 26, 1943. Enclosure to Caffery to State, Subject: Resolving Labor Legislation Difficulties for the Airport Development Program, December 3, 1943 CDF 1940-44 832.7962/101; Major A. T. Goodwyn, Acting District Engineer, to The Division Engineer of the South Atlantic Division, May 16, 1944, Subject: Legal Problems in Brazil under the A.D.P. Contract. RG 77, Entry 1011 Security Classified Subject Files 1940-45, Box 80, Folder A.D.P. (Labor) NARA.

118. Rihl to Pryor, January 11, 1944.

119. Manoel Costa Vieira e outros, CNT11275/43, TRT-8.

120. Caffery to Secretary of State, May 5, 1944, 832.7962/110, RG 59, NARA.

121. Haner to Caffery, April 23, 1944, enclosure to Caffery to Secretary of State, May 5, 1944, 832.7962/110, RG 59, NARA.

122. Filinto Müller, August 3, 1944, Circular CNT-DJT-278/44, second enclosure to dispatch 17407 of August 21, 1944, from the Embassy at Rio de Janeiro, Folder A.D.P. (Labor), Box 80, Security Classified Subject Files 1940-45, RG 77, NARA; Richard P. Momsen to Mr. Theodore A. Xanthaky, American Embassy, August 4, 1944, 3rd Enclosure to Dispatch 17407 of August 21, 1944, from the Embassy at Rio de Janeiro, Folder A.D.P. (Labor), Box 80, Security Classified Subject Files 1940-45, RG 77, NARA.
123. Pan American Airways' Response to Ross and Condra Second Report, Folder 20, Box 61, Accession II, Pan Am Records, UM.
124. Valença to Crosson, July 4, 1945.
125. Valença to Crosson, July 4, 1945.
126. Unlike the situation in San Antonio de los Baños, Cuba, where the United States assumed administrative control of the base when Cayuga's construction was complete, in Brazil, Pan Am continued to be responsible for maintaining bases long after they had begun to be used by the US armed forces.
127. Carlos Aguirre and Ricardo D. Salvatore, "Introduction: Writing the History of Law, Crime and Punishment in Latin America," in *Crime and Punishment in Latin America: Law and Society since Late Colonial Times*, ed. Ricardo D. Salvatore, Carlos Aguirre, and Gilbert M. Joseph (Durham, NC: Duke University Press, 2001).

CHAPTER 4

1. "Agria pugna racial en el canal existe entre los trabajadores de distinto países," August 29, 1941, enclosure to The Panama Canal Periodical Reference Form, 2-P-59 (6), Box 419, Record Group 185: Records of the Panama Canal Zone (hereafter RG 185), National Archives College Park (hereafter NARA).
2. The trend of reimagining race and citizenship during this period was region-wide, but given the demographic diversity of Latin America, the particular place of blackness or indigeneity in these processes cannot be generalized for the entire region. For an introduction to the major themes in the literature on race and nationality in Latin America, see Nancy P. Appelbaum, Anne S. Macpherson, and Karin Alejandra Rosemblatt, "Introduction: Racial Nations," in *Race and Nation in Modern Latin America*, ed. Appelbaum, Macpherson, and Rosemblatt (Chapel Hill: University of North Carolina Press, 2003), 1–31.
3. Marixa Lasso argues that the presence of black West Indians in Panama even inadvertently helped to facilitate the integration of Afro-descended Panamanians who traced their roots in Panama to the colonial era, as the inclusion of so-called colonial black Panamanians in the mestizo category bolstered nationalist claims that West Indian exclusion was a cultural issue rather than a racial one. Marixa Lasso de Paulis, "Race and Ethnicity in the Formation of Panamanian National Identity: Panamanian Discrimination Against Chinese and West Indians in the Thirties," *Revista panameña de política* 4 (2007): 61–92. See also George Priestley, "Ethnicity, Class and the National Question in Panama," in *Emerging Perspectives on the Black Diaspora*, ed. Aubrey W. Bonnett and G. Llewellyn Watson (New York: University Press of America, 1990), 215–237, and "Afro-Antillanos o Afro-Panameños," in *Piel oscura Panamá: ensayos y reflexiones al filo del centenario*, ed. Alberto Barrow and George Priestley (Panama City: Editorial Universitaria de Panamá), 185–231.
4. On labor in the Canal Zone during the construction period see Michael Conniff, *Black Labor on a White Canal: Panama 1904–1981* (Pittsburgh: University of Pittsburgh Press, 1985); Joan Flores-Villalobos, "Colón Women: West

Indian Women in the Construction of the Panama Canal, 1904–1911" (PhD diss., New York University, 2018); Julie Greene, *The Canal Builders: Making America's Empire at the Panama Canal* (New York: Penguin Press, 2009), and "Spaniards on the Silver Roll: Labor Troubles and Liminality in the Panama Canal Zone, 1904–1914," *International Labor and Working-Class History* 66 (Fall 2004): 78–98; Gerardo Maloney, *El Canal de Panamá y los trabajadores antillanos* (Panamá: Universidad de Panamá, 1989); Yolanda Marco Serra, *Los obreros españoles en la construcción del Canal de Panama: La emigración españa la hacia Panamá vista desde a través de la prensa española* (Panamá: Portobelo, 1997); Luis Navas, *El movimiento obrero en Panamá, 1880–1914* (San José, Costa Rica: Universitaria Centroamericana, 1979); Velma Newton, *The Silver Men: West Indian Labour Migration to Panama, 1850–1914* (Kingston, Jamaica: Ian Randle, 2004); Reyes Rivas and Eyra Marcela, *El trabajo de las mujeres en la historia de la construcción del Canal de Panamá, 1881–1914* (Panamá: Universidad de Panamá, Instituto de la Mujer, 2000).

5. In practice, there were ample examples of silver and gold jobs that required performance of identical duties for different pay, such as "chauffeur" or "painter." In such instances, only a worker's race and/or nationality could explain the roll to which they were assigned, a point commonly raised to debunk the notion that the system was based solely on skill set. Gold workers made as much as six times the wages of silver workers doing the same work.

6. In the United States, the Good Neighbor policy weighed on debates over the "whiteness" of Mexicans and Mexican Americans. See, e.g., Mark Brilliant, *The Color of America Has Changed: How Racial Diversity Shaped Civil Rights Reform in California, 1941–1978* (New York: Oxford University Press, 2010), chap. 3; Thomas Guglielmo, "Fighting for Caucasian Rights: Mexicans, Mexican Americans, and the Transnational Struggle for Civil Rights in World War II Texas," *Journal of American History* 92 (March 2006): 1212–1237; Natalie Mendoza, "The Good Neighbor Comes Home: The State, Mexicans and Mexican Americans, and Regional Consciousness in the US Southwest during World War II" (PhD diss., UC Berkeley, 2016), chap. 2; Mark Overmyer-Velázquez, "Good Neighbors and White Mexicans: Constructing Race and Nation on the Mexico-US Border," *Journal of American Ethnic History* 33, no. 1 (2013): 5–24. In Latin America, nineteenth- and twentieth-century elites had long been preoccupied with their nations' whiteness. See, e.g., Diego Armus, "Eugenics in Buenos Aires: Discourses, Practices, and Historiography," *História, Ciências, Saúde-Manguinhos* 23, Suppl. 1 (2016): 149–170; Nancy Leys Stepan, *"The Hour of Eugenics": Race, Gender and Nation in Latin America* (Ithaca, NY: Cornell University Press, 1991).

7. The way that race shaped US relations with each American Republic at this juncture varied substantially. Jessica Lynn Graham offers a fascinating analysis of the role that myths of racial democracy played in the US-Brazilian wartime alliance, and the ways that each state managed images of race and democracy in wartime propaganda, in *Shifting the Meaning of Democracy: Race, Politics and Culture in the United States and Brazil.* (Oakland: University of California Press, 2019), chapters 5 and 6. On wartime cultural exchange between black Americans and black Panamanians, see Zien, *Sovereign Acts*, chap 3.

8. Memorandum presented by (Ambassador) Jorge E. Boyd to the President of the United States, February 9, enclosed in Boyd to Garay, February 9, 1940,

Embajada de Panama en EUA, Volume 86: Boyd, Ministerio de Relaciones Exteriores de Panamá, Panama City, Panama (hereafter MRE Panama).

9. Rather than be embedded in the treaty, the equal employment opportunity stipulation was instead indicated in a "Memo of Understanding" attached thereto.

10. The AFL originally lobbied for an amendment to the funding bill that would limit all employment on the project to US citizens only—when the cost of that proposition made it a non-starter, the AFL settled for an amendment stipulating that all skilled and technical positions would be reserved for US citizens. John Major, *Prize Possession: The United States and the Panama Canal, 1903–1979* (Cambridge: Cambridge University Press, 1993).

11. On West Indians, West Indian Panamanians, and race in Panama and the Canal Zone, see Conniff, *Black Labor on a White Canal*; Kaysha Corinealdi, *Panama in Black: Afro-Caribbean World Making and the Promise of Diaspora* (Durham, NC: Duke University Press, 2022); Michael Donoghue, *Borderland on the Isthmus: Race, Culture and the Struggle for the Canal Zone* (Durham, NC: Duke University Press, 2014); Marixa Lasso, *Erased: The Untold Story of the Panama Canal* (Cambridge, MA: Harvard University Press, 2019); Priestley, "Ethnicity, Class and the National Question in Panama"' Maloney, *El Canal de Panamá y los trabajadores antillanos*; Newton, *The Silver Men*; Trevor O'Reggio, *Between Alienation to Citizenship: The Evolution of Black West Indian Society in Panama 1914–1964* (Lanham, MD: University Press of America, 2006); George W. Westerman, *Los inmigrantes antillanos en Panamá* (Panamá: G. W. Westerman, 1980); Katherine Zien, *Sovereign Acts: Performing Race, Space and Belonging in Panama and the Canal Zone* (New Brunswick, NJ: Rutgers University Press, 2017).

12. See David FitzGerald and David Cook-Martin, *Culling the Masses: The Democratic Origins of Racist Immigration Policy in the Americas* (Cambridge, MA: Harvard University Press, 2014); and Lara Putnam, *Radical Moves: Caribbean Migrants and the Politics of Race in the Jazz Age* (Chapel Hill: University of North Carolina Press, 2013).

13. On the complicated figure and legacy of Arnulfo Arias, see Jorge Conte Porras, *Arnulfo Arias Madrid* (Panamá: J. Conte Porras, 1980); and William Francis Robinson, "Panama for the Panamanians: The Populism of Arnulfo Arias Madrid," in *Populism in Latin America*, ed. Michael Conniff, 2nd ed. (Tuscaloosa: University of Alabama Press, 2012), 184–200. On the rise of *panameñismo*, see Alberto McKay, "Las primeras crisis políticas," in *Historia General de Panamá, Vol III, Tomo II*, ed. Alfredo Castillero Calvo (Panamá: Comité Nacional del Centenario de la República, 2004).

14. Memorandum presented by (Ambassador) Jorge E. Boyd to the President of the United States, February 9, 1940.

15. Ley n. 13, October 23, 1926, and Ley 54 of 1938, Constitución de la República de Panamá de 1941. The exclusion of other groups, including Chinese, Syrian, and Turkish migrants, began as early as 1904 shortly after the founding of the Republic. For an overview of the history of racialized immigration restrictions in Panama, see Virginia Arango Durling, "La inmigración prohibida en Panamá y sus prejuicios raciales" (Panamá: PUBLIPAN, 1999).

16. Constitución de la República de Panamá de 1941.

17. Stepan, *"The Hour of Eugenics."*

18. In Panama, attacks on the West Indian population were usually couched in that community's perceived failure to assimilate (the extent to which one supposed

marker of this, English-language skills, gave them an advantage in obtaining coveted Canal Zone jobs was not insignificant).

19. "La traída de antillanos de es una violación la leyes de inmigración de este país: la sociedad afirmación nacional dirige importante carta al Dr. Augusto Boyd," *El Panamá América*, January 18, 1940.
20. "Panama Will Fight Move to Import Alien Labor President Boyd States," *Star & Herald*, January 22, 1940.
21. See Putnam, *Radical Moves*, chap. 3; and FitzGerald and Cook-Martin, *Culling the Masses*.
22. "La traída de antillanos de es una violación de la leyes de inmigración de este país."
23. Linda Smart Chubb, "The British West Indians and British Representations on the Isthmus of Panama," annex to report entitled "The Forgotten People: A Report on the Condition of the British West Indians on the Isthmus of Panama" composed by the British Vice Consulate in Colón, Panama. March 1943. CO 318/447/6, The National Archives of the UK (hereafter TNA).
24. Boyd to Garay, February 9, 1940, Embajada de Panama en EUA Volume 86: Boyd, Archive del Ministerio de Relaciones Exteriores de Panama (hereafter MRE Panama).
25. Boyd to Garay, February 9, 1940.
26. Duggan to State, January 23, 1940, 811F.504/203, RG 59, National Archives and Records Administration of the United States, College Park, MD (hereafter NARA); Memorandum of Conversation re: Recruitment of Labor in the Construction of the Third Set of Locks of the Panama Canal, Participants Duggan, Finley, Barber, Gov. Ridley, January 22, 1940, 811f.504/188, RG 59, NARA.
27. "Estimates of Total Number of Silver Alien Employees and Number of West Indian Employees and Other Alien Employees by Major Organizational Units of the Panama Canal and Panama Railroad," appended to Ellis S. Stone to Governor Mehaffey. September 4, 1944, 2-P-59, Folder 1, Box 419, RG 185, NARA.
28. Major, *Prize Possession*, 212. There is also evidence in the archives that Hondurans were recruited but I have not been able to determine how many.
29. William Dawson to State, March 1941, 811f.504/385, RG 59, NARA.
30. Greene examines a similar incompatibility in the early twentieth century in "Spaniards on the Silver Roll."
31. Edgerton to Lawrence W. Cramer, May 1, 1942, Folder 2-C-55, Box 121, RG 185, NARA.
32. In the past, black US citizens were hired to work in some senior positions, for instance, managing the "silver" clubhouses, but when the color line was reified during the war in ways that relied on racializing nationality, Canal Zone employers stopped hiring black US citizens. F. H. Wang Executive Secretary, Memorandum to Governor, December 30, 1944, 2-C-55, RG 185, NARA.
33. Memo for the Executive Secretary, February 24, 1943.
34. Memo for Chief of Police and Fire Division, July 9, 1940, 2-P-59, Box 419, RG 185, NARA.
35. Memo for Chief of Police and Fire Division, July 9, 1940.
36. Cocoli Silver Camp Riot, July 28, 1941; Gatun Lake Silver Camp Riot, July 24–25, 1941; La Boca Labor Mess Hall Incident April 18, 1941, July 13, 1942.

37. "Dificultades en la Zona del Canal" and "Batalla Campal en la Zona del Canal entre Obreros," July 26, 1941, Embajada de Panama en EUA Volume 88, MRE Panama.

38. Memo for Chief of Division regarding Disturbances between West Indians and Latin Americans at Cocoli, November 29, 1941, 2-P-59 (5), Box 419, RG 185, NARA. The atmosphere was enough to make some West Indians seek a way home. In the wake of the Cocoli incident, some Jamaican workers, who were in the minority at that camp, requested to be transferred to another camp or else to be repatriated to Jamaica, because they "did not want to get mixed up in any trouble with the Latins." The camp housed 188 Jamaicans and 1,551 "mixed Latins," and the latter also advocated that the Jamaicans be transferred. The official who wrote a report on the incident agreed such a transfer might be necessary to "to avoid any serious disturbances in the future." Jerome Barras, Assistant to the Chief Quartermaster, "Transfer of Jamaican Contract Laborers to La Boca," December 10, 1941, 2-P-59 (5), Box 419, RG 185, NARA; Vincent Mowatt to T. C. Coleman, Assistant Supervisor Pedro Miguel Locks, December 6, 1941, 2-P-59 (5), Box 419, RG 185, NARA.

39. On race and United Fruit's labor management practices in Guatemala and Costa Rica, see Jason Colby, The Business of Empire: United Fruit, Race and US Expansion in Central America (Ithaca, NY: Cornell University Press, 2011).

40. "Riot between W. I. and Latin American Workers in Canal Zone Quelled by Police," July 28, 1941, The Panama American. Memo for Chief of Division regarding Disturbances between West Indians and Latin Americans at Cocoli, November 29, 1941. Barras, "Transfer of Jamaican Contract Laborers to La Boca"; Mowatt to Coleman, December 6, 1941.

41. Walter Thurston to State, "Recruitment of Salvadoran Labor for the Panama Canal," May 20, 1943, 811f.504/443 RG 59, NARA.

42. Walter Thurston to State, "Recruitment of Salvadoran labor for the Panama Canal."

43. Victor Urrutia, "Relaciones interamericanas en la Zona del Canal: memorandum para el licenciado Vicente Lombardo Toledano, presidente de la Confederación de Trabajadores de America Latina," 811f.504, RG 59, NACP.

44. Victor Urrutia et al. to Franklin Roosevelt, October 3, 1943, 811f.504, RG 59, NARA. Urrutia, "Relaciones interamericanas en la Zona del Canal."

45. Urrutia, "Relaciones interamericanos en la Zona del Canal." Emphasis original.

46. Urrutia, "Relaciones interamericanas en la Zona del Canal." Emphasis original.

47. On CTAL see Patricio Herrera, "El asedio a la Clase Obrera Organizada en los inicios de la Guerra Fría: El caso de la CTAL, 1943–1953," Revista divergencia 6 (July 2016): 29–39; Daniela Spenser, En combate: la vida de Lombardo Toledano (Mexico City: Editorial Debate, 2018).

48. Muccio to State, April 28, 1944, 811f.504/456, RG 59, NARA.

49. Urrutia, "Relaciones interamericanos en la Zona del Canal." Emphasis original.

50. This was not the first time that Executive Order 8802 was invoked to denounce the discriminatory employment practices in the Canal Zone. In 1941, the NAACP submitted similar allegations to the Fair Employment Practices Committee. The committee's investigation led nowhere, as Governor Edgerton failed to supply the information upon which the committee might have built a case.

51. Victor Urrutia, "Relaciones interamericanas en la Zona del Canal."

52. Memorandum, April 6, 1944. Enclosure to Muccio to State, April 28, 1944.

53. Charles Dodd to J. A. Thwaites, May 12, 1942. He further noted, "they are working here temporarily on emergency work, and they should be willing to put up with a certain amount of inconvenience, or even hardship, without complaining. If they gain the notion that they or their spokesman, may run to you as chicks to the hen for trifles, there is a danger that our whole situation here vis a vis the Canal Zone authorities will be stultified," CO 318/447/6 TNA. Thwaites, the author of the "Forgotten People" report, was more sympathetic, but the civil servants' handwritten correspondence on the file in the Colonial Office archive suggests that Thwaites was certainly the exception rather than the rule; CO 318/447/6 TNA. The British and US governments acted to mitigate the complaints—the British created a new Labor Representative position in the British consulate in Panama dedicated to mediating conflicts between workers and Canal Zone employers and, at the United States' request, Britain launched a propaganda campaign designed to convince black British subjects in the Canal of the importance of the war effort. C. Greaves Hill, January 26, 1944, "Report for the year January 27th 1943 to January 26th 1944," FO 986/72 TNA. "British Propaganda in Panama Canal Zone," January 8, 1943, FO 371/34185 TNA.

54. W. K. Smith to Foreign Office, May 9, 1944, FO 986/72 TNA. Nonetheless, West Indian contract workers too framed their plight in the language of the global moment in appeals to US and British authorities. A common strategic trope in correspondence with the British government was to perform loyalty, as when members of the Dunbar Cultural League asked the British legation, "Does it not occur to you that Britain's future position in world affairs may require the bolstering influence of her loyal blacks? . . . She will have use for us, the loyal and the true." Dunbar Cultural League to British Vice Consul in Colon, Panama, February 20, 1943, Annex to "The Forgotten People," CO 318/447/6 TNA.

55. "Zone Labor and the I.L.O.," *Panama Tribune*, April 23, 1944.

56. On the complex evolution of West Indian Panamanian identities during this period, see Corinealdi, *Panama in Black*. For two different perspectives on George Westerman's legacy, see Conniff, *Black Labor*; and Priestley, "Race and Nationalism in Panama: George Westerman and the Antillean Question, 1941–1960," *Wadabagei: A Journal of the Caribbean and Its Diaspora* 7, no. 1 (2004): 1–58.

57. "Organize Now for the Campaign of Full Citizenship Rights, the Sacred Heritage of All Peoples in a Democracy," Political ad, *Panama Tribune*, July 30, 1944. "1000 Signatures to Petition to Lift 'Citizenship' Ban," *Panama Tribune*, July 23, 1944. Besides creating civic and advocacy organizations within Panama and the Canal Zone, Westerman fostered ties with African American leaders and artists. On his efforts to foster an appreciation of black excellence in both Panama and the Zone by sponsoring cultural exchange, see Zien, *Sovereign Acts*, chap. 3.

58. George H. Butler to State, November 23, 1944. "Meeting of the Congreso de la Juventud Istmeña de la Raza Negra," RG 59, CDF 1940–1944, 811f.504/11-2344.

59. For instance, "Racial Bias in Panama Opposed by Renovador," *Panama Tribune*, October 1, 1944; "Don Domingo Diaz Favors Citizenship for All Born in Republic," *Panama Tribune*, October 29, 1944; "Vote for Pedro Rhodes," *Panama Tribune*, April 22, 1944; "Help Him to Serve You," *Panama Tribune*, April 29, 1944.

60. "Más de cinco mil obreros de la Zona envían exposición a la Conf. Internl. del Trabajo," *Estrella de Panama*, April 1, 1944.

61. Diógenes de la Rosa, International Labour Conference Record of Proceedings, Twenty-Sixth Session Philadelphia, 1944.

62. "Zone Labor and the I.L.O."

63. Warren to State re: Labor Policies of the United States Agencies in the Canal Zone, August 7, 1944, 811f.504/8-744, RG 59, NARA.

64. Letter drafted by Jonathan Daniels for FRD to send to Brig. Gen. J. C. Mehaffey, Acting Governor of the Panama Canal Zone, May 13, 1944, enclosure to State Department Memorandum by R. G. McGregor Jr., May 15, 1944, 811f.504/458, RG 59, NARA.

65. John J. Muccio, Chargé d'Affaires US Embassy in Panama City to Secretary of State, April 28, 1944, 811f.504/456, RG 59, NARA.

66. Governor Glen E. Edgerton, Memorandum to Chief of Office, April 15, 1944, enclosure to Muccio to Secretary of State, April 28, 1944.

67. Laurence Duggan, Director of the Office of American Republic Affairs, Memorandum of Conversation with Enrique A. Jimenez, Ambassador of Panama and Ricardo A. Morales, Counselor of the Panamanian Embassy, May 3, 1944.

68. McGregor, Labor Practices in the Canal Zone, May 4, 1944, 811f.504/5-444, RG 59, NARA. The Fair Employment Practices Commission was also prevented from looking deeply into discrimination against people of Mexican descent in the United States during the war for the same reason. See Justin Hart, "Making Democracy Safe for the World: Race, Propaganda, and the Transformation of US Foreign Policy during World War II," *Pacific Historical Review* 73 (2004): 49–84.

69. Division of Caribbean and Central American Affairs, "Labor Problems in the Canal Zone," 811f.504/454, RG 59, NARA.

70. Department of State Division of the American Republics, Memo for the files: Labor, 811f.504/12-944, RG 59, NARA.

71. Letter drafted by Jonathan Daniels for FDR to send to Brig. Gen. J. C. Mehaffey. Department of State Division of the American Republics, Memo for the files: Labor, 811f.504/12-944, RG 59, NARA.

72. Memorandum of Conversation between Samuel Lewis, Minister of Foreign Affairs of Panama, Enrique Jimenez, Ambassador of Panama, Mario de Diego, Director of Protocol of Panama, Narciso E. Garay, First Secretary of the Embassy of Panama, Otis Mulliken, Chief of International Labor, Social and Health Affairs, December 12, 1944, 811f.504/12-1244; Memorandum of Conversation between Warren, Wilson, Mulliken, and Farber, December 16, 1944, 811f.504/12-1644, RG 59, NARA.

73. Secret Memorandum of Conversation, Subject: Racial Discrimination in the Panama Canal Zone between John Muccio, Howard Wilson, and Bonnie Farber, 811f.504/9-2544, RG 59, NARA.

74. Secret Memorandum of Conversation, Subject: Racial Discrimination in the Panama Canal Zone.

75. Muccio to State, May 3, 1944, 811f.504/458, RG 59, NARA.

76. Warren to State, September 19, 1944, 811f.504/9-1944, RG 59, NARA.

77. Warren to State, October 11, 1944, 811f.504/10-1144, RG 59, NARA.

78. Memorandum of Conversation between Lewis, Jimenez, Diego, Garay, Mulliken, December 12, 1944.

79. They organized with the reluctant blessing of the canal administration, in part because they were deemed preferable to the openly anti-imperialist CTAL, which might otherwise step in to take similar actions. Though the CIO was in some

ways an "honorary member" of CTAL, Canal Zone officials preferred for US citizens to play a hand in any ongoing organizing.

80. Editorial, July 4, 1946, *Ac-CIÓ-n*, Biblioteca Nacional de Panamá, Panama City.
81. Note from President Jimenez, July 2, 1946, printed in *Ac-CIÓ-n*, July 4, 1946.
82. On the continued struggle against Canal Zone discrimination in the context of the Cold War, decolonization, and transformations in Panamanian domestic politics, see Rebecca Herman, "The Global Politics of Anti-Racism: A View from the Canal Zone," *American Historical Review* 124, no. 2 (April 2020): 460–486.
83. Record of Proceedings, International Labour Conference, Thirty-Seventh Session, Geneva, 1954, ILO.

CHAPTER 5

1. Author interview with Rui Moreira Lima in Rio de Janeiro, November 6, 2012.
2. Blanchard Girão, *A invasão dos cabelos dourados: do USO aos AbUSOs no tempo das "Coca-Colas"* (São Paulo: ABC Editora, 2008), 71.
3. Gender histories of bases constitute a rich literature that is far too extensive to catalog here. For an introduction to some of the most salient themes in the field, see Rowena Ward and Christine de Matos, eds., *Gender, Power and Military Occupations: Asia Pacific and the Middle East since 1945* (New York: Routledge, 2012); and Maria Höhn and Seungsook Moon, eds., *Over There: Living with the US Military Empire from World War Two to the Present* (Durham, NC: Duke University Press, 2010).
4. In both Brazil and Panama, female suffrage was still effectively limited after these dates. In Panama, Law 81 of July 5, 1941, permitted women to vote in municipal elections if they were twenty-one years old or above and had certain advanced educational qualifications. Women gained the right to vote in presidential elections only with the new Constitution of 1946. Yolanda Marco Serra, "El movimiento sufragista en Panamá y la construcción de la mujer moderna," in *Historia de los movimientos de mujeres en Panamá en el siglo XX*, ed. Fernando Aparicio, Yolanda Marco Serra, Miriam Miranda, and Josefina Zurita, 45–132 (Panamá: Universidad de Panamá, 2002). In Brazil, persistent limitations on the right to vote disqualified many women even after the advent of female suffrage and, when Vargas declared the Estado Novo and suspended elections, suffrage became inconsequential. The limited utility of suffrage in political systems that were not always democratic was part of the reason many Latin American feminists did not view voting rights as the highest priority in their struggle for female emancipation, in contrast to US feminists. On the relative importance of suffrage for different feminist movements in the Americas during this period, see Katherine M. Marino, *Feminism for the Americas: The Making of an International Human Rights Movement* (Chapel Hill: University of North Carolina Press, 2019).
5. For an overview of women and gender in Latin American history, see Nara Milanich, "Women, Gender and Family in Latin America, 1820–2000," in *A Companion to Latin American History*, ed. Thomas H. Holloway (New York: John Wiley & Sons, 2010), 461–479. For a historiographical overview of gender in Latin American historiography, see Sueann Caulfield, "The History of Gender in the Historiography of Latin America," *Hispanic American Historical Review* 81, no. 3–4 (August 2001): 449–490.
6. Girão, *A invasão dos cabelos dourados*, 70.

7. On whether World War II cultural exchange amounted to an "Americanization" of Brazil as some hypothesized during and after the war, see Gerson Moura, *Tio Sam chega ao Brasil: a penetração cultural Americana* (São Paulo: Brasilense, 1984); Ursula Prutsch, "Americanization of Brazil or a Pragmatic Wartime Alliance? The Politics of Nelson Rockefeller's Office of Inter-American Affairs in Brazil during World War II," *Passagens: Revista internacional de história política e cultura jurídica* 2, no. 4 (May–August 2010): 181–216; Antônio Pedro Tota, *O imperialismo sedutor: a americanização do Brasil na época da Segunda Guerra* (São Paulo: Companhia das Letras, 2000).

8. Girão, *A invasão dos cabelos dourados*, 81.

9. Sueann Caulfield, "The Changing Politics of Freedom and Virginity in Rio de Janeiro, 1920–1940," in *Honor, Status and Law in Modern Latin America*, ed. Sueann Caulfield, Sarah C. Chambers, and Lara Putnam (Durham, NC: Duke University Press, 2005), 223–246, and *In Defense of Honor: Sexual Morality, Modernity and Nation in Early Twentieth Century Brazil* (Durham, NC: Duke University Press, 2000), chap. 3. On sex, honor, and the state in Brazil, see Susan K. Besse, *Restructuring Patriarchy: The Modernization of Gender Inequity in Brazil, 1914–1940* (Chapel Hill: University of North Carolina Press, 1996).

10. For a summary of some significant points of change and continuity between the 1890 and 1940 Penal Codes, see Caulfield, *In Defense of Honor*, 191–194.

11. Jane Derarovele Semeão e Silva, "O 'Esforço de Guerra' em Fortaleza: atividade patriótica e participação feminina nos anos de 1940," *Saeculum—Revista de história* 30 (June 2014): 289–303; Jane Derarovele Semeão e Silva, "Comportamento feminino em Fortaleza: entre o tradicional e o moderno durante a Segunda Guerra Mundial," in *Fortaleza: história e cotidiano*, ed. Simone Souza and Federico de Castro Neves (Fortaleza: Demócrito Rocha, 2002), 17–52.

12. Appendix to Braddock Report, Daniel M. Braddock to Jefferson Caffery, Report: Relations Between Brazilians and Americans in Para, July 14, 1944, 711.32/7-1944, Central Decimal Files (hereafter CDF) 1940–1944, Record Group 59: General Records of the Department of State (hereafter RG 59), US National Archives and Records Administration (hereafter NARA). Sexual violence is a common feature of US overseas basing that has been well documented by historians in other regions of the world. It is safe to assume US bases in Brazil were no exception, but it is difficult, based on the existing archival record, to discern instances of consensual versus nonconsensual sex between US personnel and local women. The archives I consulted did not reveal formal allegations of rape, but traced instead broader perceptions of moral degradation, to which both rape and consensual extramarital sex would have contributed. For a recent reflection on scholarship and the challenges of researching sexual violence during World War II, see Ruth Lawlor, "Contested Crimes: Race, Gender and Nation in Histories of GI Sexual Violence, World War II," *Journal of Military History* 84 (April 2020): 541–569. Another significant silence in the archive was the absence of any records of queer sex, consensual or nonconsensual, which also surely occurred but did not appear in the records that I consulted. Research by other historians has uncovered archival evidence of male-victim sexual violence by US soldiers elsewhere during World War II. See, e.g., R. M. Douglas, "The US Army and Male Rape during the Second World War," *Journal of Contemporary History* 56, no. 2 (2021): 268–293.

13. Morris Berg, "Interim Report—Secret and Confidential Remarks" for Nelson Rockefeller, March 29, 1943, Folder 27, Box 4, Series O, Subseries 1, NAR, RG 4, RAC.

14. W. N. Walmsley Jr., Strictly Confidential Report: "Americans in Brazil," April 9, 1943, 811.24532/35, Confidential CDF 1940–1944, RG 59, NARA.

15. Walmsley, Strictly Confidential Report: "Americans in Brazil."

16. Daniel M. Braddock to Jefferson Caffery, Report: Relations Between Brazilians and Americans in Pará, July 14, 1944, 711.32/7-1944, CDF 1940–1944, RG 59, NARA.

17. U. G. Keener and Townsend Munson to Earl, February 6, 1943, Box 1277, Entry 99, Record Group 229: Records of the Office of Inter-American Affairs (hereafter RG 229), NARA.

18. Joseph F. Brown to Captain Harold Dodd, June 2, 1944, Box 1309, Entry 99, RG 229, NARA.

19. Translated transcription of untitled story from *La Vanguardia*, April 12, 1940, CDF 1940-44, RG 59, NARA.

20. Yolanda Marco Serra, "Ruptura de la tradición, construcción de la mujer moderna y resistencia del patriarcado liberal en Panamá en las décadas de 1920 y 1930," *Diálogos* 5 (2004); Yolanda Marco Serra, "El feminismo de los años veinte y la redefinición de la femineidad en Panamá," in *Entre silencios y voces: género e historia en América Central (1750–1990)*, ed. Eugenia Rodríguez Sáenz (San José, Costa Rica: Editorial Porvenir, 1997), 183–196.

21. Michael Donoghue, *Borderland on the Isthmus: Race, Culture, and the Struggle for the Canal Zone* (Durham, NC: Duke University Press, 2014), 14.

22. Panama Canal Periodical Reference Form, Translation of article in *El Tiempo*, May 4, 1942, titled "Brawl in Panama Yesterday between American Soldiers and Panamanian Police," Folder 62-B-199, Box 1852, Record Group 185: Records of the Panama Canal (hereafter RG 185), NARA.

23. Foreign Minister Octavio Fábrega to Ambassador Edwin Wilson, September 14, 1942, Zona del Canal, Vol. 17, Archivo del Ministerio de Relaciones Exteriores de Panamá, Panama City, Panama (hereafter MRE Panama); Virgilio Angulo, Alcalde Municipal, to the Governor of the Province of Panama, January 23, 1942, Zona del Canal, Vol. 17, MRE Panama.

24. Black US soldiers sent to Panama had to contend with both the racial politics within the US military and the racial politics of blackness that they confronted on the ground in Panama. On these kinds of intersections in military deployments around the globe in World War II, see Khary Oronde Polk, *Contagions of Empire: Scientific Racism, Sexuality and Black Military Workers Abroad, 1898–1948* (Chapel Hill: University of North Carolina Press, 2020), 188–194.

25. "El Cabaret Almendra," *Acción Comunal*, July 1943.

26. Michael Donoghue, *Borderlands on the Isthmus*.

27. O. C. Wenger, Senior Surgeon, Division of Venereal Diseases, Public Health Service, Special Consultant to the Chief Health Officer Panama Canal Health Department, April 1, 1943, "The Venereal Disease Situation in the Panama Canal Zone and the New Control Program," 75, Albert and Shirley Small Special Collections, University of Virginia, Charlottesville, Virginia (hereafter UVA).

28. J. E. Moore to Thomas Parran, Surgeon General, US Public Health Service, December 3, 1941, Box 1653, Health and Sanitation, RG 229, NARA.

29. These sorts of gray-area relationships were common across defense sites in Latin America, a most extreme example of which occurred in Salinas Ecuador, where the city's Office of Sanitation reportedly provided US servicemen with a list of women who did not have other means of income, and a soldier could opt to assume responsibility for a woman on the list after signing an agreement. Lt. Colonel Eugene Cunningham, Air Corps, Confidential Memo, May 20, 1944, Enclosure to despatch 790 of May 26, 1944 Harold L. Williamson, American Consul General at Guayaquil to Secretary of State, 811.24522/88, RG 59, NARA.

30. US servicemen had liberty every evening in Caimanera (5 miles away) and Guantánamo on weekends (25 miles). Enlisted men could travel to Santiago de Cuba 40 miles away on payday.

31. Katherine Lynn Stoner, *From the House to the Streets: The Cuban Woman's Movement for Legal Reform, 1898–1940* (Durham, NC: Duke University Press), 147.

32. On the history of women and Cuban legal reform see Stoner, *From the House to the Streets*.

33. For more on this debate, see Sarah R. Arvey, "'Labyrinths of Love': Sexual Propriety, Family and Social Reform in the Second Cuban Republic, 1902–1958" (PhD diss., University of Michigan, 2007).

34. Orestes Robledo Reyes, "Estudio de la Comunidad de San Antonio de los Baños" (thesis, Universidad de la Habana, 1952), Archivo del Museo de San Antonio de los Baños, San Antonio de los Baños, Cuba (hereafter Museo de San Antonio de los Baños).

35. Robledo Reyes, "Estudio de la Comunidad," 387.

36. Robledo Reyes, "Estudio de la Comunidad," 221.

37. Robledo Reyes, "Estudio de la Comunidad," 388.

38. Robledo Reyes, "Estudio de la Comunidad," 386.

39. Rene Misa, "Notas politicas," *La Tribuna*, August 21, 1942; Robledo Reyes, "Estudio de la Comunidad," 388.

40. Robledo Reyes, "Estudio de la Comunidad," 388.

41. Robledo Reyes, "Estudio de la Comunidad," 222.

42. John Corbin to Joyce, August 25, 1942, Box 168, General Records of the United States Embassy in Havana, Record Group 84: Records of the Foreign Service Posts (hereafter RG 84), NARA.

43. Corbin to Joyce, August 25, 1942.

44. "Párrafos del director," *La Tribuna*, September 26, 1943.

45. "Párrafos del director," *La Tribuna*, September 26, 1943. *Ariguabense* is the word that San Antonio residents use to describe themselves, in reference to the town's location on the Ariguanabo river

46. "Párrafos del director," *La Tribuna*, September 26, 1943.

47. Robledo Reyes, "Estudio de la Comunidad," 249–252. Robledo also insisted that women's lack of a sexual education, in particular, posed a threat to marital and social stability because it left women ill-equipped to lead fulfilling sex lives within marriage. On marital stability, female frigidity and the promise of sexual education, see Sarah R. Arvey, "Sex and the Ordinary Cuban: Cuban Physicians, Eugenics and Marital Sexuality in the 1940s and 1950s," *Journal of the History of Sexuality* 21, no. 1 (2012): 93–120.

48. Robledo Reyes, "Estudio de la Comunidad," 391.

49. Irwin F. Gellman, *Roosevelt and Batista: Good Neighbor Diplomacy in Cuba, 1933–1945* (Albuquerque: University of New Mexico Press, 1973), 217.

50. Jefferson Caffery to State, November 30, 1942, 711.32/149, CDF 1940-44, RG 59, NARA.
51. Caffery to State, December 24, 1942.
52. Given that there was no combat in the region during World War II, venereal disease proved to be the greatest threat to the well-being of US troops in Latin America. For an expansive, nuts-and-bolts history of venereal disease as a medical concern during World War II, see Thomas H. Sternberg, Ernest B. Howard, Leonard A. Dewey, and Paul Padget, "Venereal Disease," chap. 10 in *Preventative Medicine in World War II Volume V: Communicable Diseases* (Washington, DC: Office of the Surgeon General Department of the Army, 1958). On concerns about venereal disease in US history, see Allan M. Brandt, *No Magic Bullet: A Social History of Venereal Disease in the United States since 1880* (New York: Oxford University Press, 1987).
53. See Cramer and Prutsch, "Introduction," in ¡*Américas Unidas!: Nelson A. Rockefeller's Office of Inter-American Affairs, 1940–1946*, ed. Gisela Cramer and Ursula Prutsch (Madrid: Iberoamericana Vervuert, 2012).
54. Christine Ehrich, "Buenas Vecinas?: Latin American Women and US Radio Propaganda during World War II," *Feminist Media Histories* 5, no. 3 (Summer 2019): 60–84.
55. Semeão, "Comportamento feminino em Fortaleza," 28
56. Brazil Coordinating Committee Annual Report 1943, Box 1259, Entry 99, RG 229, NARA.
57. Frank Nattier Jr., Reports on Visits to Belém and Recife, November 9, 1944, Box 1277, Entry 99, RG 229, NARA. Boletim do S.E.S.P. do Ministerio de Educação e Saúde, August 1945, Fontes para a Historia da Fundação de Saúde Pública, Seção: Administração, Serie: Organização e Funcionamento, Code: A/00/OF/03, Arquivo Fundação Osvaldo Cruz, Rio de Janeiro (hereafter FIOCRUZ).
58. Peter T. Seidl to Edgar Chermont, December 26, 1944, Box 1277, Entry 99, RG 229, NARA; Seidl to Chermont, December 21, 1944, Box 1277, Entry 99, RG 229, NARA. US officials also invested some energy and resources into efforts to educate US personnel in ways that might prevent them from offending local residents in the first place. Among its wartime projects, the Coordinator's Office ran a massive stateside campaign in the US to convince US Americans of the Pan-American cause and cultivate admiration and respect for Latin American cultures by introducing US Americans to various genres of Latin American literature, music, and film, encouraging Pan-American clubs and celebrations, and supporting the expansion of Spanish and Portuguese-language instruction. When ill will proved rampant in the areas surrounding base sites, the Coordinator's Office sought to extend the sentiment behind this nationwide campaign to the US overseas bases.
59. Brown to Dodd, June 2, 1944.
60. Office of Strategic Services: Research and Analysis Branch, Short Guide to Brazil, Report No 60, July 10, 1942, Box 225, Entry 47, RG 319, NARA. I'm grateful to Alexandre Fortes for sharing these sources with me.
61. Office of the Control Officer, Air Transport Command—Belém, Brazil, "Information for Transient Enlisted Men—Belem," July 14, 1942, Box 225, Entry 47, Record Group 319: Records of the Army Staff (hereafter RG 319), NARA. I'm grateful to Alexandre Fortes for sharing these sources with me.
62. Major Hugh J. Denney of the Adjutant General's Office to the Adjutant General, October 6, 1941, Folder AG 726.1 1941, Box 1002 (721.5–726.3), Entry 360,

Record Group 407: Records of the Adjutant General (hereafter RG 407), NARA. John Corbin to Joyce, August 25, 1942, Box 168, General Records of the United States Embassy in Havana, RG 84, NARA.

63. Walmsley, Strictly Confidential Report: "Americans in Brazil."

64. On the development of recreation options as a means of addressing the threat posed by venereal disease in Latin America, see United States Policy on Venereal Disease Control in the Caribbean, October 21, 1943, Box 1, Entry 66, Record Group 215: Community War Services (hereafter RG 215), NARA.

65. "Report of Val de Cans Air Field," December 12, 1942. Box 276, Entry 26 E, Record Group 159: Office of the Inspector General (hereafter RG 159), NARA.

66. Wenger, "The Venereal Disease Situation in the Panama Canal Zone and the New Control Program," 174.

67. Berg, "Interim Report—Secret and Confidential Remarks," March 29, 1943.

68. Berg, "Interim Report—Secret and Confidential Remarks," March 29, 1943, 7.

69. Berg, "Interim Report—Secret and Confidential Remarks," March 29, 1943, 8.

70. Conrad Van Hyning, Coordinator of Welfare Services to Mr. Charles P. Taft, Community War Services, Director Community War Services, Report on Visit to the Caribbean Area, February 27–May 31, 1943, Folder Venereal Disease Control Program 3 of 4, Box 1, Entry 66, RG 215, NARA. Ideas about race, morality and sexuality had shaped the US presence in Panama since the period of canal construction; on this earlier period, see Joan Flores-Villalobos, "Colón Women: West Indian Women in the Construction of the Panama Canal, 1904–1911" (PhD diss., New York University, 2018). The same official made similar remarks about the promiscuity of Brazilian women of "the lower economic classes" after a visit to Brazil the following year. Conrad Van Hyning to Dean Snyder, Subject: Attached Report on Brazil, Dutch Guiana, British Guiana, and Trinidad, July 3, 1944, Box 1, Entry 66, RG 215, NARA.

71. Wenger, "The Venereal Disease Situation in the Panama Canal Zone and the New Control Program," 120.

72. John J. Hurley, Field Representative, Social Protection Section, "Survey of the Canal Zone," October 8–November 6, 1942, Box 11, Entry 40, RG 215, NARA.

73. Wenger, "The Venereal Disease Situation in the Panama Canal Zone and the New Control Program," 116.

74. Wenger, "The Venereal Disease Situation in the Panama Canal Zone and the New Control Program," 116–117.

75. Contrary to this approach, historian Michael Donoghue has noted instances in Panama when US officials intentionally directed servicemen to lower-class and foreign sex workers in order to avoid offending Panamanian elites. Donoghue, *Borderlands on the Isthmus.*

76. "A Preliminary Statement on the Program of the United Service Organizations for National Defense, Inc." Undated, Folder United Service Organizations, Box 10, Correspondence of Secretary of War Stimson 1940–1945, Record Group 107: Office of the Secretary of War (hereafter RG 107), NARA.

77. "A Preliminary Statement on the Program," United Service Organizations for National Defense, Inc. Undated. Box 10, Correspondence of Secretary of War Stimson 1940–1945, RG 107, NARA.

78. Van Hyning to Snyder, Report on Brazil, Dutch Guiana, British Guiana, and Trinidad.

79. Van Hyning to Snyder, Report on Brazil, Dutch Guiana, British Guiana, and Trinidad.

80. Vice Consul Edward McLaughlin to State, July 21, 1943, Box 46, United States Consulate in Belém, RG 84, NARA.

81. McLaughlin to State, July 21, 1943.

82. McLaughlin to State, July 21, 1943.

83. Van Hyning to Snyder, Report on Brazil, Dutch Guiana, British Guiana, and Trinidad; Van Hyning to Taft, Report on Visit to the Caribbean Area.

84. Van Hyning to Taft, Report on Visit to the Caribbean Area.

85. American Consul Edward McLaughlin to Secretary of State, Subject: Special Relationships between the Americans and Brazilians of Belém, October 30, 1943, 711.32/191, RG 59, NARA.

86. Van Hyning to Snyder, Report on Brazil, Dutch Guiana, British Guiana, and Trinidad.

87. Kara Vuic, *The Girls Next Door: Bringing the Home Front to the Front Lines* (Cambridge, MA: Harvard University Press, 2019),) 68.

88. Brazil Red Cross Files, NARA. My thanks to Kara Vuic for generously sharing her Brazil Red Cross files with me during the pandemic.

89. Semeão, "O 'Esforço de Guerra,'" 295.

90. Blanchard Girão, *A invasão dos cabelos dourados*, 75.

91. Semeão, "Comportamento feminino em Fortaleza."

92. Antonio J. C. dos Reis to Minister of War, May 9, 1944, Arquivo do Ministério de Relações Exteriores (Itamaraty), Brasília, Brazil (hereafter Itamaraty—Brasília).

93. "Moralizando os Cinemas," *Folha do Norte*, April 14, 1944.

94. "Moralizando os Cinemas."

95. Van Hyning to Taft, Report on Visit to the Caribbean Area.

96. "Beautiful Models Greet GIs at Jungle Outpost," *Estrella de Panama*, December 1, 1944. On the systematic effort to recruit US women to boost US soldiers' morale overseas, see Vuic, *The Girls Next Door*.

97. Bolivar Avenue USO Club, Pan American Day Program, Expediente 282, Caja 91, Fondo Presidencia, Archivo Nacional de Panamá, Panama City, Panama (hereafter ANP).

98. T. N. Casserly, Chairman and S. D. Freeman, Acting Director of the Cristobal USO Club to President Ricardo Adolfo de la Guardia, September 9, 1944, Expediente 282, Caja 91, Fondo Presidencia, ANP.

99. "500 GIs Attend 'Wonderland' Dance at USO: Colon Officials Guests at Festive Holiday Party in Cristobal," *Estrella de Panamá*, December 31, 1944; Headquarters Panama Canal Department, "Memorandum: Pan-American Premiere of *Her's to Hold*," August 31, 1943, Expediente 282, Caja 91, Fondo Presidencia, ANP. Casserly and Freeman to de la Guardia, September 9, 1944. Hugh A. Kelly, Presidente del Comité Administrativo and Louis Famucci, Director del Tivoli USO Club to Presidente Ricardo Adolfo de la Guardia, November 20, 1944, Expediente 282, Caja 91, Fondo Presidencia, ANP.

100. Berg, "Interim Report—Secret and Confidential Remarks," March 29, 1943, 10.

101. The practice by which US officials regulated sexual encounters between US personnel and sex workers overseas was not unique to Cuba and Brazil, nor was it unique to World War II basing. For a few examples of historical scholarship on these kinds of practices across time and space, see Paul A. Kramer, "The Military-Sexual Complex: Prostitution, Disease and the Boundaries of Empire during the Philippine-American War," *Asia-Pacific Journal* 9, no. 2 (July 2011): 1–35; Katharine H. S. Moon, *Sex among Allies: Military Prostitution in US-Korea Relations* (New York: Columbia University Press, 1997); Seungsook Moon,

"Camptown Prostitution and the Imperial SOFA: Abuse and Violence against Transnational Camptown Women in South Korea," in Höhn and Moon, eds. *Over There*; Mire Koikari, *Pedagogy of Democracy: Feminism and the Cold War in the US Occupation of Japan* (Philadelphia: Temple University Press, 2008), chap. 5; Beth Bailey and David Farber, *The First Strange Place: The Alchemy of Race and Sex in WWII Hawaii* (New York: Free Press, 1992), chap. 3; Mary Louise Roberts, *What Soldiers Do: Sex and the American GI in World War II France* (Chicago: University of Chicago Press, 2013).

102. Jeffrey W. Parker, "Sex Work on the Isthmus of Panama," in *Trafficking in Women (1924–1926): The Paul Kinsie Reports for the League of Nations, Vol. I* (Geneva: United Nations Publications, 2017), 166–171.

103. The immigration of sex workers to Panama was technically prohibited, so women arrived proclaiming themselves to be artists and entertainers. Wenger, "The Venereal Disease Situation in the Panama Canal Zone and the New Control Program," 73. In perhaps his only successful effort at repressing prostitution, the Canal Zone health officer on one occasion sent a letter to Panamanian immigration authorities with the names and nationalities of a number of foreign-born women who were infected with venereal disease and suggested they be deported—and they were. Minutes of Community War Services Conference on Health, Caribbean Defense Command, June 28, 1943, 62, Box 3, Entry 41, RG 215, NARA.

104. Minutes of Community War Services Conference on Health, Caribbean Defense Command, June 28, 1943, 59. He was commenting on a Panamanian official who reportedly used a diplomatic passport in order to travel to other countries to recruit women to work in the sex industry.

105. Moore to Parran, December 3, 1941, 6.

106. Van Hyning to Taft, Report on Visit to the Caribbean Area, 11.

107. Minutes of Community War Services Conference on Health, Caribbean Defense Command, June 28, 1943, 66.

108. Minutes of Community War Services Conference on Health, Caribbean Defense Command, June 28, 1943, 67.

109. On sex worker activism in shaping the Panamanian system of prostitution regulation between 1908 and 1932, see Jeffrey Wayne Parker, "Empire's Angst: The Politics of Race, Migration, and Sex Work in Panama, 1903–1945" (PhD diss., University of Texas at Austin, 2013), chap. 3.

110. Juan Perdomo, Inspector de Meretrices to President Ricardo de la Guardia, September 30, 1942, Expediente 256, Caja 80, Prevención social y Salud Pública, Documentación del Ministerio de Trabajo, Fondo Presidencia, ANP.

111. Perdomo to de la Guardia, August 26, 1942, Expediente 256, Caja 80, Prevención social y Salud Pública, Documentación del Ministerio de Trabajo, Archivo de la Presidencia, ANP. According to one report, the mayor's order to suspend the detention of sex workers was due to the fact that there was no space left in the women's jails for them. Memo para el Dr. Guillermo Garcia de Paredes, Director de la Sección de Salubridad, September 18, 1943, Expediente 256, Caja 80, Prevención social y Salud Pública, Documentación del Ministerio de Trabajo, Fondo Presidencia, ANP.

112. Parker, "Empire's Angst," 315.

113. Wenger, "The Venereal Disease Situation in the Panama Canal Zone and the New Control Program," 87. "Información confidencial," January 19, 1943, Fondo Presidencia, ANP. Documentación del Ministerio de Trabajo prevención social

y salud pública, Expediente 256, Caja 80, Fondo Presidencia, ANP; Minutes of Community War Services Conference on Health, Caribbean Defense Command, June 28, 1943, 58–59, Box 3, Entry 41, RG 215, NARA.

114. Moore to Parran, December 3, 1941, 6.

115. One example of this that I came across in my research in the Archivo Nacional de Panama were allegations against Beatriz Castillo in Entrada No. 491, Fiscalia Tercera del Circuito, Caso Contra Lewis F. Quigley, Jack Hedgepeth, Gilber Genereux y Paul Leroy Lucas, Iniciado June 16, 1942, Sección de Judiciales, ANP. Jeffrey Parker examines a larger cluster of these cases in Colón during World War II in "Empire's Angst," 326–339.

116. Parker, "Empire's Angst," 326–339.

117. Stayer to Moore, January 12, 1942, Folder 37-H-10 (7), Box 1444, RG 185, NARA. In 1941, a specialist from the US Public Health Service did an assessment of the venereal disease situation in Panama and suggested a plan for expanding the treatment of VD both within the terminal cities with red light districts and in the interior of the Republic, and this became the basis for the proposal to the Panamanian government. He discouraged a solution that simply offered aid to the Panamanian Health Department and instead insisted that a Division of Venereal Disease Control be created within the Canal Zone Health Department to make progress in reducing the rates of venereal disease among US personnel and Canal Zone employees. The program proposed to build treatment clinics for venereal disease in Panama City, Colón, and every smaller city in which at least 500 US troops were stationed. In addition, the program would enlarge the existing hospital for women with venereal disease. Finally, the program would train one of that hospital's doctors at Johns Hopkins University. Stayer to Dr. Julio Jimenez, Director of the Section of Public Health, Panama, March 5, 1942, Folder 37-H-10 (7), Box 1444, RG 185, NARA.

118. Stayer to Dr. P. J. Crawford, March 14, 1942, Folder 37-H-10 (7), Box 1444, RG 185, NARA.

119. In addition to new facilities in the major cities, they would create two mobile units that would travel to smaller towns for the treatment of patients living throughout the area, and open further facilities in temporary buildings in the interior. Wenger, "The Venereal Disease Situation in the Panama Canal Zone and the New Control Program," 121, 128.

120. Anticipating objections from War Department officials in Washington to the fact that the cooperative program elaborated by a US Public Health Service called for the examination of sex workers, in his report on the new control program, the US official who oversaw the program passed the buck, stating: "this examination of these women should not be interpreted as a recognition or toleration of prostitution by our government. It is a case finding measure, carried out in a foreign country, in conformance with the laws of that country, and under supervision of the Director of Health of that country. . . . Whatever the shortcomings of the measure, it is the only measure of protection which can be employed for the protection of our nationals in Panama at this particular time." Wenger, "The Venereal Disease Situation in the Panama Canal Zone and the New Control Program," 140.

121. Wenger, "The Venereal Disease Situation in the Panama Canal Zone and the New Control Program," 144.

122. "Pro-Moralidad Pública," Acción Comunal, July 1943. Acción Comunal expressed skepticism about the plan, reminding readers than many of the politicians who

were to be charged with the plan's execution were themselves implicated in the corruption that had allowed clandestine prostitution to flourish.

123. "A Highly Important Campaign," *Star and Herald*, September 10, 1943.

124. "Ciudadanos de David Elevan un Reclamo," Reproduction of Petition from Celia de Obaldía et al. to the Minister of Government and Justice dated July 1943, reprinted in *Acción Comunal*, August 12, 1943.

125. "Junior Chamber of Commerce Is Interested in the Transfer of the Red Light District," August 20, 1944, Box 1937, 64-Y-4(2a), RG 185, NARA. Emphasis original.

126. "Junior Chamber of Commerce Is Interested in the Transfer of the Red Light District." Emphasis original.

127. "Junior Chamber of Commerce Is Interested in the Transfer of the Red Light District." Emphasis original.

128. Berg, "Interim Report—Secret and Confidential Remarks," March 29, 1943, 8; Hurley, "Survey of the Canal Zone."

129. On policing prostitution in early twentieth-century Rio, see Caulfield, *In Defense of Honor*, and "The Birth of Mangue: Race, Nation and the Politics of Prostitution in Rio de Janeiro, 1850–1942," in *Sex and Sexuality in Latin America*, ed. Daniel Balderston and Donna Guy (New York: New York University Press, 1997), 86–100; Christiana Schettini Pereira, "Prostitutes and the Law: The Uses of Court Cases over Pandering in Rio de Janeiro at the Beginning of the Twentieth Century," in *Honor, Status and Law in Modern Latin America*, ed. Caulfield, Chambers, and Putnam.

130. According to US reports, the Brazilian Ministry of Health's Federal Venereal Disease Control Division proved relatively ineffective in the North due to insufficient staffing and budgeting. Van Hyning to Snyder, Report on Brazil, Dutch Guiana, British Guiana, and Trinidad.

131. Van Hyning to Snyder, Report on Brazil, Dutch Guiana, British Guiana, and Trinidad.

132. Márcio Couto Enrique and Luiza Helena Miranda Amador, "Da *Belle Epoque* à cidade do vício: o combate à sífilis em Belém do Pará, 1921–1924," *História, Ciências, Saúde—Manguinhos, Rio de Janeiro* 23 (April–June 2016): 359–378.

133. Typically this meant rubbing calomel ointment on their genitals to prevent infection.

134. Van Hyning to Snyder, Report on Brazil, Dutch Guiana, British Guiana, and Trinidad.

135. Another conspicuous absence in the archival record is the work of male sex workers. Male prostitution almost certainly existed, though it did not appear in the available sources.

136. Transcribed excerpt from *The Times Herald*, Washington DC, May 12, 1945, Folder 726.1 1943, Box 3320, Entry 360, RG 407, NARA.

137. Berg, "Interim Report—Secret and Confidential Remarks," March 29, 1943, 9.

138. The history of formal regulation of prostitution in Cuba dated back to the mid-nineteenth century, when Spanish colonial officials experimented with the French system of regulation in order to protect imperial soldiers' health. In 1873 they elaborated a set of public hygiene laws that purported to offer a means of coping with the sex industry that would contain the moral degeneration associated with prostitution while allowing the state to tax the industry as it would any other. During the US occupation from 1898 to 1902, the US military government maintained Spain's regulatory system. But after independence, in

line with trends elsewhere, Cuban intellectuals, social reformers, and nation-builders denounced prostitution regulation as an exploitative system given to corruption, a relic of backward Spanish colonialism unbefitting a modern nation. Tiffany A. Sippial, *Prostitution, Modernity and the Making of the Cuban Republic, 1840–1920* (Chapel Hill: University of North Carolina Press, 2013); Amalia L. Cabezas, "Havana's Sex Trade," in *Trafficking in Women*, ed. Chaumont, Rodriguez, and Servais, 82–89.

139. Sidney O'Donoghue to Ellis Briggs, Memorandum, September 11, 1941, enclosure to Despatch No. 2616 of September 11, 1941, from Embassy at Habana, Cuba, Box 135, General Records of the United States Embassy in Havana, RG 84, NARA.

140. Van Hyning to Taft, Report on Visit to the Caribbean Area, 24.

141. The Navy Surgeon in Guantánamo Bay advocated the creation of an isolation hospital, arguing that the practice of expelling an infected woman from town simply circulated those women carrying venereal disease between the three cities that troops visited on leave—Caimanera, Guantánamo, and Santiago. Van Hyning to Taft, Report on Visit to the Caribbean Area, 6.

142. Van Hyning to Taft, Report on Visit to the Caribbean Area, 5.

143. Van Hyning to Taft, Report on Visit to the Caribbean Area, 6.

144. One official reflected, "In discussing the job with Mr. Taft at the time I took the position, it was hoped that the CWS representative might be effective in securing the cooperation of foreign governments in the Caribbean Area and South America, where American armed services were stationed, for the purpose of limiting sex contacts and reducing venereal disease infection to a minimum." However, while progress was being made in Puerto Rico and the Virgin Islands to these ends, the official determined "as to foreign countries in the Caribbean and South America, I have finally come to the conclusion that the original conception of the job is not valid." Conrad Van Hyning to Mark McCloskey, Director of Community War Services, July 3, 1944, Box 2, Entry 66, RG 215, NARA.

145. Van Hyning to McCloskey, July 3, 1944.

CHAPTER 6

1. SOFAs have not resolved all problems relating to jurisdiction and have themselves often been the source of great conflict, but they did create a template for carving out overseas bases as anomalous legal zones that deviated from the usual rules of Westphalian sovereignty. On the rise of SOFAs in the broader history of US extraterritoriality, see Kal Raustiala, *Does the Constitution Follow the Flag? The Evolution of Territoriality in American Law* (New York: Oxford University Press, 2009), chap. 4; and Peter Rowe, "Historical Developments Influencing the Present Law of Visiting Forces," in *The Handbook of the Law of Visiting Forces*, ed. Dieter Fleck, 2nd ed. (Oxford: Oxford University Press, 2018), 13–32. Fumi Inoue theorizes what she calls a postwar "U.S. military legal regime of exception" in her research on SOFAs and the politics of extraterritoriality in postwar Japan and Okinawa in "The Politics of Extraterritoriality in Post-Occupation Japan and U.S.-Occupied Okinawa, 1952–1972" (PhD diss., Boston College, 2021).

2. US Vice Consul Harold Sims to Chief of Police Colonel Alexandre Moss Simões dos Reis, May 19, 1944, Enclosure to Despatch No 16621 of June 27, 1944, from the Embassy at Rio de Janeiro, 811.24532/6-2744, Central Decimal Files (hereafter CDF) 1940–1944, Record Group 59: General Records of

the Department of State (hereafter RG 59), National Archives and Records Administration (hereafter NARA).

3. Abílio Cesar Cavalcanti of the Department of Public Security to Chief of State Police, Colonel Alexandre Moss Simões dos Reis, May 26, 1944, Enclosure to Despatch No 16621 of June 27, 1944, from the Embassy at Rio de Janeiro, 811.24532/6-2744, CDF 1940–1944, RG 59, NARA.

4. On international law as an essential tool of US imperialist foreign policy in Latin America in the early twentieth century, see Benjamin Allen Coates, *Legalist Empire: International Law and Ameircan Foreign Relations in the Early Twentieth Century* (New York: Oxford University Press, 2016), especially chaps. 2 and 5.

5. Teemu Ruskola, "Canton Is Not Boston: The Invention of American Imperial Sovereignty," *American Quarterly* 57, no. 3 (2005): 859–884, and "Colonialism without Colonies: On the Extraterritorial Jurisprudence of the US Court for China," *Law and Contemporary Problems*, June 22, 2008; Eileen Scully, *Bargaining with the State from Afar* (New York: Columbia University Press, 2001); Francis C. Jones, *Extraterritoriality in Japan, and the Diplomatic Relations Resulting in Its Abolition, 1853–1899* (New York: AMS Press, 1931). The United States was not the least bit exceptional in its exertion of extraterritorial authority in the Asia Pacific. A comparative reflection on US and European practices of extraterritoriality is beyond the scope of this book. For a recent volume the contemplates extraterritoriality across time and space, see Daniel S. Margolies, Umut Özsu, Maïa Pal, and Ntina Tzouvala, *The Extraterritoriality of Law: History, Theory, Politics* (New York: Routledge, 2019). For deeper dives into extraterritoriality, law, and European power, see Lauren Benton, *A Search of Sovereignty: Law and Geography in European Empires: 1400–1900* (Cambridge: Cambridge University Press, 2010); and Turan Kayaoğlu, *Legal Imperialism: Sovereignty and Extraterritoriality in Japan, the Ottoman Empire and China* (Cambridge: Cambridge University Press, 2010).

6. France was hardly in a strong position to bargain at the time. The United States also exercised jurisdiction over US troops in England during World War I, but there, England never consented to a formal arrangement of this sort. Instead, something of a "gentlemen's agreement" was reached.

7. For instance, see Lauren Benton, "Constructing Sovereignty: Extraterritoriality in the Oriental Republic of Uruguay," in *Law and Colonial Cultures: Legal Regimes in World History, 1400–1900* (New York and Cambridge: Cambridge University Press, 2001), 210–252.

8. Theodore Roosevelt, Annual Message to Congress, December 6, 1904.

9. In *Mestizo International Law*, Arnulf Becker Lorca contends that nineteenth-century jurists in Latin America and elsewhere on the "semi-periphery" adopted and adapted international law during this period, in part to assert their own civilization, but they did so as a counter-hegemonic technique to advance their own objectives, Arnulf Becker Lorca, *Mestizo International Law: A Global Intellectual History, 1842–1933* (New York: Cambridge University Press, 2015). Similarly, Liliana Obregón argues that Creole elites in nineteenth-century Latin America appropriated civilizing discourse "to avoid being excluded from the rights and entitlements assigned (by Europe) to other members of the 'community of civilized nations'" but that Latin American elites also asserted their own conceptions of international law outside of the European framework. Liliana Obregón, "Completing Civilization: Creole Consciousness and International Law in Nineteenth-Century Latin America," in *International*

Law and Its Others, ed. Anne Orford (Cambridge University Press, 2009), 247–264. Juan Pablo Scarfi's work on US–Latin American cooperation in articulating an American international law complicates the picture a bit, by demonstrating how some prominent South American lawyers believed in the "civilizing mission" of international law and sometimes supported interventions carried out under this banner, for instance in Cuba, though their multilateral vision differentiated their vision from the unilateral impulses the US government. Juan Pablo Scarfi, *The Hidden History of International Law in the Americas: Empire and Legal Networks* (New York: Oxford University Press, 2017).

10. That said, Calvo did appear to agree that international law provided for extraterritorial jurisdiction over soldiers transiting or garrisoned in a friendly foreign country. He wrote that consent to allow foreign soldiers to pass through a nation's territory marked "the implicit abandonment" jurisdiction over those soldiers. Carlos Calvo, *Le Droit International: Théorie et practice précédé d'un historique des gens* (Paris: Rousseau, 1896), 3:341.

11. Antonio J. C. dos Reis, Commander of the Eighth Military Region in Brazil, to the Brazilian Ministry of War, May 9, 1944, enclosure to Ambassador Jefferson Caffery to Secretary of State, 811.24532/62, CDF 1940–1944, RG 59, NARA.

12. The British originally sought, as they had during World War I, to exercise jurisdiction over US troops, and the British Allied Forces Act of 1940 explicitly preserved British jurisdiction over crimes committed against British law by all foreign servicemen. But the US refused to accept the terms. When the British sought to retain jurisdiction at least over crimes committed by US troops when off base and off duty, US officials reasoned that since US soldiers could be conscripted against their will and sent overseas, then they were *always* on duty. After drawn-out negotiations on the matter, the United States of America Visiting Forces Act, which became law in August 1943, created an exception to the British Allied Forces Act of 1940 and granted US troops immunity from UK courts. United States of America (Visiting Forces) Act 1942, August 6, 1942. On this history, see David Reynolds, *Rich Relations: The American Occupation of Britain, 1942–1945* (New York: Random House, 1995); and Steven High, *Base Colonies in the Western Hemisphere, 1940–1967* (Palgrave Macmillan, 2008), 159.

13. "Contra Wilbert L. Schwartzfiger, por homicidio por imprudencia," Registro Judicial: Órgano del Poder Judicial de la República, August 18, 1926, Vol. XXIV, N 83, 772–775.

14. William Dawson to Secretary of State, March 20, 1940, 711f.1914/135, CDF 1940–1944, RG 59, NARA.

15. Sumner Welles (for the Secretary of State) to Ambassador Wilson, June 29, 1943, 711f.1914/709, Document 529, *Foreign Relations of the United States, 1943, The American Republics, Vol. VI.* Acta Confidencial de una conversación tenida por el excelentísimo Señor Presidente de la Republica con el Embajador de los Estados Unidos en Panama, Sr. William Dawson, January 7, 1941, and accompanying Aide Memoire January 7, 1941. Archivo del Ministerio de Relaciones Exteriores, Panamá, Panama City, Panama (hereafter MRE Panama).

16. Declaración de Inocencia Flores taken by District Attorney Luis A. Carrasco and Secretary C. Dario Sandoval, February 26, 1942, Vol. 20, MRE Panama.

17. Declaración de Tomas Frendega taken by District Attorney Luis A. Carrasco and Secretary C. Dario Sandoval, February 15, 1942, Embajada de Estados Unidos, Vol. 20, MRE Panama.

18. Declaración de Leonidas Castillo, February 15, 1942.

19. Declaración de Eric Gilkes, recorded and signed by Police Officer V. Bellido, District Attorney Luis A. Carrasco M. to Attorney General V. A. de Leon S. transcribed in letter from Panamanian Attorney General V. A. de Leon S. to Minister of Government and Justice, March 7, 1942, Embajada de Estados Unidos, Vol. 20, MRE Panama. Statement by Inocencia Flores taken by Carrasco Sandoval, February 26, 1942.

20. Declaración de Patrocinia Castillo taken by District Attorney Luis A. Carrasco and Secretary C. Dario Sandoval, February 15, 1942, Embajada de Estados Unidos, Vol. 20, MRE Panama.

21. Declaración de Patrocinia Castillo, February 15, 1942.

22. Declaración de Inocencia Flores, February 26, 1942.

23. Declaración de Eric Gilkes, March 7, 1942.

24. District Attorney Luis A. Carrasco M. to Attorney General V. A. de Leon S., reproduced in letter from Panamanian Attorney General V. A. de Leon S. to Minister of Government and Justice, March 7, 1942, Embajada de Estados Unidos, Vol. 20, MRE Panama.

25. Fábrega to Wilson, April 20, 1942, Embajada de Estados Unidos, Vol. 20, MRE Panama.

26. Fábrega to Wilson, April 20, 1942.

27. Wilson to Fábrega, April 27, 1940, Embajada de Estados Unidos, Vol. 20, MRE Panama.

28. Wilson to Fábrega, May 5, 1942, Embajada de Estados Unidos, Vol. 20, MRE Panama. Major General Wm. E. Shedd to Wilson, May 2, 1942, Embajada de Estados Unidos, Vol. 20, MRE Panama.

29. Shedd to Muccio, July 10, 1942, Embajada de Estados Unidos, Vol. 20, MRE Panama.

30. Fábrega to Muccio, June 18, 1942, Embajada de Estados Unidos, Vol. 20, MRE Panama.

31. Fábrega to Muccio, August 10, 1942, Embajada de Estados Unidos, Vol. 20, MRE Panama.

32. Transcribed in Muccio to Fábrega, September 8, 1942, Embajada de Estados Unidos, Vol. 20, MRE Panama.

33. Fábrega to Wilson, October 30, 1942, Embajada de Estados Unidos, Vol. 20, MRE Panama.

34. Fábrega to Muccio, August 10, 1942.

35. Martin Olson, May 28, 1944, Embajada de Estados Unidos, Vol. 20, MRE Panama. Another strategy for shielding US servicemen from the Panamanian justice system in situations in which Panama was entitled to jurisdiction was to send the men overseas before a custody transfer could be requested, and then inform the Panamanian government that the servicemen could not be turned over for trial because they had left the country "for military reasons." Case file against Lewis F. Quigley, Jack Hedgepeth, Gilbert Joseph Genereux and Paul Leroy Lucas, June 16, 1942, Sección de Judiciales, Archivo Nacional de Panamá, Panama City, Panama (hereafter ANP).

36. Fábrega to de Leon, July 14, 1943 (P1120170), Embajada de Estados Unidos, Vol. 20, MRE. Comunicado July 16, 1943, Embajada de Estados Unidos, Vol. 20, MRE Panama.

37. Wilson to Fábrega, March 22, 1943, Embajada de Estados Unidos, Vol. 20, MRE Panama. Wilson to Interim Minister of Foreign Relations Victor Goytia, May 21, 1943, Embajada de Estados Unidos, Vol. 20, MRE Panama. In another

example, Filewicz was not allowed to use the phone at the police station to call his superiors in the Canal Zone, and when US authorities protested this, the minister of justice explained that this was because the police officers were not permitted to use the phone for long-distance calls. De la Guardia to Fábrega August 4, 1943, Embajada de Estados Unidos, Vol. 20, MRE Panama.

38. Wilson to Fábrega, March 22, 1943. Wilson to Goytia, May 21, 1943.

39. Wilson to Goytia, May 21, 1943.

40. Entrada No. 123, Tribunal Superior del Primer Distrito Judicial, Juicio Contra Douglas David Boyd, por lesiones personales, Repartido: April 20, 1944 (assault occurred June 6, 1941), Sección de Judiciales, Archivo Nacional de Panamá (hereafter ANP).

41. A medical inspection revealed that Castillo did not have gonorrhea, and the court found in Castillo's favor on the matter.

42. Entrada No 491, Fiscalia Tercera del Circuito, Caso Contra Lewis F. Quigley, Jack Hedgepeth, Gilber Genereux y Paul Leroy Lucas, Iniciado June 16, 1942, Sección de Judiciales, ANP.

43. Virgilio Angulo, Alcalde Municipal, to the Governor of the Province of Panama, January 23, 1942, Zona del Canal Vol. 17, MRE Panama.

44. Foreign Minister Octavio Fábrega to Ambassador Edwin Wilson, September 14, 1942, Zona del Canal Vol. 17, MRE Panama.

45. See also High, *Base Colonies in the Western Hemisphere*, 157.

46. "While on the one hand the United States recognizes the continuance of the ultimate sovereignty of the Republic of Cuba over the above described areas of land and water, on the other hand the Republic of Cuba consents that during the period of the occupation by the United States of said areas under the terms of this agreement the United States shall exercise complete jurisdiction and control over and within said areas" "Agreement Between the United States and Cuba for the Lease of Lands for Coaling and Naval Stations," February 23, 1903.

47. Supreme Court Resolution dated April l 3, 1918, reproduced in "No serán juzgados por nuestros tribunales los soldados de EE.UU. que delincan en Cuba," *El Mundo*, October 9, 1942.

48. Once US officials agreed in theory to the idea of a Joint Military Zone, the question of who would exercise jurisdiction there was impossible to reconcile. The State Department agreed to remove any mention of jurisdiction due to failure to agree and concern on the part of US officials that the agreement on Guantanamo might serve as a model for agreements reached elsewhere in the Americas. Welles to Knox, August 7, 1941, Box 135, General Records of the United States Embassy in Havana, Record Group 84: Records of the Foreign Service Posts of the Department of State (hereafter RG 84), NARA. In the meantime, airbase construction progressed in the British colonies, where jurisdiction proved somewhat easier to sort out. The airbase in Jamaica decreased the need for an expanded Guantanamo base, and US officials abandoned the project.

49. Jana Lipman offers an excellent analysis of this case in, "Guantánamo and the Case of Kid Chicle: Private Contract Labor and the Development of the US Military," in *Colonial Crucible: Empire in the Making of the Modern American State*, ed. Alfred McCoy and Francisco Scarano (Madison: University of Wisconsin Press, 2009), 452–460.

50. James Forrestal, Acting Secretary of the Navy to Secretary of State, January 6, 1941, Box 137, General Records of the United States Embassy in Havana, RG

84, NARA; Ralph A. Bard, Acting Secretary of the Navy, to Amassador George Messersmith, April 22, 1941, Box 172, General Records of the United States Embassy in Havana, RG 84, NARA.

51. Article IX, Agreement for Military Cooperation signed in Havana, June 19, 1942.
52. Major Guillermo Pierluisi to Commanding Officer of US Troops in Cuba re: Disorders between American troops and Cuban police, June 29, 1943, Box 206, General Records of the United States Embassy in Havana, RG 84, NARA.
53. Boletin 187, "La voz de la calle," July 9, 1943, Box 206, General Records of the United States Embassy in Havana, RG 84, NARA.
54. Vice Consul Franklin Hawley to Briggs, June 19, 1943, Box 206, General Records of the United States Embassy in Havana, RG 84, NARA.
55. Pierluisi to Commanding Officer of US Troops in Cuba, June 29, 1943.
56. Garret Ackerson, Strictly Confidential Memorandum, July 26, 1943, Box 206, General Records of the United States Embassy in Havana, RG 84, NARA.
57. Pierluisi to Commanding Officer of US Troops in Cuba, June 29, 1943.
58. Samuel McGreery to Base Commander, January 27, 1943, Subject: Punishment of an unauthorized vendor, Box 207, General Records of the United States Embassy in Havana, RG 84, NARA.
59. McGreery to Base Commander, January 27, 1943.
60. Woodward to Secretary of State, May 24, 1946. Re: Resume of Jurisdictional matters affecting United States Armed Forces personnel stationed at wartime bases in Cuba, 811.203/5-2446, CDF 1940–1944, RG 59, NARA.
61. Sargeant Antonio Fortez Valdes, December 5, 1943, Box 277, General Records of the United States Embassy in Havana, RG 84, NARA.
62. Valdes, December 5, 1943.
63. Commanding Officer Leigh Wade to Ambassdor Spruille Braden, April 27, 1944, Box 277, General Records of the United States Embassy in Havana, RG 84, NARA.
64. Major Fred R. Panico by order of Colonel Wade, May 15, 1944, Box 277, General Records of the United States Embassy in Havana, RG 84, NARA.
65. Braden to Mañach, May 24, 1944, Box 277, General Records of the United States Embassy in Havana, RG 84, NARA.
66. Mañach to Braden, June 2, 1944, Box 3, Serie: Asuntos Militares 1944–1959, Subserie Asuntos Políticos Militares 1900–1959, Archivo del Ministerio de Relaciones Exteriores de Cuba, Havana, Cuba (hereafter MRE Cuba).
67. Mañach to Braden, June 22, 1944, Box 277, General Records of the United States Embassy in Havana, RG 84, NARA.
68. Orestes Robledo Reyes, "Estudio de la Comunidad de San Antonio de los Baños" (Thesis, Universidad de la Habana, 1952), Archivo del Museo de San Antonio de los Baños, San Antonio de los Baños, Cuba (hereafter Museo de San Antonio de los Baños), 391.
69. Robledo Reyes, "Estudio de la Comunidad," 393.
70. Robledo Reyes, "Estudio de la Comunidad," 393–394.
71. Draft enclosure to Colonel L. Mathewson to Walter M. Walmsley, Division of American Republics, State Department, November 7, 1942, 811.203/199, CDF 1940–1944, RG 59, NARA.
72. Draft enclosure to Colonel L. Mathewson to Walter M. Walmsley, November 7, 1942.
73. Braden to Secretary of State, September 8, 1943, 837.30/88, CDF 1940–1944, RG 59, NARA.

74. Appendix to Braddock Report, 13. Consul Daniel M. Braddock to Jefferson Caffery, Report: Relations Between Brazilians and Americans in Para, July 14, 1944, 711.32/7-1944, CDF 1940–1944, RG 59, NARA.
75. Appendix to Braddock Report, 7.
76. Consul Edward D. McLaughlin to Ambassador Jefferson Caffery, September 10, 1942, Enclosure to John F. Simmons, Counselor of Embassy to State, September 19, 1942, 810.20 DEFENSE/3267, CDF 1940-1944, RG 59, NARA.
77. McLaughlin to Caffery, September 10, 1942.
78. McLaughlin to Caffery, September 15, 1942, Enclosure to John F. Simmons, Counselor of Embassy to State, September 19, 1942, 810.20 DEFENSE/3267, CDF 1940-1944, RG 59, NARA.
79. McLaughlin to Caffery, September 10, 1942.
80. R. L. Walsh and Jonas H. Ingram to Colonel Byron T. Burt, September 15, 1942, Enclosure to John F. Simmons, Counselor of Embassy to State, September 19, 1942, 810.20 DEFENSE/3267, CDF 1940-1944, RG 59, NARA.
81. Appendix to Braddock Report, 7.
82. dos Reis to the Brazilian Ministry of War, May 9, 1944. "Moralizando os Cinemas," *Folha do Norte*, April 14, 1944.
83. Daniel M. Braddock to Jefferson Caffery, Report: Relations Between Brazilians and Americans in Para, July 14, 1944, RG 59, CDF 1940–1944, 711.32/7-1944; W. N. Walmsley Jr., June 22, 1944, 811.24532/63, CDF 1940–1944, RG 59, NARA. Conrad Van Hyning to Dean Snyder, Subject: Attached Report on Brazil, Dutch Guiana, British Guiana, and Trinidad, July 3, 1944, Box 1, Entry 66, Record Group 215: Community War Services, NARA. Vice Consul John H. Burns to the Secretary of State, May 3, 1944, 811.24532/59, CDF 1940–1944, RG 59, NARA. Appendix to Braddock Report. Daniel M. Braddock to Jefferson Caffery, Report: Relations Between Brazilians and Americans in Para, July 14, 1944, 711.32/7-1944, CDF 1940–1944, RG 59, NARA.
84. Burns to the Secretary of State, April 27, 1944.
85. Burns to the Secretary of State, April 27, 1944.
86. Hackworth to John H. Burns, American Vice Consul in Para, June 7, 1944, FW811.24532/59, CDF 1940–1944, RG 59, NARA.
87. Supreme Court Decision in the case of Arthur James Gilbert, Enclosure to Walter J. Donnelly, Chargé d'Affaires ad interim to Secretary of State, November 24, 1944, 811.203/11-2444, CDF 1940–1944, RG 59, NARA.
88. Conflito de Jurisdição n 1520, June 11, 1945, Arquivo do Supremo Tribunal Federal, Brasilia, Brazil.
89. Walter J. Donnelly, Chargé d'Affaires ad interim to Secretary of State, November 24, 1944, 811.203/11-2444, CDF 1940–1944, RG 59, NARA.
90. Memorandum of Conversation, January 23, 1945, Mr. Harrison and Captain Jarrell Garonzik, FW811.203/7-1145, CDF 1940–1944, RG 59, NARA.
91. Office Memo, Dearborn to Wells and Briggs, June 19, 1946, 811.24522/6-546, CDF 1945–1949, RG 59, NARA.

CHAPTER 7

1. Capitolino Antonio Filós to the President of the Republic, January 26, 1948, Expediente 322, Caja 107, Fondo de la Presidencia, Bases Militares o Sitios de Defensa de Estados Unidos en Panama, Archivo Nacional de Panamá, Panama City, Panama (hereafter ANP).

2. Bruno Bellido, Secretario de Actas de la Union General de Trabajadores de la República, January 26, 1948, Expediente 322, Caja 107, Fondo de la Presidencia. Bases Militares o Sitios de Defensa de Estados Unidos en Panama, ANP.

3. L. A. Guerra to Minister of Finance, November 6, 1947, Expediente 322, Caja 107, Fondo de la Presidencia, Bases Militares o Sitios de Defensa de Estados Unidos en Panama, ANP.

4. Flavio Velásquez Jr. and Prudencio Ayala, Commander of the Firefighter Corps of la Chorrera, October 17. 1948. Governor of Veraguas to President Jiménez, October 14, 1946; Mayor Isaías Díaz to President of the Republic, August 28, 1947, Expediente 322, Caja 107, Fondo de la Presidencia, Bases Militares o Sitios de Defensa de Estados Unidos en Panama, ANP.

5. Flavio Velásquez and Jose Iraiarte, August 16, 1946, Expediente 322, Caja 107, Fondo de la Presidencia, Bases Militares o Sitios de Defensa de Estados Unidos en Panama, ANP. Guerra to Minister of Finance, November 6, 1947. Flavio Velásquez Jr., Governor, Tomás Guardia Jr., Public Works Engineer, José R. Luttrell Jr., Provincial Engineer, and Narciso A. Ayala, Visiting Education Inspector, "Plan de construcción de escuelas en la provincia aprovechando el material que hay en las bases recientamente devueltas a la república," October 8, 1946, Expediente 322, Caja 107, Fondo de la Presidencia, Bases Militares o Sitios de Defensa de Estados Unidos en Panama, ANP. Flavio Velásquez Jr. to the Mayor of Arraiján, October 17, 1946, Expediente 322, Caja 107, Fondo de la Presidencia, Bases Militares o Sitios de Defensa de Estados Unidos en Panama, ANP. Delgado Capipuerto to Minister of Finance, December 13, Expediente 322, Caja 107, Fondo de la Presidencia, Bases Militares o Sitios de Defensa de Estados Unidos en Panama, ANP.

6. Thomas L. Pearcy, *We Answer Only to God: Politics and the Military in Panama, 1903–1947* (Albuquerque: University of New Mexico Press, 1998), 125.

7. "Resolution XXV: Post-War Problems, Final Act of the Third Meeting of Ministers of Foreign Affairs of the American Republics," *American Journal of International Law* 6, no. 2 (April 1942): 83.

8. Melvyn P. Leffler, "The American Conception of National Security and the Beginnings of the Cold War, 1945–48," *American Historical Review* 89, no. 2 (April 1984): 346–381; Stephen Wertheim, *Tomorrow, the World: The Birth of US Global Supremacy* (Cambridge, MA: Belknap Press, 2020).

9. On these efforts see Tom Long, "Historical Antecedents and Post–World War II Regionalism in the Americas," *World Politics* 72, no. 2 (April 2020): 214–253; Stella Krepp, *The Decline of the Western Hemisphere*, unpublished manuscript, chap. 2; Christy Thornton, *Revolution in Development: Mexico and the Governance of the Global Economy* (Oakland: University of California Press, 2021); Corinne A. Pernet, "Shifting Position to the Global South: Latin America's Initiatives in the Early Years at the United Nations," in *Latin America, 1810–2010: Dreams and Legacies*, ed. Claude Auroi and Aline Helg, 83–100 (London: Imperial College Press, 2012); Elizabeth Borgwardt, *New Deal for the World* (Cambridge, MA: Harvard University Press, 2007); John Childs, *Unequal Alliance: The Inter-American Military System, 1938–1979* (Boulder, CO: Westview Press, 1980); David Green, *The Containment of Latin America: A History of the Myths and Realities of the Good Neighbor Policy* (Chicago: Quadrangle Books, 1971).

10. On Brazil's quest to obtain a seat on the UN Security Council, see Eugenio Vargas Garcia, *O sexto membro permanente: o Brasil e a criação da ONU* (Rio de Janeiro: Editora Contraponto, 2012).

11. See Thornton, *Revolution in Development*, chap. 4; and Eric Helleiner, *Forgotten Foundations of Bretton Woods: International Development and the Making of the Postwar Order* (Ithaca, NY: Cornell University Press, 2016).

12. Pernet, "Shifting Position to the Global South." Pernet also describes subsequent efforts by Latin American delegates to insist on a greater focus on social democratic rights in the UN Declaration of Human Rights. On this topic, see also Katherine Marino, *Feminism for the Americas: The Making of an International Human Rights Movement* (Chapel Hill: University of North Carolina Press, 2019).

13. Thornton, *Revolution in Development*, 107–119. Pernet, "Shifting Position to the Global South," 87.

14. Laurence Duggan, Memorandum on Proposed Allocation of Funds of the Coordinator's Basic Economy and Health and Sanitation Programs, 810.12/177, Central Decimal Files (hereafter CDF) 1940–1944, Record Group 59: General Records of the Department of State (hereafter RG 59), National Archives and Records Administration (hereafter NARA). Nelson Rockefeller, as head of the OIAA, the wartime agency that devised and administered many of the development assistance programs in Latin America during World War II, also anticipated that problems would follow when the agency's work inevitably came to an end at the war's conclusion. Rockefeller cautioned against any rapid diminution of programs at the war's end. When possible, Rockefeller had built some protections against this eventuality into the structure of OIAA programs, structuring them in such a way that would allow them to continue beyond the duration of the war, even though his office likely would not continue in peacetime. For example, public health programs followed the Rockefeller Foundation's model of establishing cooperative arrangements that would, over time, become fully sustained by the host government. In 1943, looking forward, Rockefeller sought to create subsidiary corporations to administer certain OIAA activities and to transfer the administration of other programs from his wartime office to permanent agencies within the government to ensure their postwar survival. Rockefeller to Stettinius, October 21, 1943, NAR, RG 4, Series o, Subseries 1, Box 10, Folder 83, Rockefeller Archive Center, Tarrytown, New York (hereafter RAC). *History of the Office of the Coordinator of Inter-American Affairs* (Washington, DC: Government Printing Office, 1947).

15. Leffler, "The American Conception of National Security," 355.

16. Quoted in Leffler, "The American Conception of National Security, 355.

17. *Foreign Relations of the United States*, 1944, Vol. VII, 87–92. Child, *Unequal Alliance*, 73. Green, *The Containment of Latin America*, 180–181.

18. Child, *Unequal Alliance*, 77.

19. For more on the Inter-American Military Bill, see Chester Pach Jr. , "The Containment of US Military Aid to Latin America, 1944–49," *Diplomatic History* 6, no. 3 (July 1982): 225–244; John Child, *Unequal Alliance*; Stephen Rabe, "Inter-American Military Cooperation, 1944–1951," *World Affairs* 137, no. 2 (Fall 1974): 132–149.

20. These tensions were also evident in an inter-agency tussle over whether State Department officials should play a significant role in the 1944 Staff Conversations. Memorandum for the President, Subject: Forthcoming Bilateral Staff Conversations, November 1, 1944, 810.20 DEFENSE/9-2044, CDF 1940–1944, RG 59, NARA. On these tensions and their impact on the IAMS more broadly, see Child, *Unequal Alliance*, 75–110.

21. Child, *Unequal Alliance*, 79.
22. Child, *Unequal Alliance*, 78.
23. Mark A. Stoler, *Allies and Adversaries: The Joint Chiefs of Staff, the Grand Alliance, and US Strategy in World War II* (Chapel Hill: University of North Carolina Press, 2003), 239–240.
24. Resolution IV of the Act of Chapultepec, Adopted at the Inter-American Conference held in Chapultepec Mexico from February 21 to March 7, 1945, signed March 6, 1945.
25. Joint Chiefs of Staff, "Over-All Examination of US Requirements for Military Bases and Rights," October 25, 1945, Joint Chiefs of Staff 570/34, CDF 1945–1949, RG 59, NARA.
26. Joint Chiefs of Staff, "Over-All Examination of US Requirements for Military Bases and Rights," October 25, 1945.
27. Leffler, "The American Conception of National Security"; Vine, *Base Nation*, 30.
28. Joint Chiefs of Staff, Policy on Post-War Military Problems, November 15, 1943, FW 811.24500/11-1543, CDF 1940–1944, RG 59, NARA. The JCS outlined projected US basing needs in three phases. First, the period after German defeat but before Japanese defeat. Second, the immediate period after the war ended, before the creation of a global organization for collective security. And third, a period after a United Nations was created. The JCS contended that basing requirements for the third period would have to be determined as the United Nations organization took shape, but the JCS did advance basing needs for the first two phases at this time.
29. Admiral William D. Leahy to President Roosevelt, November 15, 1943, 811.24500/11-1543, CDF 1940–1944, RG 59, NARA; Military Air Base Requirements—Period I, Map, Enclosure to Joint Chiefs of Staff, Policy on Post-War Military Problems, November 15, 1943; and Military Air Base Requirements—Period II, Map, Enclosure to Joint Chiefs of Staff, Policy on Post-War Military Problems, November 15, 1943.
30. Joint Chiefs of Staff, "Over-All Examination of US Requirements for Military Bases and Rights," October 25, 1945.
31. Roosevelt to State, January 7, 1944, 811.24500/1-744, CDF 1940–1944, RG 59, NARA.
32. "Nazis Assail US over Latin Bases," *New York Times*, August 9. 1941.
33. Strictly Confidential Daily Information Bulletin, February 16, 1944, NAR, RG 4, Series O, Subseries 1, Box 10, Folder 81, RAC.
34. FA 6 Official Japanese Broadcasts, Latin American Affairs, NAR, RG 4, Series O, Subseries 1, Box 10, Folder 81, RAC.
35. Department of State Division of Current Information, Memorandum of the Press Conference Saturday, March 6, 1943, 811.24522/60, CDF 1940–1944, RG 59, NARA.
36. Harold Williamson to Secretary of State, May 9, 1944, 811.24510/17, CDF 1940–1944, RG 59, NARA.
37. Francisco de Assis Chateaubriand, "O penedo," *O Jornal*, September 24, 1944.
38. Virginia Prewett, "Our Postwar Designs: Nazis Make Charges," *Washington Post*, March 13, 1943.
39. Editorial in *El Comercio*, May 10, 1944, enclosure to despatch from George H. Butler, First Secretary of US Embassy in Peru to Secretary of State, May 10, 1944, 811.24510/16, CDF 1940–1944, RG 59, NARA.
40. Assis Chateaubriand, "O penedo."

41. "No Need to Fear US on Bases, Says Hull: Utterly Absurd for Any Latin American Nations to Suspect Our Plans," *New York Times*, June 13, 1944.

42. William C. Grey Jr. to President Truman, May 18, 1945, 811.24510/5-1845, CDF 1945–1949, RG 59, NARA.

43. Stimson to Hull, January 14, 1944, 811.24500/1-1444, CDF 1940–1944, RG 59, NARA.

44. Memorandum for the President, April 7, 1944, 811.24500/2-144, CDF 1940–1944, RG 59, NARA.

45. Military Aviation Agreement Between the United States and Brazil, June 14, 1944. Enclosure to Caffery to State, June 14, 1944, 711.322/131, CDF 1940–1944, RG 59, NARA; *Foreign Relations of the United States, Diplomatic Papers*, 1944. The American Republics, 560–565. Also at times referred to as the "Strategic Air Base Agreement" and the "Secret Base Agreement."

46. Military Aviation Agreement Between the United States and Brazil, June 14, 1944.

47. Walmsley to Bonsal and Duggan, February 24, 1944, 711.3227/47, *Foreign Relations of the United States, Diplomatic Papers*, 1944, The American Republics, 554–555.

48. Frank L. Kluckhoh, "Brazilians Cooler to US 'Occupation': Some Opinion Seen Affronted by Profusion of Our Men Now That War Is Over," *New York Times*, January 5, 1946.

49. American Vice Consul Donald W. Lamm to Paul C. Daniels, Esquire, Chargé d'Affaires ad interim US Embassy Brazil, January 28, 1946, enclosure to Paul C. Daniels to Daniel M. Braddock, Division of Brazilian Affairs, State Department, February 6, 1946, 811.24532/2-646, CDF 1945–1949, RG 59, NARA.

50. Lamm to Daniels, January 28, 1946.

51. Interview with Diógenes Arruda, June 1979, Portal Vermelho, Transcrição Diego Grossi Pacheco, http://www.marxists.org/portugues/arruda/1979/06/entrevista.htm (accessed December 14, 2021).

52. Rio Embassy to State, April 3, 1946, "Subject: Prestes Attacks Permanence of American Soldiers on Bases," 811.24532/4-346, CDF 1945–1949, RG 59, NARA.

53. "Os americanos no Brasil," *Folha da Mañha*, September 25, 1946, and "Não falou pelo povo," *Folha do Povo*, September 26, 1946.

54. Various, DPS 198 v3, Folhas 1336 a 1512, Setor Geral, Notação 26N, Fundo Policias Politicas do Rio de Janeiro, Arquivo Público do Estado do Rio de Janeiro, Rio de Janeiro, Brazil (hereafter APERJ).

55. Francisco de Assis Chateaubriand, "Malaise," *O Jornal*, March 30, 1946.

56. Daniels to State, March 28, 1946, Subject: Recent Publicity Relating to Air Bases in Brazil and Strategic Air Bases Agreement, 811.24532/3-2846, CDF 1945–1949, RG 59, NARA.

57. Carlos Lacerda, "O brigadeiro disse: Nunca," *Tribuna da Imprensa*, April 28, 1945.

58. Clarence Brooks, Chargé d'Affaires ad interim to Secretary of State, April 16, 1947, Subject: Withdrawal of United States Armed Forces from the Brazilian Airports, 811.24532/4-1647, CDF 1945–1949, RG 59, NARA.

59. *Gazeta de Noticias* quoted in unsigned report from US embassy in Rio, Subject: Editorial Comment on the Return of Airport Installations to Brazilian Government, April 18, 1947, RG 59, 811.24532/4-1847, CDF 1945–1949, RG 59, NARA.

60. Prestes to Brazilian Foreign Office, quoted in unsigned report from US embassy in Rio, Subject: Editorial Comment on the Return of Airport Installations to Brazilian Government, April 18, 1947, 811.24532/4-1847, CDF 1945–1949, RG 59, NARA.

61. Alberto F. Nufer to State, August 9, 1944, Box 12, Classified General Records of the United States Embassy in Havana, Record Group 84: Records of the Foreign Service Posts of the Department of State (hereafter RG 84), NARA.

62. "Entregadas al gobierno cubano las bases militares por los EE.UU.," and Juan Simplon, "Boberías," *Hoy*, May 21, 1946. "Cuban para los cubanos," *Siempre*, May 21, 1946.

63. Braden to State, January 12, 1945, Subject: Post-war use of military air bases in Cuba, 811.24537/1-1245, CDF 1945–1949, RG 59, NARA.

64. Braden to State, January 12, 1945.

65. Braden to State, January 12, 1945.

66. Department of State Memorandum of Conversation, Subject: Post-war Use of Military Air Bases in Cuba, Participants Major General George Strong, Major General Collins, Colonel Hamilton, Captain F. P. Thomas, Captain H. W. Ruble, Ambassador Spruille Braden, Mr. John Hickerson, Mr. George F. Scherer, January 25, 1945, 811.24537/1-2545, CDF 1945–1949, RG 59, NARA.

67. Braden to State, January 12, 1945.

68. Agreement between the United States and Cuba for Military Cooperation, signed in Havana, June 19, 1942.

69. For instances in which the outcome of legal cases hung on the surprisingly opaque answer to the question "When Was World War II?" see Mary Dudziak, *War Time: An Idea, Its History, Its Consequences* (New York: Oxford University Press, 2013), chap. 2.

70. Norweb to State, Subject: Policy regarding postwar operation of United States bases in Cuba established under Agreement of September 7, 1942, August 22, 1945, 811.24537/8-2245, CDF 1945–1949, RG 59, NARA.

71. "Necesaria la unión de los pueblos de América para una paz justa, dijo Grau," *El Mundo*, May 21, 1946.

72. "Entregadas al gobierno cubano las bases militares por los EE.UU.," *Hoy*, May 21, 1946.

73. These withdrawals proceeded in a much more bureaucratic, mundane fashion than the ceremonies elsewhere. The US State Department would simply send a note indicating the US abandonment of a particular site, and request that it be removed from the list included with the lease agreement. John Muccio to Fábrega, April 28, 1944, Secretaria de Relaciones Exteriores/Ministerio— Expediente de Bases Militares o Sitios de Defensa de Estados Unidos de Panama (Zona del Canal), Expediente 282, Caja 91, Archivo Nacional de Panamá, Panama City, Panama (hereafter ANP). By October 1945, US troops had abandoned about one quarter of the occupied land. Brigadier General W. C. Christy to Eduardo Valdes, Director of Relations with the Canal Zone, October 3, 1945, Sitios de Defensa Volumen XII, Archivo del Ministerio de Relaciones Exteriores, Panamá, Panama City, Panama (hereafter MRE Panama).

74. Lecture by Doctor Jorge Illueca at the University of Panama on the twenty-fifth anniversary of the rejection of the Filós-Hines Treaty, December 12, 1972, Convenio sobre Sitios de Defensa entre Panama y Los Estados Unidos de America Parte II, MRE Panama.

75. On the transformation of the Canal's strategic utility, see John Major, *Prize Possession: The United States Government and the Panama Canal, 1903–1979* (New York: Cambridge University Press, 1993); Walter LeFeber, *The Panama Canal: The Crisis in Historical Perspective* (New York: Oxford University Press, 1990); and Michael Conniff, *Panama and the United States: The Forced Alliance* (Athens: University of Georgia Press, 2001).

76. Article I, "Agreement for the Lease of Defense Sites in the Republic of Panama," signed May 18, 1942 (Washington, DC: Government Printing Office, 1944).

77. Major, *Prize Possession*, 311.

78. Jiménez to Alfaro, December 5, 1946, Bases Militares o Sitios de Defensa de Estados Unidos en Panama (Zona del Canal) Expediente 322, Caja 107, Fondo de la Presidencia, ANP.

79. Major, *Prize Possession*, 318.

80. Discurso de Ricardo Alfaro frente el Comité Político de la Asamblea General de las Naciones Unidas, November 21, 1946, Bases Militares o Sitios de Defensa de Estados Unidos en Panamá (Zona del Canal) Expediente 322, Caja 107, Fondo de la Presidencia, ANP.

81. LeFeber, *The Panama Canal*, 100.

82. Ambassador Hines to the Secretary of State, December 11, 1947, 711F.1914/12–1147: Telegram, *Foreign Relations of the United States*, 1947, The American Republics, Vol. VIII, Document 793.

83. Alfaro fought to make the renewal of the ten-year lease at Rio Hato dependent on the approval of both nations, but US officials sought exclusive rights to renew the lease, asserting that in light of the improvements the US sought to make to the installations at Rio Hato, the investment of those resources would be worth it only if the US were guaranteed a minimum of twenty years. Ricardo Alfaro to President Jiménez, November 14, 1947, Bases Militares o Sitios de Defensa de Estados Unidos en Panama (Zona del Canal) Expediente 322, Caja 107, Fondo de la Presidencia, ANP.

84. Enrique A. Jiménez to National Assembly, December 12, 1947, Convenio sobre Sitios de Defensa entre Panamá y Los Estados Unidos de America Parte II, MRE Panama.

85. Pearcy, *We Answer Only to God*, 127.

86. David Acosta, *La influencia decisiva de la opinión pública en el rechazo del Convenio Filós-Hines de 1947*, 3rd ed. (Panamá: Impresora de la Nación, 1983).

87. "Desprecio a la opinión pública," *La Hora*, December 10, 1947, reproduced in Acosta, *La influencia decisiva de la opinión pública*, 398.

88. Acosta, *La influencia decisiva de la opinión pública*, 423.

89. Interview with Cleto Manuel Sousa Batista, undated, in Acosta, *La influencia decisiva de la opinión pública*, 313.

90. Interview with Marta Matamoros, July 18, 1977, in Acosta, *La influencia decisiva de la opinión pública*, 245.

91. Interview with Matamoros, July 18, 1977.

92. Informe de la Comisión (majority opinion; Luis E. García de Paredes, Jacinto López y León, Gregorio de los Ríos, Manuel Varela Jr., Manuel Pino R., José M. Herrera G.), December 19, 1947, Convenio sobre Sitios de Defensa entre Panama y Los Estados Unidos de America Parte II, MRE Panama.

93. Hines to Mario de Diego, February 16, 1948, Volume XVII Sitios de Defensa, MRE Panama.

94. Interview with Camilo O. Pérez, undated, in Acosta, *La influencia decisiva de la opinión pública*, 136. See also Bona Fide, "Anatomía de un Rechazo" (Panamá: Ediciones Autodeterminación, 1974).

95. Ambassador Edwin J. Kyle of the US Embassy in Guatemala to Secretary of State, Subject: Recommending Early Termination of Air Base Agreement and Evacuation Remaining United States Armed Forces from Guatemala, January 21, 1948, 811.24514/1-2148, CDF 1945–1949, RG 59, NARA; Ambassador Richard C. Patterson Jr. to Secretary of State, June 15, 1949, Closing of Guatemala City Military Air Base under Consideration by Caribbean Air Command, 811.24514/6-1549, CDF 1944–1949, RG 59; US Air Force Sub-Base at Guatemala City transferred to the Guatemala Government; Texts of Speeches Attached November 4, 1949, 811.24514/11-449, CDF 1945–1949, RG 59, NARA; Return of the 5712th Air Squadron Base to Nicaraguan Authorities and Abandonment of Services, Except Weather Reporting, October 5, 1948, 811.24517/10-1548, CDF 1944–1949, RG 59. On anti-basing protests in Ecuador, see Marc Becker, "Ecuador's Early No-Foreign Military Bases Movement" *Diplomatic History* 41, no. 3, 2017: 518-542.

96. "Viva la farsa!" *La Patria*, October 15, 1947.

97. JCS Report 570/51 Re: Military Arrangements Pertaining to Bases Deriving from Act of Chapultepec, January 25, 1946, FW811.24500/2-25, CDF 1945–1949, RG 59, NARA.

98. JCS Report 570/51 Re: Military Arrangements Pertaining to Bases Deriving from Act of Chapultepec, January 25, 1946.

99. Federico Gil, "The Latin-American Viewpoint," *Inter-American Economic Affairs* 2, no. 4 (1949): 50.

100. Child, *Unequal Alliance*, 91.

101. Child *Unequal Alliance*, 96; Krepp, *Decline of the Western Hemisphere*, 68.

102. Krepp, *Decline of the Western Hemisphere*, 61.

103. Child, *Unequal Alliance*, 102.

104. Krepp, *Decline of the Western Hemisphere*, 7.

105. Charter of the Organization of American States, 1948.

106. Claude Erb attributes much of the Point Four program to the experience of the Institute for Inter-American Affairs, the organization created to execute health and sanitation projects in Latin America as part of the Office of the Coordinator of Inter-American Affairs. See Claude Erb, "Prelude to Point Four: The Institute of Inter-American Affairs," *Diplomatic History* 9, no. 3 (July 1985): 249–269; Merle Curti and Kendal Birr trace the precedents for the Point Four program back further, charting US "advice aid" over the course of the previous century, primarily toward Latin America and the Far East, in *Prelude to Point Four: American Technical Missions Overseas, 1838–1938* (Westport, CT: Praeger, 1978).

107. "Circular Telegram from the Department of State to All Posts in Latin America," April 23, 1961, *Foreign Relations of the United States*, 1961–1963, Volume X, Cuba, January 1961–September 1962, Document 171.

108. "Circular Telegram from the Department of State to All Posts in Latin America," April 23, 1961.

109. Inter-American Treaty of Reciprocal Assistance, September 2, 1947.

110. "Circular Telegram from the Department of State to All Posts in the American Republics," June 24, 1961, *FRUS, 1961–63, Vol. XII, American Republics*, Document 114.

111. Telegram from the Embassy in Colombia to the Department of State, May 6, 1961, *Foreign Relations of the United States* 1961–1962, Vol. XII, American Republics, Document 111. For a sampling of responses that the State Department received to its telegram and to what came to be known as the "Lleras Plan," see the documents published under the heading "The Cuban Question in Latin America" in *Foreign Relations of the United States, 1961–1963, Vol. XII, American Republics*, Documents 109–171.

112. The United States' renewed interest in Latin America, and the increased power of the Defense Department relative to State, finally facilitated new legislation to enable US military aid to Latin America to resume in larger quantities than US defense officials had sought and failed to obtain between 1945 and 1947. Resolution III of the Fourth Foreign Ministers meeting declared that the American Republics should "strengthen their armed forces and collaborate in military matters for Continental Defense," and the 1951 Mutual Security Act created a legal means for the United States to embark upon a series of bilateral agreements with Latin American countries to deliver weapons and advisers. Resolution III: Inter-American Military Cooperation, Final Act of Fourth Foreign Ministers Meeting, Signed in Washington, DC. By the end of the 1950s, every Latin American country except Mexico and Argentina had signed Mutual Defense Assistance Agreements with the United States. When the United States sought Latin American support in alienating Jacobo Arbenz at a meeting of the OAS in 1954, Latin American delegates refused to support intervention and watered down the consensus resolution that the US delegation sought. But they did take the opportunity to resurrect their calls for collaboration in addressing the economic and social problems of the region, and some traded their support for the US delegation's objectives in relation to Guatemala for quid pro quo assistance. See Max Paul Friedman, "Fracas in Caracas: Latin American Diplomatic Resistance to United States Intervention in Guatemala in 1954," *Diplomacy & Statecraft* 21, no. 4 (December 2010): 669–689.

113. Text of speech by Osvaldo Dorticós, reproduced in full in *Hoy*, January 27, 1962. The Cuban Foreign Ministry similarly impugned the Rio Treaty as a "diplomatic instrument whose purpose is to incorporate the Latin American armed forces into the war machinery of the United States of America." El Tratado de Rio y Las Reuniones de Consulta, undated, ca. 1962, Serie 31: Guerra, Archivo del Ministerio de Relaciones Exteriores de Cuba, Havana, Cuba (MRE Cuba).

CONCLUSION

1. David Acosta, *Influencia decisiva de la opinión pública en el rechazo del Convenio Filós-Hines de 1947*, 3rd ed. (Panamá: Impresora de la Nación, 1983), 38.

2. I borrow this concept of "elasticity" in Latin American legal culture from Carlos Aguirre and Ricardo D. Salvatore, "Introduction: Writing the History of Law, Crime and Punishment in Latin America," in *Crime and Punishment in Latin America: Law and Society since Late Colonial Times*, ed. Ricardo D. Salvatore, Carlos Aguirre, Gilbert M. Joseph (Durham, NC: Duke University Press, 2001).

3. For instance, in the mid-1950s, the United States sought to establish a guided missile facility on the island of Fernando de Noronha off the coast of northeastern Brazil and a naval refueling station in Pernambuco. In negotiations with the United States, Brazilian president Juscelino Kubitschek insisted that if he allowed the United States to establish new military sites on Brazilian soil he would do so at great political risk in an already delicate political context, and he

requested military assistance to bolster supportive factions within the armed forces and economic aid to more generally advance his developmentalist goals for the nation in order to offset the risks he would incur by cooperating. Briggs to State, December 18, 1956, FRUS, 1955–1957, American Republics: Central and South America, Volume VII. Telegram from the Ambassador in Brazil (Briggs) to the Department of State, January 2, 1957, FRUS, 1955–1957, American Republics: Central and South America, Volume VII. Text of the agreement, December 22, 1956, FRUS 1955–1957, 732–734. For more on the base at Fernando de Noronha and US-Brazilian relations under Kubitschek, see Grazielle Nascimento, "Fernando de Noronha e os ventos da guerra fria" (Disertação de mestrado, Universidade Federal de Pernambuco, Recife, 2009). See also Moniz Bandeira, *A presença dos Estados Unidos no Brasil*.

4. On the negotiations over the canal treaties, see Omar Jaén Suárez, *Las Negociaciones sobre el Canal de Panamá: 1964–1970* (Grupo Editorial Norma, 2002) and *Las Negociaciones de los Tratados Torrijos-Carter 1970–1979* (Autoridad del Canal de Panamá, 2005). See also Rómulo Escobar Bethancourt, *Torrijos: Colonia Americana, No!* (Bogotá: C. Valencia Editores, 1981), 257.

5. Luiz Inácio Lula da Silva of Brazil, for instance, vetoed a bill upon assuming the presidency that had been negotiated by his predecessor to give the US military control over a section of Brazil's Alcântara facility. More recently, right-wing president Jair Bolsonaro has flirted with the idea of permitting a US base in Brazil.

6. Sebastian Bitar, *US Military Bases, Quasi-Bases, and Domestic Politics in Latin America* (New York: Palgrave Macmillan, 2016).

7. Teo Ballvé, "US Military Looks to Colombia to Replace Base in Ecuador," *North American Congress on Latin America*, June 6, 2008.

8. Quoted in Lester D. Langley, "Negotiating New Treaties with Panama: 1936," *Hispanic American Historical Review* 48, no. 2 (May 1968): 232.

BIBLIOGRAPHY

ARCHIVES
Brazil
Arquivo da Fundação Oswaldo Cruz (FIOCRUZ), Rio de Janeiro
Arquivo Histórico do Exército, Rio de Janeiro
Arquivo do Ministério de Relações Exteriores, Itamaraty, Brasília
Arquivo do Ministério de Relações Exteriores, Itamaraty, Rio de Janeiro
Arquivo Nacional do Brasil, Rio de Janeiro
Arquivo Público Estadual Jordão Emerenciano, Recife, Pernambuco
Arquivo Público do Estado do Pará, Belém, Pará
Arquivo Público do Estado do Rio de Janeiro (APERJ)
Arquivo Público do Estado do Rio Grande do Norte, Natal, Rio Grande do Norte
Arquivo do Supremo Tribunal Federal, Brasília
Arquivo do Tribunal Regional do Trabalho—Região 8, Ananindeua, Pará, Brasil
Biblioteca Pública Arthur Vianna, Belém, Pará
Centro de Memória da Amazônia, Universidade Federal do Pará, Belém, Pará
Centro de Pesquisa e Documentação da História Contemporânea do Brasil (CPDOC),
    Fundação Getúlio Vargas (FGV), Rio de Janeiro
Fundação Rampa, Natal, Rio Grande do Norte
Instituto Histórico e Geográfico do Rio Grande do Norte, Natal, Rio Grande do Norte

Cuba
Archivo Histórico Provincial de Camagüey, Camagüey
Archivo Histórico Provincial de Pinar del Rio, Pinar del Rio
Archivo del Ministerio de Relaciones Exteriores de Cuba, Havana
Archivo Nacional de Cuba, Havana
Biblioteca Provincial de Camagüey, Camagüey
Instituto de Historia de Cuba, Havana
Museo de San Antonio de los Baños, San Antonio de los Baños, Artemisa

Panama
Archivo Nacional de Panamá, Panama City (ANP)
Archivo del Ministerio de Relaciones Exteriores de Panamá, Panama City
Hermeroteca, Biblioteca Nacional de Panamá, Panama City

United Kingdom
The National Archives of the United Kingdom

The United States
Federal Bureau of Investigation. Files Obtained through Freedom of Information Act Request #1471928-000
Franklin Roosevelt Presidential Library, Hyde Park, New York
U.S. National Archives and Records Administration, College Park, Maryland (NARA)
   Record Group 59: General Records of the Department of State
   Record Group 60: Department of Justice
   Record Group 77: Records of the Office of the Chief of Engineers
   Record Group 84: General Records of the Foreign Service Posts of the Department of State
   Record Group 107: Office of the Secretary of War
   Record Group 159: Office of the Inspector General
   Record Group 165: Records of the War Department General and Special Staffs
   Record Group 185: Records of the Panama Canal Zone
   Record Group 215: Community War Services
   Record Group 229: Records of the Office of Inter-American Affairs
   Record Group 319: Records of the Army Staff
   Record Group 407: Records of the Adjutant General
Hoover Institution, Stanford University, Stanford, California
Rockefeller Archive Center (RAC), Tarrytown, New York
University of Miami Special Collections, Coral Gables, Florida
   Pan American World Airways Records*
Albert and Shirley Small Special Collections, University of Virginia, Charlottesville, Virginia

*This collection has been reorganized since I used it in 2014.

NEWSPAPERS, MAGAZINES, AND JOURNALS
Brazil
Diário Oficial
Folha do Norte
Folha da Manhã
Folha do Povo
Folha Vespertina
O Globo
O Jornal
Tribuna da Imprensa

Colombia
El Siglo

Cuba
El Camagueyano
Hoy
El Mundo
Siempre
La Tribuna: Periódico Político y de Interés General San Antonio de los Baños
Boletin Oficial de la Cámara de Comercio e Industriales de San Antonio de los Baños

Ecuador
La Patria

Panama
Ac-CIÓ-n
Acción Comunal
Estrella de Panama
El Panamá América
The Star and Herald

Peru
El Comercio

United States
Life Magazine
The New York Times
The Washington Post
Time Magazine

Uruguay
El Debate
La Tribuna Popular

INTERVIEWS
Major-Brigadeiro Rui Moreira Lima
Comandante Lucas Antonio Monteiro de Barros Bastos
Uilde Monteiro

WORKS CITED

Acosta, David. *Influencia decisiva de la opinión pública en el rechazo del Convenio Filós-Hines de 1947*. 3rd ed. Panamá: Impresora de la Nación, 1983.

Aguirre, Carlos, and Ricardo D. Salvatore. "Introduction: Writing the History of Law, Crime and Punishment in Latin America." In *Crime and Punishment in Latin America: Law and Society since Late Colonial Times*, edited by Ricardo D. Salvatore, Carlos Aguirre, and Gilbert M. Joseph. Durham, NC: Duke University Press, 2001.

Alves, Vágner Camilo. *O Brasil e a segunda guerra mundial: história de um envolvimento forçado*. Coleção Ciências sociais 3. Rio de Janeiro: Editora PUC-Rio, 2002.

Amado, Jorge. *Hora da guerra: a Segunda Guerra Mundial vista da Bahia: crônicas (1942–1944)*. Coleção Jorge Amado. São Paulo, SP: Companhia das Letras, 2008.

Appelbaum, Nancy P., Anne S. Macpherson, and Karin Alejandra Rosemblatt, eds. *Race and Nation in Modern Latin America*. Chapel Hill: University of North Carolina Press, 2003.

Argote-Freyre, Frank. *Fulgencio Batista: From Revolutionary to Strongman*. New Brunswick, NJ: Rutgers University Press, 2006.

Armus, Diego. "Eugenics in Buenos Aires: Discourses, Practices, and Historiography." *Historia, Ciencias, Saúde—Manguinhos* 23, suppl. 1 (December 2016): 149–170.

Aron, Stephen. "Frontiers, Borderlands, Wests." In *American History Now*, edited by Eric Foner and Lisa McGirr. Philadelphia: Temple University Press, 2011.

Arvey, Sarah R. "'Labyrinths of Love': Sexual Propriety, Family and Social Reform in the Second Cuban Republic, 1902–1958." PhD diss., University of Michigan, 2007.

Arvey, Sarah R. "Sex and the Ordinary Cuban: Cuban Physicians, Eugenics, and Marital Sexuality, 1933–1958." *Journal of the History of Sexuality* 21, no. 1 (2012): 93–120.

Atkins, G. Pope. *Encyclopedia of the Inter-American System*. Westport, CT: Greenwood, 1997.

Avery, Molly. "Promoting a 'Pinochetazo': The Chilean Dictatorship's Foreign Policy in El Salvador during the Carter Years, 1977–81." *Journal of Latin American Studies* 52, no. 4 (November 2020): 759–784.

Baggio, Kátia Gerab. "A 'outra' América: A América Latina na visão dos intelectuais brasileiros das primeiras décadas republicanas." Universidade de São Paulo, 1999.

Bailey, Beth, and David Farber. *The First Strange Place: The Alchemy of Race and Sex in World War II Hawaii*. New York: Free Press, 1992.

Baker, Anni P. *American Soldiers Overseas: The Global Military Presence*. Westport, CT: Praeger, 2004.

Becker, Marc. "Ecuador's Early No-Foreign Military Bases Movement." *Diplomatic History* 41, no. 3 (2017): 518–542.

Becker, Marc. *The FBI in Latin America: The Ecuador Files*. Durham, NC: Duke University Press, 2017.

Benton, Lauren. *Law and Colonial Cultures: Legal Regimes in World History, 1400–1900*. Cambridge: Cambridge University Press, 2001.

Benton, Lauren. *A Search for Sovereignty: Law and Geography in European Empires, 1400–1900*. Cambridge: Cambridge University Press, 2010.

Beruff, Jorge Rodríguez. *Strategy as Politics: Puerto Rico on the Eve of the Second World War*. San Juan: Editorial Universidad de Puerto Rico, 2007.

Beruff, Jorge Rodríguez, and José L. Bolivar, eds. *Puerto Rico en la Segunda Guerra Mundial: Baluarte del Caribe / Puerto Rico in World War II: Caribbean Bulwark*. San Juan, Puerto Rico: Ediciones Callejon Inc., 2012.

Besse, Susan K. *Restructuring Patriarchy: The Modernization of Gender Inequality in Brazil, 1914–1940*. Chapel Hill: University of North Carolina Press, 1996.

Bethell, Leslie. "Brazil and 'Latin America.'" *Journal of Latin American Studies* 42, no. 3 (August 2010): 457–485.

Blower, Brooke L. "Nation of Outposts: Forts, Factories, Bases, and the Making of American Power." *Diplomatic History* 41, no. 3 (2017): 439–459.

Borgwardt, Elizabeth. *A New Deal for the World: America's Vision for Human Rights*. Cambridge, MA: Belknap Press, 2007.

Brandt, Allan M. *No Magic Bullet: A Social History of Venereal Disease in the United States since 1880*. 2nd ed. Oxford: University Press, 2020.

Brilliant, Mark. *The Color of America Has Changed: How Racial Diversity Shaped Civil Rights Reform in California, 1941–1978*. New York: Oxford University Press, 2012.

Burns, E. Bradford. *The Unwritten Alliance: Rio-Branco and Brazilian-American Relations*. New York: Columbia University Press, 1966.

Cabezas, Amalia L. "Havana's Sex Trade." In *Trafficking in Women 1924–1926: The Paul Kinsie Reports for the League of Nations*, edited by Jean-Michel Chaumont, Magaly Rodriguez Garcia, and Paul Servais, 82–89. Historical Series 2. Geneva: United Nations Publications, 2017.

Calvo, Carlos. *Derecho internacional teórico y práctico de Europa y América.*
Paris: D'Amyot, 1868.

Cameselle-Pesce, Pedro M. "Forgotten Neighbors: The Challenge of Uruguay–United
States Relations during the Era of Franklin D. Roosevelt, 1929–1945." PhD
diss., Fordham University, 2016.

Campbell, Courtney. "Four Fisherman, Orson Welles, and the Making of the Brazilian
Northeast." *Past & Present* 234, no. 1 (2017): 173–212.

Campos, André Luiz Vieira de. *Políticas internacionais de saúde na era
Vargas: o serviço especial de saúde pública, 1942–1960.* Rio de Janeiro: Editora
Fiocruz, 2006.

Cándida Smith, Richard. *Improvised Continent: Pan-Americanism and Cultural Exchange.*
Philadelphia: University of Pennsylvania Press, 2017.

Carr, Barry. "Pioneering Transnational Solidarity in the Americas: The Movement
in Support of Augusto C. Sandino 1927–1934." *Journal of Iberian and Latin
American Research* 20, no. 2 (2014): 141–152.

Caulfield, Sueann. "The Birth of Mangue: Race, Nation and the Politics of Prostitution
in Rio de Janeiro, 1850–1942." In *Sex and Sexuality in Latin America: An
Interdisciplinary Reader*, edited by Daniel Balderston and Donna J. Guy, 86–100.
New York: New York University Press, 1997.

Caulfield, Sueann. "The Changing Politics of Freedom and Virginity in Rio de Janeiro,
1920–1940." In *Honor, Status, and Law in Modern Latin America*, edited by
Sarah C. Chambers, Lara Putnam, and Sueann Caulfield, 223–246. Durham,
NC: Duke University Press, 2005.

Caulfield, Sueann. "The History of Gender in the Historiography of Latin America."
Hispanic American Historical Review 81, no. 3–4 (2001): 449–490.

Caulfield, Sueann. *In Defense of Honor: Sexual Morality, Modernity, and Nation in Early-
Twentieth-Century Brazil.* Durham, NC: Duke University Press, 2000.

Child, John. *Unequal Alliance: The Inter-American Military System, 1938–1978.* Boulder,
CO: Westview Press, 1980.

Clemans, Paul. "Unwilling Tools of Empire: Pan American Airways, Brazil
and the Quest for Air Hegemony, 1929–1945." PhD diss., Florida State
University, 2019.

Coates, Benjamin Allen. *Legalist Empire: International Law and American Foreign
Relations in the Early Twentieth Century.* New York: Oxford University
Press, 2016.

Colby, Jason M. *The Business of Empire: United Fruit, Race, and U.S. Expansion in Central
America.* Ithaca, NY: Cornell University Press, 2013.

Coletta, Paolo Enrico, and K. Jack Bauer. *United States Navy and Marine Corps Bases,
Overseas.* Westport, CT: Greenwood Press, 1985.

Conn, Stetson, Rose C. Engelman, and Byron Fairchild. *The Western
Hemisphere: Guarding the United States and Its Outposts.* Washington, DC: Office
of the Chief of Military History, Department of the Army, 1964.

Conn, Stetson, and Byron Fairchild. *The Framework of Hemisphere Defense.*
Washington, DC: Government Printing Office, 1960.

Conniff, Michael L. *Black Labor on a White Canal: Panama, 1904–1981.*
Pittsburgh: University of Pittsburgh Press, 1985.

Conniff, Michael L. *Panama and the United States: The Forced Alliance.*
Athens: University of Georgia Press, 2001.

Conte Porras, J. *Arnulfo Arias Madrid.* Panamá: J. Conte-Porras, 1980.

Cooke, Morris Llewellyn. *Brazil on the March, a Study in International Cooperation; Reflections on the Report of the American Technical Mission to Brazil.* New York: Whittlesey House, McGraw-Hill, 1944.

Cooley, Alexander. *Base Politics: Democratic Change and the U.S. Military Overseas.* Ithaca, NY: Cornell University Press, 2008.

Corinealdi, Kaysha. *Panama in Black: Afro-Caribbean World Making and the Promise of Diaspora.* Durham, NC: Duke University Press, 2022.

Coronil, Fernando. "Foreword." In *Close Encounters of Empire: Writing the Cultural History of U.S.–Latin American Relations*, edited by Gilbert M. Joseph, Catherine LeGrand, and Ricardo D. Salvatore. Durham, NC: Duke University Press, 1998.

Cortina, José Manuel. *Ideales internacionales de Cuba.* 2nd ed. Habana: El Siglo XX, 1926.

Cramer, Gisela, and Ursula Prutsch. *¡Américas Unidas!: Nelson A. Rockefeller's Office of Inter-American Affairs (1940–46).* Madrid: Iberoamericana Vervuert, 2012.

Cuba. *Constitución de la República de Cuba: publicada en la Gaceta Oficial de Julio 8 de 1940.* Habana: Compañía Editora de Libros y Folletos, 1940.

Curti, Merle Eugene, and Kendall Birr. *Prelude to Point Four: American Technical Missions Overseas, 1838–1938.* Westport, CT: Praeger, 1978.

Daley, Robert. *An American Saga: Juan Trippe and His Pan Am Empire.* New York: Random House, 1980.

Davies, Ronald Edward George. *Airlines of Latin America: Since 1919.* London: Putnam, 1984.

De Matos, Christine, and Rowena Ward. *Gender, Power, and Military Occupations: Asia Pacific and the Middle East since 1945.* New York: Routledge, 2012.

Dinius, Oliver. *Brazil's Steel City: Developmentalism, Strategic Power, and Industrial Relations in Volta Redonda, 1941–1964.* Stanford, CA: Stanford University Press, 2010.

Donoghue, Michael E. *Borderland on the Isthmus: Race, Culture, and the Struggle for the Canal Zone.* Durham, NC: Duke University Press, 2014.

Douglas, R. M. "The US Army and Male Rape during the Second World War." *Journal of Contemporary History* 56, no. 2 (2021): 268–293.

Dudziak, Mary L. *War Time: An Idea, Its History, Its Consequences.* New York: Oxford University Press, 2013.

Dudziak, Mary L., and Leti Volpp, eds. *Legal Borderlands: Law and the Construction of American Borders.* Baltimore: Johns Hopkins University Press, 2006.

Ehrick, Christine. "Buenas Vecinas? Latin American Women and US Radio Propaganda during World War II." *Feminist Media Histories* 5, no. 3 (2019): 60–84.

Erb, Claude C. "Prelude to Point Four: The Institute of Inter-American Affairs." *Diplomatic History* 9, no. 3 (1985): 249–269.

Falcão, João. *O Brasil e a Segunda Guerra Mundial: testemunho e depoimento de um soldado convocado.* Brasília, DF: Editora UnB, 1998.

Fajardo, Margarita. *The World that Latin America Created: The United Nations Economic Commission for Latin America in the Development Era.* Cambridge: Harvard University Press, 2022.

Ferrer, Ada. "Cuba, 1898: Rethinking Race, Nation, and Empire." *Radical History Review* 1999, no. 73 (1999): 22–46.

Fischer, Brodwyn. *A Poverty of Rights: Citizenship and Inequality in Twentieth-Century Rio de Janeiro.* Stanford, CA: Stanford University Press, 2010.

FitzGerald, David, and David Cook-Martín. *Culling the Masses: The Democratic Origins of Racist Immigration Policy in the Americas*. Cambridge, MA: Harvard University Press, 2014.

Flores-Villalobos, Joan. "Colón Women: West Indian Women in the Construction of the Panama Canal, 1904–1911." PhD diss., New York University, 2018.

Fontes, Paulo, and Alexandre Fortes. "Brazilian Labour History—Recent Trends and Perspectives: An Introduction." *Moving the Social* 49 (2013): 5–10.

Foreign Relations of the United States, 1940. Volume V, The American Republics. Washington, DC: Government Printing Office, 1961.

Foreign Relations of the United States, 1941. Volume VII, The American Republics. Washington, DC: Government Printing Office, 1962.

Foreign Relations of the United States, 1942. Volume VI, The American Republics. Washington, DC: Government Printing Office, 1963.

Fortes, Alexandre. "A espionagem Aliada no Brasil durante a Segunda Guerra Mundial: cotidiano e política em Belém na visão da inteligencia militar norte-americana." *Esboços* 22, no. 34 (2016): 81–115.

Fortes, Alexandre. "A Segunda Guerra Mundial e a sociedade brasileira." In *A Era Vargas 1930–1945, Volume II*, edited by Marco Aurélio Vannucchi and Luciano Aronne de Abreu. Porto Alegre, Brasil: EDIPUCRS, 2021.

Fortes, Alexandre. "Trabalho, raça e política: o olhar norte-americano sobre o Brasil no contexto da Segunda Guerra Mundial." In *Trabalho & labor: histórias compartilhadas, Brasil e Estados Unidos, século XX*, edited by Alexandre Fortes and Fernando Teixeira da Silva. Salvador, Brasil: Editora Sagga, 2020.

French, John D. *Drowning in Laws: Labor Law and Brazilian Political Culture*. Chapel Hill: University of North Carolina Press, 2004.

Friedman, Max Paul. "Fracas in Caracas: Latin American Diplomatic Resistance to United States Intervention in Guatemala in 1954." *Diplomacy & Statecraft* 21, no. 4 (December 2010): 669–689.

Friedman, Max Paul. *Nazis and Good Neighbors: The United States Campaign against the Germans of Latin America in World War II*. New York: Cambridge University Press, 2005.

Friedman, Max Paul. "Retiring the Puppets, Bringing Latin America Back In: Recent Scholarship on United States–Latin American Relations." *Diplomatic History* 27, no. 5 (2003): 621–636.

Friedman, Max Paul, and Tom Long. "Soft Balancing in the Americas: Latin American Opposition to U.S. Intervention, 1898–1936." *International Security* 40, no. 1 (July 2015): 120–156.

Gambini, Roberto. *O duplo jogo de Getúlio Vargas: influência americana e alemã no Estado Novo*. Coleção Ensaio e memória 4. São Paulo: Edições Símbolo, 1977.

Garcia, Eugenio Vargas. *O sexto membro permanente: o Brasil e a criação da ONU*. Rio de Janeiro: Contraponto, 2012.

Garfield, Seth. *In Search of the Amazon: Brazil, the United States, and the Nature of a Region*. Durham, NC: Duke University Press, 2013.

Gellman, Irwin F. *Roosevelt and Batista: Good Neighbor Diplomacy in Cuba, 1933–1945*. Albuquerque: University of New Mexico Press, 1973.

Gil, Federico. "The Latin-American Viewpoint." *Inter-American Economic Affairs* 2, no. 4 (1949).

Girão, Blanchard. *A invasão dos cabelos dourados: do 'uso' aos abusos no tempo das "Coca-Colas."* Fortaleza: ABC Editora, 2008.

Gobat, Michel. *Confronting the American Dream: Nicaragua under U.S. Imperial Rule.* Durham, NC: Duke University Press, 2005.

Gobat, Michel. "The Invention of Latin America: A Transnational History of Anti-Imperialism, Democracy, and Race." *American Historical Review* 118, no. 5 (December 2013): 1345–1375.

Gomes, Ângela de Castro, and Fernando Teixeira da Silva, eds. *A justiça do trabalho e sua história.* Campinas: Editora Unicamp, 2013.

González, Patricio Herrera. "El asedio a la clase obrera organizada en los inicios de la guerra fría: el caso de La CTAL, 1943–1953." *Revista Divergencia* 5, no. 6 (July 2016): 29–39.

Graham, Jessica Lynn. *Shifting the Meaning of Democracy: Race, Politics, and Culture in the United States and Brazil.* Oakland: University of California Press, 2019.

Grandin, Greg. "The Liberal Traditions in the Americas: Rights, Sovereignty, and the Origins of Liberal Multilateralism." *American Historical Review* 117, no. 1 (2012): 68–91.

Grandin, Greg. "Your Americanism and Mine: Americanism and Anti-Americanism in the Americas." *American Historical Review* 111, no. 4 (October 2006): 1042–1066.

Green, David. *The Containment of Latin America: A History of the Myths and Realities of the Good Neighbor Policy.* Chicago: Quadrangle Books, 1971.

Greene, Julie. *The Canal Builders: Making America's Empire at the Panama Canal.* New York: Penguin Press, 2009.

Greene, Julie. "Spaniards on the Silver Roll: Labor Troubles and Liminality in the Panama Canal Zone, 1904–1914." *International Labor and Working-Class History*, no. 66 (2004): 78–98.

Guglielmo, Thomas A. "Fighting for Caucasian Rights: Mexicans, Mexican Americans, and the Transnational Struggle for Civil Rights in World War II Texas." *Journal of American History* 92, no. 4 (March 2006): 1212–1237.

Guridy, Frank Andre. *Forging Diaspora: Afro-Cubans and African Americans in a World of Empire and Jim Crow.* Chapel Hill: University of North Carolina Press, 2010.

Hagedorn, Dan. *Conquistadors of the Sky: A History of Aviation in Latin America.* Tallahassee: University Press of Florida, 2010.

Haglund, David G. *Latin America and the Transformation of U.S. Strategic Thought, 1936–1940.* Albuquerque: University of New Mexico Press, 1984.

Harkavy, Robert E. *Bases Abroad: The Global Foreign Military Presence.* Oxford: Oxford University Press, 1989.

Harmer, Tanya. "Brazil's Cold War in the Southern Cone, 1970–1975." *Cold War History* 12, no. 4 (November 2012): 659–681.

Harmer, Tanya. "Fractious Allies: Chile, the United States, and the Cold War, 1973–76." *Diplomatic History* 37, no. 1 (2013): 109–143.

Hart, Justin. "Making Democracy Safe for the World: Race, Propaganda, and the Transformation of U.S. Foreign Policy during World War II." *Pacific Historical Review* 73, no. 1 (February 2004): 49–84.

Helleiner, Eric. *Forgotten Foundations of Bretton Woods: International Development and the Making of the Postwar Order.* Ithaca, NY: Cornell University Press, 2016.

Henrique, Márcio Couto, and Luiza Helena Miranda Amador. "Da Belle Époque à cidade do vício: o combate à sífilis em Belém do Pará, 1921–1924." *Análise* 23, no. 2 (June 2016): 359–378.

Herman, Rebecca. "The Global Politics of Anti-Racism: A View from the Canal Zone." *American Historical Review* 125, no. 2 (April 2020): 460–486.

Herrera González, Patricio, and Juan Carlos Yáñez Andrade. "Saberes compartidos entre América Latina y la Organización Internacional del Trabajo: un recuento historiográfico contemporáneo." *Anos 90* 27 (September 2020): 1–14.

High, Steven. *Base Colonies in the Western Hemisphere, 1940–1967*. New York: Palgrave Macmillan, 2009.

Hilton, Stanley E. *Suástica sobre o Brasil: a história da espionagem alemã no Brasil, 1939–1944*. Coleção Retratos do Brasil 105. Rio de Janeiro: Civilização Brasileira, 1977.

Höhn, Maria, and Seungsook Moon, eds. *Over There: Living with the U.S. Military Empire from World War Two to the Present*. Durham, NC: Duke University Press, 2010.

Huggins, Martha Knisely. *Political Policing: The United States and Latin America*. Durham, NC: Duke University Press, 1998.

Iber, Patrick. *Neither Peace nor Freedom: The Cultural Cold War in Latin America*. Cambridge, MA: Harvard University Press, 2015.

Immerwahr, Daniel. *How to Hide an Empire: A History of the Greater United States*. New York: Picador, 2020.

Inoue, Fumi. "The Politics of Extraterritoriality in Post-Occupation Japan and US-Occupied Okinawa, 1952–1972." PhD diss., Boston College, 2021.

Inoue, Masamichi. *Okinawa and the U.S. Military: Identity Making in the Age of Globalization*. New York: Columbia University Press, 2007.

Johnson, Chalmers. *Dismantling the Empire: America's Last Best Hope*. New York: Metropolitan Books, 2010.

Jones, Francis Clifford. *Extraterritoriality in Japan and the Diplomatic Relations Resulting in Its Abolition, 1853–1899*. New York: AMS Press, 1931.

Joseph, Gilbert M., Catherine LeGrand, and Ricardo D. Salvatore, eds. *Close Encounters of Empire: Writing the Cultural History of U.S.–Latin American Relations*. Durham, NC: Duke University Press, 1998.

Kayaoğlu, Turan. *Legal Imperialism: Sovereignty and Extraterritoriality in Japan, the Ottoman Empire, and China*. Cambridge: Cambridge University Press, 2010.

Kramer, Paul A. "The Military-Sexual Complex: Prostitution, Disease and the Boundaries of Empire during the Philippine-American War." *Asia-Pacific Journal: Japan Focus* 9, no. 30 (July 2011): 1–35.

Krasner, Stephen D. *Sovereignty: Organized Hypocrisy*. Princeton, NJ: Princeton University Press, 1999.

Kraus, Theresa L. "The Establishment of United States Army Air Corps Bases in Brazil, 1938–1945." PhD diss., University of Maryland, 1986.

Krepp, Stella. *The Decline of the Western Hemisphere: The History of Inter-American Relations since 1941*. Unpublished manuscript.

LaFeber, Walter. *The Panama Canal: The Crisis in Historical Perspective*. New York: Oxford University Press, 1990.

Langer, William Leonard, and S. Everett Gleason. *The Undeclared War, 1940–1941: The World Crisis and American Foreign Policy*. New York: Harper & Brothers, 1953.

Langley, Lester D. *America and the Americas: The United States in the Western Hemisphere*. Athens: University of Georgia Press, 1989.

Langley, Lester D. "Negotiating New Treaties with Panama: 1936." *Hispanic American Historical Review* 48, no. 2 (May 1968): 220–233.

Lasso, Marixa. *Erased: The Untold Story of the Panama Canal*. Cambridge, MA: Harvard University Press, 2019.

Lasso, Marixa. "Race and Ethnicity in the Formation of Panamanian National Identity: Panamanian Discrimination against Chinese and West Indians in the Thirties." *Revista panameña de política* 4 (2007): 61–92.

Lawlor, Ruth. "Contested Crimes: Race, Gender, and Nation in Histories of GI Sexual Violence, World War II." *Journal of Military History* 84, no. 2 (April 2020): 541–569.

Lease of Defense Sites: Agreement between the United States of America and Panama, Signed at Panama, May 18, 1942; Effective May 11, 1943, and Exchange of Notes. Executive Agreement Series 359. Washington, DC: Government Printing Office, 1944.

Leffler, Melvyn P. "The American Conception of National Security and the Beginnings of the Cold War, 1945–48." *American Historical Review* 89, no. 2 (1984): 346–381.

Leite, Mauro Renault, and Novelli Júnior. *Marechal Eurico Gaspar Dutra: o dever da verdade.* Coleção Brasil século 20. Rio de Janeiro: Editora Nova Fronteira, 1983.

Leonard, Thomas M., and John F. Bratzel, eds. *Latin America during World War II.* Lanham, MD: Rowman & Littlefield Publishers, 2013.

Lichtenstein, Nelson. *Labor's War at Home: The CIO in World War II.* New York: Cambridge University Press, 1982.

Lima, Rui Moreira. *Senta a pua!* Rio de Janeiro: Biblioteca do Exército Editora, 1980.

Lindsay-Poland, John. *Emperors in the Jungle: The Hidden History of the U.S. in Panama.* Durham, NC: Duke University Press, 2003.

Lipman, Jana K. "Guantánamo and the Case of Kid Chicle: Private Contract Labor and the Development of the US Military." In *Colonial Crucible: Empire in the Making of the Modern American State,* edited by Alfred W. McCoy and Francisco A. Scarano. Madison: University of Wisconsin Press, 2009, 452–460.

Lipman, Jana K. *Guantánamo: A Working-Class History between Empire and Revolution.* American Crossroads 25. Berkeley: University of California Press, 2009.

Long, Tom. "Historical Antecedents and Post–World War II Regionalism in the Americas." *World Politics* 72, no. 2 (April 2020): 214–253.

Long, Tom, and Carsten-Andreas Schulz. "Republican Internationalism: The Nineteenth-Century Roots of Latin American Contributions to International Order." *Cambridge Review of International Affairs* (July 16, 2021): 1–23. DOI: 10.1080/09557571.2021.1944983.

Lorca, Arnulf Becker. *Mestizo International Law: A Global Intellectual History 1842–1933.* Cambridge: Cambridge University Press, 2016.

Lutz, Catherine, ed. *The Bases of Empire: The Global Struggle against U.S. Military Posts.* New York: New York University Press, 2009.

Lutz, Catherine, ed. "Introduction: Bases, Empire and Global Response." In *The Bases of Empire: The Global Struggle against U.S. Military Posts.* New York: New York University Press, 2009.

Mahan, Alfred Thayer. *The Interest of America in Sea Power, Present and Future.* Boston: Little, Brown and Company, 1897.

Major, John. *Prize Possession: The United States Government and the Panama Canal 1903–1979.* New York: Cambridge University Press, 1993.

Maloney, George. *El Canal de Panamá y los trabajadores antillanos.* Panamá: Universidad de Panamá, 1989.

Marco Serra, Yolanda. "El feminismo de los años veinte y la redefinición de la femineidad en Panamá." In *Entre silencios y voces: género e historia en América*

Central (1750–1990), edited by Eugenia Rodríguez Sáenz, 183–196. San José, Costa Rica: Editorial Porvenir, 1997.

Marco Serra, Yolanda. "'El movimiento sufragista en Panamá y la construcción de la mujer moderna.'" In *Historia de los movimientos de mujeres en Panamá en el siglo XX*, edited by Fernando Aparicio, Yolanda Marco Serra, Miriam Miranda, and Josefina Zurita, 45–132. Colección Agenda de género del centenario. Panamá: Universidad de Panamá, 2002.

Marco Serra, Yolanda. *Los obreros españoles en la construcción del Canal de Panama: la emigración Españá la hacia Panamá vista desde a través de la prensa española.* Panamá: Portobelo, 1997.

Marco Serra, Yolanda. "Ruptura de la tradición, construcción de la mujer moderna y resistencia del patriarcado liberal en Panamá en las décadas de 1920 y 1930." *Diálogos* 5, no. 1–2 (2004).

Margolies, Daniel S., Umut Özsu, Maïa Pal, and Ntina Tzouvala, eds. *The Extraterritoriality of Law: History, Theory, Politics.* New York: Routledge, 2019.

Marino, Katherine M. *Feminism for the Americas: The Making of an International Human Rights Movement.* Illustrated edition. Chapel Hill: University of North Carolina Press, 2019.

Maximiano, Cesar Campiani. *Barbudos, sujos e fatigados: soldados brasileiros na Segunda Guerra Mundial.* São Paulo: Grua Livros, 2010.

McCaffrey, Katherine T. *Military Power and Popular Protest: The U.S. Navy in Vieques, Puerto Rico.* New Brunswick, NJ: Rutgers University Press, 2002.

McCann, Frank D. *Brazil and the United States during World War II and Its Aftermath: Negotiating Alliance and Balancing Giants.* Cham, Switzerland: Palgrave Macmillan, 2018.

McCann, Frank D. *The Brazilian-American Alliance, 1937–1945.* Princeton, NJ: Princeton University Press, 1974.

McCoy, Mary Ellene Chenevey. "Guantanamo Bay: The United States Naval Base and Its Relationship with Cuba." PhD diss., University of Akron, 1995.

McGillivray, Gillian. "Cuba: Depression, Imperialism, and Revolution, 1920–1940." In *The Great Depression in Latin America*, edited by Paulo Drinot and Alan Knight, 246–275. Durham, NC: Duke University Press, 2014.

McKay, Alberto. "Las primeras crisis políticas." In *Historia general de Panamá, Volumen III, Tomo II*, edited by Alfredo Castillero Calvo. Panamá: Comité Nacional del Centenario de la República, 2004.

McPherson, Alan. *The Invaded: How Latin Americans and Their Allies Fought and Ended U.S. Occupations.* New York: Oxford University Press, 2016.

McPherson, Alan. "World War I and US Empire in the Americas." In *Empires in World War I: Shifting Frontiers and Imperial Dynamics in a Global Conflict*, edited by Richard S. Fogarty and Andrew Tait Jarboe, 328–350. London: I. B. Tauris, 2014.

McPherson, Alan, and Yannick Wehrli, eds. *Beyond Geopolitics: New Histories of Latin America at the League of Nations.* Albuquerque: University of New Mexico Press, 2015.

Memorias que el Ministro de Relaciones Exteriores presenta a La Asamblea Nacional en sus sesiones ordinarias. Panamá: Ministerio de Relaciones Exteriores, 1943.

Mendoza, Natalie. "The Good Neighbor Comes Home: The State, Mexicans and Mexican Americans, and Regional Consciousness in the US Southwest during World War II." PhD diss., University of California, Berkeley, 2016.

Milanich, Nara. "Women, Gender, and Family in Latin America, 1820–2000." In *A Companion to Latin American History*, edited by Thomas H. Holloway, 461–479. New York: John Wiley & Sons, 2010.

Moon, Katharine H. S. *Sex among Allies: Military Prostitution in US-Korea Relations*. New York: Columbia University Press, 1997.

Morgenfeld, Leandro Ariel. *Vecinos en conflicto: Argentina y Estados Unidos en las conferencias panamericanas (1880–1955)*. Buenos Aires: Ediciones Continente, 2011.

Moura, Gerson. *Autonomia na dependência: a política externa brasileira de 1935 a 1942*. Brasil—século 20. Rio de Janeiro: Editora Nova Fronteira, 1980.

Moura, Gerson. *Sucessos e ilusões: relações internacionais do Brasil durante e após a Segunda Guerra Mundial*. Rio de Janeiro: FGV, Editora da Fundação Getúlio Vargas, 1991.

Moura, Gerson. *Tio Sam chega ao Brasil: a penetração cultural americana*. São Paulo: Brasiliense, 1984.

Navas, Luis. *El movimiento obrero en Panamá, 1880–1914*. San José, Costa Rica: Universitaria Centroamericana, 1979.

Neptune, Harvey R. *Caliban and the Yankees: Trinidad and the United States Occupation*. Chapel Hill: University of North Carolina Press, 2007.

Newton, Velma. *The Silver Men: West Indian Labour Migration to Panama, 1850–1914*. Kingston, Jamaica: Ian Randle, 2004.

Obregón, Liliana. "Completing Civilization: Creole Consciousness and International Law in Nineteenth-Century Latin America." In *International Law and Its Others*, edited by Anne Orford, 247–264. Cambridge: Cambridge University Press, 2009.

Offner, Amy C. *Sorting Out the Mixed Economy: The Rise and Fall of Welfare and Developmental States in the Americas*. Princeton: Princeton University Press, 2021.

Olcott, Jocelyn. *International Women's Year: The Greatest Consciousness-Raising Event in History*. New York: Oxford University Press, 2017.

Oliveira Lima, Manuel de. *Pan-americanismo (Monroe-Bolivar-Roosevelt)*. Rio de Janeiro: H. Garnier, 1907.

Olsson, Tore C. *Agrarian Crossings: Reformers and the Remaking of the US and Mexican Countryside*. Princeton: Princeton University Press, 2017.

O'Reggio, Trevor. *Between Alienation and Citizenship: The Evolution of Black West Indian Society in Panama, 1914–1964*. Lanham, MD: University Press of America, 2006.

Overmyer-Velázquez, Mark. "Good Neighbors and White Mexicans: Constructing Race and Nation on the Mexico-U.S. Border." *Journal of American Ethnic History* 33, no. 1 (2013): 5–34.

Pach, Chester J. "The Containment of U.S. Military Aid to Latin America, 1944–49." *Diplomatic History* 6, no. 3 (July 1982): 225–244.

Palacio, Juan Manuel. "From Social Legislation to Labor Justice: The Common Background in the Americas." In *Labor Justice across the Americas*, edited by Leon Fink and Juan Manuel Palacio, 16–43. Champaign: University of Illinois Press, 2017.

Parker, Jeffrey W. "Empire's Angst: The Politics of Race, Migration, and Sex Work in Panama, 1903–1945." PhD diss., University of Texas, Austin, 2013.

Parker, Jeffrey W. "Sex Work on the Isthmus of Panama." In *Trafficking in Women 1924–1926: The Paul Kinsie Reports for the League of Nations*, edited by

Jean-Michel Chaumont, Magaly Rodriguez Garcia, and Paul Servais, 166–171. Historical Series 2. Geneva: United Nations Publications, 2017.

Pearcy, Thomas L. "Panama's Generation of '31: Patriots, Praetorians, and a Decade of Discord." *Hispanic American Historical Review* 76, no. 4 (1996): 691–719.

Pearcy, Thomas L. *We Answer Only to God: Politics and the Military in Panama, 1903–1947*. Albuquerque: University of New Mexico Press, 1998.

Pereira, Christiana Schettini. "Prostitutes and the Law: The Uses of Court Cases over Pandering in Rio de Janeiro at the Beginning of the Twentieth Century." In *Honor, Status, and Law in Modern Latin America*, edited by Sarah C. Chambers, Lara Putnam, and Sueann Caulfield, 273–294. Durham, NC: Duke University Press, 2005.

Pérez, Louis A., Jr. *Army Politics in Cuba, 1898–1958*. Pittsburgh: University of Pittsburgh Press, 1976.

Pérez, Louis A., Jr. "Incurring a Debt of Gratitude: 1898 and the Moral Sources of United States Hegemony in Cuba." *American Historical Review* 104, no. 2 (April 1999): 356–398.

Pérez, Louis A., Jr. *The War of 1898: The United States and Cuba in History and Historiography*. Chapel Hill: University of North Carolina Press, 1998.

Pérez, Orlando J. "Panama: Nationalism and the Challenge to Canal Security." In *Latin America During World War II*, edited by Thomas M. Leonard and John F. Bratzel, 54–74. Lanham, MD: Rowman & Littlefield, 2006.

Pernet, Corinne. "Shifting Position to the Global South: Latin America's Initiatives in the Early Years at the United Nations." In *Latin America 1810–2010: Dreams and Legacies*, edited by Claude Auroi and Aline Helg, 83–100. London: Imperial College Press, 2011.

Piñero Cádiz, Gerardo M. *Puerto Rico: el Gibraltar del Caribe: intereses estratégicos estadounidenses y la base aeronaval Roosevelt Roads*. San Juan, PR: Editorial Isla Negra, 2008.

Polk, Khary Oronde. *Contagions of Empire: Scientific Racism, Sexuality, and Black Military Workers Abroad, 1898–1948*. Chapel Hill: University of North Carolina Press, 2020.

Ponsa, Christina Duffy. "Contingent Constitutions: Empire and Law in the Americas." PhD diss., Princeton University, 2010.

Prado, Eduardo. *A ilusão americana*. 2nd ed. Paris: Armand Colin, 1895.

Priestley, George. "Afro-Antillanos o Afro-Panameños." In *Piel oscura Panamá: ensayos y reflexiones al filo del centenario*, edited by George Priestley and Alberto Barrow, 185–231. Panamá: Editorial Universitaria de Panamá, 2003.

Priestley, George. "Ethnicity, Class and the National Question in Panama." In *Emerging Perspectives on the Black Diaspora*, edited by Aubrey W. Bonnett and G. Llewellyn Watson, 215–237. New York: University Press of America, 1990.

Prutsch, Ursula. "Americanization of Brazil or Pragmatic Wartime Alliance? The Politics of Nelson Rockefeller's Office of Inter-American Affairs in Brazil during World War II." *Passagens revista internacional de história política e cultura jurídica* 2 (January 2010): 181–216.

Putnam, Lara. *Radical Moves: Caribbean Migrants and the Politics of Race in the Jazz Age*. Chapel Hill: University of North Carolina Press, 2013.

Rabe, Stephen G. "Inter-American Military Cooperation, 1944–1951." *World Affairs* 137, no. 2 (1974): 132–149.

Rankin, William. *After the Map: Cartography, Navigation, and the Transformation of Territory in the Twentieth Century*. Chicago: University of Chicago Press, 2018.

Raustiala, Kal. *Does the Constitution Follow the Flag?: The Evolution of Territoriality in American Law*. New York: Oxford University Press, 2009.

Reyes Rivas, Eyra Marcela. *El trabajo de las mujeres en la historia de la construcción del Canal de Panamá, 1881–1914*. Panamá: Universidad de Panamá, 2000.

Reynolds, David. *Rich Relations: The American Occupation of Britain 1942–1945*. London: Phoenix, 2001.

Rivera, Jorge Nieves. "De Puerto Rico a Puerto Guerra: Las alteraciones al paisaje puertorriqueño con fines militares, entre 1939 a 1945." *Diálogos revista electrónica* 22, no. 1 (n.d.): 134–155.

Roberts, Mary Louise. *What Soldiers Do: Sex and the American GI in World War II France*. Chicago: University of Chicago Press, 2013.

Robinson, William Francis. "Panama for the Panamanians: The Populism of Arnulfo Arias Madrid." In *Populism in Latin America*, edited by Michael L. Conniff. Tuscaloosa: University Alabama Press, 1999.

Robinson, William Francis. "Panama for the Panamanians: The Populism of Arnulfo Arias Madrid." In *Populism in Latin America*, 2nd ed., edited by Michael L. Conniff, 184–200. Tuscaloosa: University of Alabama Press, 2012.

Robledo Reyes, Orestes. "Estudio de la Comunidad de San Antonio de Los Baños." Thesis, Universidad de la Habana, 1952.

Roosevelt, Franklin D. *The Public Papers and Addresses of Franklin D. Roosevelt, 1938 Volume*. New York: Macmillan, 1941.

Roosevelt, Theodore. "Fourth Annual Message to Congress," December 6, 1904.

Rosenberg, Emily. *Spreading the American Dream: American Economic and Cultural Expansion, 1890–1945*. New York: Hill and Wang, 2011.

Rout, Leslie B., Jr., and John F. Bratzel. *The Shadow War: German Espionage and United States Counterespionage in Latin America during World War II*. Frederick, MD: University Publications of America, 1986.

Rowe, Peter. "Historical Developments Influencing the Present Law of Visiting Forces." In *The Handbook of the Law of Visiting Forces*, edited by Dieter Fleck, 11–44. Oxford: Oxford University Press, 2018.

Ruskola, Teemu. "Canton Is Not Boston: The Invention of American Imperial Sovereignty." *American Quarterly* 57, no. 3 (2005): 859–884.

Ruskola, Teemu. "Colonialism without Colonies: On the Extraterritorial Jurisprudence of the U.S. Court for China." *Law and Contemporary Problems* 71, no. 3 (October 2008): 217–242.

Sadlier, Darlene J. *Americans All: Good Neighbor Cultural Diplomacy in World War II*. Austin: University of Texas Press, 2012.

Sandars, C. T. *America's Overseas Garrisons: The Leasehold Empire*. Oxford: Oxford University Press, 2000.

Scarfi, Juan Pablo. *The Hidden History of International Law in the Americas: Empire and Legal Networks*. New York: Oxford University Press, 2017.

Scarfi, Juan Pablo. "In the Name of the Americas: The Pan-American Redefinition of the Monroe Doctrine and the Emerging Language of American International Law in the Western Hemisphere, 1898–1933." *Diplomatic History* 40, no. 2 (April 2016): 189–218.

Schoultz, Lars. *Beneath the United States: A History of U.S. Policy toward Latin America*. Cambridge, MA: Harvard University Press, 1998.

Schulz, Carsten-Andreas. "Civilisation, Barbarism and the Making of Latin America's Place in 19th-Century International Society." *Millennium* 42, no. 3 (June 2014): 837–859.

Schrader, Stuart. *Badges without Borders: How Global Counterinsurgency Transformed American Policing*. Oakland: University of California Press, 2019.

Scully, Eileen P. *Bargaining with the State from Afar: American Citizenship in Treaty Port China, 1844-1942*. New York: Columbia University Press, 2001.

Secreto, María Verónica. *Soldados de borracha: trabalhadores entre o sertão e a Amazônia no governo Vargas*. São Paulo: Editora Perseu Abramo, 2007.

Seitenfus, Ricardo Antônio Silva. *O Brasil de Getúlio Vargas e a formação dos blocos, 1930–1942: o processo do envolvimento brasileiro na II Guerra Mundial*. São Paulo: Companhia Editora Nacional, 1985.

Semeão e Silva, Jane Derarovele. "Comportamento feminino em Fortaleza: entre o tradicional e o moderno durante a Segunda Guerra Mundial." In *Gênero: Fortaleza, história e cotidiano*, edited by Simone Souza and Frederico de Castro Neves, 17–52. Fortaleza: Demócrito Rocha, 2002.

Semeão e Silva, Jane Derarovele. "'Esforço de guerra' em Fortaleza: atividade patriótica e participação feminina nos anos de 1940." *Saeculum—Revista de história* 30 (June 2014): 289–303.

Sheinin, David. *Beyond the Ideal: Pan Americanism in Inter-American Affairs*. Westport, CT: Praeger, 2000.

Sikkink, Kathryn. "Latin America's Protagonist Role in Human Rights: How the Region Shaped Human Rights Norms Post–World War II." *Sur—International Journal on Human Rights* 12, no. 22 (December 2015): 207–219.

Sippial, Tiffany A. *Prostitution, Modernity, and the Making of the Cuban Republic, 1840–1920*. Chapel Hill: University of North Carolina Press, 2013.

Smith, Joseph. "Brazil: Benefits of Cooperation." In *Latin America during World War II*, edited by Thomas M. Leonard and John F. Bratzel, 144–161. Lanham, MD: Rowman & Littlefield, 2006.

Smith, Joseph. *Brazil and the United States: Convergence and Divergence*. Athens: University of Georgia Press, 2010.

Spenser, Daniela. *En combate: la vida de Lombardo Toledano*. Ciudad de México: Debate, 2014.

Stepan, Nancy Leys. *"The Hour of Eugenics": Race, Gender, and Nation in Latin America*. Ithaca, NY: Cornell University Press, 1996.

Sternberg, Thomas H., Ernest B. Howard, Leonard A. Dewey, and Paul Padget. "Venereal Disease." In *Preventive Medicine in World War II. Volume V: Communicable Disease*. Washington, DC: Office of the Surgeon General, Department of the Army, 1958.

Stoler, Mark A. *Allies and Adversaries: The Joint Chiefs of Staff, the Grand Alliance, and U.S. Strategy in World War II*. Chapel Hill: University of North Carolina Press, 2003.

Stoner, Kathryn Lynn. *From the House to the Streets: The Cuban Woman's Movement for Legal Reform, 1898–1940*. Durham, NC: Duke University Press, 1991.

Szok, Peter A. *La última gaviota: Liberalism and Nostalgia in Early Twentieth-Century Panama*. Westport, CT: Praeger, 2001.

Teixeira, Carlos Gustavo Poggio. *Brazil, the United States, and the South American Subsystem: Regional Politics and the Absent Empire*. Lanham, MD: Lexington Books, 2012.

"Third Meeting of Ministers of Foreign Affairs of the American Republics." *American Journal of International Law* 36, no. 2 (April 1942): 61–95.

Thornton, Christy. *Revolution in Development: Mexico and the Governance of the Global Economy*. Oakland: University of California Press, 2021.

Tillman, Andrew R., and Juan Pablo Scarfi. *Cooperation and Hegemony in US–Latin American Relations: Revisiting the Western Hemisphere Idea*. New York: Palgrave Macmillan, 2017.

Tota, Antônio Pedro. *O imperialismo sedutor: a americanização do Brasil na época da Segunda Guerra*. São Paulo: Companhia das Letras, 2000.

United States Office of Inter-American Affairs. *History of the Office of the Coordinator of Inter-American Affairs*. Historical Reports on War Administration. Washington, DC: Government Printing Office, 1947.

Valdés Sánchez, Servando. *Cuba y Estados Unidos: relaciones militares, 1933–1958*. La Habana: Editora Política, 2005.

Van Vleck, Jenifer. *Empire of the Air: Aviation and the American Ascendancy*. Cambridge, MA: Harvard University Press, 2013.

Vargas, Getúlio. *Diário, Volumen 2: 1937–1942*. Edited by Leda Saraiva Soares. São Paulo: Rio de Janeiro: Siciliano; Fundação Getúlio Vargas, 1995.

Vine, David. *Base Nation: How U.S. Military Bases Abroad Harm America and the World*. New York: Metropolitan Books, 2015.

Vine, David. *Island of Shame: The Secret History of the U.S. Military Base on Diego Garcia*. Princeton, NJ: Princeton University Press, 2009.

Vuic, Kara Dixon. *The Girls Next Door: Bringing the Home Front to the Front Lines*. Cambridge, MA: Harvard University Press, 2019.

Wertheim, Stephen. *Tomorrow, the World: The Birth of U.S. Global Supremacy*. Cambridge, MA: Belknap Press, 2020.

Westerman, George. *Los inmigrantes antillanos en Panamá*. Panamá: G. W. Westerman, 1980.

Whitney, Robert. *State and Revolution in Cuba: Mass Mobilization and Political Change, 1920–1940*. Chapel Hill: University of North Carolina Press, 2001.

Wright, Almon R. "Defense Sites Negotiations between the United States and Panama, 1936–1948." *The Department of State Bulletin* 27 (1952).

Zien, Katherine A. *Sovereign Acts: Performing Race, Space, and Belonging in Panama and the Canal Zone*. New Brunswick, NJ: Rutgers University Press, 2017.

Zolov, Eric. *The Last Good Neighbor: Mexico in the Global Sixties*. Durham, NC: Duke University Press, 2020.

INDEX

For the benefit of digital users, indexed terms that span two pages (e.g., 52–53) may, on occasion, appear on only one of those pages.